**WITHDRAWN
UTSA Libraries**

The Mobilization of the Unemployed in Europe

EUROPE IN TRANSITION: THE NYU EUROPEAN STUDIES SERIES

The Marshall Plan: Fifty Years After
  Edited by Martin Schain

Europe at the Polls: The European Elections of 1999
  Edited by Pascal Perrineau, Gérard Grunberg, and Colette Ysmal

Unions, Immigration, and Internationalization: New Challenges and Changing Coalitions in the United States and France
  By Leah Haus

Shadows Over Europe: The Development and Impact of the Extreme Right in Western Europe
  Edited by Martin Schain, Aristide Zolberg, and Patrick Hossay

Defending Europe: The EU, NATO and the Quest for European Autonomy
  Edited by Joylon Howorth and John T.S. Keeler

The Lega Nord and Contemporary Politics in Italy
  By Thomas W. Gold

Germans or Foreigners? Attitudes toward Ethnic Minorities in Post-Reunification Germany
  Edited by Richard Alba and Peter Schmidt

Germany on the Road to Normalcy? Politics and Policies of the First Red-Green Federal Government
  Edited by Werner Reutter

The Politics of Language: Essays on Languages, State and Society
  Edited by Tony Judt and Denis Lacorne

Realigning Interests: Crisis and Credibility in European Monetary Integration
  By Michele Chang

The Impact of Radical Right-Wing Parties in West European Democracies
  By Michelle Hale Williams

European Foreign Policy Making Toward the Mediterranean
  By Federica Bicchi

Sexual Equality in an Integrated Europe: Virtual Equality
  By R. Amy Elman

Politics in France and Europe
  Edited by Pascal Perrineau and Luc Rouban

Germany after the Grand Coalition: Governance and Politics in a Turbulent Environment
  Edited by Silvia Bolgherini and Florian Grotz

The New Voter in Western Europe: France and Beyond
  Edited by Bruno Cautrès and Anne Muxel

The Mobilization of the Unemployed in Europe
  Edited by Didier Chabanet and Jean Faniel

The Mobilization of the Unemployed in Europe

From Acquiescence to Protest?

Edited by

Didier Chabanet and Jean Faniel

THE MOBILIZATION OF THE UNEMPLOYED IN EUROPE
Copyright © Didier Chabanet and Jean Faniel, 2012.

All rights reserved.

First published in 2012 by
PALGRAVE MACMILLAN®
in the United States—a division of St. Martin's Press LLC,
175 Fifth Avenue, New York, NY 10010.

Where this book is distributed in the UK, Europe and the rest of the world, this is by Palgrave Macmillan, a division of Macmillan Publishers Limited, registered in England, company number 785998, of Houndmills, Basingstoke, Hampshire RG21 6XS.

Palgrave Macmillan is the global academic imprint of the above companies and has companies and representatives throughout the world.

Palgrave® and Macmillan® are registered trademarks in the United States, the United Kingdom, Europe and other countries.

ISBN: 978–0–230–61939–5

Library of Congress Cataloging-in-Publication Data

    The mobilization of the unemployed in Europe : from acquiescence to protest? / edited by Didier Chabanet and Jean Faniel.
      p. cm.—(Europe in transition)
      ISBN 978–0–230–61939–5 (alk paper)
      1. Unemployment—Europe. 2. Labor mobility—Europe. I. Chabanet, Didier. II. Faniel, Jean.

HD5764.A6M63 2011
331.12′7094—dc23   2011026823

A catalogue record of the book is available from the British Library.

Design by Newgen Imaging Systems (P) Ltd., Chennai, India.

First edition: January 2012

10 9 8 7 6 5 4 3 2 1

Printed in the United States of America.

Contents

List of Figures and Tables	vii
List of Contributors	ix

	Introduction: The Mobilization of the Unemployed in a Comparative Perspective *Didier Chabanet and Jean Faniel*	1
1	The Long History of a New Cause: The Mobilization of the Unemployed in France *Didier Chabanet*	29
2	The Mobilization of the Unemployed in Germany (1998–2004) *Britta Baumgarten and Christian Lahusen*	57
3	Inside or Outside Trade Unions? The Mobilization of the Unemployed in Belgium *Jean Faniel*	89
4	The Movement of the Unemployed in Finland *Eeva Luhtakallio and Martti Siisiäinen*	109
5	The Mobilization of the Unemployed in Italy: The Case of Naples *Simone Baglioni*	131
6	The Organization of the Unemployed in Spain: Local and Fragmented Dynamics *Sophie Béroud*	155
7	Contention over Unemployment in Britain: Unemployment Politics versus the Politics of the Unemployed *Manlio Cinalli*	175

8 Organizing the Unemployed in Ireland 195
   Frédéric Royall

9 Political Opportunities and the Mobilization of the
   Unemployed in Switzerland 221
   Michel Berclaz, Katharina Füglister, and Marco Giugni

10 The Mobilization That was Not: Explaining the Weak Politicization
   of the Issue of Unemployment in Poland 247
   Catherine Spieser and Karolina Sztandar-Sztanderska

Index 277

Figures and Tables

Figures

4.1	Registration of new associations of the unemployed in Finland (1986–2005)	115
5.1	The process of interaction between political opportunities, the unemployed, and jobs in Italy	140
5.2	Networks of unemployed organizations in Naples	146
9.1	Network of collaborations in the unemployment political field in Switzerland	234

Tables

3.1	Evolution of the regional rate of unemployment in Belgium (1948–2008)	94
3.2	Evolution of the rate of unemployment in Belgium by gender (1948–2008)	94
4.1	Unemployment rate in Finland (1990–2005)	113
4.2	Main activities in local associations of the unemployed in Finland in 2005	120
4.3	Articles concerning the collective action of the unemployed in Finland (*Helsingin Sanomat*, 1991–1995 and 2000–2004)	123
6.1	Evolution of the rate of unemployment in Spain (1978–2004)	157
8.1	Unemployment in Ireland (1980–2008)	196
9.1	Actors involved in claim-making in unemployment politics in Switzerland (1995–2002)	227

9.2	Distribution of claims in unemployment politics by party in Switzerland (1995–2002)	228
9.3	Thematic focus of claims in unemployment politics in Switzerland (1995–2002)	230
9.4	Object actors of claims in unemployment politics in Switzerland (1995–2002)	231
9.5	Form of actions used by different types of actors in Switzerland	235
10.1	Employment and unemployment in Poland (1990–2008)	256
10.2	Unemployment benefit coverage and replacement rate in Poland (1990–2007)	259

Contributors

Simone Baglioni, a political scientist, is a lecturer in politics at Glasgow Caledonian University and a research associate at Bocconi University in Milan. He is the principal investigator of the European funded (EC 7th Framework Programme) project YOUNEX (Youth, Unemployment and Exclusion in Europe: A multidimensional approach to the understanding of conditions and prospects for social and political integration of young unemployed). His research interests include unemployment and social exclusion, civil society and social capital, immigration, and asylum policies. Recent publications include: "The Public Discourse on Immigration and Unemployment in Italy in the 1990s: A Comparative Analysis" (with D. della Porta), *Politica e Società*, 1 (5), 2010; "The Role of Civil Society Actors in the Contentious Politics of Unemployment," in *The Contentious Politics of Unemployment in Europe*, Marco Giugni ed., Palgrave (2010); and "The Contentious Politics of Unemployment. The Italian Case in Comparative Perspective" (with D. della Porta and P. Graziano), *European Journal of Political Research* 47 (6), 2008.

Britta Baumgarten, a sociologist, is a research fellow at the Centre for Research and Studies in Sociology (Lisbon University Institute). Her research interests include social movements, civil society, discourse analysis, and political communication. She has worked as a postdoc researcher in the Research Group "Civil Society, Citizenship and Social Movements in Europe" at the Social Science Research Centre Berlin (WZB). Recent publications include: *Interessenvertretung aus dem Abseits. Erwerbsloseninitiativen im Diskurs über Arbeitslosigkeit*, Campus (2010); *Das Ende des sozialen Friedens? Politik und Protest in Zeiten der Hartz-Reformen* (with C. Lahusen), Campus (2010); "The Theoretical Potential of Website and Newspaper Data for Analysing Political Communication Processes" (with J. Grauel), *Historical Social Research*, 34 (1), 2009; and "Transcending Marginalization. The Mobilization of the Unemployed in France, Germany and Italy in Comparative Perspective" (with S. Baglioni, D. Chabanet, and C. Lahusen), *Mobilization*, 13 (3), 2008.

Michel Berclaz, a sociologist, is a scientific adviser at the Commission for Evaluation of Public Policies of the canton of Geneva. His research interests include collective action and social policy, especially active labor market policies. Recent publications include: "Le rôle des employeurs dans la réinsertion professionnelle," *Cahier de l'IDHEAP*, 254, 2010; "Globalization and the Contentious Politics of Unemployment: Towards Denationalization and Convergence?" (with C. Lahusen and M. Giugni), in *The Contentious Politics of Unemployment in Europe*, ed. Marco Giugni, Palgrave (2010); and "Welfare States, Labor Markets, and the Political Opportunities for Collective Action in the Unemployment Political Field: A Theoretical Framework" (with K. Füglister and M. Giugni), in *The Politics of Unemployment in Europe*, Marco Giugni ed., Ashgate (2009).

Sophie Béroud, a political scientist, is a lecturer at the University of Lyon 2, France. She has collaborated in a number of projects on topics relating to industrial relations and collective action in France. She has published widely on social movements and trade unions, in France and Spain, focusing on the mobilization of the precarious and the working poors. Recent publications include: *Quand le travail se précarise, quelles resistances collectives ?* (ed. with P. Bouffartigue), La Dispute (2009); "Les opérations 'Robins des Bois' au sein de la CGT Energie : quand la cause des chômeurs et des 'sans' contribue à la redéfinition de l'action syndicale," *Revue française de science politique*, 59 (1), 2009; "L'action syndicale au défi des travailleurs pauvres," *Sociologies pratiques*, 19, 2009; and "La mobilisation des chômeurs en Espagne : la difficile émergence d'un mouvement autonome (1988–2002)," *Politique européenne*, 21, 2007.

Didier Chabanet, a political scientist, is a Marie Curie Fellow at the European University Institute and associate research fellow at the Ecole normale supérieure de Lyon Lettres & Sciences humaines, Lyon, France. He is a well-known scholar on European Union, social exclusion, and collective action. Recent publications include: *Mobilising against Marginalisation in Europe* (ed. with F. Royall), Cambridge Scholars Publishing (2010); *European Governance and Democracy. Power and Protest in the EU* (with R. Balme), Rowman & Littlefield (2008); "When the Unemployed Challenge the EU: The European Marches as a Mode of Externalisation of Protest," *Mobilization*, 13 (3), 2008; and "Citizenship, Welfare, and the Opportunities for Political Mobilisation: Migrants and Unemployed Compared" (with M. Giugni), in *From National toward International Linkages? Civil Society and Multi-Level Governance*, Jan van Deth and William Maloney eds, Edward Elgar Publishers (2008).

Manlio Cinalli, a political scientist, is a senior researcher at Sciences Po and professor at the Institut d'Etudes politiques de Paris, France. His research focuses on political behavior, exclusion and unemployment, the politics of ethnic relations and integration, and network structures across the public and the policy domains in Europe. He is research director of the French projects for European funded (EC 7th Framework Programme) projects YOUNEX and EURISLAM. Recent publications on unemployment include: "Welfare States, Political Opportunities, and Claim Making in the Field of Unemployment Politics" (with M. Giugni), in *The Contentious Politics of Unemployment in*

Europe, Marco Giugni ed., Palgrave (2010); "Multi-Organisational Fields and Unemployment in Europe: National Publics in Britain and France," in *Mobilising against Marginalisation in Europe*, Didier Chabanet and Frédéric Royall eds, Cambridge Scholars Publishing (2010); and "Networks and Political Contention over Unemployment: A Comparison of Britain, Germany and Switzerland" (with K. Füglister), *Mobilization*, 13 (3), 2008.

Jean Faniel, a political scientist, is a researcher at the Centre de recherche et d'information socio-politiques (CRISP), Brussels, Belgium. He has published widely on trade unions, collective action of the unemployed, the relationship between trade unions and the unemployed, and Belgian politics. Recent publications include: "The Mobilization of the Unemployed: A Recurrent but Relatively Invisible Phenomenon" (with D. Chabanet), in *Unemployment and Protest*, Matthias Reiss and Matt Perry eds, Oxford University Press (2011); "Belgium: Unemployment Insurance Caught between Pressure from Europe, Regional Controversy and Fall-out from the Crisis," in *Unemployment Benefit Systems in Europe and North America*, Florence Lefresne ed., IRES/ETUI (2010); "Belgian Trade Unions, the Unemployed and the Growth of Unemployment," in *The Politics of Unemployment in Europe*, Marco Giugni ed., Ashgate (2009); and "L'Europe du chômage" (ed. with D. Chabanet), special issue of *Politique européenne*, 21, 2007.

Katharina Füglister, a political scientist, is a researcher at the Institute of Political Science at the University of Zurich, Switzerland. Her research interests include comparative politics, collective action, policy diffusion, welfare systems, and health care policies. Recent publications include: "Where Does Learning Take Place? The Role of Intergovernmental Cooperation in Policy Diffusion," *European Journal of Political Research* (forthcoming); "Learning from Others: The Diffusion of Hospital Financing Reforms in OECD Countries" (with F. Gilardi and S. Luyet), *Comparative Political Studies* 42 (4), 2009; "Welfare States, Labor Markets, and the Political Opportunities for Collective Action in the Unemployment Political Field: A Theoretical Framework" (with M. Berclaz and M. Giugni), in *The Politics of Unemployment in Europe*, Marco Giugni ed., Ashgate (2009); "Empirical Modeling of Policy Diffusion in Federal States: The Dyadic Approach" (with F. Gilardi), *Swiss Political Science Review* 14 (3), 2008; and "Networks and Political Contention over Unemployment: A Comparison of Britain, Germany and Switzerland" (with M. Cinalli), *Mobilization*, 13 (3), 2008.

Marco Giugni, a sociologist and political scientist, is a professor at the Department of Political Science and International Relations and director of the Institute of Social and Political Research (resop) at the University of Geneva, Switzerland. His research interests include social movements and collective action, immigration and ethnic relations, unemployment, and social exclusion. Recent publications include: *Social Capital, Political Participation and Migration in Europe* (ed. with L. Morales), Palgrave (2011); *The Contentious Politics of Unemployment in Europe* (ed.), Palgrave (2010); *The Politics of Unemployment* *in Europe* (ed.), Ashgate (2009); *Contested Citizenship* (with R. Koopmans, P. Statham, and F. Passy), University of Minnesota Press (2005); and *Social Protest and Policy Change*, Rowman & Littlefield (2004).

Christian Lahusen, a sociologist, is a professor of sociology at the University of Siegen, Germany. He received his PhD at the European University Institute, Italy, in 1994. He taught at the University of Düsseldorf and Bamberg, Germany. He is a well known scholar in the fields of sociological theories, political sociology, here primarily social movement analysis, European studies, unemployment, and social exclusion. Recent publications include: "Joining the Cocktail-Circuit: Social Movement Organizations at the European Union," *Mobilization*, 9 (1), 2004; "Die Fragilität kollektiven Handelns: Arbeitslosenproteste in Deutschland und Frankreich" (with B. Baumgarten), *Zeitschrift für Soziologie* 35 (2), 2006; "La main invisible de l'Union européenne et l'européanisation silencieuse des débats publics sur le chômage," *Politique européenne*, 21, 2007; and "Transcending Marginalization. The Mobilization of the Unemployed in France, Germany and Italy in a Comparative Perspective" (with B. Baumgarten, S. Baglioni, and D. Chabanet), *Mobilization*, 13 (3), 2008.

Eeva Luhtakallio, a sociologist, is a research fellow at the University of Helsinki, Finland, and a member of the Helsinki Research Group for Political Sociology. She has published on local democracy, on practices of everyday politics and citizenship, and on methodological issues in political sociology. Recent publications include: *Practicing Democracy. Local Activism and Politics in France and Finland*, Palgrave Macmillan (forthcoming); "Perceptions of Democracy in Helsinki and Lyon," in *Nordic Associations in a European Perspective*, Risto Alapuro and Henrik Stenius eds, Nomos (2010); and "Quota Trouble: Talking about Gender Quotas in Finnish Local Politics" (with A. Maria Holli and E. Raevaara), *International Feminist Journal of Politics* 8 (2), 2006.

Frédéric Royall, a political scientist, is a senior lecturer and member of the Center for European Studies at the University of Limerick, Ireland. He has published extensively in the area of contemporary European politics and society. Recent publications include: "Globalization and Political Posturing on the Left in France in the 1990s," (with C. Desbos) *French Politics*, 9 (2), 2011; "A Comparative Analysis of Pro-Traveller and Pro-Unemployed Mobilisations," *Irish Journal of Sociology*, 18 (2), 2010; "Opportunities and Perception in Pro-Traveller Mobilisations in Ireland (1960–2000)," *Journal of Contemporary European Studies*, 18 (2), 2010; "Economic Recession and the Mobilization of the Unemployed: France and Ireland Compared" (with D. Chabanet), *French Politics*, 7 (3/4), 2009; "Regards croisés : La presse frontiste face aux mouvements des 'sans' dans les années 90," *French Politics, Culture & Society*, 26 (3), 2009.

Martti Siisiäinen, a sociologist, is a professor at the University of Jyväskylä, Finland. He has published extensively on collective action, social capital, sociology of organizations and voluntary associations and networks. Recent publications include: *Fields and Capitals. Constructing Local Life* (ed. with L. Alanen), Finnish Institute for Educational Research (2011); "Voluntary Associations at the Local Level in three Nordic Countries" (with D. Wollebaek and B. Ibsen), in *Nordic Associations in a European Perspective*, Risto Alapuro and Henrik Stenius eds, Nomos (2010); "Associational Activeness and Attitudes towards Political Citizenship in Finland from a Comparative Perspective" (with R. Blom), *Journal of Civil Society*, 5 (3), 2009; and "New and Old Associations as Trusting Networks: Tracing Social Capital in Jyväskylä," in *Social Capital and Urban Networks of Trust*, Jouni Häkli and Claudio Minca eds, Ashgate (2009).

Catherine Spieser, a political scientist, is a postdoctoral researcher at the Centre d'études de l'emploi, Paris. Her PhD thesis (EUI, Florence) focused on the construction of labor market policies in Poland since 1989. Her primary research interests are in the politics of labor market adjustment, the political sociology of the welfare state, and the comparative study of labor market policies. Recent publications include: "The Politics and Policies of Labour Market Adjustment in Post-1989 Poland," in *What Capitalism? Socio-Economic Change in Central Eastern Europe*, A. Krause and V. Trappmann eds, *SFB 580 Mitteilungen*, 36, 2010; "Managing Mass Dismissals and High Unemployment. Employment Policies and Unemployment Compensation in Poland," in *Restructuring in the New EU Member States*, M.-A. Moreau and M. E. Blas-López eds, Peter Lang (2008); and "Labour Market Policies and Union Politics in Post-communist Poland. Explaining the Peaceful Institutionalisation of Unemployment," *Politique européenne*, 21, 2007.

Karolina Sztandar-Sztanderska, a sociologist and translator, is a PhD student at Sciences Po de Paris and University of Warsaw. Her thesis focuses on the activation of the unemployed at the street level in Poland. Her research interests concern social and employment policies, Central and Eastern European countries, economic and organizational sociology, and sociology of science. Recent publications include: "Activation of the Unemployed in Poland: From Policy Design to Policy Implementation," *International Journal of Sociology and Social Policy* 29 (11), 2009; "Poland. Unemployment Benefit: Haunted by a Lack of Legitimacy" (with S. Portet), in *Unemployment Benefit Systems in Europe and North America*, Florence Lefresne ed., IRES/ETUI (2010); and "Poland: Vulnerability under Pressure of Unemployment" (with S. Portet), in *Evolving World of Work in the Enlarged EU*, Daniel Vaughan-Whitehead and François Eyraud eds, European Commission and International Labour Office (2007).

Introduction: The Mobilization of the Unemployed in a Comparative Perspective

Didier Chabanet and Jean Faniel

The mobilization of the unemployed has for long been considered by specialists in the field of collective action as a highly improbable phenomenon (see Galland and Louis 1981; Russ 1990; Demazière 1996; Wolski-Prenger 1997 and 1998; Bourdieu 1998; Paugam 1998). The pioneering study carried out in Marienthal, Austria, in the early 1930s by Jahoda, Lazarsfeld, and Zeisel (1933), who emphasized the irremediable desocializing and destructuring effects of unemployment, served as a basis for this analysis. Thereafter, the obstacles that the unemployed had to overcome to get mobilized were largely documented and are essentially a throwback to the characteristics of a population subject to strong forces of social and political atomization (Schnapper 1981; Rolke 1988). The cause seems to have been heard and, by the same token, was never really questioned. It is moreover striking to note that the explanations put forward were always very similar, if not the same, whatever the countries or periods examined, rather as though the incapacity of the unemployed to claim was (virtually) taken for granted (Chabanet and Faniel 2011). On the whole, the arguments put forward can be summarized in four main categories: (1) The jobless would be deprived of a common identity, regarded as an indispensable prerequisite to any collective action. (2) Their position even as unemployed would encourage them even more to take shelter in individual survival strategies rather than to get mobilized in a situation from which they hoped to escape. (3) The weakness of their resources (financial, cultural, or even in terms of social networks) would be an almost unacceptable obstacle to the appearance of a protest movement. (4) Last, the stigmatization to which they would be subject in public would make any expression of politics almost unthinkable, and in any case illegitimate.

Without any of these arguments being unfounded—far from it—different published works over the last twenty-five years bid us to alleviate the extent.

In particular, research with a strong historical bent (Croucher 1987; van den Oord 1990; Bagguley 1991 and 1992; Flanagan 1991; Folsom 1991; Lorence 1996; Kourchid 1999; Perry 2000 and 2007; Richards 2002; Pierru 2003; Reiss 2007; Croucher et al. 2008; Reiss and Perry 2011) and some comparative studies of limited scope (Royall 1997 and 2000; Faniel 2004; Baglioni et al. 2008; Chabanet and Royall 2009) throw new light, which obliges one to reconsider the question of the mobilization of the unemployed. In the light of these works, it seems that, despite great difficulties, the unemployed got organized and made demands collectively on several occasions and in different national contexts. Consequently, nothing from this viewpoint allows one to distinguish them fundamentally from any other more socially integrated groups. The phenomenon, observable over two centuries, seems moreover not to be limited to any precise region in the world, affecting in various forms, periods, and with variable intensity those such as the United States (Rosenzweig 1976; Piven and Cloward 1977; Kerbo and Shaffer 1992), Palestine (De Vries and Bar-On 2011), Argentina (Svampa and Pereyra 2004; Fernández Álvarez and Manzano 2007), New Zealand (Locke 2011), as well as a large number of European countries (see, e.g., Giugni 2010 and the chapters in this volume).

Particularly since the end of the 1970s, it is Europe that has seen a concentration of a large number of these demonstrations, in a global context marked by high unemployment levels and the growth of social deprivation (Cameron 2001; Chabanet 2007). Mobilizations of the unemployed have already been studied at the transnational level, via the European Marches against unemployment, job insecurity, and social exclusions ("Euromarches"—Mathers 1999; Chabanet 2002 and 2008), but never systematically at the national level. This present work is, to our knowledge, the first attempt in this area, covering ten European countries: Belgium, Britain, Finland, France, Germany, Ireland, Italy, Poland, Spain, and Switzerland.[1] This broad choice is in order to put in perspective a very wide variety of situations, from a point of view as much economic as political, social, geographical, or cultural. Each study has been entrusted to specialists in social movements who carried out their research independently, including the methodological approach. The contributions, therefore, follow their own logical approach, while sharing a common analysis framework, drawn up during the initial workshop. The analyses focus basically on the period 1980–2007, that is, before the arrival of the economic and financial crisis that has affected Europe especially since 2008. The case studies of Britain and France are purposefully spread over a much longer outlook going back, respectively, to the second half of the nineteenth century, and to the 1920s. Proceeding in this manner, it was a question of taking account of the intrinsic specificities of the national situations examined, of the diversity of available sources, but also of the absence of consistent and comparative data on the subject matter, while providing us with a means of offering a global outlook allowing for the ultimate drawing up of a certain number of hypotheses on the subject. In this introduction, we proceed first with an overview of the actions initiated by the unemployed in the various European countries studied. We then draw more systematic lessons on conditions surrounding the emergence and the characteristics of the mobilization of the unemployed in Europe. Thus we are providing what may be termed a "comprehensive comparison," not based on the use of standardized data, usually mostly quantitative, but on a much more inductive analysis, of a qualitative nature, ascertaining links between the processes and the categories that emerge from the different analyses brought together here, to develop and formalize a set of proposals on the conditions of mobilization of the unemployed.

Very Variable Levels of Mobilization

The different contributions are presented in terms of the size of movements of the unemployed, which took place in each country. Thus three sets emerged according to whether the mobilization of the unemployed was major, limited, or residual. Thus, the reader is invited to follow a globally descending journey, starting with France, where the movement in winter 1997–1998 was unquestionably the biggest and most media-covered of the unemployed worker mobilizations in Europe since 1980, and ending in Poland where, in spite of a particularly high level of unemployment, the phenomenon remained insignificant.

Countries with Major Mobilizations

A first category—to which Germany and even more so France belong—corresponds to a *major* mobilization situation. France is without question the European country in which the unemployed attained the greatest visibility (chapter one by Didier Chabanet). Since the interwar period, but in a fleeting manner, groups of the unemployed collectively made claims. Over the last twenty-five years, the unemployed likewise got mobilized on a massive scale several times and showed a certain continuity in action (Demazière and Pignoni 1998). Their organizations built a network that, although of a different activity level according to the regions, displayed itself at the national level and made alliances with the trade unions or organizations on the far left, which allowed it to lessen its political isolation. In spite of resources that remain limited, the French movement of the unemployed was able to preserve a certain autonomy of action. The first national organization of the unemployed was created in 1982 by several left-wing Catholic militants. Under its impetus, a protest parade of almost 5,000 unemployed, which till today remains the biggest demonstration of this group in the country, was organized on May 30, 1985, in Paris. Four other organizations saw the light of day in ten or so years, one of them within the trade union CGT (*Confédération générale du travail*), the others on the initiative of militant Catholics, communists, union organizers, those in charge of local associations of the unemployed, or intellectuals.

This period corresponds in France with mass unemployment, the appearance of new poverty, of the failure of the left in power on employment issues, and the speeding up of the process of European integration, which, since the ratification of the Maastricht Treaty forbids, in fact, any kind of Keynesian type stimulation. It was also marked by strong deunionizing and by a growing defiance of the political groupings, two evolutions that encourage the autonomy of social movements. It is in this context that the unemployed manifested their discontent and their will to speak up themselves. Hardly able to count on the support of political parties—except sometimes that of the *Ligue communiste révolutionnaire* (LCR, Trotskyite) and of the *Parti communiste français* (PCF)—and in permanent conflict with most of the trade union organizations—except the CGT and *Solidaires Unitaires Démocratiques* (SUD)—they benefitted nevertheless from support by public opinion. First of all in November and December 1995 the unemployed found a propitious setting for their action, in taking part in the biggest social movement seen in the country since May 1968. Following that, in the winter of 1997–1998 they demanded, and finally obtained—there also in a climate of strong social agitation—a "Christmas bonus" of 1,000 francs (about 150 euros) for a single person and the provision of a special fund of a billion francs (about 150 million euros).

The mobilization of the unemployed seems, since then, to be directed increasingly toward the courts so as to challenge measures restricting allowance for job seekers, but it invariably stumbles against the absence of recognition by the public authorities of the representativity of their organizations, this status being legally reserved for trade unions and employers.

In Germany likewise, the mobilization of the unemployed has seen some significant developments over the last years, following both the growth in unemployment and a series of unprecedented postwar reforms (chapter two by Britta Baumgarten and Christian Lahusen). This mobilization intensified greatly following the German reunification and remains much stronger in the eastern part of the country, characterized by unemployment levels twice the national average. In a decentralized politico-administrative system, local movements of the unemployed mushroomed but progressively structured themselves around several national associations, in particular the *Arbeitslosenverband*, strongly embedded in the former German Democratic Republic. From the middle of the 1990s, demonstrations by the unemployed grew in numerous towns, regularly grouping together several thousand people. The mobilization phases were a response to the different stages of a package of reforms baptized "Agenda 2010," which seriously affected the social security apparatus, retirement, health and dependant insurances, as well as allowances for and job placement of the unemployed.

Two peaks in mobilization intervened in 1998 and in 2004. In the first case, each month, when the latest unemployment figures were published, processions of several tens of thousands of people were organized. In the second, in spring and summer, nearly a million people—of whom half gathered in Berlin—protested in close to 230 towns against the last strand of reforms affecting the labor market ("Hartz IV" reforms). The significance of the protests in which the unemployed were involved evidently owed much to the extent of the reforms implemented, which concerned the whole of the population. In this context, the role of the trade unions, especially the *Deutsche Gewerkschaftsbund* (DGB), was ambiguous since these unions did not condemn the reforms underway, without being able to ignore the strength of popular discontent. The organizations of the unemployed—about half of which are affiliated to a trade union structure—thus benefited from mixed support, which nevertheless proved essential. The opposition front to the reforms was such that it overflowed in part the powerful DGB and provided the unemployed in action rather favorable conditions of existence and of political expression. In particular, it tended to counteract the stigmatization effects of which the unemployed are victims in German public opinion. In a country traditionally portrayed as following a corporatist model and keeping in mind the efficiency of its system of social negotiations, these are major changes and represent opportunities for new actions for the unemployed.

As in France—but not being able to count on the same popular support nor on the same political ties—the unemployed seem to direct themselves toward more and more autonomous types of action, often rash, which translate into difficulty for the reunified Germany to resolve the growing problems linked to exclusion from the labor market.

Countries with Limited Mobilization

A second category—in which are included Belgium, Finland, Italy, and Spain—covers those countries where mobilization is more *limited*.

In Belgium, 88 percent of the unemployed are unionized (chapter three by Jean Faniel). This exceptional situation is the result of historical compromises, which led to unemployment allowances being paid mainly through the trade unions. In this system, the trade unions always ensured that the compensation conditions for the unemployed were upheld, foremost to avoid all downward pressure on wages. Even if unemployment increased considerably from the middle of the 1970s on, the level of protection of job seekers was thus maintained at a threshold above the average of other countries. For example, Belgium is the only EU country where unemployment pay does not, in principle, have a fixed duration. However, restrictive measures and, above all, stricter controls have been introduced in the past few years, especially with regard to "cohabitants," that is, those living under the same roof as a person in receipt of an income. The unemployed vigorously denounced these provisions, which gave rise to impromptu visits to the homes of those concerned, and this was generally perceived as being in breach of their private lives. The government responded to these protests by toning down these practices. Belgium thus offers an illustration of a welfare state providing a high level of protection, even when the labor market is going through a serious recession. Paradoxically, the mobilization of the unemployed certainly suffers from the efficiency of their partners, in the first place the trade unions, since it can only with difficulty nourish itself on the feeling of being ignored and sidelined by the types of social representation. From then on, when reforms aimed at lowering the compensation scheme are implemented, the tendencies of the unemployed to challenge are limited, even when trade union opposition is weak, as was the case at the time of the major reform of 2004. At the same time, a smaller and exceptional mobilization can result in strong political impacts, since it generates a positive institutional response in some cases (Faniel 2004).

In Finland, unemployment soared brutally from 3.2 percent in 1990 to 16.6 percent in 1994, stabilizing until 2000 at a level above 10 percent (chapter four by Eeva Luhtakallio and Martti Siisiäinen). This increase led to the multiplication of the number of groups of the unemployed, which stood at 220 created between 1990 and 1997, brought together in *Työttömien Valtakunnallinen Yhteistoimintaverkosto* (National Cooperation Organization of the Jobless in Finland, TVY) founded in 1991. Largely controlled by the powerful trade unions, having large resources at their disposal and playing a key role in the mechanisms of public action, these groups played a decisive role in the opposition front to the government then in power, denouncing restrictive measures by a welfare state hitherto renowned throughout the world for its generosity. The highlight of this movement was the parade of nearly 20,000 people who responded to the call of the unemployed in the streets of Helsinki on November 4, 1993, on the occasion of the *Revolution-Thursday*. This event was the biggest post–World War II national demonstration, greatly exceeding, by comparison, the 6,000 people gathered in 2002 against nuclear arms, or the 10,000 opponents of the war in Iraq in 2003. This peak, however, ended up having no tomorrow, with the arrival in 1995 of a progressive coalition resulting in the isolation of the organizations of the unemployed, orphans of the support of the trade union forces, and the parties of the left. The Finnish situation thus testifies to the possibility of mobilizing the unemployed, but also to the fragility of their action, since they depend on exceptional political circumstances over which they barely have a hold. The Finnish case also throws up paradoxes, with the unemployed being relatively well organized, capable of taking part in activities *en masse*, and even sometimes instigating them, without however having control over these protesting forces.

In Italy (chapter five by Simone Baglioni), the mobilization of the unemployed is concentrated in certain urban zones in the south, mainly Naples and its surrounding region, struck over several decades by endemic unemployment above 30 percent. Its beginnings go back to the month of June 1975, when nearly 2,000 unemployed, wearied by more than a year's protests in Naples, paraded in Rome and were received by the government. At this meeting, the government promised the creation of 10,500 new jobs intended for the unemployed in action. The same day, 700 Neapolitan unemployed in conflict obtained an employment contract for a year with the municipality, paid for out of a governmental assistance fund. Armed with this success, numerous committees of the unemployed were created in Naples, negotiating with the local or national public authorities the recruitment conditions for their members. Since that time, the inclusion in the local political landscape of these groups is established, so that today they are treated by the public authorities as legitimate counterparts, occupying a central place in the labor market, playing in some way the role of a placement agency and mitigating in part the shortcomings of the welfare state whose services in matters of unemployment benefits are among the weakest in Europe.

Italy presents a special case, characterized by a very strong regionalization of actions by the unemployed. There is doubtless no other case in Europe of an autonomous movement of the unemployed having political recognition and such important influence, which is only exercised locally and contrasts with an absence of mobilization in the rest of the country.

In Spain (chapter six by Sophie Béroud), the mobilization of the unemployed is also confined locally in a country that for over twenty years has had one of the highest rates of unemployment in the EU, bordering on 20 percent of the active population between 1982 and 1998. The exclusion of a significant portion of the people in the labor market, as well as the growing marginalization of a large fringe of wage earners, did not translate into a protest movement on the part of those who were the direct victims of this situation. Since the attainment of democracy in Spain at the end of the 1970s, the sociopolitical context seems not very conducive to the collective mobilization of the unemployed and the precarious, in any case as a social movement of national magnitude. Several explanatory factors can be highlighted here.

The major element concerns the role of the main Spanish trade union confederations, which imposed themselves on the fall of the Franco regime as "social partners," negotiating with the government and employers the establishment of social rights and welfare state, thus not presenting themselves as a figurehead of a protesting working class, opposed to the political power. Without being necessarily in line with the public policies implemented, the trade unions were actually in a partnership relationship with the public authorities. At the same time, they were extensively involved in the successive reforms inspired by neoliberalism, often led by coalitions of the left, which aimed, in particular since the early 1990s, at increasing the flexibility of work and of limiting the compensation to those who do not have a job. Over the same period, the historical players in the struggle against Francoism, such as the *Partido comunista de España* (PCE) or different factions from the far left, saw their influence wither and could not relay the cause of the most socially vulnerable. Finally, the rise in power of the autonomous communities, whose powers over social matters were progressively extended—up to the point of touching on the question of drawing up the minimum wage—also contributed to boosting the territorial and local stakes and was therefore, a contrario, a brake on the possible national convergence of the struggles of the socially excluded.

In the end, the mobilization of the unemployed remains limited to a few large urban centers, such as Barcelona, Madrid, Seville, or Valencia. It is generally the result of district associations, which do not campaign specifically for "the jobless," but which wish to struggle against economic globalization and the worsening of inequalities. In this sense, the rise of the alterglobalization movement was able to be a relatively favorable context for the ideological and organizational convergence of the struggles of the unemployed, but only at the regional level.

The national strike in Spain on June 20, 2002, to protest against the restrictions the Aznar government wanted to impose on the system of unemployment benefits, finally crystallized well the whole of these elements. The size of the mobilization—more than a million demonstrators and nearly 80 percent of strikers in the country—led the government to withdraw its original project and can, as such, be considered as a success and credited to the committed forces, but without the question of the collective organization of the unemployed ever really being at the heart of the debate. In certain autonomous communities, on the other hand, the unemployed emerged as protesting players. Thus, in Andalusia, with the support of the socialist municipalities, and in a climate where the effervescence was seething and intensified by the preparation of the alterglobalization demonstrations anticipated on the occasion of the G8 summit in Seville, held on June 21–22, 2002, some groups of unemployed could express their discontent and get mobilized repeatedly, before and after this event.

The Spanish case shows in a convincing manner that the mobilization of the unemployed is not directly related to the unemployment level and to the extent of the economic and social difficulties facing a country. The general sociopolitical context and, in this case, the absence of support by the trade unions proves to be an almost insurmountable obstacle to the protest action by the unemployed, even if the virtually federal organization of the Spanish political system and the momentum of the alterglobalization movement provides, at the local level, some action spaces.

Countries with Residual Mobilization

It is possible to differentiate a third and final category of countries—of which are Britain, Ireland, Switzerland, and Poland—marked by a *residual* mobilization capacity.

The British case is especially interesting when one puts it in a relatively long historical perspective, going back to the end of the nineteenth century (chapter seven by Manlio Cinalli). Such a horizon allows an understanding of how the space and capacities for action by the unemployed are progressively reduced, to the point of being practically inexistent today. Until the interwar period, there were frequent and large demonstrations by the unemployed, comprising one of the big elements of a working-class movement powerful in itself. The organizations defending the workers, whether from the unions or political, which sprang up at this time, as well as, in their wake, the setting up of associations representing specifically the rights of the unemployed, testify to this vitality. Strong unionization, repeated strikes, and protest movements, especially in the industrial sector, as well as the emergence in 1921 of the National Unemployed Workers' Movement (NUWM), constituted a set of factors favorable to the labor cause and to the mobilization of the unemployed, whose action was at the heart of the capital/labor antagonism, which then structured British political life. Proof of its anchorage within the labor movement, the NUWM foresaw in its statutes that almost one-third of its members were to be people holding down jobs.

From the end of the 1920s, however, this understanding cracked. This was first due to the radicalization of the unemployed, of whom many got close to the Communist International and who, by the same token, distanced themselves from the less revolutionary elements of the British labor movement. Subsequently, it was due to the growing interventionism of the state in economic and social affairs, which, following the stock exchange crash of 1929, started the foundations of a policy of the Keynesian type, of which one of the features is to involve the trade unions and employers' bodies in the drawing up of public policies, thus tending to defuse conflicts in the industrial sphere. Relations between the unemployed and trade unions then slackened, the latter seeking to put the former under their control, in particular through the creation of a national network of locally run unemployed centers that the trade unions largely controlled. In parallel, the marked fall in unemployment coming out of World War II, and continuing until the end of the 1950s, considerably weakened the organizations of the unemployed, whose capacity to mobilize declined heavily.

Despite some inclination to protest during the years 1970–1980, collective action by the unemployed was already weakened when the government of Margaret Thatcher came to power in 1979. In spite of a substantial rise in unemployment during the 1980s and several protest movements organized by the unemployed themselves—the People's Marches for Jobs in 1981 and 1983 come to mind—the New Right restricted the capacity for action by the unemployed, on the one hand with an extremely aggressive policy toward their historical allies—the trade unions—and on the other by practicing more or less direct control over the unemployed centers, which became less and less socializing points for militants, and rather more placement agencies, or agencies for service providers, embedded in bureaucratic systems. In this context, conservative governments could deploy a whole series of measures reducing the rights of the unemployed—up to the abolition of the unemployment insurance scheme, replaced with a much more restrictive jobseeker's allowance—without the people directly targeted being able to fight efficiently against these provisions.

The victory of New Labour in 1997 did not fundamentally change the deal for the unemployed. Even if social questions and the struggle against inequalities again became priority issues, the government of Tony Blair followed a policy of flexibilization of the labor market, seeking to promote "workfare," that is, combining as closely as possible work and social assistance. Like the New Right, New Labour did not involve the unemployed in its policy, nor even the traditional forces of the working-class movement, preferring to focus on the assistance and support of a multitude of organizations from civil society (voluntary groups, corporations, charities, nongovernmental associations, etc.), integrated by the public authorities in the struggle against unemployment and social exclusion. This type of governance is to neutralize what remains of the action capacity of the unemployed, contributing by different means of the New Right to weaken them and reduce them to shrinking away. In parallel, the significant fall in the numbers of the unemployed—even if accompanied by a steep rise in poverty and deprivation—and the ideology of New Labour, which tends to put the question of the fluidity of the labor market at a higher stake level than the protection of the unemployed—in other words which values the mobility of individuals more than the provisions of social assistance—are factors that do not facilitate the mobilization of the unemployed.

In Ireland, each jump in unemployment gave rise to the emergence of organizations of the unemployed (chapter eight by Frédéric Royall). This was especially the case in 1983, with the creation of the Dublin Unemployed Alliance, which rapidly came to the fore as a privileged interlocutor with the public authorities and four years later helped create the Irish National Organisation of the Unemployed (INOU). The INOU is put forward as a structured representative of the unemployed, which enjoyed a rapid expansion, incorporating more than 100 affiliated groups in 1994 and almost 180 in 2003. Devoting the core of its activity to putting forward local development assistance for the unemployed, or assessing the employment policies, the INOU constantly however turned aside from the conflictual forms of action. In a context of the strong administrative centralization, and taking into account Irish political habits, marked by a substantial deference with regard to the structures of authority, the protest that could lead to anticipating the gravity of the problems to be handled was annihilated. The INOU found itself entrusted with growing responsibilities in the field of offering services to the unemployed and could be regarded as a social peacemaking factor. By the same token the member organizations progressively toned down their demands, especially after 1996 when the eradication of unemployment ushered in an unprecedented period of prosperity for the country. The Irish example thus underlines that the associations of the unemployed do not necessarily favor the scale of protest action, especially when they are co-opted by the state apparatus (Royall 2005).

In Switzerland (chapter nine by Michel Berclaz, Katharina Füglister, and Marco Giugni), the structural weakness of the unemployment level—hardly about 1 percent of the active population—but also a high level of benefits combined with a deep stigmatization of the status of the unemployed worker seemed until the beginning of the 1990s to remove any relevance of the question of the mobilization of the unemployed. The situation evolved when unemployment reached between 3 and 4 percent of the population, leading the public authorities to restrict the conditions of compensation. The organizations of the unemployed, few in number and isolated, regrouped and called for a protest march bringing together, in February 1993, almost 10,000 people. In 1996, a law revised downward unemployed worker protection and strengthened control measures against them. The tiny *Association de défense des chômeurs de la Chaux-de-Fonds* then decided—alone—to challenge this decision and undertook to gather among the population the 50,000 signatures required for the organization of a referendum. Against all expectations, not only was this fateful threshold attained, but the consultation that followed led to the withdrawal of the law called into question. This example illustrates marvelously the paradoxes of the mobilization of the unemployed: even in an apparently inauspicious context, the reduced windows of opportunity can induce substantial political effects. The existence of a popular referendum initiative, used to effect by the players otherwise deprived of any means of significant influence, appears crucial here. Moreover, in Switzerland, the unemployed seem to accede to a political existence that, while remaining weak, was formerly inconceivable. Nevertheless, relatively favorable compensation conditions meant a structural brake on their commitment, intensified by the deep stigmatization of which they are the object.

Last, Poland presents a set of features a priori among the most conducive to the mobilization of the unemployed. Three major elements seemed to go in this direction (chapter ten by Catherine Spieser and Karolina Sztandar-Sztanderska). First, the country experiences mass unemployment since the fall of the communist regime, all the more brutal and traumatic since it was previously officially inexistent. Second, and more widely, the transition to a market economy open to free competition and international competitivity—devoted somehow by Poland's entry into the EU in 2004—seemed inevitably to give rise to large movements of discontent on the part of the fringe of wage earners, previously protected, who found themselves weakened and marginalized by this change. Last, the working-class movement and the trade unions, who played a crucial role in the democratic transition of the 1980s, established themselves since that period as one of the inescapable players in the national political game.

However, it has to be noted that the Polish unemployed were never really organized collectively. This situation is better understood if one includes in the analysis, on the one hand, the question of the dominant social representations through which the unemployment experience is grasped in Polish society—what is generally called "cognitive framing"—and, on the other, the specificities of the unemployment benefit system and of social protection installed from the beginning of the 1990s.

Without a doubt, the unemployed of Poland are victims of a deep stigmatization, more so than the unemployed in all the other countries gathered in this study. In Polish society today, due to the predominance of individualistic values, unemployment is in fact and above all considered to be the consequence of personal failure. The phenomenon is not therefore seen so much as a collective problem, whose fundamental causes are to be sought in the global economico-political process, as from a moral viewpoint, highlighting the responsibility of the unemployed. It is striking to note that the latter share to a great degree these portrayals and have, in common with the population as a whole, a guilt-ridden view of their situation, which evidently does not encourage them to protest.

Moreover, the apparatus for social protection put in place to accompany the economic upheavals faced by Poland at the end of communism played an essential role in the defusing of social tensions and the discontent that this situation did not fail to induce. The explosion in the unemployment rate in 1989 led the public authorities to put in place a benefit system both advantageous and not very selective, at least at the outset. The authorities negotiated at the same time the early redundancy conditions of workers unsuited to the new rules of a competitive economy, especially in strongly unionized sectors, such as industry or the mines, where the emergence of social conflicts were potentially more common. Not only did these very stimulating sectoral measures neutralize the inclinations to protest by the most experienced of the workers, but they prevented likewise the elevation of the question of the benefit system into horizontal stakes, which could have been the cornerstone of a united opposition front.

Even if the rights of the unemployed were rapidly and drastically revised downward in the middle of the 1990s, the unemployed never constituted an organized collective force, the entry into the EU allowing, furthermore, numerous Poles in search of work to emigrate abroad, reducing somewhat the political pertinence of the subject. Above all, the principal trade unions, just like *Solidarność* whose wild anticommunism accommodated itself perfectly to the conversion to neoliberalism, accompanied and defended the passage to a market economy and largely guaranteed the policies then put into effect, including when the rights of the unemployed were questioned.

Taken as a whole, the Polish trade union movement played, over the last thirty years, a decisive role as social partner, benefiting from an incontestable political legitimacy, despite ideological divisions and a fall in the number of its members. In a cognitive context highly unfavorable to their cause, and deprived of trade union support, the unemployed were never in a position to structure themselves collectively, whereas unemployment remains one of the main ills of Polish society.

Discussion and Preliminary Hypotheses

This European overview allows for discussing some elements relating to the conditions of mobilization of the unemployed, but also to their limits. Despite the peaks in mobilization in certain countries, it is indeed the sporadic—if not marginal—nature of the action of the unemployed that stands out clearly. One of the paradoxes of the European democracies is that the most insecure of its population should not be able to organize itself sustainably and, above all, give perennial and structured political advice on the principal sickness hanging over European societies for several decades.

The studies presented in this volume suggest that the periods of strong mobilization generally correspond with phases of acute unemployment. The relationship is, nevertheless, neither direct nor automatic. The Polish and Spanish cases remind us that a very high level of unemployment does not necessarily entail protest movements on the part of those who are victims of this situation. Conversely, the Swiss example shows that in a context close to full employment, but marked by a rapid increase in unemployment, a local association of the unemployed can get mobilized and take advantage of a favorable institutional context to secure a major modification to the unemployment benefit system. One can draw three lessons from this first analysis.

1. Much more than the level of unemployment as such, it is indeed the trend of the increase of this phenomenon—even when it remains limited in absolute terms—that constitutes fertile ground for the organization of and protests by the unemployed.

2. A high rate of unemployment is not mechanically linked to a high level of protest. Other organizational, political, or cognitive factors also play an essential role in the expression (or not) of a protest movement.
3. The generalization (of the fear) of unemployment generates feelings of frustration and anger all the more vivid when expectations have been raised (Gurr 1970). In other words, the demands of the unemployed increase with the rights at their disposal, giving rise to ever stronger protests when these rights are questioned and diminish. This disclaimed version of the theorem of de Tocqueville—by virtue of which the subjective dynamic of a social phenomenon counts for more than its objective gravity—constitutes a key element of understanding. One of the configurations most conducive to the mobilization of the unemployed is therefore the one involving a high level of protection coupled with reforms aimed at restricting these benefits.

Between Local Anchorage and Globalization

When it takes place, the mobilization of the unemployed grows out of regional focal points, in a confrontational relationship aimed primarily at local actors, usually employment agencies or municipalities. Concerning movements of the unemployed in Great Britain in the 1930s, Bagguley (1991) had already shown that the phenomenon was generally limited geographically, which does not even prevent the development at national or international levels of coordinations of the unemployed (Royall 2002). In fact it seems that the process of raising the political awareness of the unemployed can only take place on a local basis, closest to their concerns and close to the places to which they go. Maurer (2001) demonstrated perfectly that the political commitment of the unemployed is most often the consequence, uncertain and very random, of a long process of reconstruction of oneself, of mutual aid and socialization, which is done through routine activities, included on a day-to-day basis, carried out within an associative framework, or just simply groups established de facto. These are exchanges that enable the unemployed to escape from their isolation and, occasionally, to build a collective challenge in which they will potentially take part.

Moreover, to thrive, a protest movement must make sense to those who are its protagonists, a fortiori when it is a question of people whose political competencies are limited. This requires clearly identifying a number of pertinent institutional targets. This is the reason why local public authorities or the job centers generally concentrate on the vindictiveness of the unemployed—suffering in the event of occupations, sequestrations even of the staff—much more often than the national institutions, which are at the same time geographically and symbolically more remote, even when they specify the struggle against unemployment, and the implementation of social devices relating thereto. This anchorage to the local explains that, in the same country at the same time, levels of mobilization are extremely mixed from one town to another. This variation stresses by the same token the difficulty in having a genuine national movement of the unemployed. This localization of mobilization is not done by chance. It is concentrated in the zones or the regions most exposed to the economic crisis and to unemployment. In Italy, it is the region of Naples, not the more prosperous north, that, for thirty-five years, has been the leading scene for mobilizations of the unemployed. In Germany it is the *Länder* of the former German Democratic Republic, hit by an unemployment rate twice that of the national average, that provide the main focus of mobilizations. In Belgium, the mobilization of the unemployed has entirely disappeared in Flanders since this rate fell below 10 percent. Mobilizations are the stuff of the unemployed from Wallonia and Brussels, with the unemployment rate approaching and even exceeding 20 percent. The Belgian towns where mobilization is the strongest are also those where the unemployment rate is highest, after having known a prosperous industrial past. This situation resembles that found in France. The former industrial basins of the Nord-Pas-de-Calais, of the Paris region, and the Bouches-du-Rhône took the full force of the recession. They were the departure points of the mobilization of the French unemployed. Last, it is Andalusia that, in Spain, is the region most involved in mobilizations of the jobless and which is also one of those most affected by the economic crisis.

In all the countries where significant mobilizations of the unemployed emerged, an organizational network whose boundaries and operating rules are often little formalized was first and above all put in place at the local level. Taking up the thesis of Hobsbawm (1984, 292–6) on the necessity for the poor people's movements to acquire organizations in support of their struggle, Baglioni shows in this volume the importance of these structures in the arrival and conduct of mobilizations of the unemployed in Naples. The juridical status of these groups varies from country to country, some among them having simply no legal existence, or claim only the status of "collective," just like *Agir ensemble contre le chômage* ("Act together against unemployment"—AC!) in France, or of *Chômeur pas chien!* ("Unemployed, but not dogs!") in Belgium. In Germany or Spain many groups are committed to their independence, inhibiting the emergence of national coordination or preventing them from gaining meaningful influence. At the same time, to break out from their isolation and make up the numbers, these organizations operate as a network, fully using modern means of information and communication to coordinate their actions. In doing this, they look for a point of balance between, on one side, an anchorage site indispensable to the enlistment of the unemployed and, on the other, the need to give magnitude to their mobilization and enhance its visibility. In Ireland and in Finland, the national organization (INOU and TVY, respectively) relies on a dense fabric of local organizations, the relationship between these two based on a certain division of tasks. Ensuring the representation of the unemployed and playing a lobbying role with regard to the public authorities, the INOU and the TVY have assumed a predominant place in the sociopolitical landscape of their countries. This structure nevertheless takes on the appearance of bureaucratization, which may contribute to defuse the protest potential of the unemployed, thus concurring with the thesis of Piven and Cloward (1977) according to which their mobilization is boosted by a low level of institutionalization of their organizations. Ultimately, if the existence of organizations appears to be an indispensable prerequisite for the mobilization of the unemployed in accordance with Hobsbawm, the way in which they are structured responds to relatively specific forces, which aim to conserve a local closeness to the unemployed and to have the largest possible action network, which allows it to spread and gain in magnitude.

This local anchorage and link with the concerns of the unemployed do not prevent the movements for the unemployed to enroll the defense of their cause within much larger types of protest, especially that of the alterglobalization. In an often difficult national context, characterized by indifference, hostility even toward them from the government parties, the unemployed thus found opportunities in the organization of European countersummits, and more widely in demonstrations opposing international neoliberalism to get themselves heard, thus turning down a particular version of "glocalism"—"think global, act local" (on the concrete relationship of the two levels, see Pleyers 2010, 202–18)—as shown in the chapters on Belgium, Germany, Italy, and Spain.

In this perspective, the devolved or decentralized politico-administrative systems—whose most pronounced form is doubtless the federal state—seem the most favorable toward collective action by the unemployed (Bagguley 1991 and 1992). The jobless target the institutions that handle specifically their files and are in a position to give them satisfaction. Among the studies brought together here, those dealing with Spain and a contrario with Ireland are particularly instructive from this point of view. In Spain, a state where federalism is quite advanced, the autonomous communities created assistance-like welfare payments. These regimes are nonetheless developed in an uneven manner from region to region. Andalusia, which has developed a subsidy of this kind, appears as the main center of mobilization of the jobless in Spain. Conversely, the very centralized decision-making system in Ireland regarding unemployment slowed the rise of mobilizations, bearers of protests at local level, even though institutions exist at this level, but having trivial power. The strategy followed by the INOU had in fact consisted of concentrating effort on the work carried out with the government in Dublin, without weaving links with the local agencies. Contrary to what one may have thought, the case of France, where it is known that the politico-administrative system is traditionally very centralized, does not represent here a counterexample, to the extent that many social benefits rely, at least in part, on local collective bodies, and that the ASSEDIC enjoyed a certain decision-making autonomy. It is by drawing on this setting that the CGT jobless workers' committees sought to obtain over several years, at the local level, a Christmas bonus for the unemployed, a demand that constituted the heart of the protest movement of the winter of 1997–1998. In brief, the associations of the unemployed found more room for action at the local level, insofar as this level provides a pertinent political arena for building up social undertakings and the defense of their cause.

Opportunities or Constraints? The Search for Alliances

The unemployed in action are for the most part sustained by other types of organization, thus seeming to permanently hover between a will of assertion of their own—which emphasizes their cause and their representation as such—and the practical need to take into consideration largely exogenous power relationships, which determine in large part the conditions of their action. This tension is not the privilege of the unemployed, but it arises in particularly crucial terms for a weakened population, with limited resources, which has to rely on outside support to have a hope of being heard. As Lipsky (1970) emphasized "the 'problem of the powerless' in protest activity is to activate 'third parties' to enter the implicit or explicit bargaining arena in ways favorable to the protestors" (2).

One knows in general the importance of political opportunity structures to understand the conditions for mobilization of social groups. In its classical definition, the concept is very state-centered (Kitschelt 1986; McAdam 1996; Tarrow 1996) and only attaches importance to strictly political variables or actors. In a very convincing manner, Giugni (2008) has shown (see also Berclaz, Füglister, and Giugni in this volume) that collective group action of the socially excluded depends closely on specific opportunities, which are not directly linked with the political system *stricto sensu*. In this regard, the attitude of the trade unions plays a determining role in the mobilization of the unemployed, even though other types of actor—one thinks in particular of the churches in Finland or Germany, of different groups coming from the anarchist domain, the far left, or even from social Catholicism—may also be valued allies.

Because they have vocation to relay social discontent and are considered by the public authorities as legitimate interlocutors, the trade unions are de facto often indispensable supports to mobilizations of the unemployed. The relations between the two sides are however highly complex and ambiguous (Ness 1998; van Berkel and Vlek 1998, 226–7; Richards 2000; Faniel 2009, 102–5; Linders and Kalander 2010). Equipped with resources and the legitimacy of which the organizations of the unemployed are deprived, the union movement is reluctant to openly support the mobilizations over which it does not have total control, which claim for their specificity, occasionally their autonomy, and in any case are beyond the hard core of the working class. Historically anchored in the area of work, the trade unions ensure above all the defense of the most active sections of the wage earners who enjoy good job stability. Without necessarily losing interest in the fate of the unemployed, the trade unions rarely give priority to their situation. Generally, the unions concentrate their attention on the struggle for employment, regarding this combat as benefiting eventually the unemployed. Very often they have trouble taking into account the real concerns of the jobless and translating them into demands capable of being borne by the trade union movement.

Moreover, since the end of World War II, the trade union organizations are consulted and even often associated in most European countries with the unemployment insurance system, very often acting as "social partners," to the detriment of the defense of the specific demands of the unemployed. Integrated thus into the system, a good number of trade union confederations go along with, foster even, welfare state reforms that reduce the protection of the unemployed, which in part anesthetizes the inclination to protest of the unemployed (see in this volume the chapter on Poland) and in part creates tensions with the movements for the unemployed there where they exist (see the chapter on France). One has, in this respect, to separate the situation where unemployment benefits are distributed mainly through the trade unions (as is the case in Belgium and Finland, to take those countries studied in this book, but also in Denmark and Sweden). In direct contact with their unemployed members, and representing the majority of the unemployed in the country, the trade unions placed in this situation seem more inclined to take greater account of the situation of the jobless and to be more vigilant in ensuring the defense of the social rights of the unemployed. In these countries, and in others, the unions have developed services addressed mainly to the unemployed, so as to help them, for example, in their search for a job or in their training path (see, e.g., the chapters about Britain and Ireland). These encouragements, often useful and important to the unemployed in their day-to-day life, can nevertheless have the effect of limiting their capacity for organization and be a brake on their collective mobilization.

Nevertheless, some unions have gone further than others in this direction, going as far as to set up committees of the unemployed among them. Two scenarios are possible in this context. Either the dominant trade unions, sensitive to the concerns of the unemployed, choose to organize them, especially to avoid seeing them develop an autonomous mobilization of the unemployed, which would be beyond them (see, e.g., the chapters about Belgium and Finland). Or the union members at the base of this organization are from minority, even marginalized, unions who on the whole are more radical than the dominant trade unions (see, e.g., the chapters about France, Italy, and Spain). From this point of view, the creation over the last decades of trade unions breaking with the traditional unions and challenging their dominant position (e.g., the *cobas* and *sincobas* in Italy, or the *SUD* in France) has been able to offer major support to the collective organization of the unemployed and to their mobilization.

More widely, the division and fragmentation of trade unions generally offer more opportunities for action to groups of the unemployed, who can benefit from their possible rivalry and find room to maneuver in the multiplicity of possible alliances. While the INOU and the TVY face the (quasi-)union monopoly of, respectively, the ICTU in Ireland and of the SAK in Finland, and since they are therefore in part dependent on the strategic choices of these two confederations, the organizations of the unemployed in France and in Spain can seek out allies from among the smallest and more marginalized trade unions, in the hope of influencing indirectly the dominant unions. Beyond, it is the trade union landscape as a whole and its ability to influence the political arena that guide the actions of the unemployed. In virtually all the European countries, union density has declined strongly in relation to the 1970s and the capacity for mobilization of the unions has receded (Visser 2006). This evolution is not moreover unrelated with the strong rise in unemployment, which contributed to undermining the position of the trade unions against the employers and to lessen the representativity and, hence, the legitimacy of the union movement. This evolution has several consequences. The two main Spanish trade unions (CC.OO and UGT) thus fell back on the most protected core of the wage earners, showing little regard for the concerns of the unemployed (Polavieja and Richards 2001). A number of unions close to the governing parties went along with the reforms affecting the different unemployment schemes in Europe, seeking to strengthen their legitimacy by the confirmation of their institutional acknowledgment by the public authorities. Others on the contrary attempt to establish their legitimacy by mobilizing audiences considered more difficult to organize collectively (Dufour and Hege 2010), and are more prone to construct links with other movements, such as the unemployed. A major cleavage emerges here between the trade unions that could be described as reformists who generally approve of measures restricting the benefits of the unemployed, and those often less powerful and more anchored in a tradition of opposition who support the unemployed. Such support is then likely to enhance the tensions between the dominant trade unions and the movements of the unemployed.

Even when they are united in action, the rivalry and distrust between the unemployed and the unions never completely go away, the one and the other referring fundamentally to identities, to interests, and to widely divergent conceptions of action. For the unions, such collaboration always risks stirring up tensions with the interests of the active workers, and to place them under stresses difficult to overcome. On the side of the unemployed, the main fear is being used as instruments, and even sacrificed on the altar of global tactico-political considerations to which they are indifferent or go beyond them. It is true that, even when they support their action, the union organizations register their initiatives in a wide political game, which can lead them to defuse an unemployed workers' movement to avoid it or even to torpedo it (by different methods, the chapters devoted to Belgium, to Finland, to France, to Germany, and to Ireland illustrate that). In this context, the relations the unions have with the political parties largely determine their position with regard to the demands of the unemployed and can vary depending on considerations that have nothing to do with the interests of the latter. In most cases, if the support of the unions is of the kind that makes up for the difficulties of organization of the unemployed, it can also act as a constraint on their collective emancipation.

Historically, a similar role was played by numerous communist parties. In the interwar period, the *Kommunistiche Partei Deutschlands* (KPD) in Germany, the PCF in France, or the Communist Party of Great Britain (CPGB) were thus crucial actors in the organization and mobilization of the unemployed (Croucher 1987; McElligott 1987; Bagguley 1991, section 4.6; Kourchid 1999; Perry 2007 and 2012; Pierru 2007). This support was also dependent on a wide political strategy, as well as, very often, orders coming from Moscow via the intervention of the *Komintern*. As with the unions, these parties brought precious assistance to the movements of the unemployed during this period but this faded at certain times for reasons largely external to the unemployed themselves. More recently, the decline, disappearance even of the communist parties in Europe led, on the one hand, to a drop in organizational resources, and the possibilities of alliances being proffered to organizations of the unemployed, on the other, an opening of the prospect of alliances with other political forces, in particular the Trotskyite parties or the anarchist movements, whose importance has nevertheless nothing in common with what was formerly the communist movement.

Between Stigmatization and Principle of Solidarity: The Importance of the Cultural Framework

Beyond the organizational context in which the mobilization of the unemployed develops, the cultural, ideological, and cognitive environment of a society also plays an essential role in the conditions for emergence of a movement of the unemployed. The political invisibility to which the unemployed are generally confined is inseparable from a certain number of misconceptions, of stereotypes, stigmas even, which are opposed to their mobilization, or which tend to discredit them when they do manage to organize themselves collectively. The neo-institutionalist approach has emphasized the importance of the elements of cultural framing (Snow and Benford, 2000), that is, "configurations or formations that constrain and enable action by structuring actors' normative commitments and their understandings of the world and of their own possibilities within it" (Emirbayer and Goodwin 1996, 365). Even though these factors are always difficult to evaluate concretely, they play an essential role in the prospects for action of the unemployed and the social acceptability of their political demands.

Two closely linked elements deserve to be highlighted here to open the way to a mobilization. First, unemployment has of necessity to be treated as a structural problem, requiring global economic reforms; otherwise public opinion and those responsible in politics accentuate the individual responsibility of those who are jobless. After that, the fact of being unemployed has to be understood as an involuntary situation of suffering, which does not in this regard entail any particular doubt. If these two conditions are not fulfilled, the mobilization of the unemployed may appear devoid of legitimacy and even seem shocking to some. Now, from these two aspects, the unemployed are rarely exempt of all suspicion even if the idea, according to which some are said to take advantage of existing social assistance, is very variable depending particularly on the economic situation and national contexts.

In this sense, a recent study based on six European countries[2] showed that it is in Italy that public speeches are the most supportive of the unemployed, way ahead of France, Great Britain, and Switzerland, which lie in an intermediate zone, while Germany and Sweden are conspicuous for their comparatively closed discursive opportunities. These differences refer to a number of explanatory factors, among which the place accorded to the value of work, and as a corollary, the degree of stigmatization to which the deprived are victims. In regions under Protestant influence, these phenomena can play a certain part. On average, however, the stances taken at the national level were rather of benevolent neutrality, if this is not support for the unemployed. Such an attitude by public opinion and several actors is all the more indispensable in that it allows the unemployed to compensate, at least in part, for their political isolation and enables alternative strategies of questioning public opinion.

The studies brought together in this volume emphasize well the influence of the cultural, ideological, and cognitive contexts in the mobilization of the unemployed. Thus, in the case of Poland, the strong stigmatization that weighs on the unemployed seems to be a determining factor of their incapacity to act collectively. Not only is the debate on unemployment monopolized by different types of expert and excludes the unemployed themselves, but in addition, the media broadcast strongly stigmatizing material about the jobless, concentrating on the responsibilities of the individuals themselves and not on the profound changes suffered by the country in a very short space of time. In contrast, social opprobrium seems lesser in other countries, especially those where the principle of unemployment benefits, in a relatively generous manner, is globally accepted, as in Belgium, France, Finland, Germany, or even Italy. This cultural opposition translates into very different conceptions of individual responsibility, but also the system of social welfare and *in fine* of national solidarity.

Several chapters also stress the deep ideological transformation that European societies have gone through between, on the one hand, the interwar period, and on the other the last three decades. Along the lines of other studies (e.g., Croucher 1987; Bagguley 1991), the contributions devoted to Britain and to France highlight the ideological role of the communist parties in the construction and dissemination of a framework conducive to the mobilization of the unemployed. By criticizing unemployment as a major outcome of a capitalist system, which they denounced moreover, the CP contributed to portraying the unemployed as victims of an injustice of a systemic nature. The near-disappearance of these parties, but also the sharp decline among wage earners of class consciousness, understood in the Marxist sense of the term, and the rise of a discourse inspired by neoliberalism focused on individual responsibility significantly complicate the conditions of mobilization of the unemployed, as pointed out in the chapters on Poland or on Britain.

From Welfare States to Mobilization

The countries that emphasize individual initiative the most are usually those that encourage mobility the most in and outside the labor market and which have a "liberal" or "residual" system of social protection (Esping-Andersen 1990). In the socially dominant representations, social inequalities—and thus unemployment—have therefore their roots in the behavior of individuals who have, as such, heavy responsibility in their situation. Conversely, the countries where the social tie is above all founded on the principles of solidarity and social justice have set up a right to work but also a more protective system of cover and of unemployment benefits. Here it is indeed the cohesion, security, and social justice that are defended—more than the question of individual merit or responsibility—on the grounds that anyone can, one day or another, find themselves in a precarious situation or one of social exclusion. One sees the link between dominant cultural values in a given society and the system of protection and, more specifically, of unemployment benefits this society establishes. In turn, "the dominant vision of the welfare state specific to a country shapes what one could call the 'protestation policy of unemployment', that is to say the public discussions and collective mobilizations regarding unemployment" (Berclaz, Füglister, and Giugni 2004, 427).

In theory, one would have thought that discontent and the propensity to protest of the unemployed would be the highest in the countries providing few rights to the jobless, at the same time prone to protest to try and improve their situation. The different contributions to this book, as well as work previously carried out on the same subject (Chabanet and Giugni 2008; Giugni 2008), suggest however that the relation is the reverse: in most cases, it is in the most socially advanced countries, whose welfare regime, and unemployment scheme particularly, is the most advantageous that the unemployed are the most likely to get mobilized.

In picking up the typology of Gallie and Paugam (2000), we may thus differentiate on one side Great Britain, Ireland, and Poland, where the unemployment welfare regime is liberal/minimal and in which the mobilization of the unemployed is weak or almost inexistent, and on the other side France or Germany, where the level of protection is much higher and where mobilizations are more pronounced. The low-level protection regimes, such as Italy and Spain, offering to the unemployed less-than-subsistence-level protection, are more ambiguous and are marked by limited mobilization, and in any case focused on quite specific urban areas such as Naples or, to a lesser degree, Andalusia. In the light of this analysis, one might have expected the mobilization of the unemployed to be more marked in Belgium or in Finland—which, with a high level of protection and open principles of eligibility, resembles the universalistic model—but other determining factors, related especially to the role of trade union organizations, explain convincingly that this is not the case. It is to be emphasized moreover that even if it was a question of an isolated event, the Finnish unemployed were behind the biggest demonstration the country has seen since World War II, which bears witness at least occasionally to their capacity for mobilization. Only Switzerland could appear as a counterexample since, despite a fairly generous system for the jobless, there has never been a major mobilization of the unemployed. The paradox is however only apparent. On the one hand, the main mobilization of the unemployed in Switzerland, whose political impact was significant, occurred exactly when the parliament adopted a quite restrictive reform of the unemployment law. On the other hand, the near-absence of unemployment in this country is a determining explanatory factor of the weakness of mobilizations of the unemployed.

All the countries studied in this volume have, over the last years, gone through numerous and often thorough reforms of their unemployment schemes. Carried out at the national level, in different ways and at different paces according to the characteristics of each state, these changes interpose themselves in the common framework of the European Employment Strategy (Lévy 2003; Lefresne 2010). Whatever the majorities in power, the so-called policies of activation of employment are often translated into a constraint on the conditions of unemployment benefit, which provokes the discontent of the unemployed. Thus, several reforms brought in by right-wing or center-right coalitions clash with large social movements in which the unemployed take part. In this framework, the organizations of the unemployed can rely on the trade union movement, usually linked to the parties on the left, or directly on the latter when they are in opposition. The chapters devoted to Belgium, Finland, France, Germany, and Spain provide examples of similar patterns. But the discontent is sometimes even more lively when the reforms are carried out by governments on the left or center-left, supposedly more inclined to defend the interests of the poor, the excluded, and the unemployed. In France, the movement of the unemployed started to get organized when the left, after being two years in power, had demonstrated its incapacity to halt the rise in unemployment and had adopted the *tournant de la rigueur* in 1983. In Germany, the most major mobilizations of the unemployed were triggered by the "Hartz IV" reforms introduced by the coalition of the Social-Democrat chancellor Gerhard Schröder. In Belgium, the last reform to trigger mobilizations of the unemployed was introduced in 2004 by a minister member of the Flemish Socialist Party. One can clearly see here the importance of subjective phenomena of letdown, anger even, of the unemployed—but also of a part of the political or trade union left—when they have the feeling that the reforms implemented by the majorities of so-called progressives go counter to the defense of the most disadvantaged.

Conclusion

This overview in a comparative perspective highlights the complexity and multifactorial nature of the mobilization of the unemployed in Europe. The case studies compiled in this volume clearly show that the collective organization and mobilization of the unemployed are difficult and dependent on a multitude of factors. These contributions suggest however that the mobilization of the unemployed is not only possible, but is also more widespread than sometimes thought. If, evidently, the sociological characteristics of the unemployed do not easily encourage them to mobilize, a host of other factors, endogenous and exogenous, have therefore to be taken into consideration to understand the circumstances of their mobilization: the resources of the unemployed, understood in the broad sense (feeling of injustice, personal militant directions, the networks woven from the paths trod, the organizations of the unemployed, above all at local level), the alliances with other important sociopolitical actors, the cultural, cognitive, ideological, or institutional context, as well as the features of the benefit system and its evolutions.

Having analyzed the conditions of the emergence (or not) of the mobilization of the unemployed, one may briefly raise the shapes these actions take on. The repertoire to which the mobilized unemployed have access is relatively extensive. Interestingly, Perry (2012) attempted to classify them according to their degree of infringement of legality and moral standards. The studies brought together here also show that these types of action enjoy more or less a consensus (petition or demonstration) or are violent (riots). In Finland or in Ireland, the national organization of the unemployed specialized in particular in lobbying the public authorities, developing a certain expertise getting involved in negotiations with governmental representatives. In the early 1980s, marches for employment were organized in several countries, such as Belgium or Britain. Sit-ins and demonstrations are organized in a good number of cases, providing the opportunity in particular for the movements of the unemployed to distribute leaflets and to make known their demands and their organizations. In some cases, these demonstrations form part of a particular local tradition, such as the Monday demonstrations reminiscent of the gatherings held in the GDR before the fall of the Berlin Wall. Specific kinds of demonstration, the marches (see Pigenet and Tartakowsky 2003) represent from the nineteenth century on a type of action typical of the movements of the unemployed. Perry (2012) even regards the hunger marches as the only form of action specific to just the unemployed. In Belgium, France, or Italy, public, or particularly symbolic, buildings (unemployment centers, employers' organizations, temporary work agencies, etc.) are sometimes occupied. The launch of a referendum allowed Swiss unemployed to defeat a reform of unemployment insurance. Along the lines of the French "recalculated," the unemployed sometimes have recourse to the courts to try and cancel the effects of certain reforms. Expressive and spectacular forms, rarely violent (hunger strikes, burning of buses, or trash cans by the Italian unemployed, "requisition of food" by French unemployed, sketches and custard pie attacks by the Belgian unemployed, or even playful and ironic actions by the "happy unemployed" in Germany), are also used by the mobilized unemployed to question public opinion and *in fine* the public authorities. Finally therein lies not the least of paradoxes: whereas unemployment has, for three decades, been one of the major problems of European societies, the unemployed are constrained to compensate for a large gap in their visibility—that is to say to demonstrate their collective existence.

Notes

1. It is the realization of a long process of collective work, which began in June 2005 with the holding of an international colloquium entitled "The Mobilization of the Unemployed in Europe," organized by the Maison française d'Oxford and the SciencesPo Research Group of the Department of Politics and International Relations. We wish to warmly thank these two institutions for their support, all of the participants at this event, as well as Sophie Duchesne (Centre d'études européennes de SciencesPo) without whom this project would not have been possible.
2. See Marco Giugni, *The Political Mobilization of the Unemployed in comparative perspective*, in particular table 2, p. 16 (http://www.eurpolcom.eu/exhibits/ch10-comparative.pdf, last accessed March 21, 2011). See the results in Giugni (2010).

References

Bagguley, Paul. 1991. *From Protest to Acquiescence? Political Movements of the Unemployed.* London: Macmillan.

———. 1992. Protest, acquiescence and the unemployed: A comparative analysis of the 1930s and 1980s. *British Journal of Sociology* 43(3): 443–61.

Baglioni, Simone, Britta Baumgarten, Didier Chabanet, and Christian Lahusen. 2008. Transcending Marginalization: The Mobilization of the Unemployed in France, Germany and Italy in a Comparative Perspective. *Mobilization: An International Journal* 13(3): 323–35.

Berclaz, Michel, Katharina Füglister, and Marco Giugni. 2004. États-providence, opportunités politiques et mobilisation des chômeurs: Une approche néo-institutionnaliste. *Swiss Journal of Sociology* 30 (3): 421–40.

Bourdieu, Pierre. 1998. *Contre-feux.* Paris: Liber/Raisons d'agir.

Cameron, David. 2001. Unemployment, Job Creation, and Economic and Monetary Union. In *Unemployment in the New Europe*, ed. Nancy Bermeo, 7–51. Cambridge: Cambridge University Press.

Chabanet, Didier. 2002. Les marches européennes contre le chômage, la précarité et les exclusions. In *L'action collective en Europe. Collective Action in Europe*, ed. Richard Balme, Didier Chabanet, and Vincent Wright, 461–93. Paris: Presses de Sciences Po.

———. 2007. Chômage et exclusion : l'échec européen. *Politique européenne* 21: 159–90.

———. 2008. When the Unemployed Challenge the European Union: The European Marches as Externalization of Protest. *Mobilization: An International Journal* 13(3): 311–22.

Chabanet, Didier, and Marco Giugni. 2008. Citizenship, Welfare, and the Opportunities for Political Mobilisation: Migrants and Unemployed Compared. In *From National toward International Linkages? Civil Society and Multi-Level Governance*, ed. Jan van Deth and William Maloney, 127–47. Cheltenham: Edward Elgar Publishers.

Chabanet, Didier, and Frédéric Royall. 2009. Economic Recession and the Mobilization of the Unemployed: France and Ireland Compared. *French Politics* 7(4): 268–93.

Chabanet, Didier, and Jean Faniel. 2011. The Mobilization of the Unemployed: A Recurrent but Relatively Invisible Phenomenon. In *Unemployment and Protest: New Perspectives on Two Centuries of Contention*, ed. Matthias Reiss and Matt Perry, 387–405. Oxford: Oxford University Press.

Croucher, Richard. 1987. *We Refuse to Starve in Silence. A History of the National Unemployed Workers' Movement, 1920–46.* London: Lawrence & Wishart.

Croucher, Richard, et al. 2008. Special Issue on Unemployed Protest and Unemployed Movements. *Labour History Review* 73(1), 1–180.

Demazière, Didier. 1996. Des chômeurs sans représentation collective : une fatalité ? *Esprit* 226: 12–32.

Demazière, Didier, and Maria-Teresa Pignoni. 1998. *Chômeurs : du silence à la révolte.* Paris: Hachette.

De Vries, David, and Shani Bar-On. 2011. Politicization of Unemployment in British-Ruled Palestine. In *Unemployment and Protest: New Perspectives on Two Centuries of Contention*, ed. Matthias Reiss and Matt Perry, 199–219. Oxford: Oxford University Press.

Dufour, Christian, and Adelheid Hege. 2010. The Legitimacy of Collective Actors and Trade Union Renewal. *Transfer* 16(3): 351–67.

Emirbayer, Mustafa, and Jeff Goodwin. 1996. Symbols, Positions, Objects: Toward a New Theory of Revolutions and Collective Action. *History and Theory* 35(3): 358–74.

Esping-Andersen, Gøsta. 1990. *The Three Worlds of Welfare Capitalism*. Cambridge: Polity Press.

Faniel, Jean. 2004. Chômeurs en Belgique et en France : des mobilisations différentes. *Revue internationale de politique comparée* 11(4): 493–505.

———. 2009. Belgian Trade Unions, the Unemployed and the Growth of Unemployment. In *The Politics of Unemployment in Europe: Policy Responses and Collective Action*, ed. Marco Giugni, 101–15. Farnham: Ashgate.

Fernández Álvarez, María Inés, and Virginia Manzano. 2007. Desempleo, acción estatal y movilización social en Argentina. *Política y Cultura* 27: 143–66.

Flanagan, Richard. 1991. *"Parish-Fed Bastards": A History of the Politics of the Unemployed in Britain, 1884–1939*. New York: Greenwood Press.

Folsom, Franklin. 1991. *Impatient Armies of the Poor: The Story of Collective Action of the Unemployed 1808–1942*. Niwot: University Press of Colorado.

Galland, Olivier, and Marie-Victoire Louis. 1981. Chômage et action collective. *Sociologie du travail* 23(2): 173–91.

Gallie, Duncan, and Serge Paugam, ed. 2000. *Welfare Regimes and the Experience of Unemployment in Europe*. Oxford: Oxford University Press.

Giugni, Marco. 2008. Welfare States, Political Opportunities, and the Mobilization of the Unemployed: A Cross-National Analysis. *Mobilization* 13(3): 297–310.

———, ed. 2010. *The Contentious Politics of Unemployment in Europe*. New York: Palgrave.

Gurr, Ted Robert. 1970. *Why Men Rebel*. Princeton: Princeton University Press.

Hobsbawm, Eric J. 1984. *Worlds of Labour. Further Studies in the History of Labour*. London: Weidenfeld and Nicolson.

Jahoda, Marie, Paul F. Lazarsfeld, and Hans Zeisel. 1933. *Die Arbeitslosen von Marienthal. Ein soziographischer Versuch*. Leipzig: Hirzel. 1971. *Marienthal: The Sociography of an Unemployed Community*. London: Tavistock.

Kerbo, Harold R., and Richard A. Shaffer. 1992. Lower Class Insurgency and the Political Process: The Response of the U.S. Unemployed, 1890–1940. *Social Problems* 39(2): 139–54.

Kitschelt, Herbert. 1986. Political Opportunity Structures and Political Protest. Anti-Nuclear Movements in Four Democracies. *British Journal of Political Science* 16: 57–85.

Kourchid, Olivier. 1999. Les mouvements de chômeurs en France, 1919–1935, historiographie selon la Vie Ouvrière. In *Images et mouvements du siècle. Tome II, Les raisins de la colère*. Ivry-sur-Seine: éditions France Progrès/France découvertes/Institut CGT d'Histoire sociale.

Lefresne, Florence, ed. 2010. *Unemployment Benefit Systems in Europe and North America: Reforms and Crisis*. Brussels : IRES/ETUI.

Lévy, Catherine. 2003. *Vivre au minimum. Enquête dans l'Europe de la précarité*. Paris: La Dispute.

Linders, Annulla, and Marina Kalander. 2010. A Precarious Balance of Interests: Unions and the Unemployed in Europe. In *The Contentious Politics of Unemployment in Europe*, ed. Marco Giugni, 97–126. New York: Palgrave.

Lipsky, Michael. 1970. *Protest in City Politics. Rent Strikes, Housing and the Power of the Poor*. Chicago: Rand MacNally.

Locke, Cybèle. 2011. Fractious Factions: The Organized Unemployed and the Labour Movement in New Zealand, 1978–1990. In *Unemployment and Protest: New Perspectives on Two Centuries of Contention*, ed. Matthias Reiss and Matt Perry, 345–66. Oxford: Oxford University Press.
Lorence, James J. 1996. *Organizing the Unemployed: Community and Union Activists in the Industrial Heartland*. Albany: State University of New York Press.
Mathers, Andy. 1999. Euromarch—The Struggle for a Social Europe. *Capital & Class* 68: 15–19.
Maurer, Sophie. 2001. *Les chômeurs en action (décembre 1997–mars 1998). Mobilisation collective et ressources compensatoires*. Paris: L'Harmattan.
McAdam, Doug. 1996. Political Opportunities: Conceptual origins, current problems, future directions. In *Comparative Perspectives on Social Movements: Political Opportunities, Mobilizing structures and Cultural Framings. Applications of Contemporary Movement Theory*, ed. Doug McAdam, John D. McCarthy, and Mayer N. Zald, 23–40. Cambridge: Cambridge University Press.
McCarthy, John D., and Mayer N. Zald. 1977. Resource Mobilization and Social Movements: A Partial Theory. *American Journal of Sociology* 82: 1212–41.
McElligott, Anthony. 1987. Mobilising the Unemployed: the KPD and the Unemployed Workers' Movement in Hamburg Altona during the Weimar Republic. In *The German Unemployed. Experiences and Consequences of Mass Unemployment from the Weimar Republic to the Third Reich*, 228–60. London/Sydney: Croom Helm.
Ness, Immanuel. 1998. *Trade Unions and the Betrayal of the Unemployed. Labor Conflicts during the 1990s*. New York/London: Garland.
Paugam, Serge. 1998. La révolte des chômeurs : un mouvement sans précédent. *Magazine Littéraire* May: 73–6.
Perry, Matt. 2000. *Bread and Work: The Experience of Unemployment 1918–1939*. London: Pluto Press.
———. 2007. *Prisoners of Want. The Experience and Protest of the Unemployed in France, 1921–45*. Aldershot: Ashgate.
———. 2012. The British and French Hunger Marches of the 1930s: An Exclusive Mode of Protest, a Cultural Transfer and a Fulcrum. In *Economic, Political and Social Movements in Asia and Europe*, ed. Bernadette Andreosso-O'Callaghan and Frédéric Royall, 135–50. Heidelberg: Springer.
Pierru, Emmanuel. 2003. *L'Ombre des chômeurs. Chronique d'une indignité sociale et politique depuis les années 30*. PhD diss., University of Amiens.
———. 2007. "Mobiliser 'la vie fragile'. Les communistes et les chômeurs dans les années 1930." *Sociétés contemporaines* 65(1): 113–45.
Pigenet, Michel, and Danielle Tartakowsky, ed. 2003. Les marches. *Le Mouvement social* 202: 3–182.
Piven, Frances Fox, and Richard A. Cloward. 1979 [1977]. *Poor People's Movements: Why They Succeed, How They Fail*. New York: Vintage Books.
Pleyers, Geoffrey. 2010. *Alter-Globalization. Becoming Actors in the Global Age*. Cambridge: Polity Press.
Polavieja, Javier G., and Andrew Richards. 2001. Trade Unions, Unemployement, and Working Class Fragmentation in Spain. In *Unemployment in the New Europe*, ed. Nancy Bermeo, 203–44. Cambridge: Cambridge University Press.
Reiss, Matthias. 2007. Marching on the Capital: National Protest Marches of the British Unemployed in the 1920s and 1930s. In *The Street as Stage: Protest Marches and Public Rallies since the Nineteenth Century*, ed. Matthias Reiss, 147–68. Oxford: Oxford University Press.

Reiss, Matthias, and Matt Perry, ed. 2011. *Unemployment and Protest: New Perspectives on Two Centuries of Contention*. Oxford: Oxford University Press.
Richards, Andrew. 2000. Trade Unionism and the Unemployed in the European Union. *La lettre de la Maison française d'Oxford* 12: 153–81.
———. 2002. Mobilizing the Powerless: Collective Protest action of the Unemployed in the Interwar Period. *Estudios Working Papers* 175. Madrid, Centro de Estudios Avanzados en Ciencias Sociales–Instituto Juan March.
Rolke, Lothar. 1988. Millionen im Griff: Warum es (noch?) keine Arbeitslosenbewegung gibt. *Forschungsjournal Neue soziale Bewegungen* 2, 45–50.
Rosenzweig, Roy. 1976. Organizing the Unemployed: The Early Years of the Great Depression, 1929-1933. *Radical America* 10 (4), 37–60.
Royall, Frédéric. 1997. Problems of collective action for associations of the unemployed in France and in Ireland. In *The Political Context of Collective Action. Power, Argumentation and Democracy*, ed. Ricca Edmondson, 146–62. London: Routledge.
———. 2000. Collective Actions and Disadvantaged Groups in Ireland and France 1987-99: The Case of the Unemployed. *Irish Political Studies* 15, 83–103.
———. 2002. Building Solidarity Across National Boundaries: The Case of Affiliates of the European Network of the Unemployed. *Journal of European Area Studies* 10(2): 243–58.
———. 2005. *Mobilisations de chômeurs en Irlande (1985–1995)*. Paris : L'Harmattan.
Russ, Wolfgang. 1990. Zwischen Protest und Resignation: Arbeitslose und Arbeitslosenbewegung in der Zeit der Weltwirtschaftskrise. *Österreichische Zeitschrift für Geschichtswissenschaften* 1(2): 23–52.
Schnapper, Dominique. 1981. *L'épreuve du chômage*. Paris: Gallimard.
Snow, David A., and Robert D. Benford. 2000. Framing Processes and Social Movements: An Overview and Assessment. *Annual Review of Sociology* 26: 611–39.
Svampa, Maristella, and Sebastian Pereyra. 2004. Les dimensions de l'expérience piquetera : Tensions et cadres communs dans l'organisation et la mobilisation des chômeurs en Argentine. *Revue Tiers monde* 178, 419–41.
Tarrow, Sidney. 1996. States and Opportunities: The Political Structuring of Social Movements. In *Comparative Perspectives on Social Movements: Political Opportunities, Mobilizing structures and Cultural Framings. Applications of Contemporary Movement Theory*, ed. Doug McAdam, John D. McCarthy, and Mayer N. Zald, 41–61. Cambridge: Cambridge University Press.
van Berkel, Rik, and Ruud Vlek. 1998. Epilogue. In *Beyond Marginality? Social movements of social security claimants in the European Union*, ed. Rik van Berkel, Harry Coenen, and Ruud Vlek, 221–31. Aldershot: Ashgate.
van den Oord, Ad. 1990. *Voor arbeid en brood, arbeidersbeweging en collectieve actie van werklozen in Nederland, een vergelijkende studie van de jaren dertig en tachtig*. Amsterdam: Thesis Publishers.
Visser, Jelle. 2006. Union Membership Statistics in 24 Countries. *Monthly Labor Review* January, 38–49.
Wolski-Prenger, Friedhelm. 1997. Marginalität und Widerstand: Mobilisierungsprobleme der Arbeitslosenbewegung. *Forschungsjournal Neue Soziale Bewegungen* 10 (2), 63–9.
———. 1998. Projects for the Unemployed in Germany. In *Beyond Marginality? Social Movements of Social Security Claimants in the European Union*, ed. Rik van Berkel, Harry Coenen, and Ruud Vlek, 95–117. Aldershot: Ashgate.

CHAPTER 1

The Long History of a New Cause: The Mobilization of the Unemployed in France

Didier Chabanet

In the winter of 1997–1998, the unemployed were for long months in the "headlines" of social and political news for demanding loudly and clearly an increase in the minimum social payments and a Christmas bonus of 3,000 francs (about 450 euros). The mobilization on this occasion was sufficiently important—a hundred thousand at its height in January 1998 (Maurer 2000, 3)—to turn upside down usual analyses. Faced with the unexpected size of the movement, comments were in fact at first marked by astonishment if not incredulity. A recognized specialist in poverty and precariousness, Paugam (1998) this time evoked "an unprecedented movement" (73–6) thus well emphasizing its exceptional character. In the same vein, Bourdieu (1998) described the mobilization as a "social miracle" (102), the expression being moreover copiously picked up, to the point of getting a seal of approval (e.g., Maurer and Pierru 2001). Although they have the merit of emphasizing the specific difficulties encountered by the unemployed in acting collectively, these renderings are largely erroneous. They ignore in fact former episodes, which occurred in particular in the first part of the twentieth century, marked by large and repeated demonstrations by the unemployed. To understand why[1] and above all how the unemployed get mobilized, it is essential to go back to the interwar period, since it is at this time that actions by the unemployed on a meaningful scale see the light of day. This putting in perspective does not aim to suggest some historical continuity or other, but simply to bring to the fore a certain number of consistencies, whether it is a question of the implacably episodic character of this phenomenon, or the practical necessity for the unemployed in action to find allies allowing them to break with their political isolation. This mobilization work constantly pits against each other two positions largely under stress, the one favoring autonomy for the unemployed, the other pressing the need to draw up alliances with third-party bodies, notably those from militant trade unionism. In all cases, the questioning and support of public opinion are the unavoidable stakes, given the social and political marginalization of the unemployed. Finally, we will see that for several years the movement has entered a less active phase and rather seeks recourse to legal process so as to try and emphasize the rights of the unemployed.

Mobilizations in the Interwar Period

It is in the early 1920s that the first significant mobilizations of the "out-of-work" appeared[2]; some groups of the unemployed came together in the Paris region, usually on the initiative of trade union sections seeking to capitalize on the grumbling to which the slight rise in unemployment was giving rise. In February, several gatherings, ranging in size from some tens to some hundreds of people, were thus organized and rapidly dispersed by the police forces. In the months that followed, the movement spread somewhat in the provinces but in a very sporadic fashion. In this era unemployment remained a limited phenomenon, affecting only a few thousand people, and it almost totally vanished between 1922 and 1926. Moreover, the public authorities controlled street demonstrations very severely and did not hesitate to forbid parades or to disperse them.

One had to wait for the years 1926–1927 and a small upsurge in unemployment for the wavering desires for mobilization to reappear. The example of the movements of the unemployed in neighboring countries—in the forefront Germany, Great Britain, and the Netherlands (Croucher 1987; Evans and Geary 1987; van den Oord 1990; Bagguley 1991; Richards 2002)—who were much more severely hit by unemployment than France, here played an important encouraging role. In the framework of the revolutionary strategy impulse of the Soviet Union, the French Communist Party (PCF) and its trade union right-hand man, the Confédération générale du travail unitaire (CGTU), decided to work toward the unification of the working class, even when they were deprived of employment. The mechanism put in place toward this end is very instructive of the suspicions the unemployed were arousing. It was a question in fact of encouraging the creation of committees of the unemployed devoted to facilitating the political socialization and enlistment of the latter, while taking care that this process does no prejudice to the integrity of the working class. In this sense, the Red Trade Union International[3] clearly specified:

> With regard to the unemployed belonging to the Communist party, we ask you to make every effort so that they may remain loyal to their cells within enterprises. There would be a great danger for the life of our cells and for the ideology of our members if the comrades formed a sort of split of the unemployed within our ranks. (Cited by Pierru 2002, 24)

At a time when experience of unemployment was associated with all the vices—going as far, for example, as making alcoholism one of the elements making up the legal identity of the unemployed (Willmann 1998)—it is not surprising that the bringing together of workers and the unemployed gives rise to such fears, including among those who supported them in their struggle. This tactic by the united front did not therefore exclude either the distrust or even a certain distancing from the unemployed. The setting up from January 1927, in the Paris region, of a central Committee of the unemployed under the control of the CGTU and overseeing the different committees of the unemployed—whether branches or districts—was moreover a means of encompassing a population one distrusted and over which one could exercise a certain guardianship (Kourchid 1999).[4]

Through the support provided to the unemployed, the aim of the PCF was to open a register of grievances and, if a sufficient critical mass was attained, to organize a street demonstration. This strategy met with a certain success, as illustrated by the February 4, 1927, gathering in Paris of several thousand participants,[5] followed over several weeks by other large parades. In the provinces, some mobilizations likewise saw the light of day, especially in regions such as Picardy or Nord-Pas-de-Calais, where the metallurgical, hotel, or textile industries had to face up to reductions in the workforce. Even if their role was largely a dominating factor, the communist organizations did not have the monopoly on action. Thus, in January, in Limoges, more than 3,000 unemployed gathered following a call by the Confédération générale du travail (CGT) and independent trade unions, close to the socialist or radical circles. All these initiatives remained rare and sporadic however and did not succeed in coming within the scope of a continuous process. From the month of March, the mobilization appears anyway to have virtually disappeared, which led the PCF to abandon the prospect—then in gestation—of creating a national organization of the unemployed spread throughout the nation.

The movement got its second wind at the outset of the 1930s. Once again, the international context played a decisive role in this relaunch. In this period the Komintern organized several days of struggle against unemployment and made the question of the participation of the unemployed in the battle against world capitalism one of its priority axes (Pierru 2007). The PCF, under the impetus of its new secretary-general Maurice Thorez, then put into operation a big campaign of assistance and awareness-raising toward the unemployed, strongly backed up by communist municipalities of the Paris region. This effort met with some success and led to the opening of a multitude of local committees of the unemployed, placed under the leadership of a *Union of the committees of the unemployed of the Paris region,* itself controlled by the PCF. In Paris and its near suburbs, in 1931, close on 25 demonstrations of a hundred or so demonstrators or more were recorded (Perry 2007, 82). From August of this same year to May 1932, 102 of the 108 parades recorded were demonstrations by the unemployed (Tartakowsky 1997, 249). To give greater scope and visibility to this force, two national open days of action were organized—on November 12, 1931, and on January 12, 1932. In both cases, several thousand demonstrators[6] converged on the National Assembly, which saw itself being directly harangued despite the strong-arm intervention of the forces of law and order. A few weeks later, a tragic event was at the origin of what is even to this day considered the biggest gathering of the unemployed in France. On March 17 at Vitry, an unemployed person was shot dead following brawls with the police. The agitation was considerable, to the extent that an impressive crowd of several tens of thousands of individuals followed the victim's coffin as a sign of protest on March 24.[7]

This episode was striking, both because it corresponded to an especially important peak in mobilization, but also because the public authorities decided to exercise much more drastic control over demonstrations by the unemployed in the future, even to the point of forbidding them. This hardening, combined with a significant fall in unemployment in the months following, weakened considerably the activity surrounding demands by committees of the unemployed. To relaunch the movement and try to escape police repression, militant communists decided on a change of strategy and opted for a register of more peaceful action. A first hunger march was organized on December 9, 1932, in Paris and in neighboring communes (Pigenet and Tartakowsky 2003, 84–5). In a context made dramatic for the impoverished by the rigors of winter, mobilization grew appreciably, even if it remained episodic, as witnessed by the growth in Paris of the number of local committees of the unemployed, which were about 140 at the outset of 1933 bringing together near to 55,000 of the out-of-work (Perry 2007, 99–122). In the provinces, mobilization was concentrated above all on a few centers of industrial decline—the Limousin, the Nord-Pas-de-Calais, or again Saint-Nazaire—but it remained short-lived and was not part of a coordinated and sustainable logical frame at the national level.

In autumn 1933, confronted with the prospects of a new winter of misery, but likewise to prevent the fascisation of the impoverished[8] populations, the CGTU undertook to intensify the struggles of the unemployed. To this effect, it set up a confederal commission of the unemployed, with Charles Tillon in charge. An ambitious project consisting of organizing a hunger march from Lille to Paris was put into operation. Several parades set out and converged on the capital to end up grouping together nearly 7,000 people, on December 2, 1933. In all, for ten days or so, "together, the demonstrations mobilized 32,000 people in the Nord-Pas-de-Calais [whereas] in Paris 80,000 [were] involved, of which 50,000 unemployed" (Kourchid 1999, 182). Despite the controls, the intimidations, and often the repression of the forces of law and order, the mobilization was a success. Once in Paris, a delegation of marchers tried, in vain, to be received at the National Assembly. The event was relayed by a large section of the press—positive or not—and met with substantial repercussions. As feedback, other similar marches saw the light of day in the following months in several provincial towns. The year 1934 was thus marked by a succession of marches and protests of a meaningful dimension, whether in the Nord-Pas-de-Calais still, or in the Pyrenees, the Gard or le Forez. At the end of the year, the unemployed movement seemed for the first time to have spread a little throughout France, admittedly in a somewhat disordered manner.

In several towns, the practice consisting of occupying the Town Hall building, even to the point of impounding the mayor or his deputies for several hours, is widespread. Other forms of protest, such as those of the unemployed withdrawing their children from school and inviting other parents to do likewise as a sign of solidarity so as to bring pressure on locally elected officials (Perry 2007, 173), showed great inventiveness. By different means—now peaceful so as not to leave your flank open to police repression, as seen on different organized marches, now provocative or spectacular to attract attention from the public bodies—the unemployed in action thus tried to make their cause more visible. Most of the time, the action of making demands was strongly anchored territorially and above all targeted the communes, which mastered the conditions of handing out assistance to the unemployed. It is because in this field the criteria for the allocation of resources was essentially set out and implemented at the municipal level that conflicts come above all within the scope of local forces (De Barros 2001). This competence almost mechanically turned the towns suffering badly from the economic crisis into privileged political targets. The state was aimed at more indirectly, since it distributed part of the global envelope destined for assistance to the most poverty-stricken. The communist municipalities do not moreover hesitate to harangue the national political powers on this matter, looking with more or less success to direct the discontent against them and somehow to externalize it.

Going into the winter of 1934 corresponded with a new outbreak of the vague desires for mobilization by the unemployed. A second hunger march, bringing together close to 20,000 people, was organized on January 12, 1935, in the Paris region, with a central demand for the creation of a national Fund—and no longer a departmental one—for unemployment. Other demonstrations, smaller now, took place from February to April, especially in the Ardennes, in Brittany, or Agin in the Somme. Far from being insignificant, these protests were however the fruit of local militancy little coordinated at the national level, even by the PCF and its ties. They therefore had trouble going into the long term and closed down almost totally as of the month of May, while unemployment stayed at a high level and even went up after the summer.

Once more, the international economic situation interfered with the policy of the PCF with regard to the unemployed. The Franco-Soviet Pact signed on May 2, 1935, translated into a bringing together of the PCF with the other French political parties—the SFIO (socialist) in the first place—and the rendering dormant of theses calling for the overturn of the bourgeois state. Less militant, less subversive, the PCF bypasses somewhat the question of the mobilization of the jobless. The prospects of a coalition of all the forces on the left with a calling to accede to power, which led several months later to the success of the Front populaire, involved moreover handling carefully ones potential allies, which brought the PCF to renounce concretely the launching of new hunger marches. From then on, action in favor of the unemployed would lean essentially toward a type of charitable assistance, led by the Union of the committees of the unemployed of the Paris region, henceforth integrated into the CGT.[9] If the mobilization of the unemployed did not stop abruptly and went through a number of local jolts, it entered nevertheless for several years into a cycle of recession. The start of World War II accentuated this trend.

The signature of the German-Soviet Pact in August 1939—a few weeks before France declared war on Germany—led to the banning of the PCF, whose organizational capacity was severely reduced by the repression to which it was subject and the arrest of many managers. Following the defeat of France in 1940, the communists, weakened and for some confounded by the alliance of their "Soviet Big brother" with Nazi Germany, tried to mobilize their troops and turned again toward the unemployed. In a France devastated, where the productive element was dismantled, employment problems were vast. It was on this subsoil of discontent and misery that were set up the popular committees of the unemployed,[10] established above all in the Paris region, intended to provide for the requirements of the most needy and to organize the Resistance. These committees were only active for a few months, victims at the same time of the difficulty of mobilizing distraught, and for the most part less-politicized, people during the period, but also from the end of 1940 the increasingly ferocious repression by the French and German authorities who, faced with communist militants, decapitated the movement. And more, the PCF committed itself resolutely to the Resistance from April 1941—the break-up of the German-Soviet Pact in June of the same year rendering this tendency inescapable—and therefore changed direction: the struggle in support of work and employment faded before the war effort to be provided and the need, on the contrary, to reduce the national productive resources in the hands of the Germans.

This summary of the mobilization of the unemployed in France from the beginning of the 1920s is rich in multiple lessons, at the same time for what we learn of the phenomenon in the period under consideration but also and above all because it modifies the perception of the latter over a more recent period, thus losing its supposed exceptionality. This bringing together refutes the idea that the fervent protest, which characterized the unemployed from the early 1980s, would be novel, exceptional even. On the contrary, although difficult given the specificities of the population involved, the mobilization of the unemployed was real in certain circumstances and this, well before the 1980s.

Putting the historical viewpoint shows that the efforts of the PCF and its trade union and associative ties to structure the cause of the unemployed were essential elements in the success of this enterprise, even if this support was largely instrumental and remained forever imprinted with distrust. If the modes of self-organization of the unemployed were not completely inexistent, in fact they remained exceptional. The analysis brings to the fore the close dependence of the unemployed on outside support, at the forefront of which were the communist organizations. In this manner, the influence of the PCF on French political life, itself in part subordinated to the line laid down by the USSR on the international scene, largely determined the possibilities open to the unemployed to express themselves and to take action. At the same time, the mobilization depended on local factors, mostly circumscribed by a town, more rarely a region, despite the efforts of the PCF to give a national dimension to the movement. The singularity of the processes by which the unemployed went into action likewise appeared clearly. The permanent cohesion between the availability of emergency aid—which of itself does not have direct or immediate political impact—and the work of fashioning demands, which only seems feasible in a later phase, appears thus as a strong characteristic. The repertoire of actions used show also that the unemployed knew how to find strategic adaptations to a very constraining and less-than-favorable environment. Even before being in a position to exert direct political influence, the unemployed had to create the conditions for their visibility and, for that, have recourse to audacious, often spectacular, questioning strategies. The task was all the more difficult and the authorities did not hesitate to use repression.

In the end, the volume of participation of the unemployed in the different forms of action undertaken is difficult to evaluate with certainty. It varied, most probably, a lot according to the registers used, the direct operations such as the sit-ins in public buildings doubtlessly mobilizing a much larger number of the unemployed than the hunger marches, for example, in large part thought up and organized by trade unions or political militants. If it is impossible to put forward figures with any certainty, either because the data are missing, or because they present no guarantee of reliability, it is certain that mobilization has been significant and repeated. One can therefore ask why this capacity to act has been almost totally wiped off from collective memories, to the point that the movements to meet the demands of the unemployed in the early 1980s could be presented in France as unpublished events.[11] This amnesia is doubtless to be seen with the long period of expansion and of full employment—the famous "Trente Glorieuses"—that the country experienced in the aftermath of World War II. At this time the providential French state came forward above all with the establishment of a system of social security, a guaranteed minimum wage, and a minimum old-age pension cover. One had to wait until 1958 for the appearance of laws on widespread unemployment insurance, the number of jobless remaining nevertheless extremely marginal. Unemployment only started to climb substantially at the time of the oil price shock of 1974, without the gravity of the situation becoming immediately apparent. At the time, the economic crisis was generally considered to be a passing phase that adapted policies—on the right or on the left—had to eradicate. This belief in the efficiency of public action wilted at the beginning of the 1980s, when employment policies kept piling up (Garraud 2000) and were shown to be incapable of resolving the problem.

The Emergence of an Organizational Network of the Unemployed

The organizations that today claim the right to represent specifically the interests of the unemployed and to speak in their name saw the light in the space of a dozen or so years, from 1982 onward.[12] Their appearance is understood in an ever more deteriorating economic context, which made employment a major problem, faced with which the public policies put in place are shown to be globally powerless. The contradiction between the importance of the stakes—which for decades form one of the main preoccupations of opinion—and the incapacity of successive governmental majorities to provide satisfactory responses lead a certain number of collective individuals to put themselves forward as spokesmen in the cause of the unemployed. This decade corresponded in France with widespread mass unemployment, with the appearance of the "new poverty," with the failure of the left in power on questions of the struggle for employment, and with the speeding up of the process of European integration, which, after the ratification of the Treaty of Maastricht, drastically limited the level of public deficits, thus strongly restraining the spending of the providential state. For the unemployed, these years were marked by a very net reduction in the level of cover, whether in duration or in indemnities.[13] These restrictions were moreover accompanied by the introduction of new procedures of individualized follow-up, which in many of their aspects are also means of control, and can lead to sanctions (Ebersold 2001; Dubois 2007).[14]

The conditions of protection of the unemployed deteriorated at the same time as the prospect of the eradication of unemployment by the governmental majorities in power vanished little by little. One by one, the political support liable to help the cause of the unemployed either seemed to consider that a high level of unemployment was inescapable, or were weakening and no longer able to defend their interests. In 1993, François Mitterrand, the president of the republic, made the disillusioned report that "against unemployment, we have tried everything,"[15] expressing very clearly his powerlessness while even having been elected twelve years earlier on the basis of a socially ambitious and voluntarist program. In parallel, the PCF started on its inexorable decline and found itself more and more marginalized on the political chessboard, incapable of softening the refocusing of the Socialist Party (PS). Its loss of influence and incapacity to adapt to the main sociocultural evolutions of French society inaugurated a new political era, characterized in particular by the brutal weakening of its hold on the forces of the social movement. The left as a whole was profoundly affected. Even if it won the next two presidential elections in a row, the "neoliberal watershed" (Jobert 1994) affected the sociological balances and distorted its capacity to respond to the needs of the most underprivileged members of society, at the time when inequalities and long-term unemployment were growing. The trade union movement did not escape from this evolution, at the behest of the French Democratic Work Confederation (CFDT), which, from the end of the 1970s, started to distance itself from a discourse on a break with the capitalist method of production to progressively adopt a much more reformist approach accepting market and competition rules, which it would from now on be a question of regulating than fighting against.[16] Worker unions, which saw membership drop breathtakingly,[17] were considerable weakened and were prey to ever stronger divisions and more demanding. The conjugation of all these elements led to a refocusing of militant action-associative in particular, which encouraged the emancipation of social movements (Mathieu 2002).[18] The phenomenon was general and could be observed in a multitude of fields. For those who expected to keep up the political cause of the unemployed, this configuration was evidently favorable for the creation of new collective actors.

In 1982, the national union of the unemployed (SNC) saw the light of day, on the initiative of Maurice Pagat and a few of his companions, coming for the most part from the Christian left. Pagat, then in preretirement after being out of work and without resources for several years, was a hardened militant, member of the CERES[19] and of the CFDT, and a former member of the Christian Youth workers, who took part in the setting up of the Emmaüs communities and committed himself very early on to the independence of Algeria.[20] As its name suggests, the SNC was a challenge to the traditional trade union organizations, which Pagat denounced for its disinterest with regard to the populations excluded from the labor market. The action strategy he developed swung between street demonstrations and haranguing the politico-media on the one hand—through the occupation of the offices of the ASSEDIC,[21] of the ANPE, the Ministry of Employment, the newspaper offices of *Le Monde*, or even recourse to forms of self-exhibition[22]—and an effort at information and raising levels of awareness on questions of employment, unemployment, or of social exclusion on the other hand. The aim was to better understand the mechanisms of precarization so as to confer on the unemployed a collective dimension and thus fight different forms of stigmatization and prevent them from being victimized as the guilty. Reinforced with large social capital, built up during its militant journey, but also from the financial support of the Christian Committee for solidarity with the unemployed (CCSC),[23] the SNC endowed itself with an independent press organ—the monthly *Partage* (Share). It opened as well throughout the country a network of "Maison Partage" destined to come to the assistance of the unemployed and at the same time pave the way for direct assistance to the unemployed and of autonomous collective action. These efforts materialized notably with the organization on May 30, 1985, in Paris of a parade of thousands of the unemployed or those in precarious situations.[24]

In spite of this success, the SNC did not manage to mobilize its militant base for long, made up essentially of older unemployed, and was confronted with growing internal divisions. Apart from personal quarrels, its closeness to the Catholic community gave rise to debate, leading in 1985 to the breaking away of twenty or so local associations, grouped together in a national federation of the unemployed run by Michel Vergely, and in the following year to the creation of the national movement of the unemployed and the precarious (MNCP), which brought together the SNC[25] and local associations having become much more independent. The MNCP looked above all to bring material support to the unemployed, giving less priority to the area of making demands and the political stakes linked to employment, unemployment, and the question of work. Federating today some forty or so associations, in particular in the center and the north of France, it claimed to have more than 6,000 members.[26]

In 1987, the association for employment, information, and solidarity of the unemployed and precarious workers (APEIS) was in turn born out of the unemployed of the Val-de-Marne, demanding of the ASSEDIC a more generous and transparent use of the social funds intended to respond to the urgent needs of job seekers (Bourneau and Martin 1993). Supported in particular by local communist elected officials,[27] the APEIS is a secular organization, which cooperates in particular with the Red Cross and the Secours populaire. It is very present in the Paris region and today has near to 28,000 members.[28] While drawing up a critical report on the institutions charged with the social treatment of unemployment, it favored action on the ground to defend those who find themselves in a situation of great precarity. It got known for its fight for free travel on public transport, stopping gas and electricity cuts, even blocking measures of expulsion from their dwellings of the unemployed. The APEIS plays an important role locally, proposing assistance to the unemployed from its offices and accompanying them in their efforts to get their rights respected. At the same time, these service activities are openly linked to a wider political battle, registered against the capitalist system. Compared to the SNC or the MNCP, the reports and action guidelines of the APEIS are therefore much more at odds.

> The problem with our association is our radicalization. The latter is not wished for, it is the situation, which imposes it on us. Today, there are still as many difficulties for some when everyone proclaims that things are better. What we reveal upsets and that does not help us. The day the capitalist organization no longer needs those retained for the moment, they will be faced with the same steamroller effect as today's excluded.[29]

In 1993, Act together against unemployment (AC!) was launched jointly by the trade unions, those responsible for the associations of the unemployed and intellectuals.[30] AC! presents itself as a multiform organization—including in particular the APEIS and the MNCP—whose statute and composition are relatively fluid, uncertain even, since it only exists through the local collectives that make it up. AC! attempts, through its battle on behalf of the unemployed, to reconcile the actors coming from quite varied origins, whose paths and political objectives are noticeably differentiated. Its initial scheme was thought up by militants emerging from autonomous trade union networks, which, starting from a denunciation of the democratic deficit of the classical commitment structures, expected the renewal of the practice of trade unions and the widening of its scope for mobilization. The interunion review *Collectif* was one of the privileged melting pots of this move, participating in the definition of actions that simultaneously took into account the growing precarity of a large section of the population, the trend toward the individualization of logics of engagement, and the multiplication of autonomistic expressions of social discontent and became a point of better links among them. With this perspective, the question of unemployment as presented by AC! allows for the development of a general reflection on the evolution of the wage earner and the place of work, while contributing to the implementation of relatively innovative participative practices, which formed a large part of the debate on ideas. The arrival of a growing number of unemployed at the heart of AC! modified the already fragile balance of this project and led to a head-on confrontation. For those who are distanced long-term from the labor market, these questions are only in fact of virtual interest and are very far from their immediate concerns, directed more toward strategies of urgency or of survival. More generally, a split separates quite cleanly those—the great majority of the unemployed—who refute all partisan obedience and those who advocate not an alignment, but a coming together with a number of partners situated on the left of the political chessboard. The sociological evolution of AC! meant that the relative internal strengths were reversed in several years. As Mouchard (2001) recalls, "one can roughly estimate that AC! is composed in 1994 of 80 percent wage earners and 20 percent of unemployed. In 1997, this proportion is reversed" (63). The departure of founder members, often in turbulent conditions, was thus made up for by the arrival of numerous young unemployed whose militant socialization was marked by a very big distance with regard to the existing political and trade union organizations.[31]

The fabric of the organizations of the unemployed includes at last the committees of the unemployed of the CGT, whose influence is especially strong in the South of France. Renewing the tradition of the early twentieth century aiming to represent the different component parts of the working class, even for its jobless members, the CGT put in place again from 1978 onward the "committees of the unemployed," regrouped in 1983 as a "committee of struggles and defense of the unemployed" with the rank of CGT national committee, rebaptized, from 1997 on, "national Committee for the struggle and defense of the jobless" (Pignoni 2012). This semantic slippage, far from being anecdotal, conveyed the determination of the CGT to register the question of the representation of the interests of the unemployed in that much more global one of the stakes in the labor and employment market. In the middle of the 1980s, the role of these committees became central to the local mobilization of the unemployed, in particular in the quite specific context of the Bouches-du-Rhône, marked at the same time by the extremely hard social conflicts linked to the closure of the shipyards at La Ciotat, a very high level of unemployment, and the breakthrough of the National Front, especially in the north districts of Marseille. It was above all to stem the rise of the extreme right in the popular quarters that the CGT decided to structure and intensify its support for the unemployed. This task was allocated to Charles Hoareau, CGT departmental representative, a militant communist, himself out of work at the time (Demazière and Pignoni 1998, 133–50; Hoareau 1998). The action he led with a small group of people met with a certain success and was rewarded by the CGT decision to award him, in 1993, the statute of full-time union official, which allowed him to devote himself entirely to the development of committees of the unemployed. A task of assistance, socialization, and greater mobilization was then undertaken on the ground, in the districts where the unemployed and those populations with serious social deprivation lived. The CGT jobless workers' committees had however to manage two stumbling blocks on a permanent basis: first get their legitimacy recognized even within a union organization having a somewhat instrumental conception of their existence; then, to establish links with other unemployed workers' associations, whose distrust of the trade union world and networks close to the PCF remained vivid. Despite these difficulties, the actions and demands of these committees were among the most combative and most determined that the unemployed workers' movement had known. It is due in great part to the Bouches-du-Rhône that the mobilization of the winter of 1997–1998 grew, notably around the demands for a "Christmas bonus."[32]

The "Gang of Four"

The existence over more than twenty years of several unemployed workers' organizations is in itself an essential achievement, which offers the unemployed a minimal base of resources available for action. It is in this respect significant that the expression "gang of four"—often used in the general press to denote AC!, the APEIS, the MNCP, and the CGT—was widespread, without it being denied by those principally concerned. It testifies to the recognition accorded them and, in this sense, their sustainable set-up in the French public arena. This understanding may be surprising given the differing degrees of deep and recurring divisions these organizations undergo. Two major cleavage lines, more or less linked, emerge, not only between organizations but equally, often, within them. It appears thus that the antagonism between trade unions (or the members) and associations of the unemployed (or the jobless) is strongly structuring; and the recurrent heartbreaks of a movement like the AC! is witness to the paroxysmal vivacity of these stakes. As well, a militant tradition strongly impregnated with social Catholicism opposes a more partisan commitment, close to the PCF, Trotskyism networks, or more widely to the far left. The very ambiguous relations that secular militants maintain, often of a communist allegiance, on one side, and of Christian-inspired militants on the other, translate into very different conceptions of demand-related actions and the type of support to be given to the unemployed. In the first case, the behaviors originate in a revolutionary project the exclusive core or even central axis of which does not include the unemployed, since its aim is to extend itself to other groups. In the second case, the strictly political dimension of the commitment is either less thought out, or designed for a more reformist register, but it concentrates on the unemployed and the most impoverished. These distinctions are not insurmountable, even if they refer back to well-established ideological traditions and families. On this subject Olivier Fillieule (1993, 150) justly notes that the growth of charitable action in France at the beginning of the 1980s—in reply to the rise of inequalities and the appearance of the "new poor" (Salmon 1998)—was able to put a brake on the emergence of a social movement of the unemployed. Emergency aid and assistance to people in serious difficulty contribute in fact to the improvement in living conditions of the unemployed without the participation as such in the drawing up of a political stake from which perhaps could be built a demand-related action, which it may even contribute to forestall. At the same time, the whole history of the mobilization of the unemployed shows that these two dimensions are linked in the process of mobilization, the enlistment and the political battle of the latter needing as a prerequisite a minimal degree of reassurance and (re)socialization (Maurer 2001, 90–4).

In spite of profound and recurring disagreements, these organizations continue and, even better, cooperate with each other, unifying their forces in the struggle. This capacity to act in common, even being deeply divided, has multiple reasons. First, and as has been amply emphasized by Klandermans (1988), mobilization around a certain number of stakes does not necessarily (or even rarely) imply the ideological consensus of its constituent parts. For example, the demand for a "Christmas bonus" may correspond to the needs of the unemployed at the end of their period of rights, deeply disadvantaged and little politicized, as it may satisfy the particularly hardened militant trade union members, anxious to maintain each year end a force of social protest. Here and there people meet momentarily around the same demand-led watchword, but they come from different paths and horizons, both individually and collectively. Then, the setting up of a quite fluid network of organizations not subject to a hierarchical center allows one to take account of their strong peculiarities and, at the same time, the regional or local singularities of mobilizations of the unemployed. If one excludes the CGT committees of the unemployed, which arise at least formally from the framework defined by the CGT at national level, the other associations of the unemployed leave their militant base a great deal of autonomy.

The existence of several organizations therefore goes with a mode of internal running, which favors freedom of action for those involved in the field. This structure has the advantage of being appropriate to the sociological particularities of the population potentially mobilizable, which we know to be very largely atomized and little inclined to follow strict organizational rules (Piven and Cloward 1977). Much better than could be done by a strongly centralized system, it facilitates in fact the establishment of a close relationship with the unemployed—generally founded on an assistance service—which is very often an indispensable first step to their possible mobilization. On a daily basis, this link makes possible the understanding of the stakes in the struggle and the identification of political targets making sense for the unemployed in action. If the occupation of the agencies of the ANPE or the ASSEDIC has an equally important place in their protest diary, it is evidently because of the discontent that the latter can crystallize, but also because the associations carry out locally, with the unemployed, a follow-up of files that allows for direct educational and political work. Moreover, the ASSEDIC had until 1997 a certain autonomy in the award of social funds, which favored the demand by the CGT committees in the Bouches-du-Rhône for a "Christmas bonus" for the unemployed. These administrations were perceived as likely to yield under the collective action of the jobless, which reinforced their status as potential targets (Bagguley 1991, 87–98). The mobilization of the unemployed is not therefore decreed from above, following a vertical logic, which would be applied throughout the land, but remains dependent on quota situations, anchored in particular local realities. Thus it develops in geographic zones hit hard by mass unemployment, which are in general former industrial basins, such as the Nord-pas-de-Calais, the big Paris suburbia, or the Bouches-du-Rhône.

In the economic disaster regions, the presence of organizations of the unemployed is an indispensable prerequisite to the shaping and the political expression of the discontent of the unemployed. In France, research by Maurer (2001) has thus highlighted the diffuse, chaotic, uncertain, but finally crucial role the associations of the unemployed can play in the work of self-reconstruction of individuals in a situation of grave personal and social suffering, an indispensable condition for the passage to demands-led action.[33] In offering a framework of life, these organizations also make available a set of resources that are going to facilitate, or make possible, the mobilization and commitment of the unemployed. In this sense, a doubtlessly too rapid and systematic analogy was made between "exclusion" and "annihilation." The example of the unemployed of the Bouches-du-Rhône indicates on the contrary that a strong social link can sometimes be built sustainably out of unemployment, especially when the latter links to sociability networks that remain powerful. Thus it is striking that the work of political mobilization of the unemployed undertaken by associations develops in local contexts struck certainly by the phenomena of social exclusion but which do not succumb completely to anomie, especially because of the resistance of family or associative solidarities.

This work can only be translated politically if the lived situation of the individual by the unemployed is interpreted as a social phenomenon, which exonerates at least in part their own responsibility. In a society that increasingly highlights the (in)capacities of the "individual," the task is not simple and supposes the distancing of values currently widespread. It is a question not only of overcoming stigmatizing representations often attached to the unemployed, but also of struggling against the depersonalization to which this statute contributes (see Castel 2003; Dubois 2003). Here, the "framing" (Snow et al. 1986; Snow and Benford 1988 and 2000) to which the associations of the unemployed proceed is essential and covers first of all the diagnosis of the situation in which the unemployed are living. As emphasized by Mouchard (2001), the unemployed who mobilize set out generally with negative identifications that are attributed to them—expressed as lacks, insufficiencies, uselessness, or of absences—and, rather than reject them, try to take them into their ownership so as to reverse the significance. Doing this, they take part in an extremely delicate process of negative dizalienation, to develop a more positive identification, from which a demand-led action becomes possible.[34] The "jobless," the "beggars" or the "invisibles" as they sometimes call themselves, thus serve—not without irony—as common denominations to the group. This reownership of oneself is done much more easily in a collective framework than individually. More so again than other categories of the population, the unemployed have in fact a need for cognitive resources that the organizations obtain, necessary for going into action.

Finally, the process of running the unemployed workers' associations manages deep internal divisions and preserves the aid and mobilization conditions of precarious and weakened individuals, whose social link often needs to be rebuilt in part. At the same time, these organizations are capable of presenting themselves and intervening on the public scene in a relatively unified manner, appearing as credible spokesmen, including the national level. The ability to use these organizational resources as a demand-led force nevertheless remains largely dependent on a global political environment, in particular the support brought by a certain number of outside contributors. The activities of strong protestation are as a consequence intermittent and alternate with periods of more calm where the essence of action is orientated toward material assistance for the unemployed.[35]

Between Strategies of Alliances and Will for Autonomy

The mobilization of the unemployed seems to oscillate permanently between the will of self-affirmation, which focuses on their cause and their representation as such, and the practical necessity of taking into account the political and institutional opportunities (or of constraints), which are largely exogenous, and which determine in large part the conditions of their action. This tension is without doubt not the attribute of the unemployed, but it poses itself in particularly crucial terms for a population flimsily constituted, weakened, poorly resourced, and which as a consequence has to rely on external support to have a hope of being heard. As emphasized by Michael Lipsky (1970), "the 'problem of the powerless' in protest activity is to activate 'third parties' to enter the implicit or explicit bargaining area in ways favorable to the protesters" (2). The mobilized unemployed have certainly forged links, sometimes very tenuous, with many other groups, in a variety of fields—struggle against AIDS, for the right to housing, or in support of immigrants, and so on (see Boumaza and Hamman 2007; Cadiou, Dechezelles and Roger 2007)—but without being able to reach the heights of decision-making and to have any say in the political timetable. It is really the access to the seats of power and especially the ties with the parties of government that are missing in the defense of the interests of the unemployed. Even if unemployment has for many years been one of the main concerns of French public opinion, the unemployed constituting a group as a whole are in effect almost totally off the political chessboard. This situation can be explained in a number of ways. It relates in part to the will for autonomy of the unemployed workers' organizations, which is also a vector of political marginalization and does not favor their ability for expression. It is explained also and above all in the electoral behavior of the unemployed, characterized by high abstentionism, and, to a lesser degree, by a protest vote (Pierru 2005). Not being a sufficiently stable and captive electorate, the unemployed do not bring to any party of government a significant reserve of votes and are not subject to any particular attention on their part. On the contrary, the fact that a minority but growing part of the unemployed gave its vote to the National Front[36] raised anxieties over a recent period, thus turning the unemployed vote and that of their representation in French society into a pertinent stake in the political debate (Perrineau 1997). As a whole, however, the organized unemployed have hardly the right to speak and are neither considered as politically legitimate interlocutors nor are they defended by any party to whom they might be close.

If the relation of the unemployed workers' associations with the partisan world is at least distant, the relations with the trade union organizations are tenuous but conflictual. The latter have a visibility, a militant know-how and a mobilization capacity very superior to the associations of the unemployed—and as such figure as partners with privileged potential—while being an obstacle to autonomy to which the latter aspire. The unemployed in action inherit from this point of view a very unfavorable institutional situation, because the shape of the social dialogue put progressively in place in France with the advent of the industrial society offers virtually no role to their organizations. The trade unions see themselves given the role of "social partners" and are considered to be formed of right "representatives" not only for the whole workforce but also those who are jobless.

In this context, it is not surprising that the large trade union confederations are opposed to any form of autonomous representation of the unemployed, with the exception of the CGT, which in spite of many ambiguities is not completely hostile to this idea. To different degrees, the trade unions denounce in this approach a risk of corporatism susceptible in time to weaken the defense of those who have a job as much as those who have not. In France, the question always raises lively recriminations and remains very largely a taboo.[37] The trade union organizations and the state in this regard share the same point of view and deny all strictly political legitimacy to the associations of the unemployed. On the occasion of the movement of the unemployed in the winter of 1997–1998, the prime minister, Lionel Jospin, had in a very significant way consented to award urgent assistance to the unemployed—thus noting their discontent—while reminding that

> the trade union organizations are the natural interlocutors, direct, constant of the public authorities. Their specific role on questions of negotiation inscribed in the Code of work is a key element in social relations. The unions have a calling to represent all workers, including those who have lost their jobs. (*Le Monde*, January 10, 1998)

By virtue of the same principle, the management of the unemployment-insurance system has been entrusted since 1958 to the trade unions and to the employers' organizations, under government control. This situation, which presented hardly any problems at the time of the "Trente Glorieuses," is much more open to challenge in a society officially counting three to four million unemployed. The fact that the regime of indemnities to the jobless is totally out of the hands of the associations specifically defending their interests, and that it is placed under the joint responsibility of organizations that refuse to recognize a political role for them is a source of lively complaints. Thus the grievances that the organized unemployed addressed to the CFDT are twofold and concern at the same time its role as union representative but also the one it played as president of the UNEDIC, between October 1996 and October 1998.

In search of recognition and relatively isolated, the unemployed workers' associations found some room for maneuver in the fragmentation and splits of the French trade union scene, which opened up some possibilities of alliances. For example, the relatively benevolent position of the CGT with regard to the mobilized unemployed is understandable particularly in the framework of the global evolution of the French trade union scene and the power relations it was going through. Pushing more or less openly their cause, the CGT chose to stand out from other union organizations, and first the CFDT. Well, the internal tensions in the union world and in particular the conflicts raised by the ideological reorientation of the CFDT strengthened the leadership of certain associations of the unemployed, the AC! in particular. The refocusing of the CFDT provoked numerous challenges from within, leading to the resignation or ousting of members, some of whom later brought direct support to the movement of the unemployed. Some dissidents regrouped together under CFDT-Tous ensemble (all together), which took a close part in the development of the latter. An important split developed here between the unions backing the negotiation, close to the government parties, which approved in July 1997 the reforms lowering the allocations to the unemployed, and those, often less powerful, more steeped in a culture of opposition. The movement of the unemployed benefited strongly from this recomposition and the radicalization of a part of the trade union movement. Moreover, it is interesting to note a relative situational analogy between the associations of the unemployed and certain emerging unions, who each in their turn demand the statute of representative organizations, thus challenging the institutional legitimacies.

Strengthened by this support, the unemployed manage to act collectively if only the global context gives them the chance. In November/December 1995, they find a favorable framework for expressing their cause, taking an active part in the largest social movement the country has seen since May 1968 (Béroud and Mouriaux 1997). The progress of the mobilization translated however their difficulty in imposing themselves as such and to speak for themselves. On one side, the unemployed were tempted to take advantage of the extraordinary size of the event in joining in the parade of demonstrators. This is what they did here and there throughout France, acceding to a visibility they had not had before. For example, in Marseille, "the CGT committees for the unemployed find/found in the social movement an unexpected local platform of expression, while they had only hitherto appeared in episodic fashion in the local press" (Capdevielle and Meynaud 1997, 76). On the other hand, their participation in a social movement strongly focused on the dissatisfactions with the world of work—and more precisely with its most protected sectors—and corresponded not well at all with their situation of exclusion and their specific demands. In the interprofessional parades moreover, the unemployed often made up a separate parade (81). On December 10, in Marseille—while the conflict was at the height of its mobilization—nearly 10,000 unemployed demonstrated in autonomous fashion to obtain a Christmas bonus of 3,000 francs (about 450 euros). Even if, through the struggles, signs of solidarity between trade union members, wage earners and the unemployed were visible (Martin 1997, 92 and 97), the tensions between the demands of those who had an employment and the others remained serious.

Two years later, in the winter of 1997–1998, there too in a strongly agitated climate, the unemployed were equally able to take an active part in protests. During several months, action campaigns were launched in dozens of towns, marked in particular by a multitude of demonstrations and the occupation between December and January of thirty or so ASSEDIC branches. For the first time in their history, the associations of the unemployed obtained satisfaction on several points of their demands.[38] During this period, the movement could take advantage of an original political situation, characterized in particular by the arrival in power of a "plural left" of which some component parts—the Greens and the PCF—openly backed the men and women who mobilized in the street. In this scenario, the unemployed did not escape from a relation of dependency, which goes against their will for autonomy and makes them dependent as regards tactico-political considerations, which they do not master. Even when they support collective action by the unemployed, certain trade union organizations include their initiatives in fact in the framework of a wide political game, which leads them sometimes to contain and to limit the social movement (Béroud, Gobin, and Lefèvre forthcoming). Depending on the government majorities, the positions they take differ a great deal. When the right is in power, generally it is a question of mobilizing in the most widely possible way against a clearly designated political adversary. In other situations, the strategies developed are much less readable and more ambiguous. This is notably the case of the CGT when the left is in power and, above all, when the leaders of the PCF—to which it is historically close—are present in government. In the winter of 1997–1998, the intensity of its support to the unemployed thus depended on a complex political configuration, in which the state of relations between the PS and the PCF played a major role. The pressure of the CGT on the government was then exerted with more or less force according to the degree of destabilization being sought. Thus on January 27, 1998, at the time when the unemployed in a struggle hoped to relaunch a conflict that was dying out, the CGT looked ahead to the end of the movement. By taking the initiative of three distinct rallies—the first with the unemployed in defense of the thirty-five hours and the revaluation of the social minima, the second with the federations FO (Force Ouvrière) and CFDT to safeguard the situation of the staff at the Ministry of Equipment, and the third with the federation of railway staff to protest against the plans for restructuring the SNCF (the national public railway company)—and above all by opposing the convergence of these parades, the CGT saved the government from a mass demonstration and brought a definitive halt to the mobilization of the unemployed.

The movements of the unemployed are therefore held in a tension difficult to manage. On the one hand, they put forward their organizational will and want to conserve their autonomy of action. On the other hand, for the sake of efficiency, the unemployed are faced with the need to build alliances with other stakeholders, in particular trade unions, who act according to their own logic and interests on which they have little control. These two guidelines are factors of deep division and raise among the jobless recurrent questions on the behavior to provide to the demands-led movement.

Challenge without Shocking: Social Acceptance At Stake

For those involved whose political and institutional resources are so weak, it is imperative to find alternative strategies that arouse, in one way or another, the attention and the widest approval of the population. Precisely, the cause of the struggling unemployed is rather favorably looked upon by a majority of French public opinion. Most of the polls carried out show that almost two-thirds of the people questioned "support" or "feel sympathy toward" their movement (Faniel 2004). The perception of unemployment has moreover evolved over the last twenty years. Although the phenomenon affected mostly the socially disadvantaged, it could be considered a consequence of a lack of skills and qualifications—and to some degree of motivation—attributable at least in part to the individuals concerned. At the end of the 1970s the dominant political speeches favored the hypothesis of an employment crisis, severe, but nevertheless of a transient nature. As the prospects of an eradication of unemployment faded and, above all, unemployment spread to the social groups hitherto relatively spared, opinions changed substantially (Join-Lambert 1994, 163–5). The idea that unemployment is, above all, a mass phenomenon that affects all strata of society in industrialized countries—including managers—has since largely imposed itself. The question of the responsibility of individuals for the persistence of this phenomenon has not gone away, but it is quite rarely raised explicitly today in public debate as a major explanation. This change of perspective is essential. It means that French public opinion is as a whole sensitive to the cause of the unemployed and ready to support their demands.

In this context, registering the mobilization of the unemployed on the agenda of the media becomes an inescapable issue. The unemployed are thus endowed with resources, know-how, and substantial experience in the area of communication. Over time, some of them even became experienced media players, have broken with the specific techniques that meetings with journalists require, especially rapidity and brevity. Richard Dethyre of the APEIS emphasizes "us, that makes 11 years, since our creation, that we have press relations. When I have 30 seconds to speak I say urgency" (*Libération*, December 14, 1998). Also, extremely efficient slogans, short, scathing, thought up in part for their sound effect—such as "existence," "resistance," or "a job is a right, a revenue is a due"—are witness to an adaptation to the rules of the media game. Most of the forms of demonstration and mobilization are thought up depending on the interest they can arouse with the media. As emphasized by one of the leaders of AC! "on matters such as unemployment, we have no other solutions than to arouse the sympathy of opinion" (interview by the author, March 2000). This objective was moreover reached since mobilization was never perceived by the population as a movement of agitators. For the unemployed the margin for maneuver is reduced. It is a question of getting the interest of the media through some spectacular actions with a heavy symbolic charge, in a manner to challenge public opinion, without as such provoking its indignation. The leaders therefore constantly ensured that protest actions conserved a political sense, which—even if illegal—always appeared respectable if not legitimate.

Thus, the few scenes of looting committed by the unemployed in shops were vigorously denounced by the organizations of the unemployed. These events are more detrimental since they risk discrediting other measures called "requisition of food," skillfully prepared, designed as political demands, carried out in supermarkets or in luxury food stores.[39]

For the governments in office, it is a question obviously of limiting to the utmost the impact of the movement of the unemployed. The support brought by public opinion, at least tacitly, limits the possibilities of intervention by the authorities and, for example, would make politically costly the evacuation by force of premises illicitly occupied by the unemployed. End 1995, in a social climate of exacerbated effervescence, the government of Alain Juppé preferred not to call on the forces of law and order to intervene, even if the mobilization was prolonged. In 1998, in a less tense context, the government of Lionel Jospin took an opposite line of action, getting the ASSEDIC premises evacuated.[40] Faced with this hardening, the unemployed hardly resisted and were not prepared for physical opposition. Such a strategy would have been possible and would doubtless have provoked a major media occasion. At the same time, while not protesting, or protesting very little, the unemployed presented themselves as exemplary victims of a political and police repression capable of provoking the reprobation of public opinion. This concern for acceptability, posted by the unemployed in action, is all the more important to be underlined since it permits a refinement of the hypothesis according to which the recourse to types of transgressive action would be a favored means for marginalized groups to surround the public space.[41] In this case, these practices are strictly controlled and forbid acts of violence under any circumstance. The occupation of buildings or lock-in of staff of the ASSEDIC are thus strongly theatrical and generally prepared with the assent, if not the agreement, of the people aimed at. Even if this line of conduct is regularly discussed and contested within the movement of the unemployed, the "institutional disruptions" (Piven and Cloward 1977, 24) are mastered—when they are not, they are severely condemned by the movement's leaders—and are akin to the media shocks with strong symbolic overtones. Rather than confrontation, the movements of the unemployed have thus looked for spectacular action and in this sense have shown great inventiveness. AC! has in particular specialized in operations called "requisition of jobs," which consists of entering the premises of the companies concerned—but foreseeing staff reduction plans—and presenting the management with whole piles of CVs of job seekers. This type of demonstration does not result in any recruitment, but draws the attention of the media to a situation considered problematical, shocking even.

As a whole, the media have largely covered the recent movements of the unemployed and provided quite a lot of visibility (Lagneau 2005). Those mobilized express satisfaction, almost gratitude in their regard and highlight "an extremely strong gratitude, the legitimacy acquired thanks to the media. Thanks to them there has been created a real political space."[42] At the same time, their hopes are so big that they have all the chance of being disappointed. Hubert Constancias, former president of the MNCP, recognizes that "the people, including our movement, have a tendency to think the media never does enough. We expect too much of the media that they do us a service, as if they owed us something. That creates a dephazing with our expectations" (*Libération*, December 14, 1998). The relations the unemployed maintain with the media are also globally marked by a strong distrust, which is often confined to hostility. Some, such as François Desanti of the CGT-Unemployed, would like to "see an unemployed person kicking in his empty fridge! Yes, you have to show suffering" (ibid.). Others, on the contrary, have the feeling that the media put forward a wretched vision of their situation in focusing exaggeratedly on the individual paths of the unemployed and the excluded, without including them in the political stakes and processes. The newspapers, TV bulletins in particular, are said to present an often disorderly image, confused and disconnected from a mobilization that would seem to have neither path nor organization. This is the interpretation given by Le Grignou and Patou (2001), for whom "this multiplication of details and fragmentary information, this juxtaposition of punctilious events contribute to giving an image of a blurred whole, unstructured, inhomogeneous, whose actions only acquire some semblance of unity through the reactions they provoke in the political area" (38).

Whether justified or not, the criticisms developed around the traditional media on the one hand and the will of the unemployed to be able to draw up and therefore master their own arguments on the other have encouraged for some years the multiplication of new modes of expression and of communication called "alternatives" (radios, written press, associative television, Internet sites, logs, etc.). These initiatives are revelatory of an approach seeking the reappropriation of the voice of demands of those who struggle to get themselves heard, even when it is they who are talked about. By creating their own dialogue and reflection space, the unemployed certainly do not leave the privacy to which their social situation confines them and do not get for themselves more means of questioning a wide public, but they offer themselves the luxury of proposing the meaning they attribute to their action.

Conclusion

Since the beginning of the century, the French unemployed have sporadically shown their capability for mobilization. They are endowed with organizations that, although divided and crossed with large fault lines, represent them and deliver their demands, which is an important asset. This collective structure is by itself a major factor for such a heterogeneous and splintered population. Politically isolated and maintaining conflictual relations with most of the representative trade union organizations, the unemployed in action aspire to autonomy for their movement. At the same time, they remain largely dependent on influence-peddling, which is beyond them and on which they have virtually no hold. In this sense, the difficulties they come across in committing themselves collectively depend at least as much on the slenderness of the opportunities offered them as on the sociological characteristics of the unemployed themselves. Despite the peaks of mobilization, it is in the end the episodic dimension of their action that stands out.

Today, the movement seems to be again in a phase of reflux. The associations of the unemployed remain corrupted by their divisions, which weaken the few resources available to them for demand-led action. Moreover, the process of mobilization demands such an effort that the lively forces of militancy tend to exhaust themselves over time. Generational renewal has not always been a guarantee, while a section of the historical leaders have committed themselves to other emerging causes, in particular the alterglobalization movement (Cohen 2011). For all that, the associations of the unemployed have gained a certain visibility in the public arena, particularly with the media. They have also become the privileged interlocutors for the jobless and the precarious, with whom they conduct themselves more and more like service providers. In parallel, new orientations on demands are emerging, unsure of whether they point to a substantial change in the forms of action, or to a simple bending of a more-or-less transient nature. Still, in 2003–2004, the organizations of the unemployed turned massively toward the courts to assert the rights of the people they represent. At this time, the new UNEDIC convention signed by the social partners and agreed to by the government foresaw a reduction in the period of indemnification of the unemployed to restrict the conditions of entry into this regime and, above all, to give retroactive effect to these provisions. The organizations of the unemployed contested the legality of this measure, arguing that UNEDIC had contractual links with the unemployed and consequently it was forbidden to unilaterally modify rights given to the latter. More than 200,000 "recalculated" unemployed were directly concerned with this measure, among whom a certain number of periodic performers on stage—who at the same period were demonstrating vociferously their opposition to the reform of their statute—contributed to the denunciation of this situation. The first filing of complaints in courts gave a high visibility to the challenge and, reciprocally, the mediatization of the movement encouraged the unemployed to contact militant organizations. The unemployed workers' associations, who benefited from the assistance of the lawyers of the CGT, multiplied their juridical submissions. On April 15, 2004, the Marseille tribunal issued a first judgment in favor of several unemployed, condemning the UNEDIC to damages and costs, obliging it to reinstate their rights to the unemployed. Rather than wait for other tribunals to take similar decisions in a cascade, the minister of employment announced on May 3 the reintegration of all the "recalculated" (Willemez 2006). This episode had a big impact in France and is to this day one of the most startling victories attributed to the unemployed. If the result obtained is spectacular, the recourse to the judicial path, more than the street demonstration, can also be interpreted as a sign of the breathlessness of the movement.

Notes

1. The individual and microsociological reasons for the mobilization of the unemployed have been very finely analyzed by Maurer (2001) and Pouchadon (2002).
2. If one excludes the one, symbolically strong but numerically weak, organized at the Invalides, Paris, on March 9, 1883, on the initiative of Louise Michel and Émile

Pouget. In the years that followed, the jobless manifested from time to time their discontent at the employment offices often with the help of militant workers close to an anarcho-syndicalist tradition (Perrot 1974).
3. Created in Moscow in 1921, its goal was to organize the proletarian masses in order to overturn capitalism.
4. Kourchid (1999) gives in this respect a multitude of indicators and extremely interesting witness statements. Thus he quotes the CGTU according to which: "You don't have to expect that the unemployed recognize [the unions] as guide; we have to impose ourselves as such, in the places where they gather: placement offices, factory recruitment, districts." Further, "the CGTU regrets that the mobilization has been the work of the unemployed themselves and not of the trade unions, who sent few delegates."
5. The number was 50,000 according to *L'Humanité*, and 6,000 according to the Ministry of the Interior.
6. A total of 8,000 according to the police, 23,000 according to the communist press.
7. A total of 120,000 according to the communist press, 15,000 according to the police (figures quoted by Perry 2007, 89).
8. In Germany, the electoral success of the NSDAP, supported by a large part of the popular classes, and the arrival in power of Hitler furnished at the same period a disquieting example.
9. From March 1936, the CGT and the CGTU were reunited.
10. Their number was estimated at 120 in September 1940 (Perry 2007, 223).
11. Pigenet and Tartakowsky (2003, 92) emphasize moreover that the mobilized unemployed at this time in France did not register at all in the tradition of marches of the jobless organized during the 1930s.
12. For a synthesis, see Demazière and Pignoni 1998.
13. To have the different unemployment insurance reforms put in perspective, see Daniel and Tuchszirer (1999); and Lévy (2003, 56–9).
14. This evolution is not specific to France as shown by Giraud and Braun (1999); Lévy (2003); and Faniel (2005).
15. Televised interview of July 14, 1993.
16. See the illuminating lexical analysis by Béroud and Lefèvre (2007).
17. Union density went from 20 to 25 percent in the middle of the 1970s to near 8 percent in 2003 (Pernot 2005, 123).
18. It is in this perspective that one may understand the appearance at the same period of the Beur movement, professional coordinations, and, more widely, the protestation renewal, which substantially modified mobilizations in France. See Crettiez and Sommier (2002).
19. The Centre for the Study, Research and Education of Socialists, cofounded by Jean-Pierre Chevènement, was one of the main trends of the PS, on the left of the party.
20. These biographical elements are taken from a series of interviews carried out in 2005 with the interested party. See also Fillieule (1993).
21. ASSociation pour l'Emploi dans l'Industrie et le Commerce. Up to 2007 the public employment service comprised principally of the ANPE (Agence Nationale pour l'Emploi), charged with placing job seekers, and the UNEDIC (Union Nationale pour l'Emploi dans l'Industrie et le Commerce) association managed by the wage earners' trade unions and employers' organizations, which set the rules and levels of unemployment indemnification and on which the ASSEDIC were dependent

on at the local level. The emergence of a one-stop counter and a single job seeker's document common to both organizations was progressively organized up to the creation in October 2008 of Pôle Emploi, a new public employment service that achieved the fusion of the ANPE and the ASSEDIC.
22. Maurice Pagat undertook a hunger strike in 1982.
23. See http://admi.net/ccsc/ (last accessed March 21, 2011).
24. In the press as in the scientific literature, the figures swing between 2,500 and 5,000 persons.
25. The SNC disappeared in 1992.
26. Action chômage 82, http://actionchomage82.fr/index.php?option=com_content&view=article&id=170&Itemid=36&0fa9cabed24b1b960e2d5bcccf0b4a9c=fc394c51bb1ba2fd92371ff69616ab5d (last accessed March 21, 2011).
27. It was set up and managed for a long time by Richard Dethyre, former CGT trade unionist, militant communist, metallurgical worker, and in-charge of the Young Communists, and by Malika Zediri-Corniou, former deputy mayor in the communist town of Arcueil.
28. Fodil Ourabah, "Un mauvais coup de plus du gouvernement," *2004 : l'année de la grande régression sociale*, http://survivreausida.net/IMG/pdf/afrika15.pdf (last accessed March 21, 2011).
29. APEIS, "Avec l'Apeis plus jamais seul!" http://www.apeis.org/article.php3?id_article=3 (last accessed March 21, 2011).
30. On the trajectory and heterogeneity of AC!, see especially Mathieu (2009).
31. These lines of tension are far from having been absorbed and get translated by recurrent discussions on the organizational or strategic stakes. These divergences led AC! to experience a split in October 2005.
32. This movement merged with the "week of social action" also foreseen for the end of the month of December by AC! APEIS, and the MNCP to claim a revaluation of the social minima. See Béroud and Mouriaux (1998, 80–9); Demazière and Pignoni (1998, introduction); Royall (1998, 351–65).
33. Maurer (2001) insists on the need to devise the notion of "resources" in a much broader way than do the social sciences and political science in particular. Thus, laziness and absence of social links, for example, can constitute as much incitation to rejoin a collective of the unemployed, if only to break with an unbearable solitude and to find oneself at the beginning of a process of political apprenticeship.
34. One finds here problematics finely analyzed in the work of Goffman, for whom the stigma is the product of a demeaning identification imposed by an institution or a social order on an individual or a group, but which can also be reworked by those who are its object, at the price most often of a costly resistance both socially and psychologically. See especially Goffman (1963).
35. These abeyance phases are the essential conditions for the reemergence of a social movement sometimes after a long period of dormancy, as has notably been shown in the work of Taylor (1989).
36. Basing on the presidential elections of 1995 and 2002, Pierru (2005) established that "the electoral range of the FN would be between 1 unemployed person in 19 and 1 unemployed person in 17" (192). The phenomenon is not only limited but also equally very volatile; other analyses show that the electorate systematically faithful to the FN does not exceed 3 percent (Collovald 2004, 148). Conversely, the FN adopted with regard to the "sans" ("those without") movements an ambiguous if not obliging strategy, as shown by Royall (2009).

37. Martine Aubry had infringed it in 1992, when she was minister of labor, mopping up very severe criticism for having publicly raised the question of the possible creation of a trade union for the unemployed.
38. The government unblocked in particular a billion francs on this occasion (about 150 million euros).
39. It is a question of investing collectively in a store, to select the popular consumer goods, and to leave without paying, using the force of numbers to render impossible any intervention by the security personnel. Led under the gaze of the journalists, these operations aim not just to satisfy the basic needs, but equally to denounce the contrast between their situation and the shop window of riches. One can see through this example that the relation between the unemployed and the media is not an instrumentalization one-way street, that the lower will make the higher undergo, but is more akin to a transaction during which both parties manipulate each other respectively. On the subject, see Gamson and Wolsfeld (1993).
40. Proportionately, the stake is understood in the light of the impact provoked by the conditions of the evacuation of the undocumented from the Church of Saint-Bernard, Paris, on August 23, 1996, whose doors had been smashed in with axes by the forces of law and order. The scene, filmed by TV cameras, raised emotions very high and caused some indignation among a large part of the population, becoming, over time, one of the defining moments of the social movements in France, especially the struggles of "those without."
41. Gamson (1975, 87) defends this idea.
42. Testimony of an anonymous unemployed person "Chômeurs: 'on s'en fout de ce que disent les journaux,'" http://mouv4x8.club.fr/F981214a.htm (last accessed March 21, 2011).

References

Bagguley, Paul. 1991. *From Protest to Acquiescence? Political Movements of the Unemployed*. London: Macmillan.

Béroud, Sophie, Corinne Gobin, and Josette Lefèvre, ed. Forthcoming. *Le syndicalisme au défi du politique*. Rennes: Presses universitaires de Rennes.

Béroud, Sophie, and Josette Lefèvre. 2007. Vers une démocratie économique et sociale ? Banalisation et redéploiement du vocabulaire syndical. *Mots, les langages du politique* 83: 37–51.

Béroud, Sophie, and René Mouriaux, ed. 1997. *Le souffle de décembre. Le mouvement social de 1995. Continuités, singularités, portée*. Paris: Syllepse.

Béroud, Sophie, and René Mouriaux. 1998. Le décembre des chômeurs ou la force des faibles. *Cahiers de l'atelier* 480: 80–9.

Boumaza, Magali, and Philippe Hamman, ed. 2007. *Sociologie des mouvements de précaires. Espaces mobilisés et répertoires d'action*. Paris: L'Harmattan.

Bourdieu, Pierre. 1998. *Contre-feux*. Paris: Liber/Raisons d'agir.

Bourneau, François, and Virginie Martin. 1993. Organiser les sans emploi ? L'expérience de l'APEIS dans le Val-de-Marne. In *Sociologie de la protestation. Les formes de l'action collective dans la France contemporaine*, ed. Olivier Fillieule, 157–80. Paris: L'Harmattan.

Cadiou, Stéphane, Stéphanie Dechezelles, and Antoine Roger, ed. 2007. *Passer à l'action: les mobilisations émergentes*. Paris: L'Harmattan.

Capdevielle, Jacques, and Hélène Meynaud. 1997. Des cheminots aux traminots, l'actualisation de la tradition marseillaise. In *Le souffle de décembre. Le mouvement social de 1995. Continuités, singularités, portée*, ed. Sophie Béroud and René Mouriaux, 59–82. Paris: Syllepse.

Castel, Robert. 2003. *From Manual Workers to Wage Laborers: Transformation of the Social Question*. New Brunswick: Transaction Publishers.

Cohen, Valérie. 2011. Inflexions des mobilisations collectives de chômeurs et fluctuation de l'engagement militant. In *Les mobilisations sociales à l'heure du précariat*, ed. Didier Chabanet, Pascale Dufour, and Frederic Royal. *Lien social et politiques*.

Collovald, Annie. 2004. *Le populisme du FN, un dangereux contresens*. Broissieux: éditions du Croquant.

Crettiez, Xavier, and Isabelle Sommier, ed. 2002. *La France rebelle : tous les foyers, mouvements et acteurs de la contestation*. Paris: Michalon.

Croucher, Richard. 1987. *We Refuse to Starve in Silence: A History of the National Unemployed Workers' Movement 1920–46*. London: Lawrence and Wishart.

Daniel, Christine, and Carole Tuchszirer. 1999. *L'État face aux chômeurs. L'indemnisation du chômage de 1884 à nos jours*. Paris: Flammarion.

De Barros, Françoise. 2001. Secours aux chômeurs et assistances durant l'entre-deux-guerres. Étatisation des dispositifs et structuration des espaces politiques locaux. *Politix* 14 (53): 117–44.

Demazière, Didier, and Maria-Teresa Pignoni. 1998. *Chômeurs : du silence à la révolte*. Paris: Hachette.

Dubois, Vincent. 2003. *La vie au guichet. Relation administrative et traitement de la misère*. Paris: Economica.

Dubois, Vincent. 2007. État social actif et contrôle des chômeurs : un tournant rigoriste entre tendances européennes et logiques nationales. *Politique européenne* 21: 73–95.

Ebersold, Serge. 2001. *L'invention de l'inemployable. Ou l'insertion au risque de l'exclusion*. Rennes: Presses universitaires de Rennes.

Evans, Richard J., and Dick Geary, ed. 1987. *The German Unemployed. Experiences and Consequences of Mass Unemployment from the Weimar Republic to the Third Reich*. London/Sydney: Croom Helm.

Faniel, Jean. 2004. Chômeurs en Belgique et en France : des mobilisations différentes. *Revue internationale de politique comparée* 11(4): 493–505.

———. 2005. Le contrôle des chômeurs en Belgique. Objectifs et resistances. *Informations sociales* 126: 84–91.

Fillieule, Olivier. 1993. Conscience politique, persuasion et mobilisation des engagements. L'exemple du syndicat des chômeurs, 1983–1989. In *Sociologie de la protestation. Les formes de l'action collective dans la France contemporaine*, ed. Olivier Fillieule, 123–55. Paris: L'Harmattan.

Gamson, William. 1975. *The Strategy of Social Protest*. Homewood: Dorsey Press.

Gamson, William, and Gadi Wolsfeld. 1993. Movements and Media as Interacting Systems. *Annals of the American Academy of Political and Social Science* 528: 114–25.

Garraud, Philippe. 2000. *Le chômage et l'action publique. Le "bricolage" institutionnalisé*. Paris: L'Harmattan.

Giraud, Olivier, and Dietmar Braun, ed. 1999. Les politiques de l'emploi en Suisse à la fin des années 90 : modèle(s) en transition. *Revue économique et sociale* 57: 128–224.

Goffman, Erving. 1963. *Stigma: Notes on the Management of Spoiled Identity*. Englewood Cliffs: Prentice-Hall.

Hoareau, Charles. 1998. Marseille 97–98. *Les Temps modernes* 600: 43–56.

Jobert, Bruno. 1994. *Le tournant néo-libéral en Europe*. Paris: L'Harmattan.

Join-Lambert, Marie-Thérèse. 1994. *Politiques sociales*. Paris: Presses de la Fondation Nationale des Sciences Politiques/Dalloz.

Klandermans, Bert. 1988. The Formation and Mobilization of Consensus. In *International Social Movement Research. From Structure to Action: Comparing Social Movement Research Across Cultures*, ed. Bert Klandermans, Hanspeter Kriesi, and Sidney Tarrow, 173–96. Greenwich/London: JAI Press.

Kourchid, Olivier. 1999. Les mouvements de chômeurs en France, 1919–1935, historiographie selon *la Vie Ouvrière*. In *Images et mouvements du siècle. Tome II, Les raisins de la colère*. Ivry-sur-Seine: éditions France Progrès/France découvertes/Institut CGT d'Histoire sociale.

Lagneau, Éric. 2005. Comment étudier la médiatisation des conflits ? In *Le conflit en grèves. Tendances et perspectives de la conflictualité contemporaine*, ed. Jean-Michel Denis, 59–95. Paris: La Dispute.

Le Grignou, Brigitte, and Charles Patou. 2001. Mouvement des chômeurs : mais que font les medias ? In *Les effets d'information en politique*, ed. Jacques Gerstlé, 31–54. Paris: L'Harmattan.

Lévy, Catherine. 2003. *Vivre au minimum. Enquête dans l'Europe de la précarité*. Paris: La Dispute.

Lipsky, Michael. 1970. *Protest in City Politics. Rent Strikes, Housing and the Power of the Poor*. Chicago: Rand McNally and Company.

Martin, Jean-Philippe. 1997. L'Hérault dans l'arc des luttes. In *Le souffle de décembre. Le mouvement social de 1995. Continuités, singularités, portée*, ed. Sophie Béroud and René Mouriaux, 89–102. Paris: Syllepse.

Mathieu, Lilian. 2002. Rapport au politique, dimensions cognitives et perspectives pragmatiques dans l'analyse des mouvements sociaux. *Revue française de science politique* 52 (1): 75–100.

———. 2009. Éléments pour une analyse des coalitions contestataires. *Revue française de science politique* 59 (1): 77–96.

Maurer, Sophie. 2000. Le mouvement des chômeurs de l'hiver 1997–1998. *Recherches et prévisions* 61: 3–17.

———. 2001. *Les chômeurs en action (décembre 1997–mars 1998). Mobilisation collective et ressources compensatoires*. Paris: L'Harmattan.

Maurer, Sophie, and Emmanuel Pierru. 2001. Le mouvement des chômeurs de l'hiver 1997–1998. Retour sur un "miracle social." *Revue française de science politique* 51(3): 371–407.

Mouchard, Daniel. 2001. *Les "exclus" dans l'espace public. Mobilisations et logiques de représentation dans la France contemporaine*. PhD diss., Sciences Po Paris.

Paugam, Serge. 1998. La révolte des chômeurs : un mouvement sans précédent. *Magazine Littéraire* May: 73–6.

Pernot, Jean-Marie. 2005. *Syndicats : lendemains de crise ?* Paris: Gallimard.

Perrineau, Pascal. 1997. *Le symptôme Le Pen. Radiographie des électeurs du Front national*. Paris: Fayard.

Perrot, Michelle. 1974. *Les ouvriers en grève, 1871–1890*. Paris/The Hague: Mouton (2 volumes).

Perry, Matt. 2007. *Prisoners of Want. The Experience and Protest of the Unemployed in France, 1921–45*. Aldershot: Ashgate.

Pierru, Emmanuel. 2002. La politique des "ventre creux." Stigmatisations socio-politiques du chômeur dans la grande dépression. Jalons pour une histoire compare. Paper presented at the seventh congress of the Association française de science politique, September 18–21, Lille, France.

Pierru, Emmanuel. 2005. Sur quelques faux problèmes et demi-vérités autour des effets électoraux du chômage. In *La démobilisation politique*, ed. Frédérique Matonti, 177–99. Paris: La Dispute.

Pierru, Emmanuel. 2007. "Mobiliser 'la vie fragile.' Les communistes et les chômeurs dans les années 1930." *Sociétés contemporaines* 65(1): 113–45.

Pigenet, Michel, and Danielle Tartakowsky. 2003. Les marches en France aux XIXe et XXe siècles : récurrence et métamorphose d'une démonstration collective. *Le Mouvement social* 202: 69–94.

Pignoni, Maria-Teresa. 2012. Les relations entre syndicalisme et mouvements sociaux: le cas des comités CGT des privés d'emploi. In *La mobilisation des chômeurs en France*, ed. Didier Chabanet and Jean Faniel. Paris: L'Harmattan.

Piven, Frances Fox, and Richard A. Cloward. 1979 [1977]. *Poor People's Movements: Why They Succeed, How They Fail*. New York: Vintage Books.

Pouchadon, Marie-Laure. 2002. *La mobilisation collective des chômeurs*. PhD diss., University Bordeaux 2 Victor Segalen.

Richards, Andrew. 2002. Mobilizing the Powerless: Collective Protest action of the Unemployed in the Interwar Period. *Estudios Working Papers* 175. Madrid, Centro de Estudios Avanzados en Ciencias Sociales–Instituto Juan March.

Royall, Frédéric. 1998. Le mouvement des chômeurs en France de l'hiver 1997–1998. *Modern & Contemporary France* 6 (3): 351–65.

———. 2009. Regards croisés: la presse frontiste face aux mouvements des "sans" dans les années 90. *French Politics, Culture & Society* 27 (1): 43–68.

Salmon, Jean-Marc. 1998. *Le désir de société. Des Restaurants du coeur au mouvement des chômeurs*. Paris: La Découverte.

Snow, David A., E. Burke Rochford, Jr., Steven K. Worden, and Robert D. Benford. 1986. Frame alignment processes, micromobilization, and movement participation. *American Sociological Review* 51: 464–81.

Snow, David A., and Robert D. Benford. 1988. Ideology, Frame Resonance, and Participant Mobilization. *International Social Movement Research* 1: 197–217.

———. 2000. Framing Processes and Social Movements: An Overview and Assessment. *Annual Review of Sociology* 26: 611–39.

Tartakowsky, Danielle. 1997. *Les manifestations de rue en France, 1918–68*. Paris: Publications de la Sorbonne.

Taylor, Verta. 1989. Social Movement Continuity: The Women's Movement in Abeyance. *American Sociological Review* 54(5): 761–75.

van den Oord, Ad. 1990. *Voor arbeid en brood, arbeidersbeweging en collectieve actie van werklozen in Nederland, een vergelijkende studie van de jaren dertig en tachtig*. Amsterdam: Thesis Publishers.

Willemez, Laurent. 2006. *Le droit du travail en danger. Une ressource collective pour les combats individuels*. Broissieux: éditions du Croquant.

Willmann, Christophe. 1998. *L'identité juridique du chômeur*. Paris: LGDJ.

CHAPTER 2

The Mobilization of the Unemployed in Germany (1998–2004)

Britta Baumgarten and Christian Lahusen

Arbeitslos, nicht wehrlos! (Jobless, not toothless!)
—Slogan proclaimed at demonstrations in
Germany in August 2004

From July 2004 onward a growing number of unemployed people, their supporters, and their sympathizers started to demonstrate every Monday against the reform plans of the German government, led by Gerhard Schröder and his coalition of Social Democrats (*Sozialdemokratische Partei Deutschlands*, SPD) and the Greens. These "Monday demonstrations" opposed vehemently the so-called Hartz reforms, because they would bring considerable aggravations for recipients of social benefits. What started as a small rally in Madgeburg with a couple of hundred people soon spread to other East German cities and developed into very popular, decentralized mass protests of several ten thousands of demonstrators. The discontent of the jobless was clearly pronounced by Andreas Ehrholdt, a long-term unemployed mainly responsible for kicking off these "Monday demonstrations" in Madgeburg and a well-known speaker at many of these occasions:

> Dear comrades. You will doubtlessly know that we live in a democracy. That means that we, who sweep through the streets today, we are the people. It also means, however, that Mr. Schröder and the likes of him are nothing but our employees. What would you think about signing them off? (Magdeburg, August 9, 2004; see Keßler 2005)

This quote clearly illustrates the outrage and self-affirmation of the unemployed, who felt increasingly marginalized and discredited unrightfully as a group. While these protests were mainly restricted to East German cities and began to dwindle from October 2004 onward, this protest wave was indicative of a virulent discontent among the unemployed and their readiness to rally for their causes publicly and collectively. Moreover, these activities were borne by a broad network of organizations, self-help groups, and individuals, which had been responsible for protest activities earlier. Here, we can refer most prominently to a protest campaign preceding national elections in 1998, and to two mass demonstrations against the reforms initiatives of the then re-elected Schröder administration during autumn and winter of 2003/2004. These events are of particular interest for social movement analysis, because they illustrate what other case studies within this volume unveil for other countries as well: the fact that protest by the marginalized can happen when certain beneficial conditions are in place (see also van Berkel, Coenen, and Vlek 1998; Roth 2000; Steinert and Pilgram 2003; Perry 2007; Reiss and Perry 2011).

In the present chapter we will present evidence for this proposition (see also Baumgarten 2010; Lahusen and Baumgarten 2010). On the one hand, we will portray the mobilization wave briefly sketched so far,[1] by referring to the two main protest episodes it was composed of: the nationally coordinated activities during the electoral campaign of 1998, and the collective protests against the so-called Hartz reforms that began in the year 2002 and culminated between autumn 2003 and autumn 2004. This bipolar mobilization wave had undoubtedly antecedents in a number of previous (local) activities, which need to be kept in mind. However, the seven years to be analyzed here distinguish themselves from the previous situation in that protests were much more structured, had a much clearer national outreach, and exhibited a more outspoken political program and collective self-awareness. In all these respects we cannot speak of a social movement, but certainly of a structured collective protest phenomenon with a basic organizational infrastructure, communicative architecture, and symbolic identity.

On the other hand, the chapter will dig into the conditions and circumstances that were responsible for this mobilization wave. In other words, we strive to explain the two protest episodes mentioned earlier, and we will do so by referring to well-developed theoretical arguments within social movement literature. More specifically, we will try to understand why nationwide protest arose only after 1997, although mass unemployment and marginalization had been a reality for more than one decade, although labor market and social policy reforms had tightened the pressure on the unemployed since the mid-1980s by instituting a number of consecutive cut backs in social security rights and provisions, and although organizations, initiatives, and self-help groups working for and with the jobless were in place and quite active since the early 1980s. What these latter observations demonstrate is that grievances and organizational infrastructures are a quite important and necessary condition for collective protests. However, in this chapter we will argue that political opportunity structures provide supplementary and decisive conditions, which explain why a latent discontent by the jobless and their organizations in specific localities grows to an overt and nationwide collective protest phenomenon. In fact, rising unemployment rates and shrinking economic development were responsible for fierce debates within the public sphere in general, and for considerable dissent within the political elites. Particularly the strong disagreements and conflicts between Social Democrats and unions opened a window of political opportunities, which were strongly beneficial for the protests of the jobless. At the same time, we can observe a gradual erosion of German neocorporatism in general, of German unionism in particular, which intensified precisely when Social Democrats came into power in 1998. While the early protests by the jobless were strongly supported by leftist unionists in their attempt to reassert the political leadership of the unions and to defend the consuetudinary coalition between unions and the then elected Social Democratic government, we will argue that the protests from 2002 onward were strongly conditioned by the crisis of German neocorporatism and unionism, particularly in East Germany. The fact that protests disappeared almost completely from national politics and news since the fall of 2004 illustrates that the collective action of the jobless still depended on conditions, which the unemployed could effectively capitalize on temporarily, but not influence or alter structurally.

In the following pages, we intend to develop the aforementioned arguments in four steps. First, we will provide insights into the German protests by the jobless, starting briefly with antecedents and moving then to a description of the protest phenomenon to be explained and discussed. Second, we will refer to the development of unemployment on the one hand and give an overview about the organizations and networks working on behalf of the jobless on the other hand, in order to discuss the effect of grievances, resources, and organizations on the emergence of collective protests by the unemployed. Third, following the aforementioned observations we will deal with the political opportunity structures, in order to portray how far the related developments from 1997 onward were conducive for the mobilization episodes described earlier. More specifically, we will analyze how these changing opportunity structures translated into specific protest coalitions and campaigns. Finally, we will summarize our findings and draw theoretical and empirical conclusions.

Protest "by" the German Unemployed

Protests by the jobless were present throughout the history of Germany after World War II. However, until the 1970s these activities were restricted primarily to the local level and were a strongly minoritarian phenomenon. As a reaction to economic take-off during the 1950s and 1960s (the so-called *deutsches Wirtschaftswunder* or German economic miracle), unemployment rates were negligible and joblessness restricted to specific fractions of the German economy and population. During these times, rebellions were directed primarily against low wages, and many, especially among young people, preferred to moonlight while being officially unemployed. According to them, it was better to be unemployed than to support an economic system that exploits and alienates the working population (Rein and Scherer 1993; Reister 2000). This argument, which was quite prominent until the 1970s, remained an important source of inspiration during the 1980s and 1990s also, as we will see later on.

The oil crisis of 1973 terminated the German *Wirtschaftswunder* and preluded a period of accelerated inflation, economic recession, and higher unemployment rates. More and more organizations and groups working on behalf of the jobless were set up during the late 1970s and in the course of the 1980s, and protests by the unemployed intensified, albeit with a strong local scope of action. Political activities were often spectacular with some successes at the local level (Kantelhardt 1999). With an increasing number of people affected by unemployment, the claims and orientations of collective protests changed. Criticism of the capitalist labor society remained in place, as well as discussions about alternative models of work, income, and their interrelations (Sommer 1988). However, since the late 1970s more attention was paid to the specific socioeconomic situation of the unemployed (FALZ 1994). Protests for social rights and benefits and against defamation, for the creation of jobs and against job cuts became more prominent during these years and have remained on the agenda of the unemployed until the present day. Many local organizations tried to convince counties and cities about the necessity of creating jobs and financing these programs accordingly (Gallas 1994, 539). However, during the 1980s budgetary austerity was proclaimed by the respective governments as a necessary reaction to stagnating economic development and increasing unemployment rates. This put the unemployed and their organizations in a defensive position. In fact, the latter concentrated their activities ever more strongly against the closing down of institutions and programs on behalf of the unemployed (ALSO 2004). Since the Christian Democrats (the *Christlich-Demokratische Union Deutschlands*, CDU) started to cut rights and benefits for the unemployed, calls on the government to revoke these aggravations intensified and were voiced even at the national level (Kantelhardt and Wolski-Prenger 1998; KOS 1998). In 1988 and 1989, first sporadic activities were organized at the national level by a loose network of unemployed organizations. These protests were directed against national policy reforms that were to cut the rights and benefits of the unemployed, but they proved unsuccessful concerning their organizational and political outcomes. Over the following years, the progress made during the late 1970s and 1980s in regard to the organization and mobilization of the unemployed was undone, given declining material and financial state support, scanty success of previous protests, and little media attention (Kantelhardt 1999).

During the early 1990s, organizations and groups of the unemployed faced a time of crisis. As a reaction, many followed an incipient process of professionalization and concentrated exclusively on social work for the jobless, while many unemployed, who had been active prior to this, became passive and used the organizations for the unemployed merely for gaining information and advice (FALZ 1994). After these quiet years, political activities became more prominent during the mid-1990s, but were still restricted to isolated events that opposed specific policy reforms of the governing coalition of Christian Democrats and Liberals (the *Freiheitlich-Demokratische Partei*, FDP). Here, we can name the 3,500 unemployed who demonstrated in front of national ministries in Bonn in 1995, and the approximately 5,000 people who demonstrated in front of the national Labor Office in Nuremberg in 1997.

When we try to summarize and characterize the years preceding the mobilization wave to be analyzed in the following pages, we can point, on the one hand, to the fact that the organization and mobilization of the jobless remained primarily a local enterprise. This comes as no surprise, because organizations and groups working for and with the unemployed aimed above all to ameliorate the specific living conditions of the jobless and represent their interests at those local authorities or bureaus responsible for social benefits, placement services, and municipal services. Protests by the unemployed were thus geared primarily at demanding a better performance of the local "welfare state," and at preventing a degradation of social rights and benefits. However, this local focus of activity went hand in hand with an incipient, nationwide network of organizations and groups, to which we will refer later on in more detail, and which laid the ground for the national protest activities of the late 1990s. On the other hand, it is true that local organizations and groups addressed predominantly the immediate situation of the unemployed, and were forced into a more defensive strategy during the late 1980s in their attempt to safeguard the financial and organizational status quo in view of social and labor market policy reforms by the conservative government coalition under Helmut Kohl. However, unemployed organizations and initiatives conducted also more general, albeit minoritarian, debates with some tradition within the history of the protests by the unemployed. In fact, accelerating mass unemployment rates underscored a debate about the universal right to work among the incipient nationwide network of organizations. This demand was not aimed at providing everybody with any kind of work, but claimed rather that everyone is entitled to have a decent and meaningful job. Taking up the earlier criticism of capitalism, this discourse pointed at the alienating and exploitative nature of modern labor markets, and the need to safeguard the unemployed from exposing themselves to this empire of bondage by introducing a universal and minimal income for all citizens (e.g., so-called *Existenzgeld*). These demands, which became quite prominent during the 1980s and early 1990s (Rein and Scherer 1993), embraced not only a socialist criticism of capitalist labor society, but also anarchic and situationist discourses, which have been popular among the student movement and leftist and anarchic groups since the 1970s (e.g., the *Sponti* movement). They aroused general public awareness, not least because of a small group of unemployed in Berlin, which called themselves the "Happy Unemployed," and whose pamphlet from 1996 was circulated among many unemployment groups throughout Germany and was debated also within leading German newspapers. These happy jobless engaged in well-perceived public communications (e.g., their magazine *Müßiggangster*) and conducted a number of (ironic, dadaist) actions that strived to ridicule wage labor society and oppose the enforcement of back-to-work schemes and the victorious neoliberal work ethic.

Based on these organizational and discursive developments, the mobilization of the unemployed acquired a new quality in the late 1990s and led to the two protest episodes, which will be at the center of attention of our analysis. In first instance, there was an exceptional wave of mobilization in 1998, which was coordinated for the first time at the national level. From February to September, monthly and decentralized demonstrations took place simultaneously across more than 250 cities, with more than 40,000 people participating at most of these actions (KOS 1998). Participants mainly belonged to the group of the long-term unemployed, and more than half of the demonstrators came from Eastern Germany (Reister 2000, 12). Protests were directed against the policies of the conservative government and were stamped by the forthcoming national elections in Germany, which eventually led to a new government of Social Democrats and the Greens. Moreover, activities were motivated also by the strong protests of the unemployed in France, and by the first Euromarches against Unemployment, Job Insecurity, and Social Exclusions converging in 1997 in Amsterdam. After the national elections in September 1998, however, all of the mobilizations ended abruptly. The protest campaign was followed by a phase of low activity, restricted mainly to protests at the local level and to the participation of German groups in the Euromarches between 1998 and 2002.

After these five silent years, protest activities increased in 2003 in response to major reforms of the welfare state envisioned by the Schröder administration, here, the so-called Hartz reforms. A large demonstration with about 100,000 participants on November 1, 2003, was organized by a network of antireform alliances called *Anti-Hartz-Bündnisse*, within which the organizations of the unemployed played a significant role. In April 2004, the unemployed rallied again in opposition to government plans, but now as part of a mass demonstration organized and led by the German unions. This rally was the biggest event ever set up by a union against a Social-Democratic government, as more than half a million people gathered simultaneously in Berlin, Stuttgart, and Köln. However, due to tactical considerations and to internal conflicts among the participating groups, these mass protests were discontinued (Roth 2005). From now on, local and decentralized activities came to the fore, here, in particular the so-called Monday demonstrations against the "Hartz IV" reforms. The very first rally was initiated by Andreas Ehrholdt, a long-term unemployed in Madgeburg by means of self-made flyers (Baumgarten 2004; Roth 2005). The idea of consecutive rallies was quite successful, and "Monday demonstrations" with many thousands of participants were held in many East German cities from late July 2004 onward. Demonstrations were supported by a wide alliance, including unemployed organizations, local union branches, ATTAC, welfare organizations, local parishes, small left-wing parties (primarily the German Marxist-Leninist Party, the MLPD), and others. These protests lent a voice to the unemployed, who envisioned considerable aggravations due to the reform of the German welfare system (i.e., social assistance and labor agencies) to be adopted on January 1, 2005. However, the rallies fueled a much larger discontent among East Germans about the meager social and political achievements made since German reunification in 1990, and the deteriorating situation of those without a job. The weekly demonstrations and the chanted slogans (e.g., "we are the people") were explicit reminiscences of the historic "Monday demonstrations" of the East German civil rights movement, which had played an important role in overthrowing the socialist regime of the German

Democratic Republic in 1989 and eventually opened the door to German reunification. Media attention for these protests was strong throughout the summer of 2004, also because of regional elections (Brandenburg, Saarland, Saxonia in September 2004 and North Rhine-Westphalia in May 2005), which were generally defined as important test elections for the governing coalition of Social Democrats and Greens in Berlin, given the fact that they were suffering from dwindling public support in previous elections and public opinion polls. Organizers and supporters of the "Monday demonstrations" strived to step up the pressure on the national government by joining forces and organizing national rallies for the first weekend in October. Due to internal conflicts about the ambitions of the Marxist-Leninist party to gain control of the events, two separate demonstrations were conducted, one in Berlin with 70,000 participants, and a smaller one in Leipzig with a couple of thousands people.

From October 2004 onward, however, "Monday demonstrations" suffered from low attendance and public awareness. In this way a mobilization wave came to an end, which kept politicians and mass media in suspense during an entire summer, but exposed symptoms of fatigue due to the repetitiveness of the action form, the internal conflicts among the participating organizations and individuals, the absence of measurable successes, and the dwindling interest of the mass media. Commentators expected that protest would return to dominate daily news by January 1, 2005, as a reaction to the implementation of the Hartz IV reform, because the unemployed would be in need of reapplying for social assistance, vocational training, or placement services under a much more constrictive scheme. However, collective action by the unemployed was and remained negligible. It faded away into a broad discontent, which eventually was responsible for the consecutive defeats of the coalition of Social Democrats and Greens in regional elections and the early national elections in September of 2005, which replaced the leftist government by a Great Coalition between Christian and Social Democrats under the leadership of Angela Merkel.

Collective Grievances and Protest Behavior

When we try to understand the emergence and development of this mobilization wave with its two-phased protest episodes, we need certainly to address collective grievances first. Indeed, in Germany, unemployment became a problem in the mid-1970s. Unemployment rates started to increase significantly after 1974, mounted to 9 percent for the first time in 1983, and were always higher than 10 percent since 1994, to surpass the threshold of five million jobless in January 2005. The unemployment rates in Eastern Germany are approximately twice as high as the Western ones (*Bundesagentur für Arbeit* 2004). Therefore, it comes as no surprise that unemployment attained high priority on public and government agendas, particularly since the 1990s. The conservative coalition of Christian Democrats and Liberals, in power since 1982, put an emphasis on economic development as a means to structurally solve mass unemployment, and pushed toward the reduction of nonwage labor costs and bureaucratic burdens on firms and investments. The Schröder government, which replaced Helmut Kohl's administration in 1998, promised to improve the performance of previous policies, but pledged to safeguard the high standard of social security and justice of the German welfare state at the same time. Leading Social Democrats rallied for a modernization of the system, borrowing concepts and ideas from Tony Blair's Third Way, which was to be specified and implemented along a concerted effort between the state and the social partners (i.e., the employers' associations and the unions). However, after being confirmed in power in 2002, the Schröder administration soon abandoned the badly working method of moderation and social partnership (e.g., the so-called *Bündnis für Arbeit*, Alliance for Work). At the same time, he proclaimed a unilateral reform strategy called Agenda 2010 in 2003, which stressed deregulation, privatization, and flexibilization measures and placed high emphasis on activation policies. More specific recommendations were developed by a consultative committee under the direction of Peter Hartz, former staff manager of Volkswagen. The propositions were edited and adopted by the government as the reform package Hartz I–IV from 2003 onward. Particularly the last element of these reforms, voted in on July 9, 2004, was the most ambitious, as it intended to increase the efficiency and effectiveness of the established system of social assistance and employment service. This improvement was to be achieved by integrating what had been previously distinct administrative branches of social security and social assistance,[2] and by introducing a "carrot and stick" model of activation (a policy of so-called *Fördern und Fordern*) that would establish positive and negative incentives for the jobless to accept—any kind of—labor.[3]

These developments indicate that grievances aggravated considerably from the early 1990s onward. Indeed, unemployment became a reality for a growing number of people, who additionally had to face consecutive cuts in regard to social rights and benefits. Moreover, governments became ever more adverse in regard to the jobless even publicly, and this was true also for the newly elected government, which learned quickly to blame the victim for raising unemployment figures and for meager reform successes—for instance, when Gerhard Schröder proclaimed in an interview with a leading German tabloid that "there is no right to be lazy in our society" (Bild-Zeitung, April 5, 2001). In sum, the unemployed had accumulated enough reasons to protest against social exclusion and stigmatization. However, these grievances do not explain the mobilization wave, because mass unemployment and disadvantageous policy reforms had affected a considerable number of people before, when referring, for instance, to consecutive cutbacks in social provisions and entitlements implemented in reaction to austerity measures since the 1970s (e.g., the *Haushaltsstrukturgesetz* of 1975, the *Haushaltsbegleitgesetze* of 1983 and 1984; see Rein and Scherer 1993; FALZ 1994; Schmid 1998). At the same time, it is noteworthy that the implementation of Hartz IV in January 2005 did not result in nationwide protest action by the jobless, although implying considerable hardships for most of them.

Scholarly writing has provided enough evidence for the fact that grievances do not translate automatically into protest action (Zald and McCarthy 1987). In fact, unemployment needs to be perceived and addressed as a problem that awaits collective action, instead of individual coping or problem-solving strategies (Steinert and Pilgram 2003). Hence, we might expect that the propensity to engage in collective protest is highest among long-term jobless, because they have made the experience that unemployment and exclusion cannot be solved individually. Collective action by long-term unemployed, however, is improbable as well, because it is well documented that long-term marginalization reduces those (material, social, or motivational) resources necessary to engage into collective protest. In particular, long-term unemployment underscores the erosion of social capital, and thus leads to fatalism and apathy (Jahoda, Lazarsfeld, and Zeisel 1933).

We must expect therefore that passivity is the rule, even in spite of apparent objective grievances, to which the jobless are exposed. We might even argue in accordance with collective action theory (Olson 1971; Opp 2009, 45–90) that passivity is a perfectly rational choice. On the one hand, it is more probable that the jobless opt for individual coping strategies as opposed to collective action, in view of meager resources and little chances to successfully protest and influence government agendas. On the other hand, we might assume that each individual unemployed will tend to free-ride, given the fact that she/he would benefit from protest achievements without bearing the costs of collective action. These arguments support the assumption that grievances have no direct effect on protest behavior. Instead, participation (or nonparticipation) of the jobless is determined by further, intervening factors that are strongly related to resources and organizations (Zald and McCarthy 1987; Jenkins 1999).

In this regard, scholarly writing points to two possible ways out of "rational passivity" (von Winter 1997). On the one side, Oliver, Marwell, and Teixeira (1985) have argued that collective protest becomes more probable when a group of activists is available, which is ready to make more risky and demanding contributions and pushes collective action beyond the threshold of a critical mass. This situation makes consecutive protests more probable, because these groups and their activities allow influencing preference structures and cost/benefit calculations of constituencies and by-standers, thus setting a self-reinforcing process of political protest in motion. On the other hand, the establishment of organizations is considered as a solution to the problem of free-riding (Olson 1971; Zald and McCarthy 1987). In fact, organizations are a means of securing and accumulating mobilization resources (e.g., finances, contacts, skills, and knowledge). They are thus in the position of providing selective incentives, which are necessary, for instance, to overcome individual free-riding, or, to say it in a less economist phrasing, to implicate the jobless into a process of self-empowerment and collective learning. Hence, we need to look at the organizational infrastructure fabricated since the late 1970s by a number of activists, in order to understand better the emergence of those mobilization episodes portrayed before.

Organizations and Networks of the Unemployed

An organizational infrastructure is important for the emergence and consolidation of collective action processes (Neidhardt 1985). This is particularly true for the jobless, because of the obstacles toward political protest described earlier. Regarding this infrastructure, we can observe two main developments. On the one hand, the organizational infrastructure has become denser in regard to the number of (local) groups and initiatives, and the amount of interorganizational relations and networks. From the late 1980s onward, we are speaking about a nationwide, but highly decentralized, field of organizations loosely integrated into national structures of cooperation, coordination, and communication. On the other hand, there is a trend among the organizations of the unemployed to become more professional over time, meaning that (paid and employed) staff becomes the backbone of these organizations and that routine work becomes more systematized, rationalized, and methodical. Professionalization has evolved more strongly along the lines of social work (e.g., consultation, information, assistance) during the late 1980s and the early 1990s, and of a more markedly political activism (e.g., community organizing, advocacy, and public campaigning) from then until the early 2000s.

Both processes, organization and professionalization, have been conducive for the micromobilization of the unemployed, given the impeding circumstances of social exclusion they live in. In fact, it has been argued in the literature that the decision by an unemployed person to participate in political activities is rarely determined by one's belief that one's contribution makes a (political) difference. According to Gallas (1994), it is often a staff member of an initiative or project that asks the unemployed to participate in protest action—a staff with whom the jobless often have close contact, and who they do not want to disappoint. Ongoing participation in protest activities increases their self-confidence and motivates them to join in future activities. And this process of empowerment is beneficial for the emergence of political protest, insofar as it allows to construct constituencies and thus to secure mobilization-potentials for future protest activities.

Overall, however, the degree of affiliation has always been low. According to Rein (Rein and Scherer 1993, 1), only about 0.5–3 percent of all officially registered unemployed are organized in unemployment projects.[4] Reasons for this low level of activity are to be seen in the isolation and marginality associated with unemployment, in the heterogeneity of the jobless in terms of social and occupational backgrounds, and in the lack of a community spirit and solidarity (Wacker 1987; Rolke 1988; Zoll, Bauer, and Springhorn-Schmidt 1991) due to the feeling of competition among themselves regarding the labor market (Paulus 1985). Moreover, an affiliation of the jobless to organizations and protest activities depends on their readiness to certify their unemployment publicly, which does not apply to the majority of the jobless, because these prefer to see themselves in a state of transit (Wacker 1987, 79) and trust therefore in individual coping strategies (Wolski-Prenger 1996).

Consequently, we are speaking only about a minority of jobless who join organizations and participate in their activities; and the number of those actively engaged in political action is even smaller. In fact, empirical reports and studies demonstrated that only a small fraction of those involved in unemployment initiatives were active in campaigning and protest activities—often we are speaking just about two or three activists (Wacker 1987; Gallas 1994 and 1996). Most of them have been unemployed for at least several months, are between thirty and fifty years old, and have a greater chance of reentering the labor market than those involved in the projects who do not engage politically, due to better skills, training, and occupational experiences. These observations suggest that the constituency of unemployed organizations and networks has become more heterogeneous in terms of its social structure, due to the fact that mass unemployment has been expanding into the middle classes and has made joblessness a more normal biographical episode. Hence, more people with higher levels of education and social capital (for instance, in regard to membership in voluntary organizations, civic commitments, trust, and self-confidence) were joining the ranks of the long-term unemployed since the 1980s.[5] This development is conducive for the organization and mobilization of the unemployed, because it augments the number of constituents who bring along valued resources, have been active in other causes before, and have a stronger readiness for political activities (Zorn 2003). In fact, studies have illustrated that politically active jobless have higher formal education and were organized in either unions or alternative leftist groups before they became unemployed; often they still are members of a union (FALZ 1994; Gallas 1994).

We can thus agree with Bagguley (1992) that the assumed improbability of collective action by the unemployed depends on the arguable presupposition that both individual preferences/choices and organizational constituencies are static or immutable. While it is true that the vast majority of the jobless seems prone to inactivity or apathy, we have strong indications for the emergence of a smaller community of committed, experienced, and resourced activists or supporters, which reached the necessary critical mass (Oliver, Marwell, and Teixeira 1985) to set a political process of collective action in motion (McAdam 1982). One of the primary achievements of this avant-garde was the gradual organization of the unemployed, which can be seen as a precondition of collective action, in so far as organizations allow to alter individual preferences and choices (microlevel) and engage thus into recruiting and stabilizing constituencies (mesolevel) by means of selective incentives and common learning processes. This assumption mirrors correctly the empirical development in Germany throughout the last three decades, because activists have been committed to building up an organizational infrastructure, primarily by setting up new initiatives and groups, (re-)committing existing organizations to a more political cause, engaging into interpersonal and interorganizational networking, and demanding a more overt public support for them (e.g., in terms of finances, media attention, and public endorsement).

In fact, following the available estimates, we can ascertain a steady growth of the organizational web.[6] Unemployed groups increased from around 1,000 projects during the 1980s (Rein and Scherer 1993; FALZ 1994) to 1,200 in 1989 (Wolski-Prenger 1996, 30) to about 1,500 in 1992 (Kantelhardt 1999, 19).

This means that an unemployed project existed in every mid-sized town, often with more than one group in larger cities. Thus, the unemployed could easily have access to at least one of these organizations, unless they lived in rural areas. The steady growth of the organizational field went hand in hand with its gradual differentiation in terms of organizational formats, mandates, and objectives. Until the early 1970s, we can speak only about a small number of unemployed groups, which met privately, were committed to an alternative way of life beyond the mainstream, and dissociated themselves from capitalist labor society as indicated earlier (Paulus 1985). Some of them were associated to Marxist/Leninist groups (FALZ 1994) and were geared toward an integrated alternative lifestyle. Hence, we should not speak about "groups or organizations of the unemployed" in a strict sense for that time period. Indeed, the first groups dedicated solely to the unemployed came about in 1974 as a reaction to rising unemployment figures. They organized and financed themselves autonomously, yet, belonged to urban leftist milieus. Counting their work as strictly political, they kept a critical distance from all established parties and associations including the unions, but cooperated with other small local initiatives such as the so-called Jobber[7] or refugee and women groups (Massow 1983; Sommer 1988; FALZ 1994).

In the 1980s and early 1990s, a lot of projects and groups were founded by churches and the unions in their attempt to assist the spreading number of jobless. Projects funded by the church were more geared toward caring for the unemployed by providing information, educational programs, and formation (FALZ 1994; Wolski-Prenger 1996), and by creating jobs for those unemployed with very low chances of reentering the labor market (Massow 1983; Rothardt and Wöhrmann 1996). Even today, many of these organizations not only provide information and help, but also offer a place of social contact. They aim to propel joint activity with and among the unemployed, but primarily with the intention of overcoming isolation rather than becoming a means of political interest representation (Reister 2000). Unionized groups and projects share this interest for individual assistance and consultation. Like some church organizations, they strive to politically represent the interests of the jobless toward local state authorities and agencies (Rein and Scherer 1993). Next to these majoritarian groups, we can point to a number of independent organizations with a much more pronounced political orientation. These were established explicitly in demarcation to church and union groups, which they criticized as being paternalistic.

This steady growth and differentiation of the organizational field is shaped by two developments. On the one hand, we have to refer to the increasing weight of state support and the consecutive institutionalization and professionalization of many groups and initiatives. In fact, while we have seen that at the beginning many unemployed groups exhibited higher degrees of organizational and financial autonomy, the situation changed considerably due to increasing unemployment figures, generalizing eligibility of state programs by the unemployed, and higher accessibility to public funding by organizations working for and with the jobless. These circumstances have been beneficial for the spread of organizations and projects, because they could count on financial resources, administrative support, and public attention. As a consequence, most unemployed organizations were highly dependent on financial support by the state or by the European Union.[8] This influences the organizational work and functioning of these groups, as state finances are restricted to specific mandates (e.g., information, training, and placement) and require more formal and "professional" organizational routines and structures (e.g., filling of applications, controlling, and statements of accounts).

On the other hand, German reunification has had considerable effects on the organizational differentiation described earlier. Since the "fall of the wall," the work with and for the jobless had to be organized from scratch in the new *Länder*, given the fact that unemployment was officially nonexistent in former socialist GDR (Rink 2000). Investment into organizational structure was much greater here and helps to explain the stronger (financial) dependencies of the Eastern organizations on the state, church, or unions. The establishment of a peak association for the unemployed (*Arbeitslosenverband*, ALV) institutes a further difference to the organizational structure in the West (Grehn 1996). While those organizations in the West preferred to organize (politically) from the grassroots, the main idea behind the ALV was to have an umbrella organization that would speak with one voice on behalf of the many small initiatives and projects and would work more efficiently in furthering the interests of the jobless.

The growth and differentiation of the organizational field has increased internal conflicts and cleavages, for instance, because the gradual institutionalization and professionalization has been severely criticized by many members and groups (Wolski-Prenger 1989; Rein and Scherer 1993; Gallas 1994, 550). However, it has not prevented activists from engaging in building national networks and related structures of cooperation. On the contrary, groups and organizations of the unemployed have attempted to cooperate at the regional and national level since the first meetings of unemployed groups in 1977 (FALZ 1994). A number of alliances between these initiatives developed at local and regional levels in the mid-1980s, up to the point that only a few projects had no contacts with other organizations (Gallas 1994, 565). National congresses have been organized in order to sample commonalities since 1982, and working groups were set up in order to exchange information, to find common positions, and to mobilize jointly (Rein and Scherer 1993). However, these working groups represented different constituencies. In Western Germany, for instance, the *Bundesarbeitsgruppen der Initiativen gegen Arbeitslosigkeit und Armut* (BAG, the federal working groups of initiatives against unemployment and poverty) was founded in 1982 to represent independent organizations of the unemployed. It was followed in 1999 by *BAG Erwerbslose* (the federal working groups of initiatives of the incomeless). A further organization, the *BAG Sozialhilfeinitiativen* (BAG-SHI), was established in 1991 in order to deal with issues specifically relating to social assistance. Furthermore, the *Koordinierungsstelle gewerkschaftlicher Arbeitslosengruppen* (KOS) was founded in 1986 to represent the unemployed organizations affiliated to the unions. Finally, in East Germany the ALV named earlier was founded in 1990 (Grehn 1996). Attempts were made to integrate these various networks, however, not until the late 1990s. For instance, a round table of unemployed and social assistance recipients (*Runde Tisch der Erwerbslosen- und Sozialhilfeinitiativen*) was set up in 2000, and in 2004 the two BAGs (*BAG Erwerbslose* and *BAG Sozialhilfeinitiativen*) merged.

The 1990s were thus a decade of accelerated organizational cooperation and integration at the national level. These attempts cannot be dissociated from policy changes since the mid-1990s. In fact, German governments started to change policy priorities in the mid-1990s when arguing that their emphasis is on financing jobs rather than unemployment provisions. They placed higher priority on measures directed at stimulating the labor market, primarily by means of widening the sector of low-paid jobs (Eick, Grell, and Mayer 2004). At the same time they limited programs and funds directed at passive measures (e.g., social security, assistance and support for the jobless). Opposition against this policy agenda grew among the many groups and projects of the unemployed during the 1990s, not only because of political dissent, but also because reforms challenged these groups in their basic organizational objectives and needs. In fact, we have to recall that most of these local organizations and projects—even those established and professionalized groups funded by the state, church, and unions—were under-resourced and lacked any long-term planning reliability. Their personnel comprised very often former jobless paid part-time or employed precariously themselves. Moreover, the Hartz IV reforms intensified cooperation between initiatives of the jobless and social assistance recipients, because this reform was to integrate both branches of social security and demanded a better coordination of demands and protest activities by those affected. We can assume therefore that the general direction of policy reforms has contributed to a widening congruence of interests between the more service-oriented organizations and those groups and activists committed to political mobilization and advocacy. Organizational "self-interests" were thus responsible for engaging into more cooperation and building up more tight organizational structures on the national level.[9]

In spite of all the organizational attempts mentioned so far, the national working groups and interorganizational networks had and still have loose and decentralized organizational structures, their primary aim being to exchange information and coordinate the activities of the various groups. Hence, the organizational infrastructure remains fragmented. One of the reasons is a lack of consensus about strategies and objectives, itself conditioned by different political backgrounds and alliances of the activists involved. Kantelhardt and Wolski-Prenger (1998) see a basic difference between those groups claiming for a right to work (*Recht auf Arbeit*) and those claiming for a right to income (*Recht auf Einkommen*), which result in different views on how unemployment and the aims of the unemployed are defined (532). This issue confronts Eastern and Western groups, given the fact that the right to work is a far more popular demands in East Germany, due to higher levels of structural (long-term) unemployment in these regions (Gallas 1994) and its socialist history and its lasting effects on political attitudes. In fact, historically, the right to work was part of the East German Constitution, because unemployment was considered to be a threat to human dignity. Even today, much more East Germans than West Germans are convinced that the state is responsible for the direct social well-being of its citizens (Roller 1999), and this applies particularly also to its responsibility in providing jobs to the people.

Another reason is to be found in traditions of political activism in both German societies. The associations in Western Germany discarded the idea of establishing formal organizational structures (e.g., in terms of a hierarchical peak association) in 1983 and have not changed their mind ever since (FALZ 1994). To better understand this rejection, we need to recall the traditionally strong impetus on grassroots democracy by West German movements since the 1960s (e.g., citizens' groups, antinuclear movements, and environmentalism; see Roth 1985), which resonate in the field of unemployment as well. East German groups did not share this history, and thus strongly disagreed with the organizational strategy of Western groups. Instead, these groups favored a tight organizational structure, which did not convince the Western organizations (Gallas 1994; Wolski-Prenger 2000). As a consequence, the organizational landscape still disaggregates along an East-West divide, implying also that mutual knowledge about each another and attempts to cooperate remained on a low level (Reister 2000).

When we assess these observations conjointly, we see that the organizational infrastructure helps to understand the emergence of the two mobilization episodes to be analyzed here, but leaves a number of questions unanswered. On the one hand, it is true that organizations are an important prerequisite for the mobilization of the jobless, because social marginalization establishes strong impediments to political participation. Organizations allow to transcend them by offering selective incentives and collective learning processes. Moreover, protest action is more probable, the more organizations develop proper interests in collective mobilization. On the other hand, the organizational web of unemployment groups provides just an infrastructure (a latent one) of constituencies and mobilizing resources. The activation of this latent infrastructure has to confront supplementary hurdles, as, for instance, the ideological cleavages between the different groups, the highly fragmented and decentralized structure of the organizational field, and the clear East-West divide in regard to constituencies and political traditions of activism. But what contributed to transcend this state of latency with its intricate cleavage structures? And what helped to activate the protest episodes of 1998 and 2002–2004? We propose that the answer to these questions resides in external stimuli. In particular, we want to argue that collective protest on the national level required conducive political opportunities in general, and political entrepreneurship by "third parties" in particular (Lispky 1968 and 1970; Jenkins 1999).

Political Opportunity Structures and Protest Entrepreneurship

Political protest is clearly marked by the opportunity structure of the surrounding political system. Scholars have pointed to the fact that collective action is more probable in a political environment that provides easy access to the political institutions, is characterized by instable electoral constituencies and heterogeneous elites, and provides influential allies (Kitschelt 1986; McAdam 1996; Tarrow 1996; Meyer and Minkoff 2004; Giugni 2011). These elements work as pull and push factors: on the one hand, these elements create room for maneuver and instigate social movement actors to mobilize for their cause; on the other hand, influential political actors become interested and actively engaged into forming and mobilizing political opposition within and outside political institutions, thus contributing to the formation of collective protest action (Kriesi 2004; Meyer 2004).

These descriptions capture accurately the political situation from the late 1990s onward, when compared with the political opportunities before that time. So far, unemployed and their organizations had a hard time finding access to public debates and political deliberations on the national sphere. In fact, while organizations of the unemployed had a say on the local level, this does not apply to the national policy arena, where they have been virtually ignored. In spite of the rising unemployment figures, the jobless were not only socially excluded, but also politically marginalized. The incipient organization of the jobless, which we ascertained for the national level in the previous section, did not alter this situation substantially. In 2003 we conducted a series of interviews with national policy actors, asking them, among others, to indicate actors with whom they cooperate or which they consider as influential. Only six of twenty-five interviewees at the national level mentioned at least one of the national unemployed organizations (i.e., ALV, BAG-E, BAG-SHI and KOS) to be an influential actor in the field of unemployment, and no core political actors (e.g., ministries, majority's parties) shared this opinion. Only five actors admitted to aim at influencing these organizations, but those interviewees indicated that they tried to influence nearly every other actor, too. Half of our interviewed organizations (thirteen) collaborated with at least one of the unemployed organizations at the national level, yet, these collaborators belong almost exclusively to the unions, churches, and welfare organizations. Our interviews demonstrate therefore that the organizations of the unemployed were a weak actor that had some ties to intermediary associations but no real access to the core policy domain of ministries, parties, or regulatory agencies. This can be interpreted as a missing link to institutionalized arenas of cooperation and decision-making. The same conclusion applies to the public sphere. Our content analysis of a leading daily newspaper (*Die Süddeutsche Zeitung*) for the years between 1995 and 2002 demonstrates that organizations of the jobless had no voice in public debates about unemployment issue: only 1 percent of all those 3,837 statements extracted from the many newspaper articles were made by these groups, while the state claims a share of 42 percent, unions 19 percent, and employers' associations about 26 percent (and 12 percent were made by other actors).

This political exclusion mirrors the social marginalization of the jobless, which is associated with a pronounced stigmatization and discrimination (Zoll, Bauer, and Springhorn-Schmidt 1991; Wolski-Prenger 1996). Previous studies report an "aggressive mixture of envy and contempt" (Kieser 1988, 32) toward those without a job. According to a survey by the Allensbacher Institut for the years 1975–1981, about half of the working population believed that a lot of unemployed did not want to work.[10] In 1982, about 35 percent of the population assumed that the unemployed received too much monetary assistance, and 80 percent supported the idea of greater controls of who receives benefits. News coverage in the mass media was dominated by discussion about the unemployed being too lazy to work and by questions about how reliable the official unemployment figures were (Uske 1995). "Blaming the victim" (Uske 1995; Wolski-Prenger 2000, 158) became thus a favored strategy of politicians when debating about the problem of unemployment. This approach lead to four major debates on the "lazy unemployed" (in 1975, 1981, 1993, and 2001) that were incited by governments very often before important (national or regional) elections (Oschmiansky, Kull, and Schmid 2001) and did not arouse substantial public opposition. However, this hostility toward the unemployed has been qualified somewhat in the course of time. In fact, it is symptomatic that chancellor Schröder was severely criticized in autumn of 1999 when arguing in an interview of the Bild-Zeitung that the unemployed had no right to be lazy. This claim was debated controversially in public and has become a contentious catch-phrase since then. Something had changed indeed in regard to public opinions about the jobless. When we follow available survey data, we see that public opinion about the unemployed has altered somewhat since the late 1980s. Criticism of the jobless has decreased slightly as unemployment rates have risen after 1981 (Brenke and Peter 1985). During the protest activities in 1998 and after 2003, an increasing percentage of public opinion has even sympathized with the unemployed (Kantelhardt and Wolski-Prenger 1998; Baumgarten 2004).

This new clemency is the product of a gradual atmospheric change within public opinion in general, and within fractions of the political establishment in particular. This development was to be expected, given the fact that "blaming the victim" strategies became more controversial in a situation of increasing mass unemployment (Gallas 1996). Instead, unemployment became a highly debated issue that was perceived to have dramatic social and political consequences for German society. Public concern about unemployment reached a climax in 1996, when unemployment figures were approximating the threshold of four million people. Unemployment figures were reaching a level unprecedented in German history in that year, and this development was debated within the public with unease. On the one hand, commentators recalled that the breakdown of the Weimarer Republic and the rise of the Nazi Regime were caused by high unemployment rates and an accelerated social depression. Hence, social exclusion was conceived of as a threat to the stability of German society at large, and to the democratic polity in particular. On the other hand, it was agreed upon that higher structural mass unemployment threatens the architecture of the German welfare state by eroding its financial viability. Severe policy reforms were necessary to promote economic development and safeguard the system.

In this context, cleavages emerged within the political elites, which are of particular interest for our analysis of political opportunity structures. Dissent intensified between conservative and liberal parties on the one hand, and social democratic, socialist, and green parties on the other. These camps disagreed about the political answers to these challenges, arguing either for a deconstruction or a reconstruction of the German system of social security. Particularly the leftist parties and the unions rallied vehemently for a political change in view of coming national elections in September 1998, calling for an end to sixteen years of conservative politics under Helmut Kohl. A more consequential conflict, however, evolved within one of the traditional ideological camps. Gerhard Schröder had sworn his party into a programmatic modernization and into a reorientation of electoral constituencies toward the center of society and the ideological spectrum. This strategic turn, which was corroborated by a common paper with UK's prime minister Tony Blair in 1999, was criticized by many party members and the unions. Until the end of 1998, this dissent was proclaimed cautiously in order to not endanger the electoral victory of the SPD and the Greens. Moreover, the unions were interested in reasserting the Alliance for Work, set up under the conservative Kohl administration as a neocorporatist instrument to fight mass unemployment. Unions intended to further this alliance in order to attest their political weight under Schröder's rule.

During the following years, "traditionalist" groups within the SPD and the unions remained perceivable and recurrently voiced their unease with the "modernist" rhetoric of party leadership. Dissent intensified in the second legislative period from 2002 onward, after the failure of the Alliance for Work and the unilateral adoption of the Agenda 2010 program by the Schröder administration. These conflicts radicalized considerably, leading eventually to the establishment of a dissenting group of social democrats, unionists, and activists under the banner of *Wahlalternative Arbeit und Soziale Gerechtigkeit* (WASG, electoral alternative for work and social justice) in the spring of 2004, which was formally set up later on as a party to participate in regional and national elections of that year and to provide social movements (such as the protests by the unemployed) a parliamentary platform. It has cooperated with the socialist *Partei des Demokratischen Sozialismus* (PDS), winning 54 out of 614 seats in the national parliament in 2005. It then merged with the socialist PDS to become *the* leftist alternative to the SPD and the Greens, in short: *Die Linke* (the Left).

These political developments mounted to conductive opportunity structures, because the growing internal dissent within the political elites contributed to the emergence of influential allies, which generated a particular interest in representing the interests of the marginalized. Hence, while the unemployed and their organizations remained politically excluded from the national policy domain as an autonomous actor of political agency, they became a quite important object of political contentions within the political institutions. Particularly the unions became an important political entrepreneur and sponsor that facilitated and promoted national protests by the unemployed.[11]

Initially, the unions had considerable reservations to expand their mandate to represent the interests of the *Lumpenproletariat* (Nikolaus 2000). However, since the 1980s German unions have started to support the unemployed as a reaction to the rising share of union members affected by unemployment, and due to the initiatives by the unemployed to sensitize the unions for their cause (Kantelhardt 1999). In fact, organizations of the unemployed benefited from the unions and tried to convince them to work on behalf of the jobless, because the unions could offer financial and logistical support, political influence and contacts, campaigning power and a good access to the mass media (Baumgarten 2003). As a consequence, as our interview partners reported, most of the organizations of the jobless are either financed by the unions or cooperate closely with them. At the same time, unions have been opening themselves gradually to the organization of the unemployed, as almost a million union members are unemployed. As a reaction to this sensitivity, regional branches of the *Deutsche Gewerkschaftsbund* (DGB) are allowed to support unemployed groups since 1987, and some unions admit unemployed members into their steering committees (Kantelhardt 1996; Beier 1999; Wolski-Prenger 2000). On the flip side, however, unionists were often distrusted and have never been the main engine of an unemployment movement. Unions are criticized by the unemployed for representing their interests only insofar as they do not collide with their primary aim to protect the employed from deteriorating labor and wage conditions (Uske 1995; Nikolaus 2000). Moreover, activists felt that the unions aimed primarily at extending their control over the organizations and activities of the unemployed, sometimes instrumentalizing or impeding protest actions. This has repeatedly caused conflicts between both sides (Rein and Scherer 1993, 37).

We are thus speaking of a marriage of convenience, albeit between two very different partners. On the one hand, the organizations of the unemployed have always been playing the role of a "junior partner," given the fact that German unionism is dominated by mass organizations that represent broad industrial branches, are organized as highly centralized associations, and merge their working power within the DGB, the German peak union. In 2000, the DGB represented the interests of approximately 7.7 million members. As we will see, protest action by the unemployed thus tended to move within the slipstream of the German unions, for instance, as compared to France (Lahusen and Baumgarten 2006). On the other hand, protests by the jobless were strongly affected by the fact that the unions were unreliable allies, insofar as they were torn between loyalty and dissent toward the SPD. In fact, many unionists were and are born-and-bred social democrats, who remain faithful to the party but had at the same time strong reservations about the new political orientation of the party leadership. While supporting the unemployed, they were still hesitant to endanger the traditional alliance between SPD and the unions. This shaky support was responsible to a good extent for the unstable development of protests by the unemployed.

This observation applies particularly to the monthly protest actions during the spring and summer of 1998. Collective action goes back to a public appeal endorsed by the network of unionized groups of the jobless (the "KOS"), the peak union DGB, nine leading branch unions, and the working groups of the unemployed and social assistance recipients (*BAG Erwerbslose* and *BAG Sozialhilfeempfänger*). In the following months, it was the KOS that played a crucial role in instigating, coordinating, and enhancing national protests by merging the activities of the many local groups into a national protest campaign. This organization called local groups to participate in the monthly activities, provided ideas and concepts, documented the many activities, and communicated them to the mass media (KOS 1998). However, after the Social Democrats and Greens took office in September 1998, the unions no longer supported protests by the unemployed. What followed were years of inactivity and of disenchantment about government policies (Roth 1999) and the support of the unions.

With the advent of the Schröder administration's reform program, alliances were reconstructed from 2002 onward, but remained highly fragile due to hesitant union leaders. In fact, it is indicative that the DGB did not endorse the mass demonstration organized by a network of "Anti-Hartz" groups in November 2003, although many local and regional branches of sectoral unions (e.g., the metal workers' union *IG-Metall* and the service sector's union *ver.di*) participated actively. Just a couple of months later, the unions put themselves at the head of protests when they organized the mass demonstration in April 2004 against Schröder's reform program. However, union leaders were concerned about overstretching the confrontation with the SPD and about endangering the unity within the DGB and among the sectoral unions. Shortly afterward, they publicly terminated protests and revoked their opposition to Agenda 2010. From now on, national union leaders abstained from endorsing the anti-Hartz protests, but left it at the regional and local union branches' discretion to actively participate in local protest coalitions. The organizations of the unemployed heavily criticized these tactical maneuvers and dissociated themselves from the national union leadership.

Interestingly enough, this rupture did not terminate protests, but rather spurred what had been emerging as a new strategy of political protest. In fact, since the proclamation of Schröder's reform program, local "Anti-Agenda" and "Anti-Hartz" alliances had been mushrooming throughout Germany, which brought together groups of the unemployed, local union branches, antiglobalization activists, church parishes, welfare organizations and leftist splinter parties, depending on local conditions (ALSO 2004). These local alliances joined force into the organization of the first mass demonstration mentioned before. Moreover, they provided a fertile organizational ground for the diffusion of protest activities throughout East German cities from July 2004 onward. In fact, while the first Monday demonstration was a rather spontaneous and unorganized activity, the proliferation of these demonstrations was facilitated by local activists and organizations, which had established local "Anti-Hartz" coalitions and similar "social" alliances, or were instigated by the Monday demonstrations to do so. This protest dynamic benefited strongly from a wide panoply of organizations that had generated since 2002 a pronounced interest in the protests of the unemployed and was geared to capitalize on this momentum for their own aims: dissenters within the SPD and the unions explicitly pointed to the protests in order to legitimize their move to establish a new leftist party; local unionists actively participated in local alliances and demonstrations as a means to oppose the conciliatory stance of national union leadership (sometimes with their implicit support) and to halt membership losses particularly in East-Germany; right-wing and left-wing parties rallied on these occasions as an opportunity to catch members and votes for the coming regional elections in Brandenburg or Saxony in September 2004; churches, welfare organizations, and civil rights activists committed themselves in order to put the situation of East Germany on the public agenda, and to revitalize the civil rights movements of the former demonstrations.

This broader support for the protests of the unemployed demonstrates that significant changes had been under way in regard to political opportunity structures. Indeed, we can synthesize our observations in regard to two elements, a situational and a structural one. On the one hand, we see that political protests had attracted generalized attention since 2003. This was due to increasing public unease about the course of Schröder's policy reforms and the dwindling support for the governing coalition within regional elections and public polls. Unemployment and the Hartz reforms were stylized as a paradigmatic battleground on which the future of German social democracy in particular, and of the German welfare system in general seemed to be at stake. These developments opened a window of opportunity for the jobless that was successfully used, because the Monday demonstrations were carried by a much wider discontent with government policies, both among the citizenry and among influential stakeholders.

On the other hand, a more structural change in political opportunities had been under way, which stems from the gradual erosion of German neocorporatism. While scholars still disagree about the magnitude of this erosion (Schmitter and Grote 1997; Traxler 2001; Streeck and Hassel 2004), it is uncontested that social partnership is discredited as a political instrument of macroeconomic and political steering since the disillusioning experiences with the Alliance for Work. Moreover, the social partners—and the unions in particular—are constantly losing societal support, both in terms of members and sympathies. Unionization rates have decreased between 1991 and 2002 from 38 percent to 27 percent, and this development was particularly pronounced in East Germany, where this decay started from a much higher level (50 percent to 27 percent in the same period of time; Ebbinghaus 2002). The erosion of neocorporatism in general and of unionism in particular might be detrimental for the jobless insofar as it deprives them of an important instrument of political representation. At the same time, however, this erosion is beneficial for collective protest action, because neocorporatism has tended to establish a quite pronounced monopoly of political interest representation by the social partners, which was replicated in the field of unemployed by a rather high rate of unionized jobless persons (i.e., an estimated 12.3 percent in the metal workers' union in 1998; Hassel 1999, 87; Ebbinghaus 2002). Consensual politics through social partnership and the strong position of centralized mass unions within it has discouraged political action by the jobless themselves, or has led to deradicalize and pacify protests, as illustrated by the fact that violent actions by the jobless were virtually nonexistent since the late 1970s (FALZ 1994; Gallas 1994).

Developments since the late 1990s suggest, however, that we are entering a post-neocorporatist era, particularly in East Germany, where traditions and institutions of social partnership have not been enrooted lastingly, and where national unions lose credibility due to allegiances to government policies. Here, the unemployed and their supporters could step out of the slipstream of the unions more easily. Under these circumstances, protest dynamics are more probable, not least because of internal dissent within the unions about their function within national policymaking. In fact, individual union activists and branches can play more outspokenly the role of political entrepreneurs, as illustrated by the permissive role of local and regional unionists. In sum, protests were conditioned by much more beneficial political opportunity structures.

At the same time, we have a second lesson to draw. Indeed, activists had learned to better work the system of political opportunities by stepping out of the slipstream of national unions and by committing themselves to the more tedious work of grassroots coalition building. These local alliances allowed to maintain the claims of the unemployed in the center of public attention and to repel the dominance of single actors, while broadening the range of actors participating in collective protests. However, this strategy limited the mobilization episode across time and space. First, Monday demonstrations proliferated across East German cities, to never gain ground in West Germany. On August 9, 2004, for instance, about 20,000 people rallied in Dessau, Leipzig, and Magdeburg each, while demonstrations in Cologne, Dortmund, and Gelsenkirchen counted only on the support of a couple of hundred persons. Second, local alliances and demonstrations were constantly exposed to sectarian ambitions and hostile takeovers. In fact, activists had to guard against attempts by right-wing groups to put their stamp on local demonstrations; internally, they had to resist left-wing splinter parties (here, the MLPD) to take control of local coalitions and organizing committees. Many local alliances broke up due to these internal conflicts of interest and ideologies. Third, Monday demonstrations were heavily exposed to electoral politics. Public and media attention to the protests were motivated by a series of regional elections (Saarland, Brandenburg, and Saxony in 2004, North Rhine-Westphalia in 2005), which were considered as test ballots for the national government. Electoral campaign events, such as the speech of Oskar Lafontaine (former SPD minister of finance and the future party leader of the new WASG) at a Monday demonstration on August 30, 2004, and the speech of Oskar Gysi (leader of the PDS) one week later in Madgeburg provided much publicity, yet pushed the activists toward institutionalized means of political influence taking.

In fact, activists and local coalitions were concerned about stepping up the pressure on the national government to revoke the Hartz reform. This was to be achieved by a tighter cross-regional cooperation among the various organizations involved in local Monday demonstrations, which met, however, insurmountable ideological and strategic disagreements, as demonstrated by the parallel and competing meetings in Berlin and Leipzig and the rival demonstrations on October 2 and 3. At the same time, activists became concerned about securing the support of the national unions in order to carry the protests into the West and into the center of the political system. However, as this perspective proved to be futile, more and more groups engaged in supporting the establishment of the WASG as a new parliamentary force that would represent the interests and demands of this "new social movement." Werner Halbauer, member of ATTAC and delegate at the WASG conference in Nuremberg on November 20, 2004, expressed this opinion when he declared that "each big mass movement needs also mass organizations, which are able to organize and sustain them" (quoted in Keßler 2005). Confronted with the choice between the Scilla of grassroots protest dynamics and the Charibdis of institutionalized interest representation, more and more activists opted for the latter in the hope of dissuading the government from its reform plans. This was even true for Andreas Ehrholdt, the main initiator of this protest episode, who decided to establish a new party called *Freie Bürger für soziale Gerechtigkeit* (Free Citizens for Social Justice). He and his followers yielded to these pressures, which, in the long run, turned out to be detrimental for the protest cycle.

Conclusion

The German unemployed were strongly involved in collective protest action and they have had a considerable impact on public debates and political deliberations. At the same time, the mobilization of the jobless depends on a series of factors, which help to explain protest differences across time and space. Indeed, nationwide collective action emerged in 1998 in anticipation of national elections, and climaxed between autumn 2003 and autumn 2004, particularly in East Germany. These peculiarities have to do, first, with grievances, given the fact that relative deprivations were much more pronounced in former socialist Germany when compared to the West (i.e., higher unemployment rates and lower wages and social benefits). Moreover, the reform program of the Schröder administration was to bring a "suddenly imposed grievance" (Walsh 1981) by qualifying previously granted rights and provisions (Böhnisch and Cremer-Schäfer 2003). Hence, even if we agree that grievances do not arouse political protest directly, we have to acknowledge that collective deprivations can provide important stimuli for the organization and mobilization of the jobless, particularly if they can be framed as an aggravation relative to comparable groups or previous situations, and thus as a struggle between antagonist actors about the material and symbolic dimensions of justice (Gamson 1995).

Second, political protest by the jobless is largely a matter of organization. Collective action by the unemployed has to struggle with impediments typically related to their situation of marginalization and stigmatization. Hence, it is strongly dependent on activists and organizations, which provide important incentives to politically "activate" the jobless. This applies particularly to the local level, where organized actors were able to set up a self-reinforcing political process that was perceived as a means of individual empowerment and allowed to construct collective protest constituencies. However, organizational matters were fundamental for the protest's scale shift (Tilly and Tarrow 2007, 94–7), that is, the emergence of nationwide protest campaigns as well, because local activities had to be instigated, coordinated, and communicated externally. These national protest campaigns build upon organizational networks and coalitions, which had been set up during the last three decades, and which were reassembled and integrated from 1998 onward in order to facilitate further action. The organizational structure of this field, however, remained highly decentralized and fragmented along issues, regional constituencies, and ideological orientations. This decentralized structure had advantages for protest dynamics (Gerlach 1999) because it concentrated the focus of attention on local actors and activities, which are eminently important for politically activating the jobless, and thus for transcending social and political exclusion. Moreover, a decentralized structure was responsible for the pronounced diffusion of claims and protest forms, and in particular, for the striking proliferation of Monday demonstrations throughout East Germany. At the same time, however, this decentralized structure was particularly dependent on political entrepreneurship, because it relied on external help to activate latent organizational fields at the local and national level into collective protest.

This observation illustrates that, third, collective action by the jobless was strongly dependent on beneficial political opportunity structures. Unemployment became a very important and highly controversial public issue since the mid-1990s. These conflicts have contributed to deepen cleavages between and within traditional political camps, here, most prominently by disaffecting the unions from the SPD on the one hand, and leftist parliamentarians or unionists from their leadership on the other. These circumstances instituted several pull and push factors in regard to political protest by the jobless, because more influential actors within the political establishment paid attention to claims of the unemployed or were interested in furthering their issues and activities. However, these political conflicts and their enabling consequences were strongly bound to electoral politics and thus mutable and ephemeral. In fact, with the reform program of the Schröder administration in place, a new consensus within the political establishment emerged (among, e.g., parties such as the SPD, CDU, FDP, the Greens, and the social partners), which argued that the direction of the reforms was without alternative. This consensus was virtually omnipresent after national elections in September 2005 and the arrival of the SPD–CDU/CSU coalition in government. Influential allies have dissociated from the jobless, and political attitudes toward the unemployed have become more hostile. It is interesting to note that political protest by the jobless has been virtually nonexisting in this changing political context, in spite of considerable aggravations, introduced by the Hartz IV reform in early 2005.

Compared to these situational developments, we have argued that the erosion of neocorporatism has engendered more enduring, structural changes of political opportunities. Social partnership in general and centralized unions in particular are losing ground, and with them a core institution of conventional interest representation and negotiation. In fact, unions have been strong in organizing and mobilizing the unemployed from the 1980s onward, but always along highly institutionalized patterns and according to the organizational needs and objectives of the unions. The importance of these centralized mass organizations has been questioned during the late 1990s and early 2000s, precisely under an SPD-led government, which compelled unionists to choose between loyalty and opposition. Torn between these two alternatives, national union leaders have developed a hesitant policy that has contributed to delegitimize them, particularly within the broad networks of organizations and activists confronting government reforms. This process was complemented by a long-dated trend of dwindling memberships and public sympathies, which forced and freed the jobless to look for other venues and ways of organization and mobilization. The emergence of broader local and national alliances (with the participation of local unions and other political entrepreneurs) demonstrates that this development was quite conducive for collective action by the unemployed, as it allowed them to step out of the slipstream of national unions.

In sum, however, we have to conclude that protest actions by the jobless is uncertain, fragile, and ephemeral, given the fact that collective action depends on a series of conditions and circumstances, which the unemployed cannot influence (Wolski-Prenger 2000). This lesson is necessarily to be drawn when putting an emphasis on political opportunity structures, which are by definition external to the jobless. However, we have seen that "windows of opportunity" emerge once in a while, and that public spheres and political domains tend to open themselves structurally to marginalized groups. We should expect therefore that political protest by the marginalized become a more probable and normal phenomenon. Moreover, we have to realize that the jobless have drawn their lessons as well. In the course of time, they opted for mobilization structures and strategies that strived to capitalize more effectively on their resources and to work effectively the system of political opportunities. Their attempts to stabilize and generalize protest dynamic across space and time proved to be futile, but may endorse what scholarly writing has underscored in regard to the temporal dynamics of social movements, namely, that mobilization follows cyclical dynamics but lays the (organizational, motivational, and ideational) ground for future collective action.

Notes

1. Data for this chapter came from the UNEMPOL project and from Internet sites by organizations for the unemployed. Here we refer to a newspaper analysis by the *Süddeutsche Zeitung* and interviews conducted in Germany as part of the comparative UNEMPOL research project (http://www.eurpolcom.eu/unempol/), funded by the European commission. Besides a newspaper analysis and the forty interviews that were conducted, the German team collected publications by actors in

the field of unemployment. Findings were published in the following two books: Baumgarten (2010) and Lahusen and Baumgarten (2010).
2. Prior to 2005, the system of benefits was split into three types. The people who had worked and paid mandatory unemployment insurance received *Arbeitslosengeld*, which was calculated on the basis of their former income (60 percent of the average last net-salary for unemployed individuals without children, and 67 percent for unemployed individuals with children). The duration of payment went up to thirty-two months depending on the length of time the individual had paid insurance and on their age. After having received *Arbeitslosengeld*, the unemployed received *Arbeitslosenhilfe*, which was about 10 percent lower than *Arbeitslosengeld* but was still based on previous wages. All those people who were entitled neither to *Arbeitslosengeld* nor to *Arbeitslosenhilfe* and who were poor received *Sozialhilfe*, based on a concept of basic needs. As soon as the recipient got "enough" money from another source, he/she was no longer entitled to *Sozialhilfe*. Furthermore there was an obligation for them to accept any job or measure of job training that was offered.
3. According to these reforms, from January 2005 onward *Arbeitslosengeld I* would be restricted in general to a period of twelve months, and to eighteen months for people over fifty-five. Every other person who is poor but able to work and whose savings (including the savings of close family members) do not exceed a certain amount receives *Arbeitslosengeld II* (ALG II). Questionnaires are to be filled out by the unemployed assessing their entitlement by asking in detail the financial and social circumstances of the applicant. The previous unemployment benefits did not take into consideration these factors. A lot of former recipients of *Arbeitslosenhilfe*, especially married women, have completely lost their entitlement to benefits as a result of this reform. For those who receive it, the amount of this benefit is 345 euros in Western Germany and 331 euros in Eastern Germany, which in many cases is lower than the former *Arbeitslosenhilfe*. Additionally, the costs for housing are paid only up to a reasonable amount. Those people who receive ALG II also have to take up any job offered to them, regardless of their qualifications. On top of this, those unemployed living "inadequately" will be forced to move to cheaper or smaller abodes (Bundesministerium für Wirtschaft und Arbeit 2004). As a part of Hartz IV, the so-called 1-euro-jobs were created as a highly controversial measure. Recipients of ALG II are forced to take up any of these jobs offered. They earn 1 euro per hour in addition to their state benefits. This is why these jobs are criticized not only as a waste of time for the unemployed but also for causing a decrease in regular paid jobs. A lot of money invested in measures of job creation, especially in Eastern Germany, which was also a financial resource for the organizations of the unemployed, was cut by the Hartz IV reforms (Roth 2005).
4. In 1984, Brinkmann assessed the percentage of organized unemployed to be 1 (cited in Bieber, Derichs-Kunstmann, and Höhfeld 1986). Comparing these two broad estimates shows that the unemployed have never been well organized since the 1980s.
5. A group of researchers went out to distribute questionnaires and to interview demonstrators on Monday, September 13, 2004, in four different cities (Berlin, Dortmund, Leipzig, and Magdeburg). Their data contain 1,025 demonstrators from these Monday demonstrations (see Rucht and Yang 2004). According to this survey, only about 40 percent of the demonstrators were unemployed, yet, the majority claimed that a family member was affected by joblessness. Hence, a large fraction of the demonstrators was to be affected by the reform of social assistance and placement.

More than half of the demonstrators were between forty-five and sixty-four years old. This is unsurprising as people in this age group face more difficulties trying to reenter the job market if they become unemployed. The percentage of demonstrators belonging to the group of old-age pensioners (18 percent) is surprisingly high, but shows the connection between Hartz IV and other reforms, which also concern old-age pensioners in a negative way. German Federal Government. 2004. *Agenda 2010. Questions and Answers*, http://www.bundesregierung.de/Anlage609255/Agenda+2010+brochure.pdf (last accessed January 10, 2006).

6. See Reister (2000, 22), who advises the use of these estimates with caution, given the fact that various authors provide different numbers, depending on differing methods and criteria.
7. The so-called *Jobbergruppen* were founded by people who tried to evade the capitalist system by not taking up steady jobs. They were officially registered as students and worked on a very insecure status.
8. In Western Germany about 68 percent of the financial resources came from the state, and in Eastern Germany this amount was estimated to be much higher (Reister 2000, 20). Particularly in the East, personnel were often financed by money through state measures of job creation (ABM). In Eastern Germany, besides the state, the unions had become the second most important supporter of unemployment projects (23). This creates further organizational dependencies, which apply also to private funding, because organizations do have to take into account the interests of their private donors and members in this case as well (Kantelhardt 1999; Wolski-Prenger 2002). To a certain degree this is true even for those few groups that temporarily used the offices of allied groups (e.g., unions, the socialist party PDS, or the German branch of ATTAC). While these independent groups aim to reduce organizational dependencies (e.g., also through the use of modern communication channels), the latter cannot evade completely, given the "poverty" of these groups.
9. The mobilization of the unemployed on the national and European levels led to a further emphasis on political activism when, e.g., about one hundred new organizations of the unemployed were founded, particularly in those cities where there had been no initiative previously (Reister 2000). Existing groups reported an increasing number of members (Kantelhardt and Wolski-Prenger 1998), and this applies also to the rate of politically active constituents (Gallas 1994).
10. Allensbacher Archiv. 2001. IfD-Umfrage *7002*, January/February. http://www.ifd-allensbach.de/news/prd_0106.html (last accessed February 5, 2006).
11. Another important actor for the unemployed is the Protestant Church, which was the first to support the unemployed organizations and has a long history of industrial and social rectories (Wolski-Prenger 1989, 166–8). In Eastern Germany it started working with the unemployed soon after German Unification (Wolski-Prenger 1996; Klippstein 2000). The churches are influential allies because they still carry weight as an important institution in our society (Gallas 1994), provide expertise to the politicians, and conduct surveys on unemployment and poverty (Rothardt and Wöhrmann 1996). In the 1980s, the Protestant Church started cooperating with the unions (Wolski-Prenger 1996; Klippstein 2000) and occasionally supported protest activities. Aside from the churches, German welfare organizations aimed at representing the interests of the unemployed. Due to their interventions the unemployed were publicly recognized as a group particularly affected by poverty. A big discussion on the cutbacks of unemployment insurance and social assistance benefits ensued (Leisering 1993). But cooperation with this

actor was not always welcome. Unemployment became an institutionalized area of social work, which was not favorable for mobilization and political action.

References

ALSO. 2004. Die Chronik. http://www.also-zentrum.de/index.htm (last accessed February 6, 2004).

Bagguley, Paul. 1992. Protest, Acquiescence and the Unemployed: Comparative Analysis of the 1930s and 1980s. *British Journal of Sociology* 43(3): 443–61.

Baumgarten, Britta. 2003. The German Unions and the Unions' Organisations of the Unemployed: Different Communication Strategies attempting to Shape the Discourse on Unemployment. Second ECPR Conference, *Section on Social Movements, Contentious Politics, and Social Exclusion*, September 18–21, Marburg, Germany.

———. 2004. Strong Protest by the Weak? Comparing Two Phases of High Mobilisation of the Unemployed in Germany. Conference, *Public Employment Action and Unemployed Movements*, November 19–20, Lyon, France.

———. 2010. *Interessenvertretung aus dem Abseits. Erwerbsloseninitiativen im Diskurs über Arbeitslosigkeit*. Frankfurt am Main: Campus.

Beier, Angelika. 1999. Aktionstage der Arbeitslosen(-projekte). In *Ausgrenzung und soziale Bewegungen. Dokumentation der Jahrestagung 1999 von ZEPRA*, ed. Klaus Kittler and Klaus Pape, 22–31. Hamburg: VSA-Verlag.

Bieber, Anne, Karin Derichs-Kunstmann, and Jörg Höhfeld. 1986. Gewerkschaftliche Vertretung von Arbeitslosen. In *Gilt Marienthal noch heute?*, ed. Rainer Kalbitz, 94–100. Düsseldorf: Hanns-Böckler-Stiftung.

Böhnisch, Tomke, and Helga Cremer-Schäfer. 2003. Coping with Social Exclusion. From Acceptance to Indignation. In *WelfarePolicy from Below. Struggles Against Social Exclusion in Europe*, ed. Heinz Steinert and Arno Pilgram, 77–89. Aldershot: Ashgate.

Brenke, Karl, and Michael Peter. 1985. Arbeitslosigkeit im Meinungsbild der Bevölkerung. In *Gewandelte Werte- Erstarrte Strukturen. Wie die Bürger Wirtschaft und Arbeit erleben*, ed. Michael von Klippstein and Burkhard Strümpel, 87–127. Bonn: Verlag Neue Gesellschaft.

Bundesministerium für Wirtschaft und Arbeit. 2004. *Erste Basisinformation zur Grundsicherung für Arbeitsuchende*. Stand: August.

Bundesagentur fur Arbeit. 2004. Arbeitslosenquoten 1975–2004. http://www.sozialpolitik-aktuell.de/tabellen_arbeitsmarkt.shtml#Arbeitslosenquote (last accessed January 10, 2006).

Ebbinghaus, Bernhard. 2002. Dinosaurier der Dienstleistungsgesellschaft? Der Mitgliederschwund deutscher Gewerkschaften im historischen und internationalen Vergleich. *MPIfG Working Paper* 02/3. http://www.mpi-fg-koeln.mpg.de/pu/workpap/wp02-3/wp02-3.html (last accessed June 20, 2005).

Eick, Volker, Britta Grell, and Margit Mayer. 2004. Zwischen Sozialintegration und Arbeitszwang. Gemeinnützige Beschäftigungsinitiativen in den USA und der Bundesrepublik. *WSI-Mitteilungen* 11/04: 610–16.

FALZ (Frankfurter Arbeitslosenzentrum e.V.). 1994. *Arbeitslose aller Länder vereinigt Euch*. Frankfurt: FALZ.

Gallas, Andreas. 1994. *Politische Interessenvertretung von Arbeitslosen. Eine theoretische und Empirische Analyse*. Cologne: Bund-Verlag.

———. 1996. Politische Wirkungsmöglichkeiten von Arbeitslosen. In *Arbeitslosenarbeit. Erfahrungen. Konzepte. Ziele*, ed. Friedhelm Wolski-Prenger, 169–86. Opladen: Leske & Budrich Verlag.
Gamson, William. 1995. Constructing Social Protest. In *Social Movements and Culture*, ed. Hank Johnston and Bert Klandermans, 85–106. Minneapolis: University of Minneapolis Press.
Gerlach, Luther P. 1999. The Structure of Social Movements: Environmental Activism and its Opponents. In *Waves of Protest. Social Movements Since the Sixties*, ed. Jo Freeman and Victoria Johnson, 85–97. Lanham: Rowman & Littlefield.
Giugni, Marco. 2011. Political Opportunity: Still a Useful Concept? In *Contention and Trust in Cities and States*, ed. Michael Hanagan and Chris Tilly, 271–85. Berlin: Springer.
Grehn, Klaus. 1996. Der Arbeitslosenverband Deutschland e.V. In *Arbeitslosenarbeit. Erfahrungen. Konzepte. Ziele*, ed. Friedhelm Wolski-Prenger, 67–79. Opladen: Leske & Budrich.
Hassel, Anke. 1999. *Gewerkschaften und sozialer Wandel. Mitgliederrekrutierung und Arbeitsbeziehungen in Deutschland und Großbritannien*. Baden-Baden: Nomos.
Jahoda, Marie, Paul F. Lazarsfeld, and Hans Zeisel. 1933. *Die Arbeitslosen von Marienthal. Ein soziographischer Versuch*. Leipzig: Hirzel.
Jenkins, J. Craig. 1999. The Transformation of a Constituency into a Social Movement Revisited: Farmworker Organizing in California. In *Waves of Protest. Social Movements Since the Sixties*, ed. Jo Freeman and Victoria Johnson, 277–99. Lanham: Rowman & Littlefield.
Kantelhardt, Uwe. 1996. Gewerkschaftliche Arbeitslosenarbeit. In *Arbeitslosenarbeit. Erfahrungen. Konzepte. Ziele*, ed. Friedhelm Wolski-Prenger, 137–54. Opladen: Leske & Budrich.
———. 1999. Aktionstage der Arbeitslosen(-projekte) Teil 1. In *Ausgrenzung und soziale Bewegungen. Dokumentation der Jahrestagung 1999 von ZEPRA*, ed. Klaus Kittler and Klaus Pape, 17–21. Hamburg: VSA-Verlag, Hamburg.
Kantelhardt, Uwe, and Wolski-Prenger, Friedhelm. 1998. Die neue A-Klasse. *Blätter für deutsche und internationale Politik*: 531–5.
Keßler, Martin. 2005. Neue Wut. Filmkommentar. http://www.neuewut.de /neueWUT_Kommentar.pdf (last accessed July 25, 2006).
Kieser, Albrecht. 1988. *Zwischen Siechtum und Widerstand. Sozialarbeit und Erwerbslosenbewegung*. Bielefeld: KT-Verlag.
Kitschelt, Herbert. 1986. Political Opportunity Structures and Political Protest. Anti-Nuclear Movements in Four Democracies. *British Journal of Political Science* 16: 57–85.
Klippstein, Norbert. 2000. Arbeitslosenarbeit bei Kirchen und Wohlfahrtsverbänden. In *Gesellschaftliche Organisationen und Erwerbslose*, ed. Hugo Reister, Kurt Nikolaus, and Norbert Klippstein, 95–128. Berlin: Karl Dietz Velag.
KOS (Koordinierungsstelle gewerkschaftlicher Arbeitslosenarbeit). 1998. *Arbeitslosen-Proteste 1998. Eine Dokumentation der KOS*. Bielefeld: KOS.
Kriesi, Hanspeter. 2004. Political Context and Opportunity. In *The Blackwell Companion to Social Movements*, ed. David A. Snow, Sarah A. Soule, and Hanspeter Kriesi, 67–90. Oxford: Blackwell.
Lahusen, Christian, and Britta Baumgarten. 2006. Die Fragilität kollektiven Handelns: Arbeitslosenproteste in Deutschland und Frankreich. *Zeitschrift für Soziologie* 35(2): 102–19.

Lahusen, Christian, and Britta Baumgarten. 2010. *Das Ende des sozialen Friedens? Politik und Protest in Zeiten der Hartz-Reformen*. Frankfurt am Main: Campus.
Leisering, Lutz. 1993. Zwischen Verdrängung und Dramatisierung. Zur Wissenssoziologie der Armut in der bundesrepublikanischen Gesellschaft. *Soziale Welt* 4: 468–511.
Lipsky, Michael. 1968. Protest as a Political Resource. *The American Political Science Review* 62: 1144–58.
———. 1970. *Protest in City Politics. Rent Strikes, Housing and the Power of the Poor*. Chicago: Rand McNally.
Massow, Martin. 1983. *Selbsthilfe für Arbeitslose*. Munich: Kösel-Verlag.
McAdam, Doug. 1982. *Political Process and the Development of Black Insurgency 1930–1970*. Chicago: University of Chicago Press.
———. 1996. Political Opportunities: Conceptual Origins, Current Problems, Future Directions. In *Comparative Perspectives on Social Movements: Political Opportunities, Mobilizing structures and Cultural Framings. Applications of Contemporary Movement Theory*, ed. Doug McAdam, John D. McCarthy, and Mayer N. Zald, 23–40. Cambridge: Cambridge University Press.
Meyer, David S. 2004. Protest and Political Opportunities. *Annual Review of Sociology* 30: 125–45.
Meyer, David S., and Debra C. Minkoff. 2004. Conceptualizing Political Opportunity. *Social Forces* 82(4): 1457–92.
Neidhardt, Friedhelm. 1985. Einige Ideen zur allgemeinen Theorie sozialer Bewegungen. In *Sozialstruktur im Umbruch*, ed. Stefan Hradil, 193–204. Opladen: Leske & Budrich.
Nikolaus, Kurt. 2000. Erwerbslosenarbeit der Gewerkschaft in den neuen Bundesländern. In *Gesellschaftliche Organisationen und Erwerbslose*, ed. Hugo Reister, Kurt Nikolaus, and Norbert Klippstein, 49–94. Berlin: Karl Dietz Verlag.
Oliver, Pamela, Gerald Marwell, and Ruy Teixeira. 1985. A Theory of Critical Mass I: Interdependence, Group Heterogeneity, and the Production of Collective Action. *American Journal of Sociology* 91: 522–56.
Olson, Mancur. 1971. *The Logic of Collective Action: Public Goods and the Theory of Groups*. Cambridge: Harvard University Press.
Opp, Karl-Dieter. 2009. *Theories of Political Protest and Social Movements. A Multidisciplinary Introduction, Critique, and Synthesis*. Abingdon: Routledge.
Oschmiansky, Frank, Silke Kull, and Günther Schmid. 2001. Faule Arbeitslose? Politische Konjunkturen einer Debatte. *Discussion Paper* FS I 01 – 206. Berlin: Wissenschaftszentrum Berlin für Sozialforschung.
Paulus, Wolfgang. 1985. Bewältigungsstrategien von Arbeitslosigkeit. Das Beispiel Arbeitslosenselbsthilfegruppen. Thesis (Diploma), Freie Universität Berlin.
Perry, Matt. 2007. *Prisoners of Want. The Experience and Protest of the Unemployed in France, 1921–45*. Aldershot: Ashgate.
Rein, Harald, and Wolfgang Scherer. 1993. *Erwerbslosigkeit und politischer Protest. Zur Neubewertung von Erwerbslosenprotest und Einwirkung sozialer Arbeit*. Frankfurt: Peter Lang.
Reiss, Matthias, and Matt Perry, ed. 2011. *Unemployment and Protest: New Perspectives on Two Centuries of Contention*. Oxford: Oxford University Press.
Reister, Hugo. 2000. Arbeitslose und Arbeitslosenorganisationen. In *Gesellschaftliche Organisationen und Erwerbslose*, ed. Hugo Reister, Kurt Nikolaus, and Norbert Klippstein, 11–47. Berlin: Karl Dietz Verlag.

Rink, Dieter. 2000. Local Citizens' Initiatives during the East German Transformation. In *Urban Movements in a Globalising World*, ed. Pierre Hamel, Henri Lustiger-Thaler, and Margit Mayer, 177–91. London: Routledge.

Rolke, Lothar. 1988. Millionen im Griff: Warum es (noch?) keine Arbeitslosenbewegung gibt. *Forschungsjournal Neue Soziale Bewegungen* 2: 45–50.

Roller, Edeltraut. 1999. Shrinking the Welfare State. Citizens' Attitudes towards Cuts in Social Spending in Germany in the 1990s. *German Politics* 8: 21–39.

Roth, Roland. 1985. Neue soziale Bewegungen in der politischen Kultur der Bundesrepublik—eine vorläufige Skizze. In *Neue soziale Bewegungen in Westeuropa und den USA. Ein internationaler Vergleich*, ed. Karl-Werner Brand, 20–82. Frankfurt: Campus.

———. 1999. Ein Jahr Rot-Grün. Ein politischer GAU für die neuen sozialen Bewegungen? *Forschungsjournal Neue Soziale Bewegungen* 12: 10–21.

———. 2000. New Social Movements, Poor People's Movements, and the Struggle for Social Citizenship. In *Urban Movements in a Globalising World*, ed. Pierre Hamel, Henri Lustiger-Thaler, and Margit Mayer, 25–44. London: Routledge.

———. 2005. The Monday Demonstrations of 2004—Continuity, Break or New Horizons in Collective Action on Unemployment in Germany? Closing Conference of the UNEMPOL Project, April 1–2, Geneva, Switzerland.

Rothardt, Dieter, and Eduard Wöhrmann. 1996. Evangelische Arbeitslosenarbeit. In *Arbeitslosenarbeit. Erfahrungen. Konzepte. Ziele*, ed. Friedhelm Wolski-Prenger, 35–42. Opladen: Leske & Budrich.

Rucht, Dieter, and Yang Mundo. 2004. Wer demonstriert gegen Hartz IV? Befragung am 13. September in vier Städten. *WZB-Mitteilungen* 106: 51–3. http://www.wz-berlin.de/publikation/pdf/wm106/51.pdf (last accessed July 3, 2006).

Schmid, Manfred G. 1998. *Sozialpolitik in Deutschland. Historische Entwicklung und internationaler Vergleich*. Wiesbaden: Leske und Budrich.

Schmitter, Philippe C., and Jürgen R. Grote. 1997. Der korporatistische Sisyphus: Vergangenheit, Gegenwart, Zukunft. *Politische Vierteljahresschrift* 38: 530–54.

Sommer, Christian. 1988. *Ausbeutung, Organisierung, Klassenkampf. Materialien zu ungeschützten Arbeitsverhältnissen und Erwerbslosigkeit*. Berlin: Eigenverlag.

Steinert, Heinz, and Arno Pilgram, ed. 2003. *Welfare Policy from Below. Struggles against Social Exclusion in Europe*. Aldershot: Ashgate.

Streeck, Wolfang, and Anke Hassel. 2004. The Crumbling Pillars of Social Partnership. In *Germany: Beyond the Stable State*, ed. Herbert Kitschelt and Wolfgang Streeck, 101–24. London: Frank Cass.

Tarrow, Sidney. 1996. States and Opportunities: The Political Structuring of Social Movements. In *Comparative Perspectives on Social Movements: Political Opportunities, Mobilizing structures and Cultural Framings. Applications of Contemporary Movement Theory*, ed. Doug McAdam, John D. McCarthy, and Mayer N. Zald, 41–61. Cambridge: Cambridge University Press.

Tilly, Charles, and Sidney Tarrow. 2007. *Contentious Politics*. Boulder: Paradigm Publishers.

Traxler, Franz. 2001. Die Metamorphosen des Korporatismus: Vom klassischen zum schlanken Muster. *Politische Vierteljahresschrift* 42: 590–623.

Uske, Hans. 1995. *Das Fest der Faulenzer. Die öffentliche Entsorgung der Arbeitslosigkeit*. Duisburg: Duisburger Institut für Sprach-und Sozialforschung (DISS).

van Berkel, Rik, Harry Coenen, and Ruud Vlek, ed. 1998. *Beyond Marginality? Social Movements of Social Security Claimants in the European Union*. Aldershot: Ashgate.

von Winter, Thomas. 1997. "Schwache Interessen": Zum kollektiven Handeln randständiger Gruppen. *Leviathan* 3: 539–66.
Wacker, Ali. 1987. Massenarbeitslosigkeit ist ein massenhaftes Schicksal, aber ein massenhaft individuelles. In *Provinz-Arbeitslosigkeit*, ed. Ulrike Rossmann, 71–91. Hamburg: Internationalismus Verlag.
Walsh, Edward J. 1981. Resource Mobilization and Citizen Protest in Communities around Three Mile Island. *Social Problems* 29(1): 1–21.
Wolski-Prenger, Friedhelm. 1989. *Arbeitslosenprojekte zwischen sozialer Arbeit und sozialer Bewegung. Eine explorative Untersuchung zu einem neuen sozialen Phänomen*. Frankfurt: Peter Lang.
———. 1996. Arbeitslosenarbeit im Überblick—Einleitende Aspekte zu einer paradoxen Aufgabe. In *Arbeitslosenarbeit. Erfahrungen. Konzepte. Ziele*, ed. Friedhelm Wolski-Prenger, 9–33. Opladen: Leske & Budrich Verlag.
———. 2000. Politikpotentiale Arbeitsloser. In *Politische Repräsentation schwacher Interessen*, ed. Ulrich Willems and Thomas von Winter, 149–69. Opladen: Leske & Budrich.
———. 2002. Arbeitslosenprojekte in der Bürgergesellschaft. In *UTOPIE kreativ* 141–142: 629–40.
Zald, Mayer N., and John D. McCarthy. 1987. *Social Movements in an Organizational Society. Collected Essays*. New Brunswick: Transaction Books.
Zoll, Rainer, Heinz Bauer, and Margrit Springhorn-Schmidt. 1991. *Arbeitslose und Gewerkschaft. Untersuchung einer schwierigen Beziehung*. Cologne: Bund Verlag.
Zorn, Annika. 2003. *Resignation oder Revolte? Welchen Anspruch haben Arbeitslose*. Thesis (Diploma), Humboldt Universität Berlin.

CHAPTER 3

Inside or Outside Trade Unions? The Mobilization of the Unemployed in Belgium

Jean Faniel

The situation of the unemployed in Belgium is distinguished by two principal elements, which set it apart from other European countries. On the one hand indemnification is, in principle, unlimited in time and young people get access to benefits from the end of their studies onward. On the other hand, the unions are deeply involved in the protection of the unemployed since they play a part in the joint management of unemployment insurance and pay out unemployment benefits to their members, which accounts for why 88 percent of the unemployed are unionized.

From the middle of the 1970s, Belgium was rocked by a rapid increase in unemployment, which rose fivefold in ten years. Different revival plans and plans for employment were implemented by the public authorities in the decades that followed. These plans met with varying fortunes in terms of job creation. They contributed to a deterioration in the quality of employment affecting particularly new entrants on the labor market such as young people and women. Moreover, on account on the one hand of the very large increase in the cost of unemployment benefit provision due to the growth in the numbers of unemployed, and on the other of the pressures exerted by employer federations and by certain right-wing parties, various measures were adopted by the Belgian government aimed at restricting or delaying access to benefits, or to making easier exclusions to unemployment insurance. More recently, the accent put at European level on the activation of the unemployed led the Belgian government to intensify checking-up procedures for the unemployed.

As a reaction to this development, the last three decades have been studded with different mobilizations of groups of the unemployed or of organizations representing them. However, these demonstrations remained episodic and brought together just a few thousand people at most. The dynamics adopted varied from region to region, especially according to the employment situation, and different traditions of struggle, be they unions, associative or political. On occasion, the mobilizations were inspired or even supported by movements emanating from abroad (in this case from neighbors France) or at the international level (the Euromarches).

Given the specific role that Belgian unions play in regard to the unemployed, the question of support or not for the organization of mobilization of the jobless is put inescapably and with a special intensity. The situation is paradoxical. Strong trade unions contribute toward the defense of the interests of the unemployed, but they often prevent them from organizing themselves in an autonomous manner. Institutionally recognized, particularly as joint managers of unemployment insurance, the unions can call moreover on powerful political ties and are, as such, quite efficient representatives of the workers and of job seekers. When they set up a mobilization, they can deploy great resources, in human and financial terms, but also from ties within these institutions managing the unemployment insurance or close to their political allies. Nevertheless, their strength often leads them to discourage attempts at self-organization by the unemployed, or in any case to view them with much reservation, distrust even. Within unions, or outside of them, with them or against them, such are the questions incessantly raised by the mobilization of the unemployed in Belgium.

To start with, we will set out the historical origins and the main current characteristics of the Belgian apparatus for unemployment indemnification. Thus, prominence will be given to the role the unions play in unemployment insurance and more widely their weight in Belgian society, especially as regards the unemployed. Following this the way in which unemployment has evolved in Belgium will be pointed out, underlining the main sociological and geographical features influencing the level of mobilization of the unemployed. This contextual viewpoint approach will allow for the painting of a panorama of mobilization of the unemployed, which has taken place over some thirty years, while underlining developments in the profile of the people taking part and the rather marked regional character of the movements. This survey will allow, in a last part, the highlighting of the role played by trade union organizations and by certain political parties in these mobilizations.

Indemnification for Unemployment and the Role of the Trade Unions

From the nineteenth century, the Belgian unions set up mutual aid funds aimed particularly at indemnifying their members who were, through no fault of their own, deprived of employment. The dual aims were: to assist colleagues deprived of all earnings and reduce the pressure toward lower wages that arises from the unemployed being prepared to work under any conditions. Progressively, thanks to the close contacts the socialist and Christian trade unions maintained with their sister parties, the union contributions were complemented by public subsidies, first at the local level, then at the national level. From the end of the nineteenth century, trade union leaders had noticed that the role of the unions in disbursing unemployment benefits guaranteed them the affiliation of a large number of workers, either unemployed or fearing to become so one day. On the creation of Social Security in 1944, the trade unions acquired the right to continue disbursing unemployment benefits to their members, although these benefits were henceforth made up solely of public funds, provided by social subscriptions deducted from wages (Vanthemsche 1985 and 1994; Faniel 2007a and 2010a). Since then, they have kept a close watch on maintaining this position, strengthening it even (Januarius 2008, 3–5).

Unemployment insurance is run by the National Employment Office (NEO), which transfers to the unions the sums of money corresponding to the unemployment benefits, all the while checking on and, where appropriate, imposing sanctions on the unemployed. The management committee of the NEO is composed of representatives of the trade unions, of the employers, and of the government. Thanks to this position, the trade unions obtained a rather favorable system for the unemployed, sometimes considered one of the most advantageous within the European Union. Thus, since 1945 Belgium has been characterized by a compulsory unemployment insurance covering all salaried employees. This scheme has certain specific features not found in other countries. The first of these concerns the period of entitlement to benefit. Once (s)he has worked for a specified period of time, any employee is entitled to claim unemployment benefit, provided that (s)he has become unemployed involuntarily and is available for work. This entitlement is in principle not time-limited. The amount of benefit is, however, reduced after a specified period of unemployment. A further specific feature is that young people who have completed compulsory education and have not found a job are entitled, after a so-called waiting period, to what is known as an "interim allowance," at a rate lower than that of unemployment benefit but subject to similar criteria (involuntary joblessness, availability for work, and benefits in principle not time-limited). Over time, the trade unions have obtained different improvements in the indemnification conditions, which raised their profile in the eyes of the workers, especially the unemployed.

This situation furthered the unionization of the Belgian unemployed to such an extent that 88 percent of them are members of one of the three trade unions. Just like (until recently) Denmark, Finland, and Sweden, Belgium even saw the number of workers unionized increase since the 1970s, unlike the trend recorded in the other Western countries. The main reason for this situation is that, in these four countries, the trade unions are directly involved in the disbursement of unemployment benefits to their out-of-work members (Western 1997; Scruggs 2002; Albrechtsen 2004; Vandaele 2006).

More widely, and in common with these three Nordic countries, Belgium distinguishes itself by having one of the highest levels of unionization in Western Europe, exceeding 50 percent (Ebbinghaus and Visser 2000; Vandaele 2009). Besides its role toward the unemployed, the Belgian trade union movement is well entrenched in firms and the three main unions (Christian, Confederation of Christian Trade Unions—CCTU; socialist, General Labor Federation of Belgium—GLFB; or liberal, General Confederation of Liberal Trade Unions in Belgium—GCLTUB)[1] are established in many socioeconomic bodies (Faniel 2010b). These bodies moreover maintain generally close links with their sister parties: the Francophone and Flemish socialist parties for the GLFB, the Christian-social parties for the CCTU, and, to far a lesser extent, the liberal parties for the GCLTUB. Within governmental coalitions, at least one of the two political families close to the main trade unions (CCTU and GLFB) is always present. In the end, since 1921, the Ministry of Employment has always been headed up by a socialist or by a Christian-social minister.

This political proximity allows trade unions to carry weight in the evolution of the country but it constrains in some cases their ability or willingness to act. Since the union leaders generally seek to handle their allies in power, they "filter" the workers' claims and tend to limit their extent or radicalness. This proves especially true regarding unemployment insurance where the principal interlocutor on whom the main grievances are concentrated is the government, represented by the minister of employment. From the middle of the 1970s, the growth in the number of unemployed gave rise to an increase in expenditure on unemployment benefits. The political instability that characterized the country at the end of this decade could have created divisions among the elites and open the political opportunity structure (Tarrow 1994, 88–9), which could have allowed the unemployed to get a better hearing. However, the socialist, Christian-social, and liberal parties had an understanding on the need to react faced with the crisis in leading an austerity policy, which particularly affected the unemployed. Successive governments therefore limited allowances paid out in the framework relation of unemployment insurance and facilitated the exclusion of the unemployed. The trade union leaders most often went along with these measures, or tried to mitigate them, without however opposing directly their political allies when the latter were in government. Although it could have been an advantage for the mobilized unemployed, the privileged relationship between the trade unions and their sister parties turned out in this respect to be an obstacle.

Thus, in thirty or so years, protection for the Belgian unemployed deteriorated significantly. In 1980 the average rate of benefit was equivalent to 41.6 percent of average gross earnings in the private sector. This replacement rate had dropped to 21.7 percent in 2004 (Faniel 2010a). Maximum benefits[2] are limited at a quite low level compared to neighboring countries. People previously earning higher wages thus face greater income differences when getting unemployed. Minimum benefits[3] as well as mean benefits are below poverty thresholds (Faniel 2010a). Living with such an income is uneasy and the financial resources of the unemployed are limited. More favorable than the other European countries in the duration of indemnification and access for young people, Belgian unemployment insurance therefore guarantees lower indemnification levels than other European countries.

In this context, the unemployed and trade unions find themselves bound together by a special dialectic. On one side, the Belgian unemployed are in regular contact with their union who manage their administrative situation. In some cases, they may benefit personally from individual (e.g., legal) assistance. This relationship allows the trade unions to get close to their jobless members and to get to know their concerns. The union representatives can thus support positions that help the jobless within the management committee of the NEO. But on the other, it can induce tensions, either because of the circumstances (material or relational) in which the unemployed are welcomed by the trade union services, or because they hold their union responsible for the negative decisions the latter have to convey in accordance with unemployment insurance rules (sanctions imposed by the NEO, recovery of sums erroneously paid out, etc.). In spite of that, most of the unemployed have a favorable attitude, even a kindly one, toward the trade unions, generally felt as organizations that stand up for them in a proper manner. Thus, only a minority of the unemployed (12 percent) chooses not to belong to a trade union and to address themselves to a public body charged with distributing their unemployment benefit (the AFPUB).

Until the 1970s, no militant collective structure exclusive to the unemployed existed within the Belgian trade unions. The latter considered the jobless as workers to be helped but hardly as militants being potential actors in their own situation. In Belgium, as elsewhere, the trade unions are, above all, organizations built historically in the workplace, mirroring the priorities of active workers (Ness 1998; Richards 2000; Faniel 2009). In this context, the unemployed have always had some trouble getting organized within trade unions, their action being perceived as even worse by the unions insofar as their demands directly concerned the welcome the unemployed got in the trade union offices, or that they challenge the policy followed by the government and pointed up, more or less explicitly, the passiveness of the trade union leaders faced with the reforms gnawing away at the rights of the unemployed. Nevertheless, the unions dreaded even more the vague organizational desires of the unemployed outside their number; they prefer, under certain conditions, to establish structures allowing the unemployed to organize themselves from within. The mobilization of the unemployed in Belgium is constantly marked by this ambivalence.

Evolution of Unemployment, Regional Disparities, and Mobilization of the Unemployed

Belgium has passed through a contrasting economic development since its independence in 1830. For a century, Flanders remained an essentially rural and relatively poor region, despite the existence of some urban industrial centers such as Antwerp and Ghent. Wallonia on the other hand experienced early and massive industrialization, becoming very early on one of the most dynamic and prosperous regions in Europe. Brussels formed a large economic zone and was the headquarters of powerful financial institutions. But the scene changed radically after World War II. Centered on the coal, steel, or glass industries, the Walloon economy was struck very hard by the economic crisis. Flanders, on the contrary, saw rapid development in the technologically advanced sectors. From

Table 3.1 Evolution of the regional rate of unemployment in Belgium (1948–2008, percentage of wage earners[a])

	1948	1953	1958	1963	1968	1973	1978	1983	1988	1993	1998	2003	2008
Belgium	4.2	9.1	5.9	2.9	4.4	3.5	10.4	18.3	14.1	15.8	14.0	12.1	10.6
Brussels[b]	N/a	7.8	4.1	2.2	2.6	2.7	10.7	20.8	17.6	23.0	21.3	19.6	19.5
Flanders	N/a	13.4	8.0	3.3	4.5	3.2	10.4	18.4	12.1	12.8	9.2	7.7	6.2
Wallonia	N/a	4.7	3.6	2.6	6.6	5.4	13.2	21.5	20.7	24.4	22.0	19.2	17.2

[a] At the regional level, the only data available are on the population of wage earners, and not the totality of the active population.
[b] With regard to the collection of data on the unemployed, the geographical limits of the Brussels area were modified in a more restrictive sense in 1975.
Source: National Employment Office (NEO).

Table 3.2 Evolution of the rate of unemployment in Belgium by gender (1948–2008, percentage of active population)

	1948	1953	1958	1963	1968	1973	1978	1983	1988	1993	1998	2003	2008
Global	N/a	N/a	3.0	1.5	2.6	2.3	6.7	11.6	8.9	10.3	8.9	8.5	7.8
Men	N/a	N/a	3.1	1.5	2.6	1.8	4.1	8.8	6.1	7.6	6.8	7.2	6.7
Women	N/a	N/a	2.6	1.4	2.8	3.2	11.3	16.1	13.1	13.8	11.6	10.0	8.7

Source: Federal Planning Bureau.

the 1970s, the whole country was hit by a rapid and high increase in unemployment (table 3.1). However, from the middle of the 1980s, Flanders succeeded better than Wallonia in overcoming this situation, some zones even confronting shortages of labor at the outset of the years 2000.

Besides the crisis in large economic sectors the pressure of unemployment was enhanced by the sizeable arrival on the labor market of the young coming out of the baby boom and a growing number of women. These two categories of worker suffered especially from the unemployment that grew from the 1970s, either because they were the first victims of redundancy, or because they had trouble finding work. In 1980, 60 percent of the unemployed were women (table 3.2) and 30 percent were under twenty-five years of age.

During the first half of the 1980s, job losses continued to mount. Young people and women remained overrepresented among the unemployed but adult male workers were also heavily struck by unemployment from then on. In total, in the space of a decade, unemployment rose fivefold in almost the whole of the country, going from 2.6 percent of the active population in 1974 to 11.6 in 1983. Since then, the rate of unemployment has remained relatively high, never dropping below 7 percent. The economic and financial crisis that occurred in 2008 again pushed unemployment up but to a lesser degree than elsewhere in Europe.

An Early Mobilization

From the middle of the 1970s and the beginnings of the rapid growth in unemployment, some groups of the jobless appeared (Caroyez 1981; Faniel

2006, 22–5). They were protesting in particular against the lack of jobs and against measures adopted by the government to reduce unemployment allowances. In Brussels at first, militants from different radical left-wing movements (communists, Maoists, or Trotskyists) set up local groups of the unemployed, of which some collaborated together. These groups were formed outside of the trade unions, whom they judged too unwilling to fight. They met with hostile resistance from the ruling bodies of the trade unions, who took these criticisms badly and refused a specific organization of the unemployed, considering that the latter were represented by the sectoral union federations. In Flanders and in Wallonia, groups of women and young people—two categories particularly hard hit by unemployment—built up as such within the regional trade union organizations, also organized mobilizations against unemployment. In November 1975, a demonstration organized by the youth union committees gathered about 5,000 people in Liège, an old Walloon city with old industries hard hit by the crisis and a characteristically strong tradition of social struggle. Save for this event, the groups of mobilized young people and women generally never counted for more than a dozen or so militants, faced with a big turnover and a lack of support from the ruling bodies of the trade unions. The predominance of the sectoral federations within these bodies left little place, and few means, for interprofessional action organized on the basis of age or gender. In Charleroi, a large city in Wallonia that had known prosperity linked to heavy industry and as a consequence had itself been hard hit by the growth in unemployment, the trade union management leaders of the CCTU and of the GLFB chose to invest large human and financial resources in the unitarian organization of the unemployed—and not in a separate manner as was the case in other regions of the country—on a coordinated basis at the level of the regional basin.

These first mobilizations showed that the relations between the unemployed and trade unions were carried out according to variable logics and they could be good or, on the contrary, tense. In all cases, the action carried out in this way was of short duration and stopped after a few years. The lack of support, opposition even, from the trade unions, but also the intrinsic difficulty of the unemployed to get themselves mobilized for the duration, even when solid means are put at their disposal to ease their action, explain the short-lived character of these actions. It has moreover to be emphasized that a big governmental back-to-work plan for the unemployed was launched in 1978, which allowed the more dynamic ones among them to find work again and had the effect of depriving the unemployed groups of their most active militants. "The gradual reduction in unemployment played the same role for the unemployed as early retirement had done for the workers, that is to say anaesthetize and thus obviate any protest movement" (Colicchio 1992, 12).

In 1980, to reduce the cost of unemployment insurance, the government created the status of cohabitant,[4] affecting women in particular. It also introduced a third period of indemnification, reduced the allowances received by quite a number of the unemployed, and extended to six months as opposed to three the period young people had to wait to receive their first allowance following the end of their studies. These modifications were the cause of the appearance of new committees of the unemployed (ibid., 13) but differed from preceding ones in that the groups who set up in 1980–1982 were above all committees created by those unemployed within the trade union framework, specifically as groups of the unemployed and no longer of women or young people. With unemployment continuing to rise, ever more of the unemployed were available for mobilizations. Among the unemployed were included more and more workers made redundant following a lengthy career and, in the case of some of them, having a certain experience of trade unions.

These elements contributed to easing the acceptance of these initiatives by trade union leaders themselves. In 1981 and 1982 the two main trade union confederations—the CCTU[5] then the GLFB—each introduced into their statutes the creation of a national commission of the unemployed, denominated significantly as "workers without employment," and a commission of the same name in each regional section. The expression thus retained emphasizes the link with active workers and the *involuntary* deprival of employment that characterizes the situation of the unemployed. These commissions were comprised of unemployed members of the union who wished to get involved in militant work. As unemployment rose, the unemployed with more militant trade union experience were made redundant. They could join with the commissions or help toward setting them up, favoring actions within the trade union framework and not autonomous groups outside it. However, the objective given to these groups was not always precise and certain unionists emphasized, for example, "The lack of clear projects on the part of the CCTU (who simply told us: you have to organize them)."[6] In reality, the role of these commissions was to inform the unemployed, to provide them with meeting space where they could bring up their problems, to enable them to maintain active contact—and not just administratively—with their trade union, provide information on the situation of the unemployed to the rest of the trade union organization, and, where appropriate, to raise the levels of awareness of the unemployed and to organize them toward their collective mobilization. These different roles are evidently somewhat linked. Maurer (2001, 66–103) underlines that as the groups of the unemployed have a function of mutual aid and of creation of links, these groups may contribute to the subsequent development of a more militant action, putting claims forward.

Unemployment Changes, the Mobilized Unemployed Also

In the same period, a committee, "women against the crisis," in which groups of women from the socialist trade union took part, organized various local actions that ended up in March 1981 in a national demonstration bringing together in Brussels over 7,000 people. At the top of their claims list was the right to work for all and a refusal of "attacks on the female unemployed." Similar demonstrations were carried out in several successive years. In parallel, different youth organizations, in particular trade unions, led in 1982 a "march of youth for employment." Preceded by different gatherings, this national demonstration[7] brought together some 30,000 people in the capital. Two years later, a new demonstration was organized around the same theme and brought together over 10,000 people. The one and other mobilizations insisted that young people have a job that is "useful, stable and creative" (Correia 1982, 79). These initiatives by women and young people were held concomitantly with the initiatives of the committees of the unemployed, but without any real collaboration with them. The profile of the militants involved in these committees had in fact evolved and corresponded essentially with that of the adult or long-term unemployed. Their concerns were somewhat different, for example, from those of the groups of young people, closer to the labor market. Besides, the youth marches were initiated by young people's organizations some of which did not belong to the trade union sphere and whose expectations were much wider and vague than the sole search for work. Finally, it emerged quite clearly that the trade unions, within which women, young people, and the unemployed organized themselves separately, hardly played a federative role in respect of these mobilizations led by groups, different of course, but with partially common interests. The attachment of trade unions to action based more on the sector of activity than on the aspects of age, gender, or holding down a job, just as their fear of seeing the emergence of a movement with wide scope and which was difficult to master, were the main reasons for this absence of coordination.

In December 1983, the government decided to impose a specific tax on unemployment benefits. The small groups of unemployed set up within the trade unions led different actions against this measure considered unjust: demonstrations of some hundreds of people and "fist punch" actions requiring few militants such as the occupation over several hours of places considered symbolic, especially the regional offices of the NEO or the national office of the employers' federation. However, these actions came to an end in the spring, without having swayed the government (Faniel 2006, 40–1). Globally weak, these actions were of unequal significance depending on the region, with regard to the economic context, but also the more-or-less benevolent attitude of the trade union bodies toward them. At the national level, the trade union bodies provided no real support to the unemployed groups, on the one hand because the sectoral federations were busy handling the consequences of ever-growing restructuring and closures of enterprises, on the other because the CCTU did not wish to make things difficult for the Christian-social parties in the coalition government, which had decided to implement the measures being fought against by the unemployed.

From 1986 to 1989 the committees of the unemployed of the GLFB got mobilized above all to improve the lot of aged jobless workers. This change reflected the evolution of the profile of the militants in the unemployed trade union committees, linked to the characteristics of unemployment itself, affecting more and more workers with long-standing employment (Faniel 2006, 49–52). These militants demanded an improvement in their status and an increase in benefits, considering that although having worked over a long period before being made redundant, they received low benefits while many of their former colleagues had been able to access more advantageous mechanisms for leaving the labor market through early retirement schemes. Various protest movements were organized, one of them drawing up to 2,500 militants in 1988. These actions had a particular characteristic in that they brought together the unemployed from around the whole country, thanks especially to the backing of the GLFB, which, mindful of the argument about the long service of these unemployed or what they had endured in the past, supported this struggle and helped toward the bringing together of different local initiatives: "These '50+' were the youth of the crisis of the 1930s. It is the generation of the Second World War, and they fought within the company and elsewhere for a social security which is both efficient and equitable."[8] These unemployed had had sometimes long experience of trade unions and personal contact with union leaders, whom they used to support their fight. The GLFB handed over this mobilization to the minister of employment and to the socialist parties, at that time in opposition faced with a government implementing a clearly neoliberal program. After the return to power of their political family in 1988, the socialist parliamentarians backed these claims inside a majority concerned to mark the break with its predecessors. This social and political configuration contributed to the creation in 1989 of a special status for the elderly unemployed, including a benefit supplement. In Flanders, where unemployment fell distinctly from the middle of the 1980s, the mobilization of the unemployed ceased on account of this measure.

New Concerns, New Groups

One had to wait several years to see again a mobilization with even a small amount of the unemployed. From 1997 to 2000, several groups of militants denounced the checks carried out on the unemployed in their own homes. Deemed to verify the truthfulness of the unemployed on their family circumstances,[9] these checks were considered by many among them as unacceptable in their respect for the private lives of the unemployed (Dryon and Krzeslo 1999; Faniel 2004, 498–501). In Charleroi, where unemployment had now reached 25 percent of the active population, the Christian and socialist trade union leaders devoted significant means to relaunch the action of their jobless workers' commissions. Stemming from the two organizations, the group "Chômeur actif" ("Active Unemployed") led different actions (press conferences, local demonstrations, occupation of the regional office of the NEO), which were widely covered in the local press. In Brussels, former trade union delegates and militants from the radical left-wing set up a small group of the unemployed within the federation of the white-collar workers of the GLFB. However, the management of the federation considered this group as being too radical and prevented it from working, which led to its quite rapid disappearance. Finally, in Liège, militant anarchists, journalists, and artists founded the group "Chômeur pas chien!" ("Unemployed, but not dogs!") in the autumn of 1997. These few militants led theatrical actions among the queues of the unemployed to encourage them to get mobilized against the checks, occupied the regional office of the NEO, and carried out a custard pie attack on the minister of employment. On several occasions they collaborated with the Charleroi trade union group and with the unemployed groups that the Liège trade union sections had re-created in this context. However, the radicalism of "Chômeur pas chien!" and the tense relationship they had with the union leaders complicated their collaboration and ended by rendering it impossible. The mobilization nevertheless carried on in a context that was relatively favorable toward the mediatization of the mobilizations of the unemployed, at the same time by means of the movement of French unemployed of 1997–1998 and of the European Marches against unemployment, job insecurity, and exclusions.

Influences from Abroad

The mobilization of the unemployed in Belgium was unquestionably dynamized by these two events. In 1997, in the wake of the marches organized in 1994 in France, came the first European March against unemployment, job insecurity, and exclusions, which ended in a parade of 50,000 demonstrators in Amsterdam (Mathers 1999; Chabanet 2008). In Belgium, as in the other countries crossed, the preparation of the welcome to the marchers gave rise to the setting up of small local groups, particularly in Brussels, Charleroi, and Liège, namely, three cities where the associative and trade union fabric is compact and unemployment is high. The militants who collaborated on this occasion came from a variety of backgrounds: unemployed, homeless, militants from the radical left (communists, Trotskyists, and anarchists), and some trade unionists in their personal capacity (Faniel 2007b). In Belgium, the 1997 spring marches and the months of preparation preceding them allowed on the one hand to attract media and public attention somewhat toward the situation of the unemployed, and on the other to give rise to the creation of groups defending the jobless.

Some months later, the French unemployed movement of the winter of 1997–1998[10] served as an example to the Belgian unemployed who were mobilizing. Not only did the French movement demonstrate that the unemployed were perfectly capable of getting mobilized, but it got some tangible results besides: payment of a Christmas bonus and establishment of a special fund to help the unemployed. In Wallonia and in Brussels, where French is the language of the majority of the population, French political life is traditionally closely followed. Despite being quite different in their claims and in organizational fabric, the French movement served as an encouragement, especially in the struggle launched against home visits by the NEO inspectors. Its repercussions also created a favorable climate within Belgian francophone public opinion, easing the development of a movement for the unemployed in Wallonia and Brussels. In Flanders, a region where right-wing political parties predominate, experiencing a noticeably better employment situation and less receptive to French topicalities, the situation hardly changed. For a long time, several nationalist or conservative parties have considered the question of unemployment as an essentially Walloon problem, linked to the idleness of the inhabitants of the South of the country and costing the decent Flemish workers dearly.

These framing elements explain in particular why the Euromarches and the French movement of 1997–1998 did not produce the same effect in Flanders, where the last unemployed mobilizations go back to the end of the 1980s.

In the spring of 1999, a second Euromarch converged on Cologne. Groups coming from France passed through Liège, where the trade union committees of the unemployed and "Chômeur pas chien!" had expanded their struggle against home visits. The parade of marchers took part in the occupation for a whole night of the regional head office of the NEO. The Belgian trade union leaders were against this kind of activity, which they judged to be too radical and "Chômeur, pas chien!," on the initiative of the occupation, had too few forces to carry this action out alone. Those occupying the premises took advantage therefore of the presence of marchers not only to benefit from their media impact, but also to use the numerical force of the parade, comprising a hundred or so people, to carry their operation to a successful conclusion. This action marked the final break in the fragile collaboration between the anarchist group and the regional trade union organizations, but it also had a particular media repercussion on the cause of the Belgian unemployed.

At the national level, the unemployed mobilizations were also taken over by the opposition Ecology parliamentarians, then by representatives of the socialist party in power. This political support to mobilization of the unemployed marks a certain division of elites at the heart of the government and a modification to political alignments, contributing to opening somewhat the political opportunity structure (Tarrow 1994, 87–9). The government then in power ended by regulating the checks that were under attack, leading to a lowering in their number. The following government, in which the Ecologists participated and within which the Employment portfolio was held by a socialist minister close to the trade unions, reduced the checks, leading to their abandonment in reality, although the specific status of cohabitants, source of the problem exposed, was retained. This relative success stimulated some trade union leaders to relaunch the activities of jobless workers' commissions in several other zones of Wallonia and Brussels.

Mobilization against the "Activation" of Checks on the Unemployed

Finally at the beginning of 2004, the federal government modified the system for checking up on the unemployed in the framework of the activation measures advocated by the European employment strategy (EES) (Faniel 2010a). Several civil society associations (organizations of the unemployed, women's movements, the Human Rights League, etc.) of Brussels and Wallonia, as well as Walloon trade union sections, mobilized hoping to prevent the government from implementing its draft project, considering it abnormal to require that the unemployed show proof of their active search for a job while the placement agencies are incapable of providing a sufficient number of job offers. Several demonstrations took place, one of which, led by the Walloon wing of the GLFB, brought together 3,000 people. The national trade union bodies were divided on this measure. The draft project was thought up and implemented by the socialist—Flemish—minister of employment. The Flemish officials of the GLFB, coming from a region plainly less touched by unemployment than their Walloon neighbors and backing the minister in the initiative of the new control system, refused to let their trade union oppose this reform more vigorously. The Walloon wing of this union nevertheless took an active part in the mobilization against this reform but came up against a categorical refusal on the part of the Francophone socialist party, in solidarity with its Flemish partner in government. The government therefore put its plan into action in July 2004 (Faniel 2005).

Movements of the Unemployed, Trade Unions, and Political Parties: What Alliances?

This survey of mobilizations of the unemployed, which occurred in Belgium over the last three decades, brings to the fore a certain number of structuring elements. Very much real, the mobilization of the unemployed presents however a discontinuous character in time and space. The public mobilized was often different, which partially explains this discontinuity. Moreover, the mobilizations have assumed a quite marked regional, local even, attachment, the cooperation of groups emanating from different regions, all the more so their convergence into a movement with a national character remaining the exception. Finally, whether it happens within or outside of the trade unions, the mobilization of the unemployed has always to deal with the weight of the unions in Belgian society. This relationship between the unions and the unemployed is complex and not without its ambivalences: the first guarantee the second a high level of social protection, while rendering them strongly dependent with regard to political situations and the games of alliances with the political parties on which the unemployed have no hold.

The Belgian trade unions serve as a framework for collective action by the unemployed. For the jobless groups they obtain human resources, both material and militant, they can transmit the claims of the unemployed, give them feedback, and bring their claims onto the political scene, thanks especially to their institutional position and their privileged relations with certain political parties. The jobless workers' commissions also constitute places that may, if need be, serve as a framework for a new collective mobilization without necessarily having to start out completely from zero. In that way, they play somewhat the role of abeyance structures, brought to the fore by Taylor (1989). The unemployed organized in union jobless workers' commissions are however closely dependent on the resources provided to them by their organization, the policy conducted by the union leaders proving to be very variable according to the periods and the regions. Thus, in Flanders, the significant drop in the level of unemployment from the end of the 1980s led to some disinterest on the part of regional trade union leaders in unemployment-related questions. Confronted on the contrary with a high and persistent level of unemployment, the Walloon and Brussels union leaders—minorities within each national confederation—came up against the indifference of Flemish officials on more than one occasion, even to the point of their refusal to organize and support the mobilization of the unemployed (Faniel 2005). The evolution of the political balances of power, and the presence or otherwise of the trade unions' sister parties in government, also has a strong influence on the degree of combativity of these organizations when it is a question of defending the rights of the unemployed, fluctuating between discreet lobbying and contentious action in support of the unemployed themselves.[11] The logic of expertise sometimes overrides collective action and conveys a break between the "base" and the apparatus of the trade union movement. The unemployed organized within the unions thus regularly criticize their difficulty in having contacts with the union representatives called upon to take part in bodies such as the management committee of the NEO, where the fate of the unemployed is at the heart of the discussions. Finally and more widely, these unemployed emphasize the lack of interest in their claims on the part of the trade union leaders and associates who have a job.

The statutory recognition of the jobless workers' commissions by the two main trade union organizations at the beginning of the 1980s was able to raise certain hopes. Thirty years later, it has to be admitted that the workings of the commissions was somewhat erratic, that the unemployed militant union members continued to raise the same kinds of criticism, and that the unemployed still had at their disposal their very weak means and weight within the trade union decision-making apparatus, albeit that they constituted in some regions a large part of the membership. This is why initiatives to mobilize the unemployed also appeared outside of the union ranks. Some union jobless workers' commissions were reactivated so as not to let the groups outside of the unions be sole occupants of the role of organizing the unemployed. Trade union leaders also transmitted claims for the suppression of home visits, made particularly by groups outside of union ranks, which furthered the change in regulations on this subject at the end of the 1990s. Nevertheless, the unavoidable weight of the trade unions in political and social life in Belgium condemned those movements outside the union ranks to a certain marginalization.

Role of the Radical Left

The different cases of mobilization in Belgium show that militants on the radical left often played a key role in this phenomenon. Some prime movers of the union jobless workers' commissions were themselves members of parties of this political tendency. On the other hand, those union officials willing to organize the unemployed did not for all that emanate from the radical left, militants from these parties being systematically kept out by the leading officials of the trade union bodies.

Outside of the unions also, several mobilizations witnessed the active participation of militants from the radical left. From the middle of the 1970s, militant communists, Maoists, and Trotskyists got involved in the setting up of the first groups of unemployed, outside the trade union organizations. Also recalled was the influence of militant anarchists at the root of "Chômeur pas chien!." At the same period, some of them, along with militant communists and Trotskyists, took a very active part in the setting up and running of the Belgian section of the Euromarches. The Trotskyists in particular, through their links with the members of the Fourth International involved in the mobilizations of the unemployed growing elsewhere in Europe, played a preponderant role in the networking of the Euromarches movement and its Belgian component (Faniel 2007b, 209–10).

In these various cases, the militants coming from the radical left made their mark on the mobilization of the unemployed in several ways. The involvement of activists in admittedly small, but generally motivated numbers, having a certain militant know-how, contacts with other associations, particularly at international level, or even a certain feedback in their press organs, constituted so much by way of resources for action. They then contributed to forging the ideological framework in which the mobilizations of the unemployed evolved by supplying the analytical grids, inducing the mobilized groups to give a more global, political, and systemic interpretation to their claims. In that respect, they played the role noted by Croucher (1987) and Bagguley (1991, 102–108) with regard to the Communist Party of Great Britain in the 1930s. Finally, the influence of these militants found expression in their recurrent claims, such as the reduction in working time, abandoned by the center-left parties, and disappearing in time from the trade union timetable, but always championed by the radical left parties. Concomitantly, an insistence on the necessity of unity of action between active and unemployed workers is likewise at the heart of the reasoning of these militants.

In Belgium, the radical left is however weak and had completely disappeared from the parliamentary scene since 1985 (Dohet and Faniel 2011). Moreover, it has a difficult relationship with the trade union movement, the latter wishing to keep control of social challenge and averse to accepting the taking of political positions and forms of action they consider too radical. At the end, one can easily see that the game of alliances to which the Belgian unemployed can turn in their mobilization is strongly constrained by a certain number of ideological splits. Besides the tensions between groups of the unemployed and union organizations, some groups of unemployed formed within the union structure and led by militants from the radical left were disbanded by their union leaders. In some respects, the assistance from the radical left in the mobilization of the unemployed could thus have served as a spur to the mobilization but it might also have acted in some cases as a factor in the isolation of these movements.

Conclusion

In the middle of the 1970s, the treatment offered to unemployed Belgians might have seemed quite favorable: the indemnification was basically unlimited in time for those made involuntarily redundant; young people had access to unemployment benefits on leaving school; and the trade unions arrived over three decades at improving unemployment benefits. The mobilizations of the unemployed started to emerge from 1975, when unemployment took root in some regions of the country. They sometimes gave rise to demonstrations of thousands of people, but the gatherings generally remained limited and were often intermittent. The Belgian example shows well that the relationship between the (high) level of unemployment and the mobilization of the unemployed is neither direct nor systematic (Chabanet and Faniel 2011, 404–405). Even if a rise in the number of jobless often precedes their entry into action, the subjective dynamics—in other words, the discontent or feelings of injustice of the unemployed—constitute key explanatory factors, which motivate their commitment. In this respect, the successive reforms aimed at lowering benefits in a relatively advantageous benefit system—in any case in relation to those of other European countries—could be transformed into a feeling of relative deprivation (Gurr 1970), which one knows well can provide not just sufficient fertile ground, but one to encourage acts of protest.

The central role that the Belgian trade unions carry out in the payment of unemployment benefits and, as a corollary, the very high level of union membership among the unemployed have led to a specific link between the latter and the trade union organizations. This link explains to a large extent both the conditions in which the unemployed mobilize themselves and the difficulties they face in doing so. In close and frequent contact with their out-of-work members, the unions endeavor to provide an efficient service and defense of the individual; they have great sociopolitical weight and take part in the management of certain institutions with direct links to the situation of the unemployed. In the framework of the social security institutions, the trade unions maintain links with the employers' representatives and political officials, particularly with members of their sister parties. Their views are somewhat influenced by this dialogue and they constitute themselves in certain respects an element of stability of the system. From then on, particularly so as to treat their negotiating partners carefully, they seek not only to keep control of social protest, but also to give importance to a peaceful and civilized repertoire of action, providing much room for the development of expertise and to their place within the management committee of the NEO. Moreover, the trade unions are above all organized around active workers and their decision-making authorities are not very open to those who are inactive (unemployed, retired, students), who have difficulty in getting their own claims placed on the trade union agenda.

The unions however also constitute for the unemployed structures capable of providing precious resources with a view to organizing themselves and acting collectively. First of all groups of young people and women, followed later by the jobless workers' commissions, served as a basis for their mobilization. In some cases, the regional trade union leaders themselves supported or organized their contentious actions. In other cases, support came rather from militants of the radical left, willing to organize the unemployed autonomously outside the union framework, or seeing here an opportunity for action. The question of alliances of the unemployed on the one hand, the trade union organizations, groups coming from the radical left, or again the Euromarches movement on the other hand is therefore at the center of their capacity for action.

As a whole, the dynamics of mobilization specific to each region, as well as the significant differences in unemployment levels from one industrial basin to another explain that the mobilization of the unemployed was of an essentially regional character, which rarely took on a national dimension. In this respect, the unions were able to serve as a decisive focal point for the organization and mobilization of the unemployed on a local basis but also represented a brake on the extension of these movements at the national level, particularly because of divergent or contradictory positions of their different regional component bodies. However, no other organization was in a position to provide more efficient support to the mobilization of the unemployed. Inside or outside trade unions, that is the question raised by the mobilization of the unemployed in Belgium.

Notes

1. The CCTU in 2008 had 1,678,373 members (or 49.4 percent of all union members), the GLFB 1,455,454 members (42.8 percent), and the GCLTUB 265,123 members (7.8 percent). The indemnification of the unemployed was spread as follows: 41.0 percent for the CCTU, 41.2 percent for the GLFB, 6.0 percent for GCLTUB, and 11.8 percent for the Auxiliary Fund for the Payment of Unemployment Benefits (AFPUB).
2. Such benefits are allocated in the first months after job loss or to the unemployed in charge of a household.
3. Such benefits are allocated after certain duration of unemployment to the unemployed living alone or with someone earning a wage or receiving a greater benefit.
4. Since then, there are three categories of the unemployed: "head of household," "person living alone," and "cohabitant" (who lives with a person enjoying an income or a higher level of benefit, see preceding note). People living alone and cohabitants receive unemployment benefits at a lower level than heads of households. Until 2004, cohabitants could be excluded from unemployment insurance for an "abnormally long" period.
5. The meeting held in 1981 by the CCTU brought together 3,500 jobless people, which can be considered a high figure.
6. Extract from the minutes of a meeting of full-time officials of the CCTU on the organization of the unemployed (1990).
7. In spite of its name, this activity is not strictly speaking a "march" in the classic sense of the term, being spread over several days and covering a great distance. On this type of mobilization, see Pigenet and Tartakowsky (2003).
8. Extract from a file sent by the GLFB to the minister of employment in 1987.
9. Given the fact that people living alone receive higher allowances than those living as cohabitants, the NEO feared that some of the unemployed unduly declared themselves as being alone.
10. See the chapter one in this volume.
11. For other examples in different contexts, see chapter two in this book; and Locke (2011, 364–6).

References

Albrechtsen, Helge. 2004. The Broken Link—Do Trade Unions Represent the Interests of the Unemployed? *Transfer* 4: 569–87.

Bagguley, Paul. 1991. *From Protest to Acquiescence? Political Movements of the Unemployed*. London: Macmillan.

Caroyez, Philippe. 1981. Les comités de chômeurs. Considérations sur l'organisation collective des sans-emploi. *La Revue nouvelle* 12: 488–95.

Chabanet, Didier. 2008. When the Unemployed Challenge the European Union: The European Marches as Externalization of Protest. *Mobilization* 13 (3): 311–22.

Chabanet, Didier, and Jean Faniel. 2011. The Mobilization of the Unemployed: A Recurrent but Relatively Invisible Phenomenon. In *Unemployment and Protest: New Perspectives on Two Centuries of Contention*, ed. Matthias Reiss and Matt Perry, 387–405. Oxford: Oxford University Press.

Colicchio, Pasquale. 1992. Groupes spécifiques en période de crise économique : remède ou syndrome de maladie ? *Alternatives Wallonnes* 79: 10–18.

Correia, Fatima. 1982. Le chômage quotidien des jeunes wallons. Réflexions à propos de la marche des jeunes pour l'emploi et ... des dernières mesures gouvernementales concernant les jeunes chômeurs. *Bulletin de la Fondation André Renard* 123-4: 57–80.

Croucher, Richard. 1987. *We Refuse to Starve in Silence: A History of the National Unemployed Workers' Movement 1920–46*. London: Lawrence and Wishart.

Dohet, Julien, and Jean Faniel. 2011. La gauche anticapitaliste en Belgique : entre fragmentation et tentatives d'unité. In *Les partis de la gauche anticapitaliste en Europe*, ed. Jean-Michel De Waele and Daniel-Louis Seiler, 263–280. Paris: Economica.

Dryon, Philippe, and Estelle Krzeslo. 1999. Les chômeurs manifestent contre le durcissement des sanctions et la suppression des allocations. Chômeurs actifs, chômeurs pas chiens ! *L'Année sociale* 1998: 209–14.

Ebbinghaus, Bernhard, and Jelle Visser. 2000. *Trade Unions in Western Europe since 1945*. London: Macmillan.

Faniel, Jean. 2004. Chômeurs en Belgique et en France : des mobilisations différentes. *Revue internationale de politique comparée* 11(4): 493–505.

———. 2005. Réactions syndicales et associatives face au "contrôle de la disponibilité des chômeurs." *L'Année sociale* 2004: 133–48.

———. 2006. L'organisation des chômeurs dans les syndicats. *Courrier hebdomadaire du CRISP* 1929–1930: 5–76.

———. 2007a. Belgique. Le système d'assurance-chômage : un particularisme en sursis ? *Chronique internationale de l'IRES* 108: 15–25.

———. 2007b. Les chômeurs entre action locale et altermondialisme. Le collectif belge des Marches européennes contre le chômage, la précarité et les exclusions. In *Contester dans un pays prospère. L'extrême gauche en Belgique et au Canada*, ed. Anne Morelli and José Gotovitch, 197–219. Brussels: Peter Lang.

———. 2009. Belgian Trade Unions, the Unemployed and the Growth of Unemployment. In *The Politics of Unemployment in Europe: Policy Responses and Collective Action*, ed. Marco Giugni, 101–15. Farnham: Ashgate.

———. 2010a. Belgium. Unemployment Insurance Caught between Pressure from Europe, Regional Controversy and Fall-out from the Crisis. In *Unemployment Benefit Systems in Europe and North America: Reforms and Crisis*, ed. Florence Lefresne, 81–99. Brussels: IRES/ETUI.

———. 2010b. Caractéristiques et spécificités des syndicats belges. In *Dynamiques de la concertation sociale*, ed. Étienne Arcq, Michel Capron, Évelyne Léonard, and Pierre Reman, 93–119. Brussels: CRISP.

Gurr, Ted Robert. 1970. *Why Men Rebel?* Princeton: Princeton University Press.

Januarius, Joeri. 2008. De werkloosheidsverzekering in de naoorlogse welvaartstaat: een blik op de werking van het ABVV. *Vlaams marxistisch tijdschrift* 42(1): 3–8.

Locke, Cybèle. 2011. Fractious Factions: The Organized Unemployed and the Labour Movement in New Zealand, 1978–1990. In *Unemployment and Protest: New Perspectives on Two Centuries of Contention*, ed. Matthias Reiss and Matt Perry, 345–66. Oxford: Oxford University Press.

Mathers, Andy. 1999. Euromarch—The Struggle for a Social Europe. *Capital & Class* 68: 15–19.

Maurer, Sophie. 2001. *Les chômeurs en action (décembre 1997–mars 1998)*. Paris: L'Harmattan.

Ness, Immanuel. 1998. *Trade Unions and the Betrayal of the Unemployed. Labor Conflicts during the 1990s*. New York/London: Garland.

Pigenet, Michel, and Danielle Tartakowsky, ed. 2003. Les marches. *Le Mouvement social* 202: 3–182.

Richards, Andrew. 2000. Trade Unionism and the Unemployed in the European Union. *La Lettre de la Maison française d'Oxford* 12: 153–81.

Scruggs, Lyle. 2002. The Ghent System and Union Membership in Europe, 1970–1996. *Political Research Quarterly* 55(2): 275–97.

Tarrow, Sidney. 1994. *Power in Movement. Social Movements, Collective Action and Politics*. Cambridge: Cambridge University Press.

Taylor, Verta. 1989. Social Movement Continuity: The Women's Movement in Abeyance. *American Sociological Review* 54(5): 761–75.

Vandaele, Kurt. 2006. A Report from the Homeland of the Ghent System: The Relationship between Unemployment and Trade Union Membership in Belgium. *Transfer* 12(4): 647–57.

———. 2009. The Ghent System, Temporary Unemployment and the Belgian trade Unions since the Economic Downturn. *Transfer* 3–4: 589–96.

Vanthemsche, Guy. 1985. De oorsprong van de werkloosheidsverzekering in België: vakbondskassen en gemeentelijke fondsen (1890–1914). *Tijdschrift voor sociale geschiedenis* 11(2): 130–64.

———. 1994. *Le chômage en Belgique de 1929 à 1940 : son histoire, son actualité*. Brussels: Labor.

Western, Bruce. 1997. *Between Class and Market. Postwar Unionization in the Capitalist Democracies*. Princeton: Princeton University Press.

CHAPTER 4

The Movement of the Unemployed in Finland

Eeva Luhtakallio and Martti Siisiäinen

Why are there no demonstrations and general strikes against the politics exercised? They are the only ways to defend our case!

—Opinion in *Helsingin Sanomat*, November 24, 1995

Well, we have not really been able to come up with any particular means of influence.

—Unemployed of Helsinki activist, 2005

Unemployment became a major political issue in Finland in the late 1970s, and has kept this status ever since. The economic depression of the first half of the 1990s, however, hiked up the unemployment rate to figures unforeseen in the country's history. Unemployment has thereafter been the number one driving force of one victorious presidential campaign (Martti Ahtisaari, 1994), and of one government program (Prime Minister Paavo Lipponen, 1995). In terms of public opinion, polls have reported for more than a decade that the Finns consider unemployment one of their most critical social problems. The issue of unemployment has thus been on the agenda from the times of the depression to the current era, marked by simultaneous economic growth and structural changes in production resulting in closing down of factories and mass redundancies. Deepening polarization in terms of growing differences in income and wealth has gained importance in public debate over the past few years (e.g., Heiskala 2006). However, a massive social movement against unemployment has never become an important transforming force in the Finnish society, despite certain attempts of mobilization during the recession. In this chapter, we examine why this is so, and what are the forms of collective action the unemployed in Finland have taken on.

The mobilization of the unemployed in Finland is an abundantly uncovered issue in Finnish social research, despite the approximately 250 registered associations of the unemployed established after the 1980s, many of which have since become important partners of local authorities (see, however, Matthies, Kotakari, and Nylund 1996; Nylund 2000). In this essay, we address the question of unemployed people's collective action especially during the 1990s and early 2000s. In order to grasp a general view of the issue, we use data triangulation from various sources. The data collected for this study include key person interviews from both national- and local-level unemployed people's associations, archives covering the period 1992–2005 (annual reports, photo archive, speeches, and communiqués), and the member association survey of the national association of the unemployed TVY, websites of the local unemployed associations, unemployment statistics of Statistics Finland, new registrations statistics of the Finnish Register of Associations, and newspaper articles concerning the collective action of the unemployed in the electronic archives of the national newspaper *Helsingin Sanomat.*

The movement of the unemployed is understood here as a process of protest against causes and consequences of unemployment for structural and policy reforms. The movement consists both of informal interaction groups and formal registered voluntary associations, of the "moving" component, and of the institutionalized part of the movement. We first outline the historical background of unemployment in the Finnish context, as well as the political and societal situation around the depression of the 1990s and onward. We then describe the emergence of the movement of the unemployed, its further formation and development, and its representations in the Finnish media.

We will observe that, in the early 1990s, Finland endured a severe social crisis—especially a fast growth of the unemployment rate—and was in a political situation likely to provoke political agitation and, more precisely, protest by the unemployed. We will show that there is indeed a great variety of activities among the unemployed, who have set up a national organization specifically dedicated to the representation and defense of their interests, but that successful mass mobilization was very sporadic. At the exception of a mobilization peak in 1993, the protest of the unemployed neither truly burst out, nor really lastingly challenged the political agenda. However, at the local level, the unemployed have organized themselves vividly, although with scarce contentious purposes. Their activities play an important social role in different local contexts, and constitute a good indicator of the place the organizations of the unemployed now occupy in Finland.

We will also show, through a media content analysis, that the public representations of the movement of the unemployed follow a path similar to the analysis from other sources. Once burning news, the situation of the unemployed slowly turned into an issue of rather remote interest. Finally, we conclude with suggestions to explain the phenomenon and its particularities in the Finnish context.

The Development of Unemployment Security in Finland, 1950–1990

The general trend of unemployment in Finland has been upward since the beginning of the twentieth century. Long-term comparisons must be done with reservations, though, because the concept of "unemployment" has not been a monolith over time.[1] Mass unemployment was, however, officially unknown in Finland before the post–World War I period. In 1917–1919, the end of the Russian demand for war material led then to a considerable decline in construction and industrial production, and hence to unforeseen numbers of unemployed workers. Following this period, the next mass unemployment developed just before the international recession, and bottomed at the beginning of the 1930s. In the 1940s the demand for labor was extremely high, and times of relatively low unemployment continued until the end of the 1950s (Keinänen 1999, 74–5).

The creation of the modern system of social—including unemployment—benefits did not start in Finland until the second half of the 1950s. Between the two world wars a great majority of Finns lived out of reach of insurance-based social security systems, and even after the recession of the 1930s, the building of a welfare state did not debut in Finland as it did in other Nordic countries. This was potentially due to the weak position of the trade unions and communist and left-socialist political movements in general. The latter were prohibited until the 1940s as a consequence of the Civil War in the beginning of the twentieth century,[2] and thus the opportunity structures with regard both to formal political institutions and to powerful allies (Tarrow 1989, 34–5) were fairly enclosed.

During the 1950s Finnish unemployment was a combination of seasonal and structural tendencies. About 200,000 workers fluctuated between wage labor and work in their own farms. Emerging rationalization of the production chain decreased the demand of forest workers. In 1957 only 20 percent of wage laborers were members of an unemployment fund. Assistance in the case of unemployment was small and the economy of the unemployment funds was dependent on conjunctures. In the 1958 elections the Leftist parties won the majority in the parliament and started preparing improvements on social security, pressured by a vast wave of protest. The main claims of the movement(s) were assertion and improvement of child benefit and social security in general, shortening of working time, and establishment of general unemployment insurance. The first draft of the law on unemployment insurance failed to come into force as planned due to the successful operation of the political Right to postpone it (Uljas 2005, 141–5). This gave impetus to a mass of demonstrations organized by trade unions and supported by leftist political forces. Local trade union organizations formed the core of the participants, along with a few other significant groups, such as mobilized housewives (62). The unemployed took part in the movement mainly in the role of actual or potential trade union members, and there was no independent movement of the unemployed. The emergence of the protest seems to have two sets of favoring prerequisites: first, the economy had started to rise, and second, the political opportunity structures characteristics had simultaneously opened for challenging groups (see Siisiäinen 1992 and 2003).

In 1959, almost 100,000 unemployed were registered, and at the end of the 1960s the figure went, for a while, up to nearly 200,000 (Keinänen 1999, 74–5). Among the political parties, two strategies on unemployment competed: the first one claimed for a universal unemployment insurance supported by the communists, its allies, some Social Democrats, and the Agrarian Union. The second line was developed by the Central Union of Finnish Employers, but the conservatives and the majority of the Social Democratic Party supported it. It was based on unemployment funds and restricted only to workers who had a relatively long, continuous employment. It excluded the majority of the workforce (agricultural and seasonal workers, short-term workers, etc.) (Uljas 2005). The new law, which finally came into force in 1960, was a compromise between these two propositions. On one hand, it was based on a system of unemployment relief organized by the state and completed by the municipalities. On the other hand, a parallel system based on unemployment funds that paid much higher compensations to their members was created.

Until the early 1990s, these funds were exclusively run by the trade union organizations. The benefits were tied to the level of income, thereby helping more the upper strata of the labor force (Uljas 2005, 158–62). This dual system was to become the cornerstone of the system of unemployment benefits in Finland for years to come. In the 1980s the average fund-based compensation for lost earnings rose to 60–70 percent of salary for five hundred days. The benefits for outsiders of the fund system, instead, were low when compared to European countries in similar phases of industrialization (Vähätalo 1998, 73). However, all bills on social security that were accepted with the assistance of mass demonstrations at the turn of the 1960s were a strong push toward the development of the modern welfare state in Finland, once well known as one of the most generous worldwide (cf. Esping-Andersen 1990). The Finnish unemployment policies have then on resulted from neocorporatist negotiations between the central unions of employers, employees, and the state.[3] The current system of unemployment benefits is a combination of a fund membership based part, depending on the level of previous income, and a basic part covering non-members and long-term unemployment (Kautto et al. 2001).

The Recession of the 1990s and the New Wave of Mass Unemployment

The 1980s was retrospectively baptized as "the crazy years" in Finland. During this decade of "casino economy," the economic growth was fast, the unemployment rate was low, and the market overheated little by little. This development resulted from both the dismantling of old regulations in, for example, the banking sector, and the runaway opening up of the country's economy. In the turn of the 1990s, a currency crisis, caused mainly by the banking sector's unpredicted breakdown, with the interaction of several other unfortunate

Table 4.1 Unemployment rate in Finland (1990–2005; values in percentages)

	1990	1991	1992	1993	1994	1995	1996	1997	1998	1999	2000	2001	2002	2003	2004	2005
Men	3.6	8.0	13.6	18.1	18.1	15.7	14.3	12.3	10.9	9.8	9.1	8.6	9.1	9.2	8.7	8.2
Women	2.7	5.1	9.6	14.4	14.8	15.1	14.9	13.0	12.0	10.7	10.6	9.7	9.1	8.9	8.9	8.6
Total	3.2	6.6	11.7	16.3	16.6	15.4	14.6	12.7	11.4	10.2	9.8	9.1	9.1	9	8.8	8.4

Note: The percentages in this table are calculated of the active workforce, not of the entire population (www.stat.fi). This table also excludes immigrant workers. Their situation was, and has remained, significantly more severe than that of Finnish-origin workers. In 1994, the unemployment rate for immigrants was 53 percent; in 2003 it remained at 29 percent. In the case of certain nationalities, the situation was a lot worse. For example, among the Somali, who had arrived in Finland at the turn of the 1990s mainly as quota refugees, the unemployment rate was 92 percent in 1994 and remained at 58 percent in 2003 (Ahmad 2005, 11).

Source: Statistics Finland 2006.

factors such as the collapse of the bilateral trade between Finland and the Soviet Union, drove the state economy to a freefall (Tainio 2006). The economic recession started in Finland earlier and with a deeper plunge than in most other European countries. This was manifested almost immediately in a very high mass unemployment rate (see Keinänen 1999; Julkunen 2001, 299). By the end of the 1980s, the unemployment rate was lower in Finland than in EU member states on an average. As shown in table 4.1, the situation degenerated rapidly: the unemployment rate nearly quintupled in five years from 1990 to 1994.

During 1993–1994 the number of unemployed job seekers was over half a million people of the total population of five million. The figures would be much higher still if involuntary part-timers and those attending training courses were included (see Helin 1998, 64–6; Keinänen 1999; Julkunen 2001; *Työpoliittinen Aikakauskirja* 2003, 53). Thereafter, the unemployment rate started to fall slowly, but stayed for a long time on a higher level than the EU average (in 1999, EU15 10 percent; Finland 14.5 percent). In 2005 the rate reached a low point of 8.4 percent, and fell below the EU average, 6.4 percent, in 2008 (Tilastokeskus 2009). The unemployment rate was in the 1990s—and still is—highest in the northern and eastern parts of Finland and lowest in the economically prosperous capital area and other southern provinces (Hokkanen 2000, 160–2; *Työpoliittinen Aikakauskirja* 2005, 52).

The participation of Finnish women in the workforce has traditionally been higher than in most other OECD countries. In Finland, the dual-breadwinner model replaced the agrarian family model rather rapidly and directly, and wage work has been traditionally regarded as the cornerstone of women's emancipation. Moreover, women's participation in the Finnish labor market has been based on full-time work, unlike in most other European and also Nordic countries, where a considerable number of women work part-time (Bergman 2002, 202). The Finnish labor market is, however, heavily gender-segregated, and wage differences between men and women remain important.[4] The unemployment crisis of the 1990s touched industries mainly using male laborers first (e.g., building), and reached the typical female sectors later (public sector and services). From 1996 on, female unemployment has been higher, and more slowly descending than male unemployment.

One of the characteristics of the 1990s unemployment was its strong influence on upper-strata and middle-class professions. In this way, the new unemployment can be seen as "negative equalization" (Weber 1976 ([1922]). In the 1990s, an important part of the senior unemployed population was forced to early retirements. Approximately half of the jobs held by persons aged fifty-five–fifty-nine vanished during the first half of the 1990s (Huovinen and Piekkola 2001, 249). By contrast, young unemployed were obliged to attend training in return for unemployment benefits. Mass unemployment also speeded up structural changes on the labor market, accelerating especially the development of a (hitherto insignificant) market of temporary jobs. The Finnish society struggled to recover from the economic recession burdened by prolonged mass unemployment, unstable labor market, and high state debt. New requirements concerning the Finnish welfare state were deduced from these economic factors, and demands for increase in the effectiveness of the administration, wide-ranging social policy reforms, development of the pension systems, and the integration of the Finnish economy to the EU were supported unanimously by all big political parties, including the "traditional" opposition forces, such as the Greens and the Left Alliance. Elite groups and power structures were thus buffered from citizen opinion and demands (Julkunen 2001, 64 and 290–8; Siisiäinen 2003, 52–3).

During this period, the Finnish societal situation was thus characterized by a strong economic recession followed by a broad consensus among the political elite in order to transform deeply the social benefits scheme. In the following, we examine the reactions of the Finnish civil society, notably the unemployed, to the crisis of the early 1990s and the societal situation followed by it.

The Movement of the Unemployed since the 1990s

On November 4, 1993, some 20,000 people gathered in the streets of Helsinki to demand actions against growing unemployment and to protest against the welfare benefit cuts that the center-right government enforced as the primary cure to the state economy's misery. Trade unions organized bus transport from different parts of Finland, and the demonstration brought together trade union activists, the unemployed, as well as general public. The demonstration that the trade union organizers named "Revolution-Thursday" was, and still remains, one of the largest mass gatherings of the post–World War II era in Finland.[5]

Notwithstanding its scale, the protest neither had any important effect on government policies, nor did it succeed to expand collective action against unemployment. A similar kind of mass mobilization never reoccurred. The main reason for the demobilization of the protest was the disengagement of the main trade unions. The latter backpedaled from supporting the unemployed, particularly since 1995. In that year, both the Social Democrats and The Left Alliance joined the government in the so-called rainbow coalition. Consequently, the most important blue-collar trade union chapter, the Central Organization of Finnish Trade Unions (SAK), thus had its own political allies in the government rows, and it refrained thence from all protest and contentious action, securing its own position in negotiations with the government.

The trade unions did, however, continue to support the associations of the unemployed financially.

Even though the unemployed were rather organized in their own associations already by 1995, they nevertheless failed to mobilize an influential protest movement on their own. Instead, they formed a network of institutionalized actors at the local as well as the national level, which enabled them to even contest issues on some occasions. The central focus of the activities, however, came to be in self-help and lobbying, not in contentious action. In sum, the protest movement of the unemployed began with an energetic mobilization, but rapidly took a more typical course within the Finnish context, and became essentially focused in associational activities.

Voluntary associations can be described as the backbone organizational form of the Finnish civil society, which can be characterized even as an "organization syndrome," with a high level of institutional organization, and difficulties in organizing collective action without going through registration formalities. New collective action tends to rapidly take the form of officially registered associations in order to gain credibility in the eyes of an organization-keen society, and thereafter to improve chances of receiving funding from the state institutions. In other words, to be taken seriously in the Finnish context, formal registration, neat paperwork, and "respectable" agenda are good bets. Gaining credibility, then, is often equal to avoiding means of protest disapproved by the established power (see Siisiäinen 1990 and 2009).

In the case of the unemployed, the model pupil image vis-à-vis the surrounding society is strong. When mass unemployment started sweeping across the country in the early 1990s, the unemployed put their first mobilization efforts into creating associations. As shown in figure 4.1, from 1992 on, new associations of the unemployed mushroomed by the dozen each year.

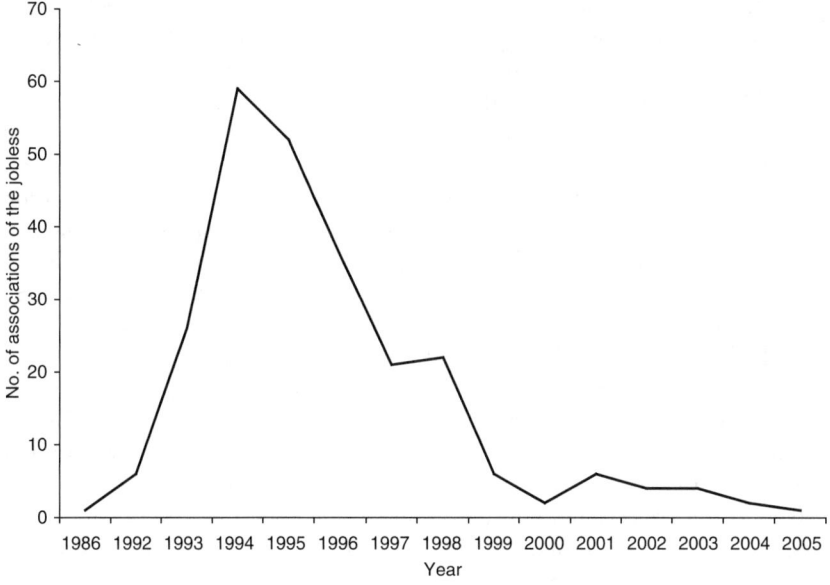

Figure 4.1 Registration of new associations of the unemployed in Finland (1986–2005).

Such an increase invites at least two main observations. First, the number of new associations grew along with the increase of the unemployment rate, reflecting the reaction of the Finnish civil society to that problem and its capacity to find forms of expression to the social problems. Second, the level of creation of new associations of the unemployed has been very low in the 2000s, slowly approaching zero, regardless of the rather stagnating unemployment rate. It would thus seem that the associations defending the unemployed nowadays form a rather stabilized field.

In the following, we look at the activities of the organization of the unemployed from three viewpoints. First, we focus on the national-level representation of the unemployed that emerged from the trade unions' armpit, but quickly became an independent umbrella organization. Second, we describe activities and activists of some local associations of the unemployed. Finally, we analyze the media representations of the activities of the unemployed.

Collective Action at the National Level: Representing the Unemployed

The National Cooperation Network of the Unemployed in Finland (*Työttömien Valtakunnallinen Yhteistoimintaverkosto*; TVY, as referred to from now on) was set up in 1991, initiated by a group of local associations of the unemployed in the middle of the dashing increase in unemployment. At best, TVY had almost 250 member organizations, and even in 2005, there were 171 associations in 164 cities or municipalities. In addition to the local scope, TVY has always been active internationally, especially in the European framework.[6] Since its creation, TVY has published a quarterly magazine *Karenssisanomat*, distributed free of charge in job centers, libraries, and in offices of the associations of the unemployed. Since 1994, TVY has organized the so-called unemployed human rights festival, an annual seminar and get-together event during which topical debates and workshops are organized alongside more recreational and social activities. In addition, TVY organizes a plethora of training and cultural events and lobbying seminars. Currently, Finland's Slot Machine Association (RAY) is TVY's main finance, whereas the Ministry of Labor and the Evangelical Lutheran Church of Finland provide minor support.

The founding idea of TVY was not only to form an umbrella organization for the associations of the unemployed, but also to create a strong lobbying and representation structure for the unemployed. The trade unions, especially the SAK, did not agree with the organization's second goal. From the trade union's point of view, TVY quickly became a threatening competitor, and after a short period of support in the beginning of the 1990s, SAK made several attempts to lessen the importance and, in practice, hinder the working of TVY. SAK's maneuvers included, for example, the creation of a central division for the unemployed within its own structures. These efforts did not put TVY off, but the rivalry was energy-consuming, as the newly founded association had to defend its right to exist not only to its political opponents, but also to hoped-for allies. However, the division for the unemployed of SAK did not manage to establish a firm foothold among the unemployed from different sectors of labor, and it soon died out without fanfare.

In the conflict-laden context of the organization's first steps, TVY's main objective, according to one of the founding members, was "to create collectiveness." Mass unemployment sweeping the country touched somewhat equally extremely different branches of employment, and thus made TVY's original recruitment and lobbying grounds challengingly heterogeneous. Alongside with political lobby and representation, the social emergency of mass unemployment was at the heart of TVY's foundation. The activists were deeply concerned about the unemployed "getting stuck inside the four walls," and thus becoming passive and marginalized. Thus, the national organization put a lot of effort in forming and supporting the creation of means to activate the unemployed on different levels. As a result, cafeterias for the unemployed were started up by dozens in order to offer budget meals, meeting places, and meaningful activities to the unemployed throughout the country. Similarly, a myriad of sports courses and happenings were rapidly organized in order to "keep up the spirit" among the unemployed.

After the "state of emergency" at the beginning of the 1990s, many of the activities TVY organized in the beginning have been taken over by the local associations of the unemployed. TVY has thus been able to concentrate increasingly on lobbying for the improvement of the unemployed status and representing its members' interests nationally.

The current lobbying practices by TVY follow in many respects the trade union model, and it has proven relatively successful, especially in terms of gaining access to high-level negotiations. According to a TVY representative, "Lobbying includes nowadays... committee visits and hearings, evaluation of bills and proposals from the point of view of the unemployed, participating in ministry working groups as well as in teamwork with different partners and cooperation networks."

TVY has made its way to ministry meetings and parliamentary committees during its fifteen years of existence, both due to their successful work and to the relatively low access threshold to ministry-level negotiations within the Finnish system of corporatism. Access, however, does not necessarily equal influence. A TVY representative's own estimation of the organization's power of influence was nevertheless rather self-confident:

> I would say that the old civic organizations have struggled for a long time to get where we are right now, sitting at the same table with the minister. The Minister of Labor, when I send her a message that I need an appointment, well, as soon as there's space in her calendar, I do get it.

The situation varies, however, due to party lines and government compositions: according to the interviewed TVY representative, the Social Democrats, the Left Alliance, and the Greens were considered as the loyal allies of TVY. The minister of labor is TVY's most crucial partner, and at the time of the interview (in 2006) the post had been occupied by first a Social Democrat and then a Green Minister, which is no doubt one reason for the very positive insight into governmental cooperation above.

The functions of TVY have undergone several transformations over the years: in the very beginning, it mainly joined the choir of the trade unions pushing forward, for example, protection of earnings. In the 2000s, a TVY representative said that their main concerns were those "undefended by the unions; those who have dropped out of the net." The configuration of alliances has also progressively shifted, slipping away from the trade union organizations to the benefit of a closer partnership with other organizations of the civil society. TVY has got increasingly engaged in various anti-marginalization projects most typically organized in cooperation with some of the biggest Finnish volunteer organizations, such as the Finnish Red Cross and the Mannerheim League for Child Protection. In addition, many TVY representatives considered the Lutheran church as the most promising partner for TVY in the future.[7]

In sum, TVY has become well integrated in the Finnish system of corporatist governance. It may have lost the most influential ally it had in the beginning, the trade unions, but it has gained a stable position as a partner of many other institutions and actors. Also, TVY's lobbying objectives have shifted from the general claim of decreasing unemployment to specifically representing the interests of the unemployed.

Collective Action at the Local Level: Actors and Activities

Many Finnish associations of the unemployed existed already before the recession, but it was in the early and mid-1990s that their numbers multiplied over a short period of time. Most of the new local associations were, to begin with, founded with a strong emphasis on social support and inexpensive recreational activities, possibilities of keeping fit, and other means of preventing exclusion. Come the 2000s, some associations have vanished, but many still have activities. What has become of the associations founded during the "heyday" of unemployed workers' movement? Who are the active members, and what do the associations do? In the following, we search for answers to these questions both by looking at TVY member associations in general, drawing from a study of the associations' websites, as well as the TVY member survey, and second, and by focusing more closely on one local association, the Unemployed of Helsinki (*Helsingin Työttömät*, HeTy).[8]

The profile of the activists in the local associations of the unemployed shared common features in the whole country. A typical activist's past occupation was a blue-collar job, s/he was over fifty years of age, had a trade union background, and a rather long experience of unemployment. The associations of the unemployed were thus marked by a certain generational divide: although the volunteer centers and cooperatives gathered people from different age groups to enjoy their services, the key activists were mostly senior long-term unemployed often with a politically active trade unionist background.

Also the founding members of the Helsinki local chapter, HeTy, were—mainly male—blue-collar trade union activists. The core group of the association's activists consisted of some 30 volunteers, accompanied by some 150 sporadically attending ones. The average age was over fifty, and the group of activists had not changed significantly during the past years: new people had not joined in droves. A familiar crowd and routine activities pleased many of the activists: "It's a good pastime when one has time." The interviewees explained the absence of young unemployed by saying that they "do not have a choice, they have to try to find a job," implying that being active in an association for the unemployed was not necessarily thought to support job seeking, but rather as an option to it.

The activists in HeTy were quasi-entirely Finno-Finnish, and the absence of immigrant-background unemployed in the associations seemed to be a dominant feature nationwide. Especially in the context of the 2000s, the absence of ethnically non-Finns becomes an outstanding issue from the viewpoint of the extremely high unemployment figures of immigrant-background workers (e.g., Ahmad 2005). The phenomenon of micro-level mobilization based on a shared ethnicity has been discussed, for instance, in studies of the feminist movement: it does not necessarily imply ethnic discrimination of any kind, but the barriers for participation of those not sharing the same cultural background can simply be so high that no attempts to participate occur (Charles 2004, 256).

Regarding the gender composition of the unemployed activists, there was a remote majority of women in positions of trust according to the lists presented on the associations' websites. In the interviews, however, gender balance in the associations was described as rather even in general, although all informants seemed to be aware of some association in which either men or women dominated the activities. These cases were typically presented as stories heard from other associations, not from the informant's immediate environment. Apparent discrimination of either gender group was unknown to the people we talked to, but in some cases, the associations' practices showed signs of structurally gendered implications:

> In some associations there is maybe male dominance, so that, I do not think that women would have deliberately been pushed away, but that it is strongly male, the activities have been developed so that there is a lot to do for men and nothing to women... So there has been male-dominant values... we have units where those values appear. (Unemployed activist, F)
>
> It might be that this division of roles has influence so that women do the sales stuff and baking, and then in other tasks there are men. Maybe it is because of the previous occupations, women have been in the service sector and they are nattier with this stuff. (Unemployed activist, M)

There is no surprise in the finding that some practices and actions taken by the associations probably followed gendered logics. The Finnish unemployed make no exception to the constant empirical result that a gendered division of labor is often a typical feature of social movements and voluntary associations (e.g., Charles 2004, 264; Luhtakallio 2007). It was, nevertheless, clear that gender was not considered a substantial issue in the associations of the unemployed. The nonidentification of the gender dimension in associational life is typical to the Finnish context. Despite, for instance, the strong gender segregation of the labor market, the Finnish society is penetrated with the idea of prevailing gender equality, often impeding the articulation of contradicting experiences (Holli, Luhtakallio, and Raevaara 2006 and 2007). Unequal or even discriminating gender relations have been identified as important demobilizing factors within social movements (e.g., Dunezat 1998). In the light of the current data it is, however, impossible to further evaluate this argument in the case of the Finnish unemployed.

In her study of the associations of the unemployed as self-help groups, Marianne Nylund (2000) suggested that in the mid-1990s "campaigning was far from being the only reason why the associations were set up; unemployed people were just motivated by the desire to meet other people in a similar situation" (102). This argument proved its strength also in our study. The raisons d'être the associations presented on their websites emphasized clearly other activities at the cost of contentious political action. In table 4.2, the activities presented and described by the associations on their websites have been structured to five main categories.

It was noteworthy that lobbying, meaning all forms of political activities from demonstrating to claims-making was presented as the association's central activity in less than half of the cases. The most frequently mentioned categories were recreational activities and service provision. The former included a variety of low-budget leisure possibilities for the unemployed: sports and dancing courses, collective trips to art exhibitions, and craft workshops. The latter consisted of services provided by the association's volunteers and employees to outsiders: catering, renovation projects and other small jobs, recycling facilities, and so on. Training and employment services were often intertwined. The associations organize a variety of courses—for example, in ADP skills and languages—in order to enhance the employability of their members.

The case of HeTy illustrated well the effort of service provision. One of the association's main activities and sources of income was catering. This has made

Table 4.2 Main activities in local associations of the unemployed in Finland in 2005 (*N* = 39)

Type of activity	Number of associations providing the activity
Recreation	36
Service provision	36
Employment	27
Training	26
Lobbying	17

Note: Only 23 percent of the TVY member associations had functioning websites at the time of the study, and are thus included in this part of the data. However, the data collected from the sites were rather homogenous and saturated quickly, which increased the reliability of the material. We also assumed that the associations with functioning websites were currently the most active ones.

the association an important actor in the social movement circles in Helsinki, as it seemed to cooperate with nearly everybody as a catering services provider. Whenever there was a mass event or a small happening—be it the Helsinki Social Forum, an annual festival of multiculturalism, or a seminar of a small citizen group challenging the city administration—the unemployed would be there with their industrial-size cooking apparatus selling soup, coffee, buns, and sausages. These activities seemed apolitical at first glance, but the interviews revealed that the association followed a certain agenda in offering their services. The price of the catering services depended somewhat on the "customer," so that HeTy would cater events organized by less institutionalized actors with scarce resources at their own risk, as an activist explained in the following:

> Like for instance students, when...they had this...demonstration [and we catered for them for free]...so in a way we give support to civic activities...because we have this point of view that more citizens are active, more they pay attention to other people's interests than their own, and thereby the political benefit will come at some point.

Another frequent form of activity in HeTy was the weekly "street kitchen," described as the associations' "most important regular mode of fieldwork." Moving from a neighborhood to another, the street kitchen group combined charity work and lobbying by distributing free soup and inviting politicians to give talks and to discuss with the crowd. The street kitchen had two main objectives: to get in touch with the unemployed who do not come to the association's premises, and to promote the image of the unemployed.

Contentious activities were marginalized in the associations of the unemployed in general, but with the example of HeTy and the underlying political logic of catering, it is possible to see a somewhat "sleeping" political agenda behind some of the associations' practices. The informants talked about cooperation with local politicians, and made it rather clear that the unemployed remained committed to their mostly leftist backgrounds, although notably the Social Democrats were heavily criticized for having "forgotten" the cause of the unemployed. Right-wing parties were never mentioned as potential partners. It seemed that the extremely slow improvement of the nationwide employment rate, and the lack of strong political acts in favor of the unemployed, combined with the wearisome personal experience of long unemployment, had made many of the activists rather pessimistic vis-à-vis their power of influence. When asked to evaluate the associations' success concerning political objectives, a long-term HeTy activist sounded rather pessimistic:

> In some scale we have succeeded [in lobbying government bills and bringing up problems] but of course it is all peanuts, the basic questions are all unsolved. It indeed is quite difficult to fix anything right now. And that of course shows in many unemployed so that many do not vote because nothing makes a difference, or at least it seems that there's no way to make a difference, no matter what one does.

Perhaps the most surprising dimension of the current development of the Finnish associations of the unemployed was their role as *employers*. According to TVY statistics concerning its member associations, there were altogether thirteen forms of employment support used by the associations to remunerate their employees, such as different state-subsidized employment measures, rehabilitation support, and municipality service budgets. The majority of the employees in the associations and cooperatives were remunerated with different combinations of support by the Social Insurance Institution of Finland (KELA), the Ministry of Labor, and the EU social and structural funds. The employees' statuses varied from employment trainees to offenders doing community service. The most common fields of employment activity were ecological community services, such as recycling, and charity or low-budget restaurant services. In several localities, the association of the unemployed was responsible for the organization of the municipal recycling center and all its activities, in which case some associations were able to have employees on their own account as well: recycling was clearly the biggest and the most profitable activity for the local associations of the unemployed.

In the case of the Helsinki unemployed, there was no goldmine recycling business at hand, but the informants explained that, nevertheless, the association had an active employment policy: it tried to "employ everyone wanting to work," and thus keep up a reputation of an open house that turned no one away. The long-term HeTy activists had a solid experience in scraping together state and city subsidies for employment. At the time of the study, there were some twenty employees in HeTy, who mainly took care of different tasks at the bureau and the cafeteria.

Nationally, the associations of the unemployed had altogether 4,235 employees in 2005. In addition, 1,282 volunteers were reported to work in the associations. This total of 5,517 paid workers or volunteers rendered the associations important employers, especially in some smaller towns and districts. For example, in Kuhmo, a small town of 11,348 inhabitants in northeastern Finland, the association of the unemployed was the second largest employer of the town, after the municipal administration (*TVY Jäsentutkimus* 2005 [Member Association Survey]). Many of the associations had actually gradually turned into social enterprises and cooperatives in the course of their existence since the early 1990s. At the same time, the share of voluntary work in the associations had declined abruptly, and correspondingly paid work had increased significantly.

If it was possible to conclude that the national organization of the unemployed, TVY, had become well integrated in the Finnish system, looking at the local activities of the unemployed provoke similar conclusions. The associations have found their niche in the Finnish civil society: they have their special branches of expertise and their own focus group. They may feel powerless vis-à-vis their *political* objectives, but they are by no means completely marginalized or excluded. On the contrary, they play an important and powerful role in several local settings as employers, volunteer centers, and service providers.

Media Representations of the Movement of the Unemployed

So far, we have described the development of unemployed workers' national- and local-level organization since the beginning of the 1990s. In order to fully assess the case of the Finnish unemployed as a social movement, we next we look at the representations of the movement in the Finnish media debate through an analysis of articles concerning the unemployed' movement in the country's leading journal *Helsingin Sanomat*.[9] The data cover two time periods: the depression era from 1991 to 1995, and the era of strong economic growth combined with the preservation of high long-term unemployment rate, from 2000 to 2004. We found a total 164 articles reporting exclusively on unemployed people's collective activities. The articles were studied using content analytical reading. As a result, we found four main categories of representation that occurred during both periods of time: self-help, support, protest, and claim-making. In table 4.3, the data have been arranged according to these categories.

Self-help consisted of a large range of the activities of the unemployed aimed at enhancing their life collectively. Right from the start, the category of self-help was by far the most common context of media representations of the activities of the unemployed. The articles included a variety of viewpoints: that of the unemployed, that of local authorities, and that of aid organizations and their volunteers. Different kinds of voluntary work projects were constantly reported, such as the unemployed organizing free food distribution and clothes recycling markets. The activities can be characterized as mainly nonpolitical: all kinds of recreational activities, such as gym classes, trips to museums, and the like, were widely represented within this category, alongside with crisis interventions, such as group therapy. In the 1990s, however, the self-help activities consisted most typically of the unemployed renovating municipality-owned real estate all over Finland in order to open clubhouses for themselves, and launching or managing cafeterias, whereas in the 2000s, they focused mainly on running training centers and employment cooperatives.

Support could be summed up as reports on helping the unemployed. The articles in this category were principally about the activities of other organizations working to ease the situation of the unemployed. Support and help given varied from food supply to assistance in employment. Typical actors mentioned in these articles were, for example, the Lutheran church and the Salvation Army. Reports of help to the unemployed lessened radically from the 1990s

Table 4.3 Articles concerning the collective action of the unemployed in Finland (*Helsingin Sanomat*, 1991–1995 and 2000–2004)

Themes/ years	Self-help	Support	Protest	Claim-making	Other	Total
1991–1995	46	23	22	25	7	*123*
2000–2004	17	9	4	11	–	*41*
Total	63	32	26	36	7	*164*

to the 2000s, and also a more qualitative change was detectable. Whereas the unemployed were incontestably the most important recipients of help from these organizations in the 1990s, in the 2000s they constituted only one of the groups in need, alongside the pauperized elderly, families with small children, and immigrants.

The category of *protest* contained stories of demonstrations, demands to organize one, and reactions to demonstrations held. During the entire period, the majority of articles in this category were reports of trade union demonstrations and strike actions in which the unemployed and their associations had taken part, but had not been the main organizers. This was the case also in 1991, the only year where the number of articles concerning demonstrations was a dominant feature of the public representations of the collective activities of the unemployed. There were, however, also a few reports on revolts of the unemployed. The most covered one was the demonstration of the so-called Revolution-Thursday in 1993 that gained media attention during several days. It is noteworthy, however, that in the 2000s all articles concerning demonstrations were, with one exception, reminiscences of the biggest demonstration in 1993 in terms of its tenth anniversary, or the like.

Claim-making consisted of other forms of political action of the unemployed. The category included public statements and demands of the organizations of the unemployed concerning different political issues. Also, there were opinions of individual unemployed, as well as of others making claims on behalf of the unemployed. In these articles, space was given to the protagonists either on the opinion section or within articles written by favorable journalists; a plethora of political suggestions to solve the problems of the unemployed, as well as the problem of unemployment altogether, entered the public debate.

The immense majority of these media representations support our previous analysis based on the interviews and other data: the unemployed were not seen as a radicalized movement in Finland in the 1990s, and even less so in the 2000s. The media representations emphasized remarkably, often ringing almost educational, the bravery and diligence of the unemployed. This emphasis is rather surprising, considered strictly from the point of view of the news media: wouldn't demonstrations and other more contentious activities supposedly make more *news* than a bunch of people renovating a house? However, the general message concerning the activities of the unemployed seemed to be that this group of people was maybe angry, but more importantly, they put their energy, paradoxically enough, to work.

However, the media representations also provided small fractures to this smooth image. First, although mainly noncontentious self-help and support activities prevailed in number, even these representations often included more or less direct criticism of the situation of the unemployed. Critical tones came up in reports, for instance, of a local priest, spending his time in ragged bars trying to find the unemployed and talk them out of the drinking spin.

Second, in mid-1990s there were several reports on the planning, realization, and launching of the new unit of the Finnish police: the Riot Police forces. In these articles, the demonstrations of the unemployed were constantly mentioned—by the journalist or by the commenting police representative—as an argument for the need of the new type of police force in Finland. This detail can be seen as a symbolically strong indicator of a more or less conscious fear of a possible radicalization of the unemployed.

Third, among the opinion-type articles in the data, people were asking why there were no demonstrations and no collective rebellion against unemployment. In rather bitter tones, these writers wondered why the unemployed were not angry, thus making it clear that they actually were. The few but straightforward opinion texts instigating more radical action against unemployment show that sentiments of frustration indeed existed regarding the somewhat lame reaction of the civil society toward mass unemployment and the fate of the unemployed. It is impossible to know how many opinions of this kind were actually sent to newspapers during the years of the recession. Nevertheless, there seems to have been a common awareness of the *possibility of a radicalization* of the protest by the unemployed, and parties that feared it, as well as parties that were hoping for it.

Conclusion

In the post-operative treatment of the recession of the 1990s the order of preference of the Finnish government was clear: first came the interests of the (export) industry (competitiveness, etc.), second the interests of the central trade unions of the private sector and their members, and only third the interests of those unemployed who were dependent on the system of general benefits provided by the state. The main line was that the reforms of social welfare systems took most away from the poorest and from those who did not have a strong organization to advance their interests (e.g., Julkunen 2001; Heiskala and Luhtakallio 2006).

The story of the mobilization of the unemployed on November 4, 1993, suggests that the political mobilization of the unemployed in Finland depended on the attitude of the trade unions toward them. In the beginning of the 1990s, strong support of the trade unions, especially SAK, helped the unemployed overcome several factors hindering mobilization. On the one hand, SAK's material and staff resources enabled concrete organization of mass gatherings. On the other hand, the support of SAK alongside with the general sentiment of societal crisis perhaps momentarily removed the stigma of unemployment and thus made the massive mobilization possible. However, after the trade unions had pulled out, the mobilization became increasingly difficult. The stigma of unemployment, especially strong in the highly work-centered Finnish culture, re-disabled mobilization, and the state of "general emergency" in the country started invoking the entire cultural reserve of (perhaps forced) consensus and common effort. The depth of the consensus—or more accurately the depth of an ethos of inevitability—becomes manifest when the government coalitions of the post-recession era are considered: between 1995 and 2003 without interruption, the farthermost left and right parties (and nearly everything in between them) belonged to the government together in the so-called rainbow coalition. This kind of a coalition is hardly imaginable in most democratic countries. In the Finnish society however, lack of political options is the predominant embodiment of the period in question. Thus, the poor chances of success for a wide, massively mobilized, and highly contentious movement of the unemployed in Finland can be reduced to the basic argument already stated by Weber (1976 [1922]): a precondition for the emergence of a social movement is the shared sentiment that things *could* be different. This sentiment was not available in 1990–2000 Finland.

According to the unemployed activists, the basic questions and problems of the unemployed are majorly the same today as during the recession. For the long-term unemployed, getting employed has not become easier. Depression and the sentiment of disability to influence one's life are blatant. In the associations of the unemployed, activists feel pessimistic about their chances of achieving any improvement to the situation on their own, and powerful allies are hard to imagine. However, the Finnish unemployed have created a professional-like lobbying network at the national level, and a somewhat dense web of local associations functioning as self-help groups and as major employers. This way, they have found their place in the current organigram of the Finnish society. The number of still active associations shows the widespread and lively nature of Finnish organizations of the unemployed. This line of development has certainly helped many unemployed in a concrete way, but it has neither gained the unemployed visibility in politics, nor gotten them to mobilize efficient social pressure to attain their goals. Analysis of the media representations of the unemployed supports this interpretation: after the first years of the recession with unemployment as striking news, the activities of the unemployed have lost most of their media visibility. Also, the issues the media found the most worth reporting were not linked to political contentiousness, but to efforts of finding useful occupations for the unemployed. In sum, it can be suggested that the Finnish unemployed movement is less about opposing unemployment, and more about creating concessions for coping with it.

In the context of hardening values and increasing polarization of the Finnish society, however, we suggest that in addition to the aforementioned facts, the movement of the unemployed failed to become a political force because there was not much discursive space for questioning the blessedness of the new direction. In the escalating rush for competitiveness, there has been only little attention available for those who fell by the wayside. The only way to stay in the game at least to some extent seems to be to become an expert in one's field, do one's job without causing trouble, and accept the predominance of the official discourse of what kind of a society Finland is, be it in whatever contradiction with one's own reality. In these partly rewarding, partly embittering tasks the Finnish unemployed have succeeded well.

Notes

The authors want to thank M.Soc.Sc Sanna Määttänen for her diligent assistance in collecting the data for this study, as well as academy research fellow Raija Julkunen and professor Risto Alapuro for their valuable comments on different versions of this text.

1. At the beginning of the last century, e.g., seasonal unemployment of farm workers was not regarded as "unemployment" at all. Due to the changing nature of the phenomenon itself, it is also difficult to distinguish collective action of the unemployed as a separate group of actors prior to the 1960s.
2. The Finnish Civil War was fought from January to May 1918, between the forces of Finland's Social Democrats led by the Red Peoples Delegation of Finland, commonly called the "Reds," and the forces of the conservative Senate, commonly called the "Whites." The Reds were supported by Bolshevist Russia, while the Whites received military assistance from the German Empire and Swedish volunteers. The White forces were victorious, but approximately 37,000 people died during the conflict, including casualties at the war fronts, deaths from political terror campaigns, and high prison camp mortality. The turmoil destroyed the economy, split the political apparatus, and divided the Finnish nation for years (e.g., Zetterberg 2003, 599–610; for a sociological analysis, see Alapuro 1988).
3. The Finnish income policy relies on the so-called tripartite negotiations. The most important and powerful representative of the employees is *Suomen Ammattiliittojen Keskusjärjestö* (SAK, The Central Organization of Finnish Trade Unions), which is the parent organization of blue-collar unions.
4. For 2005, the estimate of the Statistics Finland was that women's average wages were 80.9 percent of men's average wages (Tilastokeskus 2007).
5. In comparison, the biggest march against nuclear power gathered some 6,000 participants in 2002, and the demonstration against the U.S. war in Iraq some 10,000 people in 2003 (Villanen 2004).
6. ENU, the European Network of the Unemployed (see Royall 2002), has had a TVY delegate as its chairperson since 1999. TVY delegations also participate in the gatherings of the organizations of the unemployed in Europe, such as the meeting concerning the social security of the European unemployed organized in spring 2008 in Paris by the French organization MNCP (Vauhkonen 2008).
7. The Evangelical Lutheran Church of Finland has become increasingly active in cooperation with the civil society in the past years. It supports (financially and by offering material support and venue facilities) and participates in a plethora of activities from anti-marginalization, anti-poverty, and anti-solitude projects to social forums and the defense of refugees under threat of eviction. The church is established as a state church and it has the right to collect taxes.
8. Our analysis rests, first, on data collected from the websites of local associations in 2005, and on the TVY member association survey (2005). For the case study of the "unemployed of Helsinki", HeTy, we interviewed activists, collected and analyzed web and other material, and used the association's archive material as background information.
9. *Helsingin Sanomat* is Finland's leading newspaper and the only truly nationwide newspaper with the circulation of 430,785 in year 2005 (Sanoma WSOY Oyj 2005, 24). The newspaper data were collected through use of the electronic archives of *Helsingin Sanomat*. The entries used to get a general picture of the media coverage of the activities of the unemployed were: Unemployment + organization/Unemployed + organization; Unemployment + association/Unemployed + association; Unemployment + protest/Unemployed + protest; Unemployment + demonstration/Unemployed + demonstration; Unemployment + trade union/Unemployed + trade union.

References

Ahmad, Akhlaq. 2005. Getting a Job in Finland: The Social Networks of Immigrants from the Indian Subcontinent in the Helsinki Metropolitan Labour Market. PhD diss., University of Helsinki.

Alapuro, Risto. 1988. *State and Revolution in Finland*. Berkeley: University of California Press.

Bergman, Solveig. 2002. *The Politics of Feminism. Autonomous Feminist Movements in Finland and West-Germany from the 1960s to the 1980s*. Åbo. Åbo Akademi University Press.

Charles, Nickie. 2004. Feminism, Social Movements and the Political Order. In *Democracy and Participation: Popular Protest and New Social Movements*, ed. Gary Taylor and Malcolm Todd, 248–72. London: Merlin Press.

Dunezat, Xavier. 1998. Des mouvements sociaux sexués. *Nouvelles questions féministes* 19(2–4)/*Recherches féministes* 11(2), 161–95.

Esping-Andersen, Gøsta. 1990. *The Three Worlds of Welfare Capitalism.* Cambridge: Polity Press.

Heiskala, Risto. 2006. Sosiaaliset innovaatiot ja hegemonisten mallien muutokset: kuinka tulkita Suomen 1990-luvun murrosta? [Social Innovations and Transformations in Hegemonic Models: How to Interprete Change in Finland in the 1990s] In *Uusi jako—Miten Suomesta tuli kilpailukyky-yhteiskunta?*, ed. Risto Heiskala and Eeva Luhtakallio, 202–17. Helsinki: Gaudeamus.

Heiskala, Risto, and Eeva Luhtakallio, ed. 2006. *Uusi jako—Miten Suomesta tuli kilpailukyky-yhteiskunta?* [The New Deal – How Finland Became a Competition Society] Helsinki: Gaudeamus.

Helin, Vesa. 1998. *Trendit—Kymmenvuotiskatsaus*. [The Trends – A Decade Report] Helsinki: Tilastokeskus.

Hokkanen, Liisa. 2000. Peer support as paid work. In *The Third Sector in Finland*, ed. Martti Siisiäinen, Petri Kinnunen, and Elina Hietanen, 127–51. Helsinki: The Finnish Federation of Social Welfare and Health.

Holli, Anne Maria, Eeva Luhtakallio, and Eeva Raevaara. 2006. The Quota Trouble Talking About Gender Quotas in Finnish Local Politics. *International Feminist Journal of Politics* 8(2), 169–93.

Holli, Anne Maria, Eeva Luhtakallio, and Eeva Raevaara. 2007. *Sukupuolten valta/kunta. Politiikka, muutos ja vastarinta suomalaisissa kunnissa*. [Gender and Politics, Change, and Resistance in Finnish Municipalities] Tampere: Vastapaino.

Huovinen, Pasi, and Piekkola, Hannu. 2001. Unemployment and Early Retirements of the Finnish Aged Workers in 1989–1996. In *Down from the Heavens, Up from the Ashes. The Finnish Economic Crisis in the Light of Economic and Social Research*, ed. Jorma Kalela, Jaakko Kiander, Ullamaija Kivikuru, Heikki A. Loikkanen, and Jussi Simpura, 249–76. Helsinki: Government Institute for Economic Research.

Julkunen, Raija. 2001. *Suunnanmuutos. 1990-luvun sosiaalipoliittinen reformi Suomessa*. [Change of Direction. The 1990s Social Policy Reform in Finland] Tampere: Vastapaino.

Kautto Mikko, Johan Fritzell, Bjørn Hvinden, Jon Kvist, and Hannu Uusitalo. 2001. *Nordic Welfare States in the European context*. London: Routledge.

Keinänen, Päivi. 1999. Työttömyys. [Unemployment] In *Suomen vuosisata*, ed. Kristiina Andreasson and Vesa Helin, 74–7. Helsinki: Tilastokeskus.

Luhtakallio, Eeva. 2007. Kansalaistoiminnan ulottuvuudet. [The Dimensions of Civic Action] In *Sukupuolten valta/kunta. Politiikka, muutos ja vastarinta suomalaisissa*

kunnissa. Anne Maria Holli, Eeva Luhtakallio, and Eeva Raevaara, 167–206. Tampere: Vastapaino.
Matthies, Aila-Leena, Ulla Kotakari, and Marianne Nylund, ed. 1996. *Välittävät verkostot.* [Mediating Networks] Tampere: Vastapaino.
Nylund, Marianne. 2000. *Varieties of Mutual Support and Voluntary Action. A Study of Self-Help Groups and Volunteers.* Helsinki: The Finnish Federation for Social Welfare and Health.
Royall, Frédéric. 2002. Building Solidarity Across National Boundaries: The Case of Affiliates of the European Network of the Unemployed. *Journal of European Area Studies* 10(2) 243–58.
Sanoma WSOY Oyj. 2005. *Vuosikertomus 2005* [Annual Report 2005]. http://www.sanomawsoy.fi/Materials.aspx?f=2114&cat=2&y=2006 (last accessed December 4, 2006).
Siisiäinen, Martti. 1990. *Suomalainen protesti ja yhdistykset. Tutkimuksia yhdistyslaitoksen kehityksen ja protestijaksojen suhteesta suurlakosta 1990-luvulle.* [Finnish Protest and Civic Associations] Jyväskylä: Tutkijaliitto.
———. 1992. Social Movements, Voluntary Associations and Cycles of Protest in Finland 1905–1991. *Scandinavian Political Studies* 15(1): 21–40.
———. 2003. Vuosituhannen vaihteen yhteiskunnalliset liikkeet Suomessa. [Social Movements in Finland at the Turn of the Century] In *Liike-elämää*, ed. Pirita Juppi, Jukka Peltokoski, and Miikka Pyykkönen, 45–66. Jyväskylä: SoPhi.
———. 2009. Differentia Specifica of Voluntary Organizing in Finland. In *Civic Mind and Good Citizenship. Comparative Perspectives*, ed. Annamari Konttinen, 87–113. Tampere: Tampere University Press.
Tainio, Risto. 2006. Suomen yrityssektorin rakenteellinen ja kulttuurinen muutos. [The Structural and Cultural Transformation of the Finnish Business Sector] In *Uusi jako—Miten Suomesta tuli kilpailukyky-yhteiskunta?*, ed. Risto Heiskala and Eeva Luhtakallio, 65–81. Helsinki: Gaudeamus.
Tarrow, Sidney. 1989. *Struggle, Politics and Reform: Collective Action, Social Movements, Cycles of Protest.* Ithaca: Cornell University.
Tilastokeskus. 2007. *Palkkarakenne 2005* [Wage Statistics]. Helsinki: Tilastokeskus. http://www.stat.fi/til/pra/2005/pra_2005_2007-04-27_tie_001.html (last accessed September 28, 2009).
———. 2009. *Työttömyysaste* [Unemployment rate]. Helsinki: Tilastokeskus. http://www.stat.fi/org/historia/tyottomyysaste.html (last accessed September 28, 2009).
Työpoliittinen Aikakauskirja. 2003. [Journal of Labour Politics] 4. Helsinki: Työministeriö.
Työpoliittinen Aikakauskirja 2005. [Journal of Labour Politics] 3. Helsinki: Työministeriö.
Uljas, Päivi. 2005. *Taistelu sosiaaliturvasta. Ammattiyhdistysväen toiminta sosiaaliturvan puolesta 1957–1963.* [The Struggle for Social Security.] Helsinki: Like.
Vähätalo, Kari. 1998. *Työttömyys ja suomalainen yhteiskunta.* [Unemployment and the Finnish Society] Tampere: Gaudeamus.
Vauhkonen, Ilse. 2008. TVY ry:n edustajat Pariisissa joulukuussa 2007. [TVY Representatives in Paris] *Karenssisanomat* 2, 11–12. http://www.tvy.fi/tiedostot/karenssisanomat/karenssi0208.pdf (last accessed September 28, 2009).
Villanen, Sampo. 2004. Kaupungin ulkotilojen käyttö mielenosoituksissa—tilansosiologinen tutkielma. [The Use of Urban Space in Demonstrations] Master's thesis, University of Helsinki.
Weber, Max. 1976 [1922]. *Wirtschaft und Gesellschaft.* Tübingen: J.B.C. Mohr.
Zetterberg, Seppo, ed. 2003. *Suomen historian pikkujättiläinen. Uudistettu laitos.* [The Encyclopedia of Finnish History] Helsinki: WSOY.

CHAPTER 5

The Mobilization of the Unemployed in Italy: The Case of Naples

Simone Baglioni

The case of unemployed organizations in Naples shows that groups of resource-deprived people can organize themselves and make successful claims, overcoming their stigmatized identity. Furthermore, they are able to reverse the stigma and to organize the process that Elias (1994) defines as "counterstigmatization." How did they achieve this? This chapter shows that this has been achieved by taking advantage of the availability of small and big political opportunities (Gamson and Meyer 1996) offered to collective action by local and national political powers, through a wise use of "compensatory" resources, as suggested by recent literature (Maurer 2000), as well as by their capability of establishing viable organizations and links and practices of cooperation with groups devoted to other issues, and finally by an important activity of "framing" (Cress and Snow 2000; Snow 2004).

In the next two sections, the chapter briefly introduces the socioeconomic contexts (national and local) where the mobilization of the unemployed of Naples takes place. After this, the focus moves toward the analysis of the reasons explaining the mobilization from 1970s until the early 2000s: primarily the role of organizations and the interaction between organizations and their embedding political context. Finally, the chapter presents a typology of unemployed organizations in Naples and then discusses the network of organizations the unemployed are part of.

The Context of the Mobilization of the Unemployed in Italy

Unemployment has been a central issue in the Italian political, social, and economic debate since many decades. However, it is a phenomenon primarily affecting southern regions, the less developed and industrialized part of the country where unemployment rate reached peaks of more than 30 percent. On the contrary, from the 1970s onward, the northern regions have experienced an important process of economic development that led to a condition of full employment. In addition to this territorial differentiation, Italian unemployment is characterized by the fact that it prevalently affects women and young people (Ferrera 1993; Reyneri 1996).

However, through the 1990s, the country experienced a major process of industrial change that dramatically restructured its labor landscape with consequences also for the more developed regions. Following a general trend of industrialized countries, from 1980 to 1996 Italy reduced the weight of its manufacturing industry that lost 1.5 million workers (Berta 2006). Northern regions were able to cover this employment gap, at least in part, by creating new jobs in the service area. On the contrary, the southern regions could not exploit this shift in the economic structure of the country and remained underdeveloped. Moreover, in the 1990s the country's major state-driven industrial sectors (chemical, mechanical, food, etc.), most of them based in the south, also witnessed a drastic reduction that may qualify as evidence of an Italian "deindustrialization" process (Gallino 2003). Today, as a result, southern regions, and especially Campania, the region of Naples, are still very far from reaching satisfactory employment rates. This context description helps in understanding why the unemployed have mobilized in Naples, a city that is representative of the entire "south" of Italy.

But, to better illuminate the Italian context, it is worth mentioning also the country's system of unemployment insurance. In fact, Italian labor policies established a compulsory insurance system against unemployment, which provided the totally unemployed a modest cash benefit, but only if they have worked before. Moreover, up until mid-1950s, this provision was limited to workers of the industrial sector. There is also salary integration for partial unemployment (in cases of reduction of the working time), which corresponds to 80 percent of the salary for a period, unlimitedly renewable, of six months. For many years, this subsidy has been reserved for industrial workers. A final aspect to consider is the system of employment services that has been primarily a public function until the 1990s. This system made labor demand and supply meet, but employers and people looking for jobs were not mutually free to choose each other. This choice was indeed mediated by the state. Special local offices (*uffici di collocamento* now *centri per l'impiego*) established public lists of job seekers from which employers had to draw off their employed following the order of the employed position in the list. Unemployed with previous working experiences were excluded from this mechanism. The system changed in the 1990s when industries were allowed to engage workers by nominal appointment.

The institutionalization of this original model of labor policies has provoked relevant consequences, which still mark the Italian socioeconomic landscape: a very high youth unemployment rate (20.3 percent in 2007 according to the Italian statistical office); the impressive diffusion of different forms of irregular employment (*sommerso*, in Italian), which has been calculated to represent

15–20 percent of the GDP; the spreading of the phenomenon called *familismo*, which indicates the tendency of young Italians to leave home much later than their European homologues and to depend longer on their families to survive. Indeed, in Italy, in line with the general features of the South European Welfare State model, family is the "institution" that has played, more than others, the role of social shock absorber for generations of young people struggling to find a regular, but even an irregular, job.

The relevant social and economic difficulties of southern regions are embedded in a context of influent but fragmented trade unions. Up to end of the 1960s, the entire spectrum of trade unions activities, careers, resources, strategic decisions, and political alignment was controlled by political parties (Gualmini 1998). Indeed, the Italian union movement was shaped as unitary and democratic after World War II, when the three major parties having struggled against fascism (Christian-democratic party, communist party, and socialist party) signed an agreement of union unity. Despite that, after three years, such a unity broke down and the union movement took the fragmented form it has nowadays. CGIL (*Confederazione Generale del Lavoro*) is the biggest national trade union, politically affiliated to the left parties, in particular to the communist party; CISL (*Confederazione Italiana Sindacati Lavoratori*) is the one considered the Christian-democratic organization; and UIL (*Unione Italiana del Lavoro*) is the expression of the smaller nonreligious parties, in particular the socialist party. However, the events of 1968 and 1969, which connected the union's struggle to the students protests, led trade unions to play a more autonomous role vis-à-vis political parties. Trade unions, then, started strengthening their position, also because of their increasing membership, which, indeed, doubled between 1968 and 1977 (Accornero 1992). At the beginning of the 1980s, the three major trade unions were acknowledged by the state as crucial partners in social and economic policymaking. Moreover, this new phase started a tradition of political exchanges between government and interests groups. As a result the policymaking became distributive and permeable to parochial interests and favoritism. Concertational decision-making became more widespread in the 1990s, but it remained weakly institutionalized at the national level (Carrieri 2008).

However, we should notice that thanks to the trade unions' strategic role, the Italian system provides for very advanced workers' protection. Indeed, the *Statuto dei lavoratori* (workers statute) of 1970, which endows wide and meaningful guarantees for workers, was obtained thanks to the strong power and support of the trade union movement. On the other hand, it is exactly the strength of the trade union movement that made the Italian system focusing on protection and guarantees more for workers than for unemployed people.

To sum up, the Italian situation is characterized by three principal aspects: a marked concentration of unemployment in the poorest southern regions; some forms of social protection, partially institutionalized, partially based on the role of the family, for the most deprived persons; an increasing autonomous role of trade unions in workers' protection. These are the elements that we find also in the Neapolitan reality and that represent the overall contextual situation from which the mobilization of the unemployed starts.

The Specific Situation of Naples Regarding the Mobilization of the Unemployed

From an economic and social perspective, Naples is representative of an entire part of the country, the south (*il Mezzogiorno*), whose most typical characters can be summarized as: impressive unemployment rates, especially the juvenile one; lower occupational potentialities because of its weak industrial framework, mostly constituted by state-aided companies; high level of organized crime; diffused forms of nonregular work (*mercato nero*); inefficient local governments based upon policies of favoritism and nontransparent exchanges between public administrators and interests representatives. In order to understand the situation of the labor market of the Naples area, it is useful to take into consideration the situation of occupation in the region where it is located.

Joblessness is a peculiar characteristic of all the southern Italian regions. In Campania, as well as in Sicily and Calabria, this negative score reaches its peak. Indeed, in the year 2007, according to the Italian statistical office, the unemployment rate in Campania was the double (11.2 percent) of the Italian average (6.1 percent). Joblessness shows its most dramatic face when we consider youth unemployment. In the year 2007 Campania's rate for this kind of unemployment was 32.5 percent (when the national mean was 20.3 percent).

Despite the improvement of economic patterns witnessed by the *Mezzogiorno* in the past ten years, neither the region Campania nor, within this region, the province of Naples have been able to increase their occupational potentialities. This is in part due to the recession that affected Italy during the 1990s, but it is also due to the restructuring of different sectors, in particular public agencies. Moreover, neither the increase of temporary workers nor the increasing number of part-time workers (in any case lower then the national mean) ameliorated the occupational perspectives of the active population. However, due to the dismissals of several state-controlled industries such as Cirio, Ilva, and so on, it did not manage to reduce the unemployment rate.

Naples has a long tradition of sociopolitical radicalism: since the mid-seventeenth century popular masses (called *lazzari* or *lazzaroni*) organized protest actions aimed at obtaining both moral (public recognition) and material (jobs, money, food) rewards from the king and the aristocrats, in an optic mixing rebellions and parasitism (Hobsbawm 1959). Thus, in the Neapolitan panorama of collective mobilization, the unemployed movement is not exceptional, it is not entirely sui generis, but it is a component of a long tradition of social claims. This chapter focuses on the experience of the unemployed started from the early 1970s onward, but historical research (ibid.) provides evidence about the existence of the unemployed movement in Naples since the seventeenth century.

Looking to a more recent period, a series of events fostered collective action by the unemployed. The protest wave originating in the 1968 students' movement increased popular political engagement in the city and boosted the creation of political organizations; the outbreak of cholera in 1973 led to the abolishment of the very popular job of street sellers of mussels increasing the number of unemployed; finally, the earthquake of 1980 led to the dramatic situation of housing and added a new issue in the agenda of the city's movements.

The chapter will focus on the protest by the unemployed arguing that such mobilization could develop thanks to the following reasons:

1. Well-structured and efficient organizations succeeding in both protesting and negotiating with public powers. Such organizations are also able to regiment a consistent part of the poor [currently about 6,000–7,000 persons according to our fieldwork, but they were listed as 15,000 members in the mid-1970s according to Ginsborg (1989, 491)]. These organizations provide such poor people with symbolic and material incentives: in fact, they offer opportunities for creating a "bounded solidarity" (Portes and Sensenbrenner 1993) but they also assure their constituencies the attainment of their goals such as safe housing or a job.
2. The interaction between such organizations and the local and national political contexts, which offered multiple opportunities for the requests of the movement to be accepted, were fruitful. This led to the creation of a sort of "path-dependency process" (Sabatier and Jenkins-Smith 1993): previous successes have shown the path to be followed.
3. The unemployed organizations were able to establish a link with other important social actors such as the antiglobalization movement, which allowed the unemployed movement to widen its issues and to strengthen its political role.

Each of these points will be discussed in detail in the following sections.

Why the Unemployed Can Mobilize: The Role of the Organization

An indicator that can help understanding the Neapolitan case is the capability of its unemployed to create organizations, with formal membership, written statutes, and delegates.

Indeed, whether the establishment of an organization is an advantage for the cause of the unemployed or not is highly debated in the literature. To sum up such a debate there are two important approaches vis-à-vis this issue—the one that considers organizations as detrimental for the success of unemployed and poor peoples' movements, and the opposite one that believes that without organizations the poor would never succeed. Piven and Cloward (1979), the early theorists on the unemployed movement, belong to the "skeptical wave" vis-à-vis the organization of the unemployed movements. According to Hobsbawm (1984) their doubts do not concern mainly the danger of any bureaucratic or totalitarian degeneration but the inadequacy of the organizational spirit to meet the needs of any mass mobilization (282–96). Indeed, Piven and Cloward's skepticism is a direct consequence of their main thesis that postulates the inability of the poor to control the reactions their mobilization provokes. Capitalism is always able to face and "to metabolize" their claims (ibid.).

Piven and Cloward (1979) maintain that the real strength of a movement such as the unemployed movement consists in the revolt against those rules and authorities relevant in their daily activities. Thus, their success depends more on their ability to mobilize the largest possible number of people at the local level, even through spectacular or violent actions, than on their transformation into a real organization. Every effort in the direction of the creation of an organization leads to the institutionalization of the movement and, as a consequence, to its sclerotic inactivity. The case study that they discuss, the American unemployed mobilizations in the 1930s, is emblematic. Until the unemployed movement had preserved a sort of "primordial" organizational level it was able to concentrate most of its energy, strength, and strategic vision in putting pressure on political institutions, through occupations, marches, and pillages. It experienced double success. On the one hand, the movement transformed the personal condition of the unemployed from a private shame to a social problem, with possible political solutions. On the other hand, the movement pushed the U.S. administration, both at the local and the federal level, to try to solve or at least reduce a widespread social malaise. Once the different groups of unemployed began organizing themselves permanently through associations, their capacity to lead the movement decreased, and finally vanished. During the most active phase of the unemployed movements, "there were few membership meetings, little formal structure within each group, and very little effort to establish formal linkages among the different groups" (69).

Naples presents important differences with the analysis of the two American sociologists considering the role of the organizations, which appear since the very first experiences of the movement as successful tools in encouraging the unemployed collective action. As we can read in the first issue of the unemployed newspaper *Banchi Nuovi*:

> The old and new unemployed unified into committees: they discovered—for the first time—their great strength. They discovered that every person, individually, had to accept everyday several blackmails and had everyday to invent a new job to the detriment of another unemployed. *Together* they compelled everybody, politicians, journalists, ministries, common people, to take into consideration their needs. Their need to escape from the precariousness of illegal jobs and from the *outliving*. On the basis of this *discover*, in Naples, but not only there, the unemployed have continued to organize themselves for years.[1]

As it was told by one of the militants of the unemployed movement: "The only possibility we have to let our voices be heard is to be a mass, and an organized mass."[2] Hence, Naples seems to be better understood using Eric Hobsbawm's (1984) position, which represents the second approach, the "positive" view about the role of organizations in helping poor people movements. Hobsbawm, while reviewing Piven and Cloward's research, argues that mobilizations tend to be ephemeral when they lack organization, and they "disappear without leaving any permanent trace." Moreover, in a broader sense, the poor like other subordinate groups may become the subject, instead of the object, of the history only through formal associations of a certain consistence, whatever structure they may assume (ibid.). According to the English historian, the groups of the poor were able to reverse their unfavorable situation through their organization. The Neapolitan groups share this conviction as we can read in one of their leaflets:

> It is necessary to react and to start again organizing ourselves, to confront among proletarians and exploited people, overcoming in the unitary organized struggle the divisions to which the patrons and the government wish we restrict to.[3]

And again:

> We have to continue the mobilizations not offering any truce to our adversaries; we have to unify, in the struggle, the workers, the precarious workers, the unemployed and the immigrants to contrast employers' and government's actions.[4]

As emblematically underlined by Hobsbawm (1984) in his conclusions to the review of *Poor people's movements* (292–6), in order to be successful, a movement, like the unemployed one, has to develop strategies to lobby the authorities and, above all, it has to adopt political guidelines and *structures* to put those strategies into practice.

The importance of the organization for the mobilization process and especially in bargaining with political institutions becomes even more evident in direct discussions with interviewees. As pointed out forcefully by a militant of *Eurodisoccupati*, one of the organizations interviewed in Naples, "Only if we aggregate we count for the politicians, only by struggling we become important and they start listening to us."[5]

In this respect, Sophie Maurer (2001) speaks about the associations' detonator role[6] in the unemployed mobilizations in the French context. She argues that organizations provide that infrastructural and social environment where "poor peoples" can better exploit their own resources (such as rage, passion, and solidarity) for collective action to happen. The organizations represent the place where the unemployed, through their everyday interaction, discussions, and actions, "reconstruct" their subjective and collective condition so that they become capable of structuring a collective action on it (Maurer 2000). Indeed, there is an interdependent relationship between the individual level of participation and the organizational level of mobilization. The Neapolitan case shows that organizations served the noble purpose of boosting civic and political engagement of people who, otherwise, would have hardly been involved in some public activity. Apart, of course, from the leaders of the movement who experienced multiple and preexisting forms of political and civic involvements. As I was told by one of the activists of the *Movimento Disoccupati Autorganizzati* of Acerra:

> Like most of my comrades here I do not have previous experiences of activism or civic engagement. But I am proud to belong to this movement [of unemployed] because it has allowed me to become part of a social context and it has allowed me to claim, through the struggle, *my rights*.[7]

Furthermore, the organizations represent the instrument through which the unemployed can break their isolation, and through which they can meet other persons with whom to share sentiments, experiences, with whom to discuss and to prepare solutions to put an end to their situation of "deprived" people. The Neapolitan case suggests that organizations provide the ground on which unemployed can build the "bounded solidarity" that, according to Portes and Sensenbrenner (1993, 1325), denotes a sentiment shared by a class of people faced with common adversities—a sentiment leading to the observance of norms of mutual support, appropriable by individuals as a resource in their own pursuits. As declared by a woman actively involved in the group *Eurodisoccupati* whom I met at a public rally: "I am here, in this square, every week to meet my friends, to talk, to be together. I need to escape from my neighborhood where there is nothing to do, where I have nobody to discuss about my situation."[8]

But the organization is also the vehicle that allows the unemployed to interpret their "concern" as a social and political issue that has to alarm the whole society: in social movements theory this would be a "framing" activity (Snow 2004). In this sense, Demazière and Pignoni (1998) underline that "the association of unemployed is a social and intellectual process contributing to a new definition of the personal situation, to a new conception of society, and to a renewed perception of the role everyone can play" (217). The two authors agree that associations help the unemployed to move from a resigned and fatalistic approach vis-à-vis social structures toward an attitude of personal engagement. In this sense, organizations stimulate the process that Norbert Elias (1994) in his theories of exclusion defines as "counterstigmatization." Unemployed organizations provide their members with the opportunities to reverse the stigma and become "proud" of their struggle:

> We are not ashamed of our struggle; those who govern this city have to be ashamed because of their total incapacity to deal with unemployment. We are not the problem; unemployment is the problem concerning the whole society.[9]

The underlying idea is that even the actions of individuals may be effective in promoting social change. Furthermore, organized collective action demonstrates that unemployment does not necessarily means social death. Employment is not everything. It is possible to be unemployed and still have social value and participate in social life, as legitimate members of society, as the unemployed engagement in their organizations show. Under this perspective, the unemployment organizations are "subversive" (Demazière and Pignoni 1998). When employment becomes the supreme value, and, consequently, when unemployed people are deemed socially useless and without dignity, the organization of the unemployed has allowed them to find a new social utility, thereby connected to the social production of wealth. This new production assumes the form of charity, of militancy, of solidarity that represent "compensatory resources" for acting together (Maurer 2000). In this way, the unemployed association becomes a political project, as it represents a project of reconceptualization and reconstruction of society from its very bases (Demazière and Pignoni 1998).

As relatively permanent organizations, these unemployed associations establish durable relationships with political decision-making bodies. The political nature of the unemployed organizations and their place in the political arena is thus a useful element to understand their success as social movement.

The Interaction between Political Opportunities and Unemployed Mobilization

Social movements studies have emphasized that a social movement develops through a process of interaction between the groups of a movement and the sociopolitical environment they try to change (McAdam 1982, 40). The suggestion coming from McAdam's and similar studies (Kitschelt 1986; Kriesi 1995) is that neither internal nor exogenous factors are able to explain by themselves the origin and the development of social insurrection. Instead, we have to consider their reciprocal action. Because "opportunities open the way for political action, but movements also make opportunities" (Gamson and Meyer 1996, 276). Hence, it is worth analyzing the Neapolitan case through the interaction between the political context and the unemployed.

We can begin the analysis looking at the history of the Neapolitan unemployed movement and at its relation with the political context focusing on the last thirty years of the twentieth century. Although political groups involved in the 1968 students' and civil rights' movement had tried to organize the unemployed, the "good" opportunity to do this arrived later. In fact, in autumn 1974, the creation of the first *comitato di lotta per il lavoro* (struggle committee for work) was due to the following reasons: on the one hand, the experience of the local committees born to claim a better, salubrious urban environment after the cholera outbreak in 1973; on the other hand, to the industrial crisis of the years 1973–1975. The first organization of unemployed was called *Comitato di Vico Cinquesanti*, from the name of the street where the unemployed used to meet (Ginsborg 1989; Ferrara 1997, 7). This committee, established by former workers, artisans, long-term unemployed, and other urban poors, organized a protest campaign during 1974 and 1975 (marches, sit-in, occupation of public buildings such as the communal office of electoral certifications) to claim the intervention of the national government in jobs creation. On June 30, 1975, 2,000 unemployed went to Rome and succeeded in having a meeting with a governmental representative. On the same day, 700 unemployed of the *Comitato di vico Cinquesanti* obtained a one-year job paid by a special governmental fund for the development of Southern regions (Santoro 1997). Of course, such a success created a very attractive precedent: during autumn 1975 several new unemployed committees were formed.

This process (see figure 5.1), characterized by, on the one hand, unemployed protests and, on the other hand, governmental reactions (i.e., the creation of ad hoc public-funded working positions), has been reiterated several times in the

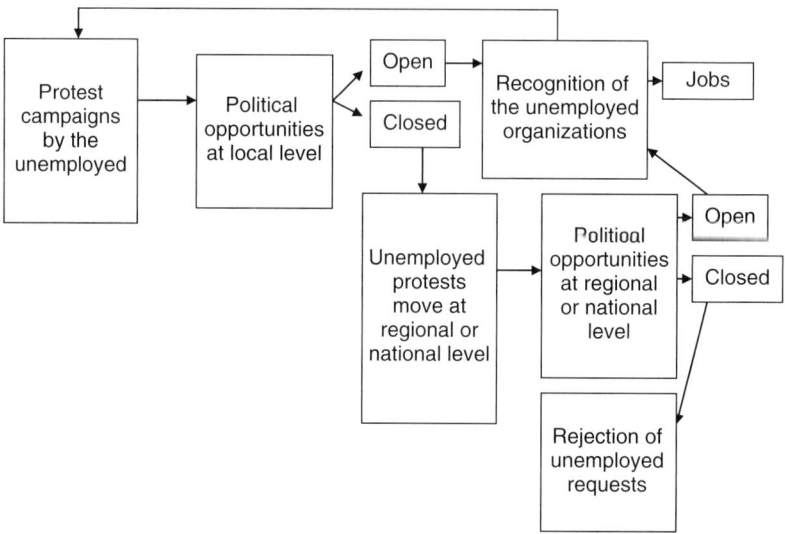

Figure 5.1 The process of interaction between political opportunities, the unemployed, and jobs in Italy.

last thirty years. For example, in 1978, the Neapolitan organizations of unemployed obtained from all local political parties the commitment to be advantaged in obtaining public jobs over other, unorganized, unemployed. In 1994, with a law shaped on the Neapolitan reality[10] the minister of labor decided to give a prioritized access to training courses to the members of unemployed organizations. Such openness of opportunities at the political structure level is due, on one hand, to the strong pressure exerted by the unemployed. On the other hand, it is a product of political parties' interest in transforming their "cooperation" into votes at the next elections, according to the well-established clientelistic modus operandi of Italian politics.

Unemployed, on their side, are proud about their priority rule claims:

> Thanks to our action we get back several thousands of millions that various institutions had hidden through bureaucracy and clientelistic practices. And it is also thanks to the action of the organized unemployed that the regional government has been obliged to speak about training courses [for unemployed people]. In the meetings that the unemployed had with ministries, president of the regional government, regional ministries and representatives of the national government it has always been said that the Plan for the training courses had to involve thousands of unemployed, without age, sex, and education limits and that *all this should have implied a material recognition for the unemployed that have concretely struggled for this.*[11]

The demand of the unemployed to have a privileged access to public resources is considered as legitimate by the unemployed themselves because, according to them, national or European public funds are allocated to Naples, or to its region, thanks also to their protest. That is not untrue, indeed.[12] As we read in another leaflet of the same organization:

> The presentation of the Plan of the training courses for unemployed by the city administration has not fallen from the sky but it is the result, although a partial one, of the struggles and battles carried out by the organizations of unemployed over the last years. The whole bureaucratic procedure could advance because in the squares of Naples the organized struggle for jobs has constantly pressed local and national authorities. This is an objective and incontestable fact with which everybody has to deal with!!! The scandal now seems to be the fact that the constituencies of the organizations of unemployed ask to be part of the training courses. Where is the scandal?[13]

This "tradition" of success in getting a priority access in public jobs has led to the strong belief among the unemployed that *La Lotta Paga* ("the struggle pays back"). As the aforementioned leaflet shows in its reference to both local and national governments, the Neapolitan organized unemployed have proved to be able of taking advantage from all political opportunities available. In fact, as social movements literature suggests (Gamson and Meyer 1996) there are different levels at which political opportunities can be seized by collective actors: if opportunities at one level are closed (for instance, if the local political structure does not accept unemployed requests), social actors can try to take advantage from opportunities at other levels (such as the regional or the national ones).

An open structure of political opportunities implies also the recognition by public authorities about the role played by the organizations of the unemployed: they are invited by different levels of government to negotiate and discuss the creation and allocation of jobs. This is a fundamental phase in the life of an organization of this kind. As we read in the jobless newspaper *Banchi Nuovi*:

> [19 October 1988] is a crucial date for the movement. In that meeting, the city council, including the opposition parties, has acknowledged the *Movimento di Lotta per il Lavoro* as a representative—not the only one, but for sure the most active one—of the needs, of the hopes, of the expectations of the Neapolitan unemployed. With such an acknowledgment obtained through the struggle a whole period is closed. The period in which we had to struggle against a wall of hostility and prejudices.[14]

However, it has happened that the unemployed had to face closed political opportunities. This is the case when local or national authorities do not accept to engage in discussions with the unemployed: they refuse to meet with their representatives. Briefly, the role of social representation of the organizations of the jobless people is not acknowledged by political institutions. This is the case with the current regional governor and former mayor of Naples Antonio Bassolino, who has inaugurated a new policy of closure vis-à-vis unemployed organizations, a policy with the aim of passing the following message: "The struggle does not pay back anymore." In fact, in 1993, when Bassolino became the new mayor of Naples as a representative of the Democrats of the Left (the former Italian Communist Party), he decided to start the new era of "clean" local government in opposition with previous corrupted administrations. Hence, he strongly discouraged some "traditions" used by previous administrators. Among these traditions, the new mayor wanted to dismantle the bargain with the unemployed (some of which had also been infiltrated by criminal groups interested in the employment funds). This type of political decision paves the way for the protest of the unemployed. At this point, their repertoire of actions is rich; it ranges from purely demonstrative activities to violent ones. The repertoire starts with marches and sit-in (they used to march twice or thrice a week, and during our field researches we counted four marches in eight days); it can evolve to occupation of public spaces or offices, and it can end up in firing buses or rubbish boxes. The use of violent strategies is not condemned by the unemployed organizations. On the contrary, it emerges from interviews that all but one group conceive the use of violence as the only strategy they can oppose to the authorities if they want to be seriously taken into account by them. Furthermore, protest and violent actions are useful also to catalyze media attention and, as underlined by Piven and Cloward (1979) as well as by Demazière and Pignoni (1998), violent and nonconventional forms of action are used by the unemployed to strengthen the cohesion of the group and their in-group trust.

The protest process can disembogue into a repressive answer by public institutions but the repression can later on turn, again, toward the opening of the negotiation procedures, because the institutions already know that the repression is not able to freeze unemployed claims for long periods. Hence, the Neapolitan case shows how important the context is to determine the length of the unemployed collective action, but it provides also evidences concerning the influence that the unemployed action itself can exert on this context.

Toward a Typology of Unemployed Organizations

The complex reality of the unemployed movement of Naples can lead to a typology of organizations according to the following criteria:

1. left-wing versus right-wing organizations;
2. multi-issue versus single-issue organizations;
3. wide versus narrow networks of organizations.

The politicization of the Italian labor policy arena, as presented earlier, with unions split following political cleavages, is replicated at the local level in the unemployment arena where unemployed organizations have been formed according to the political spectrum. There are organizations that are considered as "left-wing" political subjects and others that are "right-wing." Moreover, the diverse position in the political matrix implies other differences, which will be considered in this paragraph.

Initially, the unemployed movement born in the early 1970s was "left-oriented": it originated from different left political groups such as Marxist-Leninist groups, *Lotta continua*, or *Avanguardia operaia* (Ginsborg 1989; Ferrara 1997; Santoro 1997; Remondino 1998). The current organizations that originate from that movement are still left-oriented. Among these organizations is the *Movimento Disoccupati Autorganizzati of Acerra* (MDA) and its homologue of Naples central district, the *Movimento di Lotta per il Lavoro*. These left oriented organizations have a good relation with *Rifondazione Comunista* (Communist Refunded Party), the extreme-left party born from the split of the Italian Communist Party. Some of the unemployed organizations of this "side" and this party cooperate in political campaigning: for example, the MDA has worked with *Rifondazione* to elaborate a common proposal for a regional law establishing a minimum income and they both mobilize against neoliberal economic policies.

On the contrary, there are more recent organizations such as *Lista Flegrea*, *Lista Storica*, and *Forza Lavoro Disponibile* that are "right-oriented." They are part of a right-wing coalition close to the center-right party *Popolo della Libertà* and the extreme right-wing party called *Forza Nuova*. This more recent generation of right-wing unemployed organizations is the result of a major political reassessment of Italy between the late 1990s and early 2000s when the right-wing political field was completely reshaped by the creation of a new conservative party (*Forza Italia*, Mr. Berlusconi's party) and by the transformation of a postfascist party (*Movimento Sociale Italiano*) in a neoliberal one (*Alleanza Nazionale*). These parties have later on merged into the *Popolo della Libertà* currently governing the country. This reconfiguration of the right-wing field opened opportunities for the creation of new social organizations, including the unemployed ones. Such opportunities became even more relevant when the new right-wing coalition resulting from the alliance among *Forza Italia*, *Alleanza Nazionale*, and the *Lega Nord* succeeded at the national elections and led the country from 2001 until 2006 and from the spring of 2008 onward. Such right-wing unemployed organizations carry out joint actions, they march together, and they attack jointly public institutions. For instance, they were campaigning together, and they posted up homemade posters everywhere in town against both city and provincial governments (both run by left-wing parties). During field work we found militants of these three unemployed organizations promoting an initiative of *Alleanza Nazionale* favoring the extension of immigrants voting rights at the local level. In addition, their "right" orientation was confirmed also by a visit to their headquarters where images of past dictator Mussolini and similar typical historical "right" iconography were used as walls decorations.

The second important distinction among unemployed organizations concerns their conception of the struggle. On the one hand, there are groups that claim the respect of different rights among which the right to work is the most important, but not the only one. These groups mobilize also to claim a safe environment, a good housing, access to health care. On the other hand, there are organizations active exclusively in the field of (un)employment. A good example of the multi-issue movement is the MDA, as underlined by its spokesperson:

> The occupation of public houses has been carried out together with the struggle for jobs: the successes on one front (from 1976 onward we have occupied about 800 public flats) strengthened the determination to continue in the other one, the job one. The conviction that the struggle pays back is the result of the story of our joined campaigns for housing and jobs: a successful story, indeed we have never lost a single battle on these fronts.[15]

But among the issues of this group there is also the right to live in a salubrious environment: the same organization recently started a strong opposition to the establishment of an incinerator in the territory of their neighborhood. The activists of MDA have occupied the land where it was supposed to be built. Similarly, another organization, the *Coordinamento di Lotta per il Lavoro,* is actively engaged on different issues, as we can read in one of their leaflets diffused to protest against the introduction of a ticket to enter a public beach near Naples:

> The recent decision of the local administration to establish a ticket to accede the beach of Bacoli is a discriminatory and unjust act. This new tax will lie heavily on the miserable budget of the most popular classes. The organizations of unemployed denounce this new attack to our life conditions and launch an appeal to the public opinion for a common struggle. We claim the public availability of social spaces, including free and clean beaches.[16]

In this kind of movement there is, more in general, the demand of citizenship rights, which are perceived as denied by local, national, and transnational political institutions to which they attribute a clear exclusive will. Hence, MDA and the *Coordinamento per il Lavoro* both belong to the antiglobalization network and they mobilize also for international causes. For example, they marched against the NATO decision to bomb Yugoslavia and they marched also in favor of the Argentinean unemployed as we can read in one of their leaflets:

> The unemployed of the *Coordinamento di Lotta per il Lavoro di Napoli* are beside the Argentinean unemployed and workers against their common class enemies: employers and capitalism! The Argentinean struggle is not a local episode concerning only local masses. On the contrary, the struggles of the unemployed, workers, employees and the whole proletariat of Argentina directly concern us. Those who lead Argentinean masses to starvation, those who shoot them, those who impoverish them are the same capitalists that attack our living and working conditions.[17]

However, there are also movements of the unemployed well rooted in their context and with a relevant tradition of struggles which do not embrace a multi-issue strategy. The organization called *Sedile di Porto,* for instance, conceives itself primarily as an organization devoted to find a job for its constituency. As its spokesperson told me:

> Our conception of a movement for jobless people is that it has to be devoted to the search for a place of work for its constituencies. For examples, it has to be established in the occasion of an opportunity provided by the creation of public funded jobs (*vertenza*) with the unique aim of obtaining such jobs.[18]

The principal aim of this kind of organizations is to emerge as a recognized collective actor in the local political and economic arena and to become part of the negotiation for jobs distribution. Their most relevant aim remains, hence, a privileged access to the labor market.

But organizations of these two types of movements diverge also for the type of engagement and especially for the *formalization* of the involvement of the constituencies. In the first type of organizations (the multi-issue ones) each activist receives a membership card that fulfils a very important function. Indeed, the card is usually retained by the organization which delivers it to the concerned constituency only the day before a collective event (march, sit-in, occupation, etc.). On the day of the event the activist must give the card back to the organization that can thus check the real participation of its members. The participation to a protest event is indeed the only way to acquire the "right" to obtain one of the jobs the organization negotiates with the authorities. The "seniority" among activists is established on the basis of their participation in collective actions: the more one participates, the higher his/her chances of getting the job. This method seems a good tool to overcome some of the problems social organizations have to deal with: free riding, for instance, is not possible. There is no chance that someone not actively engaged in the organization's life could obtain the aimed job, indeed just few absences are tolerated by the organization. Moreover, such rule of behavior helps maintaining alive activists' interest and passion for the struggle. And, as pointed out by one of the interviewees, this method has played an important pedagogic role: the activists have matured the conviction that it is not through the clientele or through the familistic networks that one can obtain a job but it is through the struggle that this becomes possible.[19]

In the other type of organizations (the single-issue ones) active participation does not play such a crucial role in the determination of "who's getting the job" once the opportunities are open for that. Sure, taking part in the organization's initiatives is still important but the participation is not really controlled by the organization. This type of movement has another way of establishing "who's getting the job": it limits the number of members; it adopts the rule of restricted intake. It does not accept a constituency larger than the jobs it might take responsibility for. Hence, there is not need to establish a rank among activists.

These two groups of organizations also differ in the length of the networks in which they are involved. There are groups that have developed an intense net of contacts whereas others are more isolated. This diversity is due to the different conceptions of organizing the jobless that we have seen in the previous paragraph.

146 • Simone Baglioni

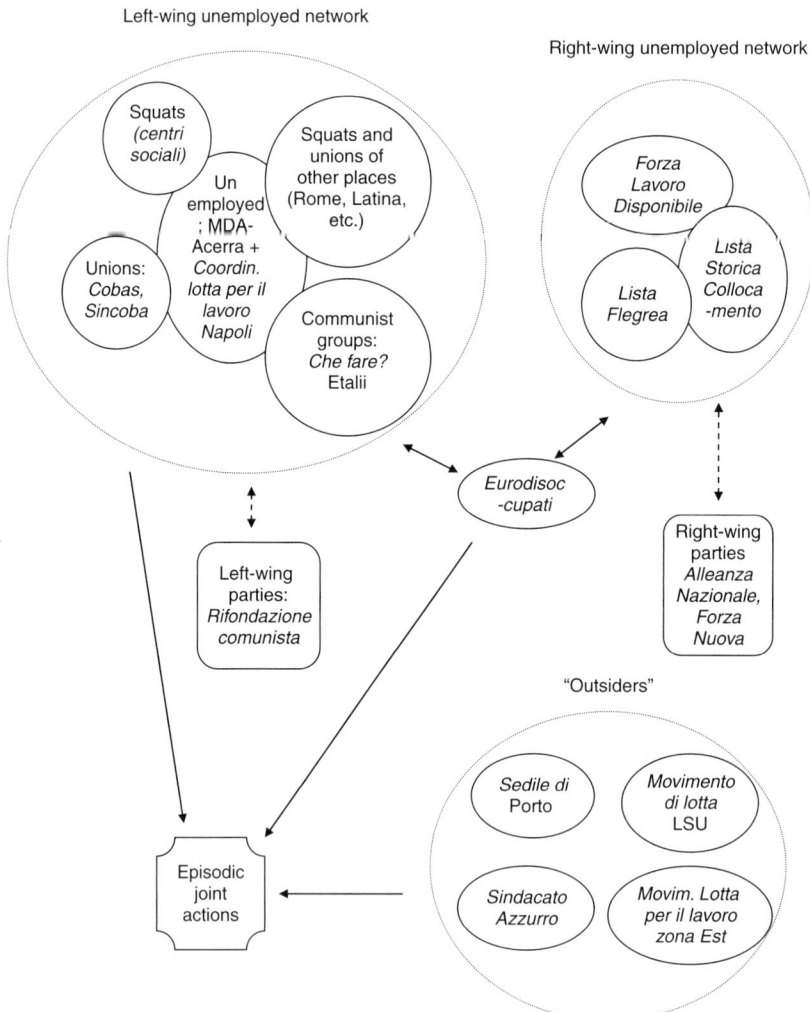

Figure 5.2 Networks of unemployed organizations in Naples.

The groups that are more endowed with social links are those defined like "multi-issue" organizations. They conceive their organization not only as a means to get a job, but as a "movement" whose claims, while encompassing the basic request for a work, embrace a richer range of issues (safe home, respect for the environment, workers' rights). In such a perspective, the struggle of the unemployed is seen as a component of the larger struggle against social exclusion—a struggle that needs to be reinforced by the establishment of links with other groups and other experiences. Some of the groups interviewed belong to this kind of organization. Two of them (MDA and *Coordinamento per il Lavoro di Napoli*) are part of the antiglobalization network (see figure 5.2): they are connected with a vast range of social actors, that is, squats (*centri sociali*), communist groups, and extreme-left unions (*cobas* and *sincobas*). These two groups of unemployed have set up a very robust network and developed strong ties, to the point that they consider themselves as two branches of the same jobless movement.

Then, there are the groups that conceive the struggle of the unemployed organizations essentially as a pure dispute engaged with public institutions to obtain a job for the organizations members (the "single-issue" movements). These are the groups that present the narrowest range of contacts. Indeed, they do not act together with other groups; they do not engage in joint actions (these groups are named "outsiders" in figure 5.2), apart from particular circumstances, when almost all groups marched together. This is the case during national general strikes or when they protest against the repression of the police vis-à-vis their action.

Finally, there is an organization of the unemployed (*Eurodisoccupati*) that has established good relations with both the left- and the right-wing organizations. This group is able to march one day with one side of the constellation of the unemployed movement, and the day after with the opposing side.

The sensibility and the attention that the more "open" organizations pay to different social and economic problems is also due to the links that these organizations have been able to establish with a multiplicity of social actors. Particularly important seems to be the link with the antiglobalization movement and with the squats: this aspect is analyzed in the following section.

Bridging Local and Global

According to previous studies, the breadth of links among unemployed organizations is one of the most relevant factors explaining their mobilization. For instance, Chabanet (2008) shows the importance of these links to organize the European Marches against unemployment, job insecurity, and exclusions.

Particularly interesting in the case of Naples is the wideness of the social network that the organizations of the movement have been able to establish. Since the creation of their first groups, the unemployed mobilized people for the right to work, and for the right to have a safe place to live. More generally, they mobilized for a better quality of life for all those citizens to whom this chance was denied. Indeed, from the very beginning, the movement was not created as a local and single-issue initiative, but as an ambitious project aimed at modifying society from its very base. In our analysis, we can consider this as a "predisposition" of the movement toward global issues. The ability to mobilize on different issues and to carry out a multifaceted identity-building process cannot be underestimated. As stated in the founding-appeal of the *Movimento di lotta per il lavoro*, one of the most important unemployed organizations,

> the aim [of the movement] is clear: to give a perspective of a unitary struggle to different social strata. The unemployed, the youth and the elderly, the vulnerable workers, the students organize themselves in the movement's centers along with those who already have a job and who are willing to bring their experience and courage as a contribution to our struggle.[20]

Similarly, one of the newspapers of the unemployed movement says that they wish their movement to be

> [a] big movement, as big as the army of unemployed people, of vulnerable workers, of workers made redundant. [A movement] being present, with its committees, in all the districts of the town and in the cities and villages of the province but also beyond these territories.
>
> A movement *open* to the participation of everyone. Because our struggle directly concerns all people: students, whose future is not really different from ours; workers who, under the weight of the unemployment of their children, accept employers' blackmails.[21]

What emerges quite clearly is their will to represent a wide group of people and, thus, to be acknowledged as politically "inclusive." They emphasize their will of avoiding a purely corporatist approach: "[The movement will be] a subject entitled with a specific representation power which will be neither corporatist nor close."[22]

But as pointed out earlier, not all unemployed organizations embrace such an inclusive and open approach to social struggles. Therefore, the links with other social actors turned out to be essential to strengthen and support the section of the movement that was interested and committed to become a multigroup representative body. What seems to be crucial, in this respect, is the relation between the unemployed and the antiglobalization movement. As one of the most important representatives of the antiglobalization movement for the South of Italy said:

> The anti-globalization network of Naples has represented a strong stimulus for the organizations of unemployed because it has encouraged them to look beyond their own reality. The struggles that we have carried out together, within the network, have pushed the unemployed to overcome their attitude toward corporatism, that is, their attitude to focus mainly on their struggle for a job *hic et nunc*.[23]

The role that social connections have played in making unemployment claims become transnational initiatives can be seen even more clearly in the history of the unemployed movement and in the analysis of their "connection channels."

First, the bonds between the unemployed and other groups have been created through symbolic actions such as the demonstration that led to the birth of the first *centro sociale* (squat) in Naples: *Officina 99*. On May 1, 1991, the unemployed, together with other associations, organized a symbolic march of nonwork. At the end of this march they occupied an abandoned building, which then became the place where different social actors could meet, share their different experiences and coordinate common actions.[24] This squat, together with another one, *SKA*, created later, has allowed the unemployed to enlarge the spectrum of their activities. It has also allowed both the unemployed and other protest groups to become multifaceted actors playing at local, regional, national, and transnational levels.

For instance, the openness of unemployed organizations to transnational issues, such as the defense of the right of migration and the struggle against EU and other international organizations' policies, has been fostered by initiatives led by the squats. *Officina 99* and *SKA* organize health consulting centers that are frequently used by undocumented immigrants that cannot go to the public ones, and they also arrange Italian-language courses. These actions make the unemployed become fully aware of the existence of other forms of social exclusion that could be added to their own cause, thereby increasing the power of marginalized people.

Furthermore, the participation of local organizations in transnational events such as the anti-G8 demonstrations is usually organized by the groups based in the squats. These groups are responsible for establishing the cooperative links with foreign groups, arranging the travel from Naples to the locality where the event occurs and other practical needs.

The antiglobalization issues have offered the leaders of the unemployed movement the possibility to continue to be perceived as sociopolitical representatives even in a period when unemployment struggles were bypassed by larger collective mobilizations such as the global movement for social justice flourished from the early 2000s. The antiglobalization movement and the constellation of its actors have so far offered the unemployed, at least to some of them, the means to avoid ending up as a closed, corporatist group. It has encouraged the movement escaping clientelism by bringing it back to its origin in the early 1970s when the movement had a clear anticlientelistic connotation and a strong antisystemic character (Ginsborg 1989). Finally, it has permitted unemployed organizations to survive when the government ignored their claims.

Moreover, by being included in local and global events, by campaigning for a "different world," the unemployed have recuperated the moral potential that inflamed their first apparitions in the public arena. In the case of Naples, notwithstanding the fact that material incentives are still there (in all the demonstrations we took part, the claim for a job was always present and relevant), it is evident that the participation is motivated also by moral demands. Most of these demands are inspired by transnational requests (stop the war in Iraq; obstruct neoliberal economic politics, and so on).

Of course, the relation between unemployed organizations and the antiglobalization movement is not unidirectional. The antiglobalization cause seems to have gained important lessons from the unemployed movement. One of the most interesting assets of the unemployed movement for the antiglobalization one is how the unemployed make use of their scarce resources. They "teach" younger groups such as the antiglobalization ones how it is possible to challenge local, national, or supranational governmental institutions even when there are no "classical" resources available to do it. For newer movements, the thirty-year experience of the unemployed organizations represents a powerful example that the struggle is possible, and can be successful, even when the actors challenged are endowed with more resources than the challengers.

The influence that the unemployed movement has exercised on the group of no-global actors is evident also when we look in detail at the types of collective action. Both sets of actors have shown a wise use of the whole spectrum of collective action, violent and nonviolent. Furthermore, the types of collective action are similar between the two forms of mobilization: the one focused on unemployment and social exclusion and the other dedicated to transnational issues such as the antiglobalization ones. The unemployed have also shown great creativity in their actions: every year in mid-August, they organize a sit-in in the famous *piazzetta di Capri* (Capri's little square), or in 1989 they sprayed buses with red paint to remind the population and the administration about the problem of unemployment. Several times, they engaged in symbolic occupations. We can find a similar range of action in the chronicles of the biggest antiglobalization meetings.

Conclusion

The research at the basis of this chapter has shown that the "poor," like the unemployed, can become social actors able to mobilize and to challenge public authorities at different levels.

In the case of Naples, the unemployed have been able to develop a strong collective identity both through a long tradition of successful *organized* struggles and through a widespread net of social connections. A consistent part of this movement of unemployed was created in the early 1970s on the basis of two local issues, unemployment and homelessness, and it continued to enlarge the spectrum of its core-issues to include other social demands, like those at the core of the antiglobalization movement. The social connectedness of the unemployed has been an important resource for their mobilization in several other countries, such as France, where contemporary organizations of the unemployed have tried to enlarge and strengthen their mobilization potential by frame bridging, that is, by undertaking several problems and linking them ideologically (Fillieule 1993, 141). The ability to bridge and bond different issues and different groups seems to be one of the "compensatory" resources that the "poor" can use for their mobilization (Baglioni et al. 2008).

Moreover, the organizations have represented for the unemployed the space or the vehicle through which they have been able to build a "bounded solidarity" as essential ingredient for collective sociopolitical struggles. Through these organizations, the unemployed have also "reframed" the reality to which they seemed to be confined forever. Indeed, they have been able to transform unemployment from a private question into a collective, thus public, political, problem—a problem that needs to be solved through joint efforts of different actors, including the unemployed and their organizations.

However, the success of this mobilization is due primarily to the availability of some opportunities offered by the different political levels to the unemployed action. Sometimes the openness of such opportunities, like the possibility to accede to subsidized jobs or to training courses, has been stimulated by the unemployed action itself. As previous studies have argued, a certain asset of opportunities can be modified also by the collective action itself. In sum, this study suggests the importance of taking in consideration different explanatory factors that contribute, all together, understanding why *even* the poor can successfully mobilize.

Appendix

Interviewed actors (interviews took place between April and October 2003):
Interview n.1: *Coordinamento di lotta per il lavoro*
Interview n.2: *Movimento Disoccupati Autorganizzati di Acerra*—MDA
Interview n.3: *Movimento di lotta LSU*
Interview n.4 *Movimento di lotta per il lavoro zona est*
Interview n.5 *Movimento di Lotta Sedile di Porto*
Interview n.6 *Disoccupati Uniti per il Lavoro*
Interview n.7 *Forza Lavoro Disponibile*
Interview n.8 *Lista Flegrea*
Interview n.9 *Eurodisoccupati italiani*
Interview n.10 *Sindacato Azzurro*
Interview n.11 *Unione Disoccupati Napoletani*—UDN
Interview n.12 Southern Italy Anti-Globalization Network
Interview n.13 Regional Minister in charge of Labor issues

Notes

This chapter is part of a large comparative research project (Unempol) concerning the contentious dimensions of unemployment policies in Europe (www.leeds.ac.uk/ics/euro/unempol). The study has been funded by the EU (HPSE-CT-2001-00053) and by the University of Florence. I am grateful to the organizations of the unemployed of Naples that accepted my interference and cooperated fully to make this research possible. I would also like to thank Didier Chabanet and Jean Faniel as well as the participants of the conference "The Mobilization of the Unemployed in Europe" at the Maison française d'Oxford, Oxford, June 2005, for their helpful comments on a previous version of this chapter.

1. *Banchi Nuovi*, February 1988, n.1; emphasis in the original.
2. *Banchi Nuovi*, June 1988, n.2.
3. Leaflet of the *Coordinamento di Lotta per il Lavoro*, June 20, 1998.
4. Leaflet of the *Coordinamento di Lotta per il Lavoro*, year 2000.
5. Interview n.9—see appendix.
6. Maurer (2001) writes: "Il semble bien que le rôle *déclencheur* des organisations soit décisif" (134; emphasis in the original).
7. Interview n.2; emphasis added.
8. Interview n.9; emphasis added.
9. Interview n.2.
10. According to several interviews during field work.
11. Leaflet of the *Coordinamento di Lotta per il Lavoro*, 2003; emphasis added.
12. As confirmed by several informed actors interviewed during field work.
13. Leaflet of the *Coordinamento di Lotta per il Lavoro*, 2003.
14. *Banchi Nuovi*, November 1988.
15. Interview n.2.
16. Leaflet of the *Coordinamento di Lotta per il Lavoro*, 2003.

17. Leaflet of the *Coordinamento di Lotta per il Lavoro*, 1999
18. Interview n.5.
19. Interview n.12.
20. *Banchi Nuovi*, June 1988.
21. *Banchi Nuovi*, February 1988; emphasis in the original.
22. *Banchi Nuovi*, May 1989.
23. Interview n.12.
24. Interview n.12.

References

Accornero, Aris. 1992. *La parabola del sindacato*. Bologna: Il Mulino.
Baglioni, Simone, Britta Baumgarten, Didier Chabanet, and Christian Lahusen. 2008. Transcending Marginalization: The Mobilization of the Unemployed in France, Germany and Italy in a Comparative Perspective. *Mobilization* 13(3): 323–35.
Berta, Giuseppe. 2006. *L'Italia delle fabbriche. Ascesa e tramonto dell'industrialismo nel Novecento*. Bologna: Il Mulino.
Carrieri, Mimmo. 2008. *L'altalena della concertazione*. Rome: Donzelli.
Chabanet, Didier. 2008. When the Unemployed Challenge the European Union: The European Marches as Externalization of Protest. *Mobilization* 13(3): 311–22.
Cress, Daniel M., and David A. Snow. 2000. The Outcomes of Homeless Mobilization: The Influence of Organization, Disruption, Political Mediation, and Framing. *American Journal of Sociology* 105(4): 1063–104.
Demazière, Didier, and Maria-Teresa Pignoni. 1998. *Chômeurs: du silence à la révolte*. Paris: Hachette.
Elias, Norbert. 1994. Introduction. In *The Established and the Outsiders*, ed. Norbert Elias and John L. Scotson, xv–li. London: Sage.
Ferrara, Luciano, ed. 1997. *È qui la festa. 1970–1997 Disoccupati organizzati a Napoli*. Rome: Ulisse Edizioni.
Ferrera, Maurizio. 1993. *Modelli di solidarietà*. Bologna: Il Mulino.
Fillieule, Olivier. 1993. Conscience politique, persuasion et mobilisation des engagements. L'exemple du syndicat des chômeurs, 1983–1989. In *Sociologie de la protestation. Les formes de l'action collective dans la France contemporaine*, ed. Olivier Fillieule, 123–55. Paris: L'Harmattan.
Gallino, Luciano. 2003. *La scomparsa dell'Italia industriale*. Turin: Einaudi.
Gamson, William A., and David S. Meyer. 1996. Framing Political Opportunity. In *Comparative Perspectives on Social Movements: Political Opportunities, Mobilizing structures and Cultural Framings. Applications of Contemporary Movement Theory*, ed. Doug McAdam, John D. McCarty, and Mayer N. Zald, 275–90. Cambridge: Cambridge University Press.
Ginsborg, Paul. 1989. *Storia d'Italia dal dopoguerra a oggi*. Turin: Einaudi.
Gualmini, Elisabetta. 1998. *La politica del lavoro*. Bologna: Il Mulino.
Hobsbawm, Eric J. 1959. *Primitive Rebels. Studies in Archaic Forms of Social Movement in the 19th and 20th Centuries*. Manchester: Manchester University Press.
———. 1984. *Worlds of Labour. Further Studies in the History of Labour*. London: Weidenfeld and Nicolson.
Kitschelt, Herbert. 1986. Political Opportunity Structures and Political Protest: Anti-Nuclear Movements in Four Democracies. *British Journal of Political Science* 16(1): 57–85.

Kriesi, Hanspeter. 1995. The Political Opportunity Structure of New Social Movements: Its Impact on their Mobilization. In *The Politics of Social Protest. Comparative Perspectives on States and Social Movements*, ed. J. Craig Jenkins and Bert Klandermans, 167–98. Minneapolis: Minnesota University Press.

Maurer, Sophie. 2000. Le mouvement des chômeurs de l'hiver 1997–1998. *Recherches et Prévisions* 61: 3–17.

Maurer, Sophie. 2001. *Les chômeurs en action (décembre 1997–mars 1998). Mobilisation collective et ressources compensatoires*. Paris: L'Harmattan.

McAdam, Doug. 1982. *The Political Process and the Development of Black Insurgency 1930–1970*. Chicago: University of Chicago Press.

Piven, Frances Fox, and Richard A. Cloward. 1979 [1977]. *Poor People's Movements: Why They Succeed, How They Fail*. New York: Vintage Books.

Portes, Alejandro, and Julia Sensenbrenner. 1993. Embeddedness and Immigration: Notes on the Social Determinants of Economic Action. *American Journal of Sociology* 98(6): 1320–50.

Remondino, Fabrizia. 1998. *Ci dicevano analfabeti. Il movimento dei disoccupati napoletani degli anni '70*. Lecce: Argo.

Reyneri, Emilio. 1996. *Il mercato del lavoro in Italia*. Bologna: Il Mulino.

Sabatier, Paul A., and Hank Jenkins-Smith. 1993. *Policy Change and Learning*. Boulder: Westview.

Santoro, Serena. 1997. Cronologia del movimento. In *È qui la festa. 1970–1997 Disoccupati organizzati a Napoli*, ed. Ferrara, Luciano, 11–35. Rome: Ulisse Edizioni.

Snow, David A. 2004. Framing Processes, Ideology, and Discursive Fields. In *The Blackwell Companion to Social Movements*, ed. David A. Snow, Sarah A. Soule, and Hanspeter Kriesi, 380–412. Oxford: Blackwell.

CHAPTER 6

The Organization of the Unemployed in Spain: Local and Fragmented Dynamics

Sophie Béroud

Spain constitutes a paradoxical case study. Despite the fact that during the 1980s and the 1990s Spain had the highest unemployment rate among the member states of the OECD, there was no national movement of the unemployed at this time. The rare attempts to create associations of the unemployed—the first of which took place toward the end of the 1980s—did not reach out beyond the local level, and their radius of action was for the most part limited to the neighborhood level and to very occasional forms of action.

Thus, the unemployed fail to appear as a collective agent taking action and therefore becoming visible in the public debate at a time when unemployment and its consequences were omnipresent in the everyday life of Spaniards. This situation leads one to examine the conjunction of factors that can explain the contrast between the strength of the social phenomenon, that is, the persistence of mass unemployment for more than two decades, and the weakness of collective protest in relation to it. This relates to the theoretical discussions fostered by other case studies such as the United Kingdom (Bagguley 1991), which attempt to grasp the elements contributing to the emergence or nonemergence of collective action by the unemployed in a given historical configuration.

In the case of Spain, and in relation to the time period examined here, which starts at the beginning of the 1980s and extends to the mid-2000s, there are three elements of defining importance. The first is the result of the attitude of the bulk of the trade union movement toward the unemployed. Despite taking a stance in the public debate on the issues of employment and job insecurity, the two main confederations—the *Union general de Trabajadores* (UGT) and the *Comisiones Obreras* (CC.OO)[1]—had not concretely concerned themselves with this group of workers who found themselves excluded from employment. This first dimension is relatively decisive to the extent that it maintains the rare associations of the unemployed in a marginal position in relation to the strongest trade unions, depriving them of potential allies and logistical support.

The second element relates to the referential universe in which these rare local associations, where unemployed workers become active, develop. If there exist associations whose activities focus on social assistance and the provision of services, such associations, which attempt to organize concretely the unemployed and engage them in forms of collective action, situate themselves in the wake of neighborhood movements (*movimiento vecinal*). These movements were strong in Spain in the last phase of the struggle against Franco's dictatorship (late 1960s and early 1970s), before declining in the early 1980s (Pérez and Sánchez León 2009). The associations aiming to fight unemployment combined various influences in this manner, notably the tradition of networks of support for the poor, of a Christian tradition (Aganzo 2003), and the influence of an anarchist tradition, through the occupation of empty housing (squat movements known as *okupas*). The political tradition of these associations focused on local action through self-organization, and were not aimed at influencing the national debate. However, the emergence of the antiglobalization movement in Spain is going to give new life to these associations and situate them in actions of a wider scope.

Finally, the third element is a consequence of the way in which the welfare state was created in Spain and of the extent to which it enjoys support within society. The creation of the welfare state and the generalization of social rights, even if levels of social protection have remained low, are linked to the return to democracy after General Franco's death in 1975. The late 1970s and the early 1980s were the periods during which the system of social protection was established and generalized while the late 1980s proved to be the period of consolidation (Rodríguez Cabrero 2008). This belated generalization of social rights contributes to the fact that the welfare state is not generally regarded by people as the result of the victories of the labor movement, but rather as a major change brought about by democracy, given the important pockets of poverty that still existed under Franco's rule.

In order to understand why collective action by the unemployed has remained weak and fragmented in Spain, we will first deal with the split between the trade union movement and the unemployed, pointing to the progressive inability of the unions to effectively represent all workers. We will then analyze the forms assumed by the small number of local initiatives, which have attempted to group together the unemployed, highlighting the changes that took place in the late 1990s in connection with the antiglobalization movement. In the third part, we will take a detailed look at a particularly significant incident, the general strike of 2002. Indeed, this strike happened because of the reform of the unemployment compensation scheme decided by the government of José María Aznar. The dynamics generated by the strike, which included a neat dissociation at the national level between the actions undertaken by the trade unions and those undertaken by the associations of the unemployed, as well as occasional encounters at the regional level, are a telling example of the contradictions one comes across in the Spanish case.[2]

The Marginalization of the Unemployed with Respect to Trade Union Activity

The transition to democracy (1976–1980) took place in Spain in a context of economic crisis. The first democratic governments had to confront the effects of this crisis. There was the need to restructure a heavy industry (steel, shipyards, and textile) inherited from the time of Franco's rule and, very soon, they had to confront the emergence of mass unemployment. Still below 8 percent in 1978, mass unemployment reached 17 percent of the labor force as early as 1982, at the time of the first democratic change in government with the coming to power of the socialist party (PSOE). These contextual data are important for understanding the attitude of the trade unions with respect to the problem of unemployment and to those groups of workers affected by it. As Richards (2000) shows very well, trade unionism lost little by little its ability, whether as an institution or a social movement, to produce wide-ranging solidarities allowing it to speak in the name of the working class (154–5). Obviously, one should not idealize these older solidarities. In Spain, the major trade union, the *Comisiones obreras* (CC.OO), was built under the rule of Franco mainly in the industrial sectors. But its oppositionist approach toward the dictatorial regime of the 1960s and 1970s gave it a political legitimacy, which extended beyond its simple presence in the workplaces. On the other hand, the importance of unemployment and the emergence of unstable employment, in particular in the services sector, have contributed since the 1980s to the transformation of the trade unions into the legitimate representatives not of the working class as a whole but of the most secure groups within it.

In the space of approximately ten years, the labor market has changed considerably. On top of the persistence of a rate of unemployment around 20 percent, there has been a massive development of insecure jobs, through temporary and most importantly part-time employment (table 6.1). The rate of job insecurity[3] exceeds the 30 percent threshold in the early 1990s (Vincent 2005, 97).

If the UGT and the CC.OO played an important political role in the period during which democratic rule was restored, through the negotiation of social contracts with the government and the employers at the national level, very quickly they found themselves in the position of having to manage the

Table 6.1 Evolution of the rate of unemployment in Spain (1978–2004, percentage of active population)

	1978	1980	1982	1984	1986	1988	1990	1992	1994	1996	1998	2000	2002	2004
Global	7.6	12.6	17.0	21.6	21.1	19.3	16.1	18.3	24.0	22.1	18.6	13.8	11.4	10.9
Men	N/a	10.8	14.8	19.0	19.4	15.2	11.9	14.3	19.8	17.4	13.5	9.5	8.2	8.1
Women	N/a	12.8	18.6	23.0	25.3	27.6	24.1	25.5	31.4	29.5	26.5	20.4	16.3	15.0

Source: Instituto Nacional de Estadistica (INE), Labour force survey.

deterioration of a segment of the labor market. As early as 1984, a legislative reform cleared the way for the unrestricted use of temporary job contracts as a means of promoting employment. Being involved in highly institutionalized forms of negotiation at the national level, the two trade unions focused during the 1980s more on preserving the interests of those workers already in employment rather than the interests of those workers entering employment or excluded from it (Polavieja and Richards 2001, 205). This situation led to a sharp polarization of the Spanish labor market, with workers having an unlimited duration contract still enjoying the benefits of a relatively protective labor law on the one hand and insecure workers on the other. It also led to a real split with unemployed workers, which can be explained in various ways.

First of all, the high degree of institutionalization of Spanish trade unionism has to do with the way in which, during the transition to democracy, the system of industrial relations was remolded through strong state intervention and the systematic quest of social contracts (Burgess 1999). The high level of dependence on the institutional recognition it enjoys, including at the financial level,[4] has led Spanish trade unionism to shift its focus to the practice of negotiations from above. This is the source of its legitimacy, not its ability to concretely organize the workers.[5] Second, the social base of Spanish trade unionism has been considerably reduced to the sole insiders, that is, those workers still employed under an unlimited duration contract in the big firms of the private and public sectors. This has led to the demands put forward by the confederations being dominated by the interests of these workers and to the de facto exclusion of other social groups (Serrano del Rosal 2000, 151–73). Finally, the UGT and the CC.OO have had to manage contentious relations with a left-wing government, which implemented policies of flexibilization of the labor market. This resulted in a weakening of the traditional links between trade unions and parties, particularly between the UGT and the PSOE (Burgess 1999), but also in a difficulty to come up with an alternative to the dominant economic discourse.

From as early as the beginning of the 1980s, the CC.OO and the UGT have maintained only a distant relationship with the unemployed. They put forward a general position on the unemployment compensation scheme and on the necessary evolution of employment norms in order to reduce unemployment, but do not attempt to organize the unemployed. A number of facts indicate that this is the case. For example, it was only as late as 1998 that a debate on the possibility of creating a specific union for the unemployed took place at the confederal conference of the UGT. Moreover, this proposal was rejected by conference (Richards 2008, 29), among fears that it would lead to the acceptance of unemployment as a permanent situation. The result was that between the early 1980s and the mid-2000s neither the UGT nor the CC.OO modified their internal organizational structures in order to create committees or federations of the unemployed, while at the same time specific organizational structures were created with the aim of strengthening trade union activities toward other groups such as the pensioners or the youth. Unemployed workers remain affiliated to their original union, which generally leads them to progressively drop out of union activity once their firm is closed down and the link with their original union is severed, since this link depends on the workplace.

Another fact worth noting is that the two trade unions did not attempt to create committees of unemployed workers on the basis of struggles against plant closures (Antentas 2007, 259–331). A number of these struggles happened, however, over a period of several months, during the 1980s and in the early 1990s, especially if one thinks of the shipyards in the principality of Asturias. Here, it is interesting to compare with the French case since similar struggles, against the closure of the shipyards in La Ciotat, near Marseilles, led the CGT to organize the unemployed (Demazière and Pignoni 1998).

The only step taken by the Spanish trade unions, in a perspective of proposing services to their members, has been to set up classes in trade union premises, both for workers in employment and for the unemployed. Trade union foundations specializing in this type of activities receive public funding—national funding or through the European Social Fund—and organize practical courses, usually oriented toward the creation of microfirms or toward specific training (e.g., becoming a "tourist development agent"). These structures prove that the relation the trade unions have with the unemployed is closer to a policy of social accompaniment than to protest strategies.

Despite being cut off from the unemployed and making no attempt to organize them or to build real links of solidarity between employed and unemployed workers, the Spanish trade unions have a general position on the system of social protection. The unemployment compensation scheme in Spain remains the responsibility of the state. Despite the fact that the funds intended for unemployment benefits come from contributions paid from wages, they are not jointly managed by the trade unions and the employers' representatives, but by the state apparatus.[6] From this point of view, the trade unions are not directly involved in the process of determination of the benefit allocation criteria. They are, however, indirectly involved through their participation in the process of agreeing to big social contracts with successive governments, which allows them to influence, or to try to influence, the orientation of employment policies.

One can identify two main phases in the evolution of the unemployment compensation scheme. The first one, from 1978 (year of the adoption of the democratic constitution) to the early 1990s, corresponds to the setting up of a real welfare state in Spain, with the creation of various welfare payments (pensions and unemployment benefit) and especially with the creation of universal coverage. The action of the state toward the unemployed is clearly socially progressive. A specific scheme of "rural unemployment compensation" (*subsidio rural*) was established in Extremadura and in Andalusia in 1984. It guaranteed a minimum income for daily agricultural laborers whose employment was discontinuous and constituted for many families a way out of poverty. The trade unions obtained in the late 1980s an increase in the level of unemployment compensation, even if it still remains limited in duration. Compensation could not exceed a twenty-four-month period and stood at 70 percent of the reference wage during the first year. However, things changed in the early 1990s. As noted by Rodríguez Cabrero (2008), the Spanish welfare state was characterized by a process of permanent restructuring, due to its belated establishment: while being in the process of consolidation, it found itself in contradiction with a trend toward restructuring and the reduction of social spending in the EU member states (101). It was the socialist government that introduced in 1993 a first reform the aim of which was to tighten the access to unemployment benefits: while this access was hitherto granted after six months of contributions, this threshold was now raised to twelve months (Tuchszirer 2002, 5). At the same time, however, the autonomous communities, and not the central state, created assistance-like welfare payments (i.e., payments to which people not having paid any social security contributions were entitled to) in the form of minimum income payments (representing 75 percent of the minimum wage and again limited to twenty-four months). Indeed, the Spanish state embarked on a process of reform tending toward federalism since the establishment of the 1978 constitution. The process notably entailed the transfer of competence on social issues to the seventeen autonomous communities (Moreno 1997). This strong tendency toward regionalization was, however, uneven from region to region and certain communities acquired more rapidly than others a range of competences. The establishment of a minimum income depended therefore on the policies decided at the regional level and did not concern the entire Spanish territory. This issue is quite important today but it remains the case that during the 1990s criticism of the recently established welfare state remained reserved.

Spanish trade unions adopted, then, a general position that criticized job insecurity and promoted the *acquis* of the welfare state. But they never presented the welfare state as something obtained through working-class struggle, as a class conquest. The establishment of social spending policies, the reduction of this spending, and the pursuit of the reform of the labor market would progressively lead the trade unions to adopt a more aggressive attitude in the late 1990s. Nonetheless, the gulf separating the trade unions and the unemployed and the lack of links with those associations aiming to organize the unemployed and those workers in insecure employment remained very pronounced. Therefore, what is important to highlight is that the trade unions could provide the associations of the unemployed with the organizational resources, as much as the "cultural" or cognitive resources, likely to contribute to an interpretative framework inciting to organize and mobilize. In his comparison of the activities of the *National Unemployed Worker's Movement* (NUWM) in the United Kingdom during the 1920s and the 1930s and those of the TUC's *Centre for the Unemployed* in the 1980s, Paul Bagguley (1992) emphasizes the cultural distance separating the two organizations. The NUWM was built as one of many organizations in a revolutionary labor movement, that is, as an organization of the working class in the service of the collective project of this class. On the other hand, the TUC's *Centre for the Unemployed* was conceived as an organism that would provide individual services in order not to lose contact with the unemployed (450–9). This analysis can be used here to shed light on the Spanish case. The notion of a social class has disappeared from the relation that the UGT and the CC.OO maintain with workers deprived of employment and the protection of the unemployed is never considered as a collective necessity, which can enable the assertion of the interests of the group when confronted with exterior entities. The relation to the state, precisely because of Spanish political history, is never conceived through the lens of a labor movement capable of relying on social conquests obtained through struggle, and on that basis capable of conferring legitimacy to the demands of the unemployed. This lack of cultural resources coming from the trade unions partly explains the fact that the associations of the unemployed have turned for inspiration to other traditions.

Between Fragmentation and Isolation: The Associations of the Unemployed in Activist Networks

The activist networks in which will emerge the small number of sporadic attempts to organize the unemployed, most often in relation with other social groups who fall victims of different forms of exclusion and deprivation, were, in effect, markedly differentiated and cut off from those workers organized by such trade unions as the UGT and the CC.OO. The connections with the world of labor were weak indeed.

It is possible to distinguish between two quite distinct types of associations. The first focuses more on providing services to specific fractions of the labor force, that is, people above forty or below thirty years of age. The second focuses more on protesting against the social order and participates in much larger activist networks.

The first group of associations is constituted by such associations as *Senun-40*, created in 1992, or the *Federación de Parados Mayores de 40* (Pérez Torres 2004, 95–116). These two associations have national offices whereas others, created and developed along the same lines, do not extend beyond the regional level (*PM-40* in Andalusia or *Xuntos 40* in Galicia). Both the activities they engage in and the conception they have of their place in society are quite close. Their role is to assist unemployed workers of more than forty years of age who, because of firms' hiring policies, have very few chances of finding a job again. The associations propose training (CV, interviews in professional orientation, etc.), psychological help, and forms of self-employment (creation of microfirms). The association *Red Araña* has specialized in the same range of services, but for young people under the age of thirty. It is present in twelve regions and has around twenty services centers. It is interesting to note that these associations only began turning their attention toward the state and presenting themselves as its interlocutors in the late 1990s. Doubtless influenced by the media impact of the movement of the unemployed in France (EIRO 1998), these associations joined forces in a *Mesa Nacional de Asociaciones para el Empleo*, on February 19, 2008, and have been putting forward two common demands: the right to employment and the improvement of social assistance programs. This attempt at national coordination has not, however, been followed through and these associations continue to carry out the same type of activities.

However, a second group of associations have very different characteristics. During the 1980s and until the early 1990s, action networks whose struggles focused on opposing unemployment appear within the framework of movements of neighborhood solidarity. The conditions that determined the emergence of these groups cannot be dissociated from a more general approach to the question of the temporality and forms of social struggle since the death of General Franco in November 1975. An intense period of social protest against the dictatorship, which took many forms, from strikes to demonstrations through nationalist demands, was followed, in effect, by a period of "disenchantment" after the vote on the Constitution in 1978 and the victory of the socialist party in 1982. As Calle (2005) reminds us, the end of the transition to democracy is accompanied in Spain by a decline of the movements that had been built in the process of everyday resistance against Franco's rule, along the lines of the movement of the neighborhood associations (115). Indeed, by *movimiento vecinal*, one usually refers to the actions undertaken by the residents of the same neighborhood for the improvement of their standard of living (e.g., by demanding infrastructures). These associations, beyond the goals that they assigned to their struggles and which could be very precise, have managed to provide the basis on which developed concrete solidarities and politicization processes (Pérez Quintana and Sánchez León 2009).

Many association networks persevered in the early 1980s but were weakened, both due to the loss of activists to the socialist party (PSOE) when it came to power in 1982 and due to the fact that many of their demands had been met—through the creation of new social policies—both of which defused the dynamics of protest. The communists and the far left were going through a period of crisis. The Spanish communist party had played a central role in the opposition to Franco's rule. But it lost a part of its influence and of its social roots to the socialist party during the democratic transition and also lost its ability to lead the association networks.

It was only after 1986 that a part of the communist and radical left began to realign. The campaign against the continued presence of NATO's military bases contributed to modifying the political situation and set in motion a new activist dynamic. While the socialist party had pledged to obtain the shutdown of these military bases, it changed its position once it came to power and called on the electorate to approve their continued presence through a referendum. The campaign provided the opportunity for the realignment of the political space at the left of the socialist party (with the constitution of the *Izquierda Unida* coalition, which brings together the Spanish communist party and various groups of the far left). It also contributes to the reactivation of the activist networks at the local level.

This is the context in which the first initiatives against unemployment materialize. In 1988 a *State coordination against unemployment, poverty and social exclusion* was created out of a small association in Madrid. It brought together neighborhood associations, inheritors of the tradition of concrete actions on precise objectives, and youth organizations linked to the Catholic movement (Aganzo 2003, 218). In this latter case, these associations—"rank and file communities" in activist jargon—share the principles of social Catholicism and aimed to promote forms of popular education. The *State coordination* was related to the conjuncture described earlier to the extent that it was quite characteristic of the first criticisms that started to surface against the social policies of the socialist government of Felipe González.

The *coordination* did not succeed however, despite its ambition, to establish stable contacts with other local groups. It did not attempt to systematically organize the unemployed, but rather to create links between the associations fighting against various social problems linked to unemployment and exclusion (drugs, prostitution, or incarceration) and to transform stigmatized people into the agents of their own struggle. Despite the fact that this attempt was not followed through, it is representative of the legacy of the *movimiento vecinal* through the philosophy of which it was the bearer.

The lack of dynamism of the far left and of the Spanish communist party, the hegemony of the PSOE, and the effects of the conjuncture linked to the "normalization" of the democratic regime explain the fact that the 1980s were not very favorable to attempts to mobilize against the socialist government's employment and unemployment compensation policies. But several elements contributed to the modification of this political situation in the mid-1990s. On the one hand, the electoral victory of José María Aznar's conservative party in 1996, after fourteen years of socialist governments, resulted in an acceleration of the policies of flexibilization of employment practices and in the introduction of measures of activation of social spending (i.e., benefits became conditional on the beneficiary making an effort to get a job) as we will see later. The fact that the right was in power contributed to the clarification of the political space. On the other hand, the influence of the movement of the unemployed that took place in France during the winter of 1997–1998[7] as well as the launching, in 1997, of the first European Marches against unemployment, job insecurity, and exclusions (Chabanet 2008) contributed to the spreading in different Spanish cities of the idea of constituting committees or assemblies of the unemployed. Despite all this, there was be no link-up with the associations referred to earlier, such as *Senun-40*, which focused more on providing services.

Aganzo (2003) remarks that "it would be disproportionate to attribute to initiatives which materialize as occasional actions against unemployment and social precariousness the quality of a social movement, in the standard sense of the term" (222).[8] These groups of unemployed workers, which made their appearance in the late 1990s and especially in the early 2000s, proved to be very heterogeneous indeed. They were part of the continuation of the already existing association networks, which reformulated a number of their demands parallel to the evolution of the political context. Having established a foothold in the big urban centers (Barcelona, Cordoba, Madrid, Valencia, and others), they continued to operate at the crossroads of several networks: the "Christian rank and file communities," the associations active on the issues of social exclusion or the support to ex-drug addicts (*Madres Unidas contra la Droga*), finally the "autonomous" movement of the *okupas* (appropriation of empty housing, cultural and social demands, creation of social centers). They also enjoyed the support of small trade unions and in particular of the CGT (*Confederacion general de Trabajadores*). Standing in the anarcho-syndicalist tradition, this organization occupied an extremely peripheral position in Spanish industrial relations, had a few thousand members, and only existed in a few sectors. Its historical legitimacy (during the second Republic and the Spanish civil war the CGT was the anarchists' emblematic organization and exercised a relative degree of influence in Catalonia and Andalusia) as well as its links with other libertarian or anarchist groups mean that it was a relatively visible actor in the far left milieu. For instance, it was representatives of the Spanish CGT who were the first contacts in Spain of the network organizing the European marches and who contributed to the participation of associations from Catalonia and Andalusia[9] in these marches.

The composition of these associations and the networks in which they participated assumed variable forms according to the local contexts. Their dissemination, although it remained limited, profited from a third factor: the development of the antiglobalization movement. Indeed, a new cycle of mobilizations took shape in Spain and fed on, both in terms of its demands and the repertoire of its actions, the wider dynamic of the antiglobalization movement at the international level (Calle 2007, 139–40). Thus, campaigns were created on particular themes (e.g., "Against the Europe of Capital") and created the possibility of bringing together relatively diversified actors who would not group together before. This was, for example, the case of the CGT mentioned earlier, of certain company trade unions that were members of the CC.OO but were also critical of the latter's leadership, of feminist associations, and so on. The antiglobalization movement also had the role of a melting-pot where new groupings and new synergies were created. Some activist associations followed, then, a process of adaptation and transformation closely resembling the process that several associations, which participated in the antiglobalization movement in France, had gone through (Agrikoliansky, Fillieule, and Mayer 2005).

There are several examples that can illustrate this dynamic. The antiglobalization movement sometimes constitutes the basis on which to create a new activist network on issues related to unemployment or can sometimes provide the impulse for the reconfiguration of older groups. For instance, committees against unemployment were created in Leganés, near Madrid, and in Moratalaza in Andalusia, in preparation for the Barcelona countersummit of 2002. Sometimes the starting point was given by more specific campaigns: the association *Rompamos el silencio* was created in Madrid at the occasion of an initiative called "Seven days of social struggle" in 1997. Another example of such activist groups that evolve and find a new dynamism is the association "*people of Baladre*."[10] This association has little by little grouped together people used to mobilizing in the popular neighborhoods of the big towns of the provinces of Valencia and of Catalonia. These activists have for the most part received their training through participation in the labor movement and in those activist groups that although part of the CC.OO are critical of its leadership. In the conjuncture that characterizes the late 1990s and the early 2000s, these associations put together a series of demands, the main one being the demand for new welfare payments in order to fight job insecurity. To the right to housing, food, electricity, education, and culture was added the right to a universal and unconditional minimum income (*renta básica*). This association thus aimed to loosely group the "local assemblies," which were united by their refusal of all manifestations of urban poverty.

An identical structure dominates in the *Rompamos el silencio* assembly—which is constituted by a network of Catalonian, Madrilenian, and Andalusian associations—and which organizes not only meetings but also action campaigns. Conceived as a "temporary union of distinct social identities," *Rompamos el silencio* was built on the basis of common concerns shared by associations working on issues such as poverty, exclusion, marginalization, or social violence. The struggle against unemployment thus took its place in a far larger and more diffuse set of demands that led to a critique of the capitalist model of society (Aganzo 2003, 228–9).

These different examples are especially useful for highlighting the fact that in Spain there are no specific organizations of the unemployed, but rather associations that link together different problems, articulating their criticisms of job insecurity and unemployment with other issues, and especially integrating these criticisms with a denunciation of economic and financial globalization, which is the main ideological reference of these associations. Despite their heterogeneity and usually their discontinuous engagement in activity (which sometimes is limited to a few months and then becomes very sporadic), these associations presented some common characteristics. Being close to the alternative or radical left (very critical of political parties), they privileged forms of direct participation, the practice of assemblies, and the search for consensus. The actions they engaged in were inspired by the tradition of nonviolent movements and of civil disobedience. Therefore, they articulated the type of actions inherited from the left-wing Catholic and left-wing humanist traditions (such as the "solidarity" meals, the mutualization of purchases, etc.)—which were the vectors of everyday resistance—and more radical initiatives of direct action. Private temporary employment agencies, as well as the networks of professional training managed by the trade unions, had become one of the targets of their protest activities (through demonstrations in front of the premises of these agencies or the distribution of leaflets). Some elements of their actions were directly influenced by the movement of the unemployed in France, such as the collective and very visible use of public transport without paying (Mouchard 2002), whereas other elements were linked to the search for convergences with other struggles. The networks that were active in the anti-globalization milieu, such as the action groups against unemployment and job insecurity, came together in their attempt to support immigrant workers who occupied in 1999, and then again in 2005, churches and notably the Barcelona bishopric (Franck 2008). The emergence of these struggles should be linked to the growing importance of immigration and notably of clandestine immigration in Spain in a context of economic growth between 1995 and 2007. This last example illustrates two important points. On the one hand, it allows us to highlight once more the flexibility of those associations not looking to specialize in one issue but rather to establish convergences between groups suffering from different forms of domination. On the other, it shows the way in which these associations develop a critique of capitalist social relations by relating the different figures of exploitation: the unemployed, the workers in unstable employment, but also illegal immigrant workers.

To summarize, these associations that make their appearance on the activist space of the alternative left between the late 1990s and the early 2000s mostly bring together young people, marginalized for want of stable employment, critical of the system, as well as fringes of older activists, sometimes with trade union experience, who are victims of long-term unemployment. These associations have not stopped evolving during the 2000s, according to the dynamic of current mobilizations, and have most importantly articulated their critique of neoliberal globalization with that of migration policies. Most often, they have not ventured beyond the very local level. In addition, they are quite attached to the principle of self-organization and to their independence with regard to political parties and institutions.

The 2002 General Strike as the Incident that Revealed Occasional Coalitions

On June 20, 2002, a general strike against the reform of the unemployment compensation scheme introduced by the conservative government of José María Aznar took place in Spain. This strike resulted in a victory for the trade unions and for all the other actors involved since the essential part of the reform was withdrawn. This event is an interesting case study in light of the elements analyzed in the first two parts of this chapter. Indeed, because of the creation of local action groups against unemployment and job insecurity in the late 1990s, as well as their inclusion in the antiglobalization networks, a general strike could have constituted an occasion to strengthen a larger movement of the unemployed. It could also have constituted a moment of encounter between activist networks that had ignored each other up to that point, or worse, which had even been hostile to each other: the network of the main trade unions (CC.OO and UGT) and that of the radical left. Therefore, we have considered it useful to test this hypothesis through an analysis of the context in which this strike took place, the way it unfolded, and its implications.

The general strike of June 20, 2002, is part of a wave of mobilizations (Koopmans 2004) linked to the intensification of the neoliberal policies implemented by José María Aznar during his second term in power (2000–2004). First, the rejection of the law on foreigners resulted in big demonstrations in 2001, the year during which the students also protested en masse against the reform of the universities. In 2002, the national hydrological plan, which provided for the decanting of water from the river Ebro, resulted in a huge protest movement in Aragon and Catalonia.[11] In June 2002 antiglobalization demonstrations were organized during the European summit of Barcelona and during the G8 in Seville. Last, in 2003, the management of the ecological disaster caused by the shipwreck of the oil tanker Prestige and then the participation in the war on Iraq side by side with the United States are punished by mobilizations of an exceptional scope in which take part millions of people (Pont Vidal 2004).

This is the context in which the trade unions decided to call a general strike against the Aznar government. The strike of June 20, 2002, occupies, however, an unusual position in this cycle of conflicts. It should be understood, before anything else, as a confrontation between the two main trade union confederations and the government on the issue of the content and the method of contractual policy. Indeed, one of the main oppositions to the reform of the unemployment compensation scheme had to do with the authoritarian character of the decision-making process. The project was announced without prior consultation of the trade unions and was finally adopted on May 25, 2002, by a decree-law, which made it possible to avoid the debate with the social partners and parliamentary procedures. In essence, this reform adopted the perspectives of the European Commission aimed at the generalization of so-called active measures promoting the return to employment. One of the aims of the reform is to force job seekers to accept an offer—refusal of which would entail penalization—even if it does not correspond to what the job seekers are asking for: they are expected to accept any job (half-time, limited, or unlimited duration) situated at a distance of less than thirty kilometers from where they live, or which entails less than two hours of commuting (the cost of which might reach up to 20 percent of the net monthly wage), including jobs that do not provide for the payment of contributions to an unemployment compensation scheme. A first refusal of a proposal, which the administration considers to be adequate, results in a suspension of unemployment benefits for three months, a second refusal in a suspension of six months, and a third one in a definitive exclusion from the unemployment compensation scheme. Moreover, after a year of being unemployed, the job seeker cannot refuse an offer, whether the latter is related to the job seeker's initial training or not. Last, the principle of the activation of resources (as above, the person receiving an unemployment benefit is expected to actively make an effort to find a job) is extended to those unemployed aged fifty-two and above, who had been spared up to then (Tuchszirer 2002).

Confronted with this neoliberal offensive, the CC.OO and the UGT responded with a planned general strike, which is a traditional element in the traditional range of actions of Spanish trade unions.[12] The strike of June 20, 2002, which paralyzed the whole of the country, was part of a rather conventional pattern that, as such, did not open up new spaces for action.

The strike constituted, however, a good indicator of the developments that took place at the time. The first issue was obviously that of the convergences between different struggles. The successive mobilizations and especially the closeness between the general strike and the antiglobalization demonstrations against the G8 in Seville in June 2002 enable us to examine the reconfiguration of the relations between the different organizations. In this regard, these relations remain, generally, quite tenuous. Of course, the CC.OO and the UGT called on their members to participate in the countersummit organized parallel to the G8. For their part, the local associations of the unemployed publicized the call of the trade unions for a general strike on June 20, 2002. But closer cooperation, entailing, for instance, the adoption of a common set of demands, did not materialize. The most important connections established between the associations of the unemployed and of workers in unstable employment and other activist groups were those with organizations linked to the antiglobalization movement.

Thus, despite the importance[13] and the success of the strike and despite its main demand (defense of the unemployment compensation scheme), it is not possible to speak at this point of a social movement for and with the unemployed. It seems more accurate to highlight the fact that the trade unions acted to defend the unemployment compensation scheme without the participation of the unemployed, that is to say without considering the possibility of organizing collective action by the latter. In this regard, the Spanish case is interesting when compared with the French case where the process of the reconfiguration of the trade union movement—that is, the creation of an internal opposition within the CFDT, the departure of activists from this organization, and the creation of the new SUD unions that are much more radical—promoted the encounter between trade unionists and association activists in order to create new organizations of struggle against unemployment (Béroud 2006). In Spain, as has already been mentioned, there also exist less important trade unions such as the CGT. But they do not have sufficient weight in terms of members and in terms of their ability to take action, which would allow them to decisively influence the line of the CC.OO and the UGT and as a result the course of the general strike.

However, this observation does not apply to the whole of the country. The importance of regional contexts results in a diversification of the opportunity structures such as they present themselves and as they are perceived by the activist groups. Indeed, the autonomous community of Andalusia has witnessed important convergences because of the existence of a specific problem, that is, the abolition of the "rural unemployment compensation" scheme. The determined mobilization of a part of the population against this governmental decision, particularly those workers excluded from employment, organized or not, triggered occasional alliances between the political parties of the left (PSOE and IU), the main trade unions (CC.OO, UGT), much less important organizations such as the SOC, of an anarcho-syndicalist tradition, and the antiglobalization associations.

One of the components of the Aznar government's reform of the unemployment compensation scheme entailed the abolition of the agrarian compensation regime, the *subsidio rural* (PER), which was created in 1984 by the socialist government for the day laborers working in Andalusia and in Extremadura. The reasons behind this move by the Aznar government remain relatively obscure, since this scheme was relevant at the time of the reform to only 200,000 people and only represented a marginal sum in the total spending of the central state.[14]

The announcement of this measure triggers in Andalusia a reaction that extends largely beyond the reach of the trade unions. A true "*mobilisation de pays*"[15] unfolds parallel to the antiglobalization demonstration against the Seville G8 summit in June 2002, enjoying a strong organizational support and benefiting from the presence of actors coming from very diversified backgrounds. During the whole of June, and in preparation for the general strike, the regional epicenter of which is Seville, numerous operations took place, most often with the support of local administrations run by the PSOE.[16] Thus, on June 1, 76 percent of Andalusian municipalities went on strike for a few hours in order to protest against the decree-law doing away with the rural unemployment compensation scheme. Groups of trade unionists and of unemployed workers peacefully occupied around forty town halls or chained themselves to the latter's grillwork, as in Seville. Motions in municipal assemblies were voted by the PSOE–IU coalitions, sometimes even together with the *Partido andalucista* (regional socialist-leaning party), in support of the strike.

The (quasi-)federal structure of the Spanish state amplified the institutional resources available to local actors. So, for instance, the Andalusian parliament adopted on June 7 a document demanding the withdrawal of the decree-law (and its examination in view of verifying its conformity with the constitution) and exceptionally authorized the two regional secretaries of the CC.OO and of the UGT to sit in the guest gallery. Almost everywhere, traveling caravans traveled to the most rural parts of Andalusia, those parts that would be the most affected by the abolition of the compensation scheme. On June 9, following the call by the regional CC.OO and UGT, but also supported by all the parties in the Andalusian parliament except the Popular Party (PP), a repetition on a regional scale of the general strike took place: 250,000 people demonstrated in the streets of Seville and challenged in particular the minister of labor, Javier Arenas, representative of the ultraliberal wing of the PP and candidate in the local elections in Andalusia. Moreover, until June 20, not less than fourteen demonstrations were organized.

Several characteristics are brought out by these events. For those actors established on the institutional sphere—whether the main trade unions such as the CC.OO and the UGT or political parties such as the PSOE and the IU—the struggle in Andalusia provided the basis for a huge confrontation with the national government. In this sense, the opposition to the abolition of the PER only marginally modified the interpretative framework in which these organizations situated themselves. The regional level allowed, therefore, the deploying of demands, such as the one aiming to obtain the transfer of national responsibility in terms of employment policies to the *Junta de Andalucía* and the creation of a *servicio andaluz del empleo*,[17] in the image of what already existed in Catalonia, which would reinforce the regional level as a space of public action.

This aim was only tenuously and marginally adhered to by smaller groups, which ran their own campaigns against the abolition of the PER. Here, the small farmers' union SOC, which was present only in Andalusia (Morales 1997), played the key role. The SOC mobilized the day laborers (and not the small plot owners) in order to defend their rights, but also with the aim of obtaining a massive agrarian reform that would eventually promote land redistribution. Not only was the SOC's social base directly affected by the project of abolishing rural unemployment compensation, but it also was one of the very few unions attempting to represent illegal immigrant workers and unemployed day laborers. If the two big demonstrations of June 9 and 20 were made possible thanks to the legitimacy that the UGT and the CC.OO drew from professional elections, only the SOC activists on the other hand were capable of creating links with the antiglobalization movement, through the organization of common actions. Although relying on the legacy of a certain anarcho-syndicalist tradition that focused on direct action and in particular on the combative tradition of agricultural laborers in Andalusia going back to the 1930s, the SOC only sporadically managed to mobilize the day laborers (Talejo Vázquez 1996). Since it did not plan to situate itself in the perspective of building a national movement of the unemployed and of workers in unstable employment, it preferred to remain geographically contained and within a very limited sector of activity. The result was that, despite having contributed in the local emergence of the political figure of the unemployed and of the worker in unstable employment in rural areas, the SOC modified neither its network of alliances nor its demands in any sustainable way.

Conclusion

Convergences remain, therefore, limited, but the occasional building of a coalition of actors against the abolition of "rural unemployment compensation" in Andalusia shows several elements. On the one hand, in spite of this not being a decision by the government of the autonomous community but by the national government, the regional framework of action assumes in this case its full importance since it enables occasional coalition work (Staggenborg 1986) involving a variety of actors, which would not otherwise cooperate (both small and big trade unions, associations of the unemployed and of workers in unstable employment, but also political parties represented at the various levels of power). However, this configuration remains specific to Andalusia. The mobilization dynamic, which exists in this autonomous community, does not have a vocation to be extended to other communities. In this regard, there is also a fragmentation of action frameworks in Spain.

On the other hand, the emergence of the framework of the autonomous community as the locus of mobilizations and of demands on the regional authorities tends to modify the relation that these organizations share with regional state institutions. The latter can, indeed, become resources on which to draw when it comes to putting pressure on the national government or to reinforcing the credibility and the legitimacy of specific demands. Two examples, distinct from the incidence of the 2002 general strike, provide strong proof of the potentialities not only for trade unions but especially for those associations having limited logistical means at their disposal and enjoying limited access to the institutional sphere. In Madrid, a campaign was run for free public transport, in the late 1990s, by the *Rompamos el silencio* action group. The campaign was supported by a petition signed by 15,000 people and put forward in the municipal assembly by the PSOE and IU groups, the representatives of the local opposition. In 2000, in the autonomous community of the Basque Country, a coalition of action groups against unemployment and poverty used the legislative device of popular initiative, provided for by the "status of autonomy."[18] The draft law included the reduction of the working week to thirty-two hours and the creation of a minimum income equivalent to the bottom wage across the different sectors. Named the "The Charter of Social Rights," this program enjoyed much wider support than just that of the small groups of the unemployed, winning in particular the support of Christian associations, researchers at the Basque Country University, and nationalist trade unions. More than 80,000 people approved of this proposal, which was partially transformed into a law, within the exclusive framework of the autonomous community, on December 27, 2000. The members of parliament reduced, however, the minimum income to 75 percent of the minimum wage, reserved the scheme to those people aged between twenty-five and sixty-five, and abandoned the idea of reducing the length of the working week (Aganzo 2003, 251–4).

These experiences clearly show that the relations between the various activist milieux and the organizations are not entirely immobile in Spain, despite the existence of an important gulf separating the main trade unions and the networks of associations attempting to mobilize the unemployed and those workers in unstable employment. New issues can contribute to the creation of a more or less lasting coalition of actors. The issue of the adoption of a minimum assistance income in the autonomous communities that do not yet dispose of one could in the years ahead provide new ground for the emergence of dynamics of struggle. These dynamics could be the opportunity to unite for a range of actors extending from left-wing parties to action groups of the unemployed and of workers in unstable employment.

Notes

1. The UGT and the CC.OO have historically been close to the Spanish Socialist Labour Party (PSOE) and the Spanish Communist Party (PCE), respectively. However, these links slackened during the 1980s, in particular those between the CC.OO and the PCE, because of the acute electoral and organizational crisis experienced by the PCE.
2. Our study is based on the perusal of the national and local press, of documents from trade unions and associations, as well as the scientific literature dealing with this issue. Moreover, during a first stay in 2005 we carried out interviews with union officials from professional federations and local unions in Madrid and Andalusia. Two other stays, in 2007 and then in 2008, gave us the opportunity to meet the people responsible for running the associations that are active on the issues of job insecurity and unemployment.
3. The rate of job insecurity is the relation between the number of insecure job contracts and the total number of contracts for the labor force.
4. Both the CC.OO and the UGT hold that the source of the bulk of their resources is the contributions paid by their members. But this does not alter the fact that they remain highly dependent on public funds, which they receive through training

schemes (reinsertion in employment) and through their participation in social and economic organisms. They also receive funds from autonomous communities and municipalities. The resources distributed by the state are linked, on the one hand, to the transfer of "trade union holdings" (notably real estate) accumulated by the old pro-Franco single trade union to the organizations that were recreated with the return of democracy and, on the other, to the share of the vote that each trade union receives during professional elections.

5. The rate of unionization fell in the early 1980s and since then stands at around 16 percent (2003 figures) of the labor force (Richards 2008, 7). The two main confederations, the CC.OO and the UGT, organize around 80 percent of unionized workers (i.e., 950,000 members for the former and 850,000 for the latter). They receive around 70 percent of the vote in professional elections, in which participate around 60 percent of workers. These results are the source of their legitimacy. From this point of view, Spanish trade unionism has become more a unionism of voters than of members (Köhler 2008, 21).
6. These funds are managed by the *Instituto Nacional del Empleo* (INEM), which determines the regulatory framework of the system of social protection against unemployment.
7. See the chapter one in this volume.
8. Translated into French by the author and then into English by the translator (translator's note).
9. As mentioned earlier, the CC.OO and the UGT exercised a quasi-monopoly on the representation of the workers of the big private and public firms. However, small trade unions from a protest tradition, strongly opposed to the "reformist" line of the two big trade union confederations, played a non-negligible role in situations of struggle. These were the CGT, the CSI (*Corriente Sindical de Izquierdas*), the SOC (*Sindicato de los Obreros del Campo*), but also the nationalist trade unions in the Basque Country and in Galicia (Köhler 2008, 36).
10. Baladre is the name of a neighborhood in Sagresto, a town situated in the north of Valencia.
11. The use of the water of one of the biggest rivers in Spain, the Ebro, refers to a solidarity problem between the arid regions (Andalusia, Extremadura) and those regions not facing this kind of problem (Aragon, Catalonia). But the decanting of water provided for by the government's plans had important ecological consequences in Aragon and Catalonia, which were the target of the demonstrators.
12. Since Spanish trade unions focus mainly on negotiated social contracts with the government, they organize general strikes when they do not succeed in influencing government policy. The idea is to paralyze during twenty-four hours the entire Spanish economy. Since the return to democracy, four such general strikes have been organized: in 1985, in 1988, in 1994, and in 2002.
13. According to the trade unions 80 percent of workers took part in the strike. Industry was completely paralyzed and so was the transport sector. Energy consumption fell by 20 percent. More than a million people took part in the demonstrations (Tuchszirer 2002, 10).
14. This piece of information was collected during an interview with Manuel Pérez Yruela, director of the *Instituto de Estudios Sociales Avanzados de Andalucía*, on April 22, 2005.
15. Here we borrow an expression invented in the study of local mobilizations linked to plant closures (Mercier and Segrestin 1983).

16. Here we rely on the systematic perusal of the *Diario de Sevilla* (May and June 2002), one of the main daily papers in Andalusia, as well as on trade union documents.
17. Interview with Rafael Roldán Vásquez, general secretary of the *Union provincial* of Grenada of the CC.OO, offices of CC.OO, April 18, 2005.
18. The Basque parliament adopted on June 26, 1986, a law on the popular legislative initiative that allows for 30,000 citizens living in the Basque Country to propose, by means of a petition, to parliament a draft law. The parliament is not obliged to position itself on the text drafted by the citizens and can redraft it.

References

Aganzo, Andrés. 2003. Movimientos sociales de parados y precarios. In *Trabajadores precarios, el proletariado del siglo XXI*, ed. Rafael Díaz-Salazar, 217–54. Madrid: Ediciones HOAC.

Agrikoliansky, Eric, Olivier Fillieule, and Nonna Mayer. 2005. Introduction : aux origines de l'altermondialisme français. In *L'Altermondialisme en France. La longue histoire d'une nouvelle cause*, ed. Eric Agrikoliansky, Olivier Fillieule, and Nonna Mayer, 13–42. Paris: Fayard.

Antentas Collderram, Josep Maria. 2007. Sindicalisme i moviment "antiglobalització": una aproximació a partir dels casos del Fòrum Social Mundial i del tancament de l'empresa Miniwatt. PhD diss., Universitat Autònoma de Barcelona.

Bagguley, Paul. 1991. *From Protest to Acquiescence? Political Movements of the Unemployed*. London: Macmillan.

———. 1992. Protest, Acquiescence and the Unemployed: A Comparative Analysis of the 1930s and 1980s. *The British Journal of Sociology* 3: 443–61.

Béroud, Sophie. 2006. La rébellion salariale. In *La France rebelle*, ed. Xavier Crettiez and Isabelle Sommier, 276–87. Paris: Michalon.

Burgess, Katrina. 1999. Unemployment and Union Strategies in Spain. *South European Society & Politics* 3: 1–31.

Calle, Angel. 2005. *Nuevos movimientos globales. Hacia la radicalidad democrática*. Madrid: Editorial Popular.

———. 2007. El estudio del impacto de los movimientos sociales. Una perspectiva global. *Revista española de investigaciones sociologicas* 120: 133–53.

Chabanet, Didier. 2008. When the Unemployed Challenge the European Union: The European Marches as Externalization of Protest. *Mobilization: An International Journal* 13(3): 311–22.

Demazière, Didier, and Maria-Teresa Pignoni. 1998. *Chômeurs : du silence à la révolte*. Paris: Hachette.

EIRO. 1998. Movilización de asociaciones de parados. Una influencia del caso francés. http://www.eurofound.europa.eu/eiro/1998/03/word/es9803249fes.doc (last accessed October 1, 2009).

Franck, Cécile. 2008. Les collectifs de sans-papiers en France et en Espagne dans les années 2000 : analyse comparative d'acteurs collectifs à faible ressource. PhD diss., Université de Montpellier.

Köhler, Holm-Detlev. 2008. Los sindicatos en España frente a los retos de la globalización y del cambio tecnológico. *Laboratorio de Alternativas* 142: 3–93.

Koopmans, Ruud. 2004. Protest in Time and Space: The Evolution of Waves of contention. In *The Blackwell Companion to Social Movements*, ed. David A. Snow, Sarah A. Soule, and Hanspeter Kriesi, 19–46. Oxford: Blackwell.

Mercier, Nicole, and Denis Segrestin. 1983. L'"effet territoire" dans la mobilisation ouvrière. Essai d'analyse de situation complexe. *Revue française de sociologie* 24: 61–79.
Morales, Rafael. 1997. Desarrollo y transformaciones históricas en el Sindicato de Obreros del Campo (1976–1994). *Sociología del Trabajo* 32: 31–51.
Moreno, Luis. 1997. *La Federalización de España, poder político y territorio*. Madrid: Siglo XXI.
Mouchard, Daniel. 2002. Les mobilisations des "sans" dans la France contemporaine : l'émergence d'un "radicalisme autolimité" ? *Revue française de science politique* 52(4): 425–47.
Pérez Quintana, Vicente, and Pablo Sánchez León, ed. 2009. *Memoria ciudadana y movimiento vicinal. Madrid, 1968–2008*. Madrid: La Catarata.
Pérez Torres, Francisco Miguel. 2004. El empleo después de los cuarenta. In *Desigualdad social y relaciones de trabajo*, ed. Joaquin Elena y Peña, 95–116. Salamanca: Ediciones Universidad Salamanca.
Polavieja, Javier G., and Andrew Richards. 2001. Trade Unions, Unemployement, and Working Class Fragmentation in Spain. In *Unemployment in the New Europe*, ed. Nancy Bermeo, 203–44. Cambridge: Cambridge University Press.
Pont Vidal, Josep. 2004. *La Ciudadanía se moviliza. Los movimientos sociales y la globalización en España*. Barcelona: Flor del Viento.
Richards, Andrew. 2000. Trade Unionism and the Unemployed in the European Union. *La lettre de la Maison française d'Oxford* 12: 153–81.
———. 2008. El sindicalismo en España. *Laboratorio de Alternativas* 135: 3–54.
Rodríguez Cabrero, Gregorio. 2008. L'État-providence espagnol : pérennité, transformations et defis. *Travail et Emploi* 115: 95–107.
Serrano del Rosal, Javier G. 2000. *Transformación y cambio del sindicalismo español contemporáneo*. Córdoba: CSIC.
Staggenborg, Suzanne. 1986. Coalition Work in the Pro-Choice Movement: Organizational and Environmental Opportunities and Obstacles. *Social Problems* 33: 374–90.
Talejo Vázquez, Felix. 1996. *Cultura jornalera, poder popular y liderazgo mesiánico*. Seville: Universidad de Sevilla.
Tuchszirer, Carole. 2002. Grève générale contre une politique de l'emploi plus contraignante pour les chômeurs. *Chronique internationale de l'IRES* 77: 3–11.
Vincent, Catherine. 2005. Espagne. De la dérégulation à la recherche d'un équilibre entre flexibilité et sécurité. *Chronique internationale de l'IRES* 97: 97–108.

CHAPTER 7

Contention over Unemployment in Britain: Unemployment Politics versus the Politics of the Unemployed

Manlio Cinalli

In Britain contention over unemployment has come to an end. In the last decade, the unemployed have stopped to voice their claims at the national level, and have resorted to occasional instances of protest only as the result of local industrial disputes (Cinalli and Statham 2005). This chapter aims first of all to assess how this long process of pacification has come about. Contention over unemployment has varied substantially across time, both in terms of intensity and forms, with the unemployed alternating waves of mobilization with periods of acquiescence. This chapter also asks whether current pacification might be reversed in the future. The main question is whether New Labour has achieved a durable settlement that can reintegrate the interest of the unemployed in the political space while keeping the unemployed themselves far from street protest. Could the unemployed return to collective action owing to an increasing rate of unemployment? In fact, unemployment may also be prioritized as a salient issue regardless of real rates of unemployment (Baxandall 2001; Giugni and Berclaz 2003; see also chapter nine in this volume), while invisible processes of contentious politics may be in act beyond the curtains of the pacified field (Melucci 1984 and 1989).[1]

The main argument of the chapter is that the British unemployed have become politically unable to impose their concerns into the public space. This process of "weakening" needs to be appraised through the analysis of the changing situation of the unemployed within a broader political space occupied by other relevant actors, such as the labor movement, employers, policy elites, the state, and civil society at large. Three main phases are identified, each capturing a piece of a longer process that has reversed the premises from which it started. The first phase goes from the end of the nineteenth century to the interwar period. This phase saw the emergence of a strong unified labor movement; it ended with a restrictive stand of the state that cleaved the labor movement along the distinction between workers and the unemployed. The second phase runs from World War II until the end of the New Right government. Strengthening of workers' organizations throughout many years of economic boom was finally reversed. The state further constrained workers and the unemployed, succeeding in marginalizing their organizations. In the third and ongoing phase, New Labour has brought the "politics of the unemployed" back at the center of institutional concerns. It has left unchallenged, however, the New Right assumption that the unemployed themselves have not a political role to play, opening up extensive opportunities for the engagement of probeneficiary organizations acting on their behalf (Cinalli 2007a).

Having discussed the relevant literature and main tools of analysis (see section titled "Theoretical Background"), this chapter provides a reconstruction of labor mobilization throughout the last century, focusing specifically on (i) the shifting relations between workers and the unemployed, and (ii) the changing mix of political opportunities and constraints impacting upon mobilization of workers and the unemployed. Indeed, this chapter shows that the state and its allies have had a crucial impact on the *continuum* between workers and the unemployed. Cleaving of this *continuum* (see section titled "First Phase: Cleaving Employed Workers from the Unemployed") brought about the marginalization of the unemployed (see section titled "Second Phase: Defeating Workers and the Unemployed"). The chapter then evaluates whether New Labour has managed to bring back the politics of unemployment at the center of British political agenda without prompting a new wave of collective mobilization, or if indeed its policy may soon be challenged by the unemployed themselves. The main argument is that New Labour has opened the field of unemployment to numerous probeneficiary groups and civil society organizations, transforming a key contentious space for competition between capital and labor into a consensual space that is immune from further mobilization and disruptive protest, at least for a long time to come (see section titled "Final Phase: Pro-unemployed and New Labour Long-lasting Pacification").

Theoretical Background

The analysis of this chapter allows for integrating a number of strands in the literature. Scholars of social movements have taken the collective action of the unemployed as their main *explananda*, investigating processes of political struggle and identity formation (Piven and Cloward 1977; Bagguley 1991 and 1992). Some of them have opened space for further analysis of the dynamics that link the mobilization of the unemployed to the opening of institutional opportunities (Berclaz and Giugni 2005; Giugni 2008). At the same time, the consideration of the delicate balance between a large number of actors within the field of unemployment calls for use of scholarship applying networks to collective action (Diani 1992; Diani and McAdam 2003) since no scholar has systematically engaged with the relations tying the unemployed to other actors over time. Here the argument is that the analysis of contention over unemployment needs to be complemented with a more detailed study of exchanges as they are forged among the state, the unemployed, unions, employers, probeneficiary organizations, and other actors that enter the field. By contrast, the analysis of this chapter takes little account of scholarship that considers unemployment as a variable that facilitates or constrains labor mobilization (Fulcher 1991; Kelly 1998). Unemployment rates are considered across the different phases under investigation, showing the presence of key longitudinal variations. Yet, in contrast with analyses that are rooted within "grievance" theories, very little space is given to comment on the explanatory role of unemployment rates. The assumption here is that grievances are ubiquitous, particularly when talking about unemployment. After all, even a tiny rate of 2 percent still indicates the presence of thousands of unemployed people, hiding the potential presence of even a bigger number of workers under threat of dismissal.

A central place is thus given to the discussion of the role of political variables, in terms of (i) top-down state policies, and (ii) bottom-up decisions of organizations when forging their own system of alliances. This chapter thus relies only marginally on knowledge about the individual characteristics of the unemployed (Jahoda, Lazarsfeld, and Zeisel 1971; Demazière and Pignoni 1998). Rather, it investigates variations of contention over unemployment drawing upon two main concepts of scholarship of contentious politics, namely, opportunities and networks. The first concept refers more precisely to the Political Opportunity Structure (POS) approach (Eisinger 1973; Tarrow 1994; Kriesi et al. 1995). This approach has focused on exogenous and stable political variables impacting on the possibility that groups, organizations, and movements have for collective action. In particular, it has mostly tackled state opportunities, rooting its first steps into the analysis of formation of the modern nation-state (Tilly 1978). The second concept refers to an emerging literature dealing with the analysis of exchanges among actors (Diani 1992; Diani and McAdam 2003). The main argument here is that the examination of exchanges within the unemployment field is necessary to account for the mobilization of the unemployed, since the relational structures within which they are embedded assign them a specific position where certain conducts become more possible than others.

The seminal work of Bagguley (1991 and 1992) on the mobilization of the unemployed had mainly relied on the POS explanatory framework. His analysis considers carefully the characteristics of the political structure that the unemployed themselves face, and in particular, the extent to which specific powers of welfare are allocated at the local level. Bagguley's focus on provisions targeting the unemployed is convincing but hardly exhaustive of the political context. This chapter approaches the political context in broader terms, dealing with a number of top-down state inputs that do not target only the unemployed. In particular, the chapter pays attention to the dynamic pattern of industrial relations in Britain (Howell 2005), since the position of the unemployed is intrinsically bound to the shape of conflict between capital and work. Bagguley also focuses on organizational structures, putting emphasis on the distinction between probeneficiary organizations and organizations of the unemployed themselves. This same distinction is at the core of this chapter, but it is tackled more systematically. In particular, attention is focused on the emergence of a crucial cleavage between workers and the unemployed, discussing the relational dynamics allowing for bridging or strengthening of this cleavage. The analysis of opportunities is thus matched with that of networks. For example, some scholars have shown that a wide range of embedded resources can be accessed through mutual ties, providing the unemployed with alternative means to disruptive protest (Piven and Cloward 1977). These ties can facilitate the flow of information about choices otherwise not available; they can also influence the agents who play a critical role in decision-making, while at the same time reinforcing identity, recognition, public acknowledgment, and support.

First Phase: Cleaving Employed Workers from the Unemployed

In the second half of the nineteenth century the increasing mechanization of production, the movement of capital across new industries, alongside with new spaces for profitable activities of financial speculation, relieved pressures on capital (McNeill 1982). These pressures were passed onto the labor movement during a key phase of self-organization for a large base of workers and unemployed people. The Land and Labour League emerged as a major mobilizing organization as early as 1870, when a major protest was staged in London (Harrison 1965; Bagguley 1991). Scholars have shown that this was not the first instance of unemployment mobilization in Britain, with first unemployed protests dating back to the early nineteenth century (Schulte Beerbühl 2011). The League, however, considered the unemployed to be a core component of the labor movement and the driving force of its mobilization. It thus laid the foundations for further political efforts of Social Democrats on the footsteps of the 1870 protest (Reiss 2011). The first Marxist political organization in Britain, the Social Democratic Federation, was set up between 1881 and 1884 with the aim of providing workers and unemployed people with more influence on policy elites and processes of decision-making (Kidd 1984; Stedman-Jones 1984). The Independent Labour Party was set up in 1893, and it launched immediately a National Unemployed Committee to coordinate protest campaigning over unemployment. This was also a period of time when union membership doubled every few years (Silver 2003). Increasing political engagement of labor translated into extensive work on a broad number of social issues, linking unemployment, unionism, strike action, labor law, poverty, women's rights, child labor, education, and disarmament. Last, the Labour Representation Committee was set up in 1900, providing the fundaments for the creation, only a few years later, of the Labour Party. Put simply, this was a time of labor assertion and growing culture of opposition to employers' interests, even if there was not a full cooperation between the different workers' organizations (Thompson 1967; Brown 1971).

Hence, increasing unionization, disruptive protests, and mass strikes in core sectors of the economy (Stearns 1975) strengthened the muscular conflict between labor and capital. The 1886 West End riot stood out as a turning point that marked the irruption of unemployed politics in Britain (Flanagan 1991). Mobilization was also matched by new patterns of urbanization that divided working neighborhoods from residence locations of the upper and middle classes (Hobsbawm 1969; Meacham 1977). A mass strike in 1889 united skilled and unskilled workers, making political sense of their increasing closeness in economic terms (Webb and Webb 1920). Furthermore, this mobilization brought together workers organized in older structures (e.g., the engineers) and those organized in new unions (such as dockers and miners). Conflict over unemployment and against threats to employment was particularly explosive. A lockout at Manningham Mills in 1891 developed into a series of mass meetings, rallies, and disruptive actions that united the unemployed, workers across different industrial sectors, and new labor representations. While mobilizing both semi- and unskilled workers, the so-called New Unionism brought about further unity between workers and the unemployed. A wave of "Labour Unrest" led to hundreds of strikes and long disruptive campaigning (Phelps Brown 1975; Cronin 1979). Employers were initially overtaken by workers' mobilization: the high proportion of compromise settlements in 1891–1892 shows that they were initially forced to settle for extensive concessions. Yet, their counteroffensive did not take too long, starting with the formalization of self-organizing structures. For example, the Engineering Employers' Federation (EEF) was set up in 1896, leading the 1897 Engineering Lockout. Furthermore, employers managed to present their actions as necessary interventions to protect national interests from foreign competition. In so doing, they called for the "legitimate" support of the state, as in the case of the Taff Vale judgment of 1901.

This was indeed a time during which the British state took a more interventionist posture in labor disputes (Scally 1975; Harris 1984) so as to intermediate between the quest for protection of employers, and the potential harming of unemployed and workers' mobilization. Key institutional developments followed, such as the setting up of many boards of conciliation and arbitration where unions and employers could meet. This process culminated in the Industrial Council of 1911–1913, that is, a national conciliation body that was composed of representatives from both employers and employees. Although the Council was hardly influential, its creation built the path toward collective bargaining, reinforcing the existing embryonic structures of industrial relations. The state continued to play the pivotal role at least until the creation of a Ministry of Labour in 1917, during a period of time of gradual reinforcement of both employers' and workers' organizations. The Trades Union Congress (TUC) acquired a central authority within the labor movement, while the employers set up the Federation of British Industries (FBI) in 1916 and the National Union of Manufacturers (NUM) in 1917.

World War I helped the state to master domestic social conflict (Taylor 1954; Levy 1989 and 1998): workers backed the state and dropped their socialist agenda. Opportunities were opened for trade unions to attract government and the employers within collective bargaining and grievance procedures (Aldcroft and Oliver 2001). Joint regulation was immediately implemented after the war through the Whitley Councils and the National Industrial Conference. While the former were meant to secure a regular consultation between capital and workers, the Conference stood out as the venue where both sides would interact. Yet, the end of war also showed that class struggle and disagreements were growing stronger. The EEF opposed the FBI, the Treasury stood against the interventionism of the Ministry of Labour, while unions put increasing emphasis on their bargaining autonomy (Fulcher 1991). Militancy, industrial disputes, and left-wing mobilizations acquired a revolutionary drive: back from war, workers engaged in a wave of labor unrest (Cronin 1979). Trade unionism was a key force behind labor mobilization. Miners, transport workers, and the railway men forged their Triple Alliance in 1914, while the TUC General Council was set up in 1921 with powers to call for unified industrial action.

The unemployed played a key role throughout the mobilization process. Following a series of local protests, the National Unemployed Workers' Movement (NUWM) was set up in 1921, drawing upon a number of groups under the leadership of former engineering shop stewards (Croucher 1987). These grassroots groups thought that an organization of the unemployed was necessary to pursue their own autonomous interests and initiative. NUWM's radical outlook, its involvement in highly visible hunger strike marches, together with its ultimate goal of a Workers Socialist Republic must be put in the context of post–World War I revolutionary years. In fact, NUWM also engaged in concrete demands to increase the level of benefits, working at the same time on caseworks for individual claims. NUWM was financed through support of its own members, rather than external political funding. While targeting unemployed people, it also had a one-third quota reserved for workers in an effort to mobilize protesters who were sharing common social class, grassroots culture, and collective interests. Local branches were at the core of overall organizational structure, with the major aim to promote full participatory democracy.

In addition, NUWM had to deal with decreasing potential for mobilization. The state elaborated a well-balanced package of opportunities and constraints that aimed to preempt demands of the unemployed. The unemployed insurance was extended to employees in the low-range earnings, duration of benefits' coverage was tripled, rates were raised, and new allowances were introduced. In the decade between 1920 and 1930 the subsidy of the unemployment fund increased from 3.4 to 37 percent of total social services expenditure (Deacon 1977, 9–10; Bagguley 1991, 92). The reform of the system of benefits also weakened local control in favor of growing centralization.

The state thus managed to shrink the long wave of mobilization. There was a drastic cut in terms of NUWM activities and membership, with a tenfold fall from 100,000 in 1922–1923 to 10,000 in 1925–1926 (Bagguley 1991, 86). Workers met with a key series of defeats. Transport and railway workers refused to support the 1921 miners' strike, bringing about the end of the Triple Alliance and substantial wage cuts in the mining industry. The engineering lockout of 1922 also ended in defeat for the labor movement. Fears that bottom-up revolutionary radicalism of the shop floor could overtake the central authority of union leaders faded away. Militants were isolated and the rank-and-file were brought back under the leadership of central union's officials (Cole and Cole 1937). A stabilizing process was imposed through economic concentration, restoration of the gold standard, strengthening of employers' organizations, consolidation of Treasury, and increasing government control. In particular, unemployment was used as an instrument of industrial struggle that employers could use to contain workers' aspirations and innovation at the shop-floor level (Hinton and Hyman 1975). The 1926 General Strike showed once and for all that industrial action was destined to fail in a context of mass unemployment.

This was the turning point in the break-up of the British labor movement, marking the deepening of cleavage between workers and the unemployed. Facing demobilization, the NUWM had to stress its radical tones to single out its own "unique" mission and to attract new members. In so doing, it modified its internal balance by giving predominance to the ideological action of national officials rather than to the pragmatic leadership of local branches. Costs were huge in terms of internal relationship between workers on the one hand and the unemployed on the other. For example, in 1927 the sharp offensive against communist militants in mining areas brought about a new wave of mobilizations that did not gain the support of other workers (Bagguley 1991, 87). If the unemployed radicalized, broadening the scope of their aspirations in a way to include those of international communism, the same process of centralization brought about opposite consequences on the workers' side of the labor movement. Moderate trade unionism, and their leaders at the national level, gained back power on radical shop stewards: priority was given to the achievement of pragmatic goals, such as the forty-seven-hour week and wage rises.

By the beginning of the 1930s, the labor movement was split, employers were back in control of workplaces, and government mastered sophisticated packages of policies to keep control of bottom-up pressures. In 1931, the conservative passed a reform that enabled a large number of disallowed unemployed claimants to apply for transitional payment under the jurisdiction of local authorities. That is, the unemployed gained the power to influence through their vote the officials who sat on the local benefits committees (Bagguley 1991, 94). Yet, one should also consider the creation of the Unemployment Assistance Board under the 1934 Unemployment Act[2] as well as the application of means-testing, which stood out as the ultimate "symbol of the injustice and wrongs" (Flanagan 1991, 181). Combination of facilitations and constrictions brought about full revitalization of protest (Croucher 1987; Ward 2011). NUWM was again the protagonist of this widespread action against restrictive legislative and administrative measures (Evans 1999). Nevertheless, the new wave of mobilization was short-lived. Channels were open at the national level for interest organizations of labor and capital, as well as for pressure groups of the poverty lobby operating at the national level (Whiteley and Winyard 1987), but only a marginal space was available for locally organized mobilization. Conditions for revolutionary protest at the beginning of the 1920s had thus been reversed through an attentive series of state interventions. The final defeat of protesters indicated a potential return to cutting of wages and social services, with the effective retrenchment of unions and labor organizations. However, the Wall Street crash had also damaged the credibility of liberal policies, calling for state intervention to promote economic development and compensate market failures. The state had by now engaged extensively with workers' rights and it could hardly stand back: its interventions brought about the reshaping of the field, with a series of innovative institutions of regulation. Laissez-faire policies could now be resisted, at least better then ever before.

Second Phase: Defeating Workers and the Unemployed

World War II marked a true watershed in terms of labor market and unemployment politics, placing the 1945 Labour government in the right condition to launch an innovative and long-lasting period of social reforming (Atkinson 1975). With the end of a unified labor movement, the unemployed were no longer close to workers. On the one hand, workers and their labor leaders focused on new organizational problems, for example, where new industries were opening in places without working neighborhoods. Smaller-scale and radical actions only survived in old industries under economic distress. Hence, moderate trade unionism continued to centralize, bureaucratize, and erode workshop organization, imposing pragmatic goals in terms of wages and working conditions over ideological goals of revolutionary justice. Unions strengthened their dialogue with employers throughout years of economic growth: employers felt no longer under labor siege as in previous decades. On the other hand, the issue of unemployment lost salience in the public debate: economic growth brought about decreasing rates of unemployment, thus weakening visibility of the unemployed as well as the very object of their grievance. Unemployment rate, which was over 10 percent in 1939, dropped down to approximately 3 percent in the mid-1940s, remaining around the 2 percent threshold between the late 1940s and the late 1950s (Cronin 1979, 228). Furthermore, the organizations of the unemployed had been in full decline since the 1930s. NUWM had no role to play after World War II, nor was any space available for other oppositional groups of the revolutionary left. The long distance dividing workers from the unemployed was also matched by a new configuration of the political context. Policymakers were willing to have more responsibilities for public intervention. Institutional developments had been succeeding since the beginning of the century, but it was only now that the state decided to engage fully with regulation of conflict between work and capital.

Throughout the 1940s and 1950s, workers sustained the government and withdrew from actions that could affect industrial peace. Keynesian compromise between labor and capital, with its exchanges linking government, unions, and businesses, emerged as a third way between socialization of the economy and laissez-faire politics. Even the conservatives put on the side their traditional laissez-faire and, for three times in a row, persuaded British voters that they were the best party to manage the public sector. Unions were included in policy processes, with the launching of new tripartite institutions such as the

National Economic Development Council. In particular, unions were committed to keeping wage demands in line with capitalist growth, while fostering the creation of rules and grievance procedures at the shop floor level so as to reach a stable framework for solution of conflicts. As regards the unemployed, they lost ground for mobilization just at the same time when workers were gaining influence on decision-making. Having been cut off from the labor movement, the unemployed could hardly liaise with communist groups at a time of escalating Cold War. What is more, government had by now learned to constrain their action. No doubt, this long period of Keynesian pacification conveyed the belief that labor unrest was over for good (Ross and Hartman 1960).

A wave of small protests at the end of the 1950s marked the starting crisis of consensus. Plant bargaining and unofficial strikes stood out as forms of mobilization that workers could use to resist wage cuts and other restrictive measures. The rich setting of shop stewards and workshop committees within key unions such as the Engineers and the TGWU provided the basis for increasing militancy. The state supported the employers, for example, backing the EEF in its confrontation with unions about their claims for pay rises (Macmillan 1971). It then engaged between the late 1960s and early 1970s in the elaboration of an antilabor reform targeting voluntary collective bargaining (Whiting 2007). The conservative government of Heath also started to dismantle many channels for public intervention, such as the Prices and Income Board and the Industrial Re-organization Corporation. Crucially, unemployment was put back at the core of the reemerging struggle. For example, actions of solidarity were conducted against redundancies among engineering workers at Wigan in 1972. Altruist protests soon spread in the name of other workers under threat of dismissals. The miners' strikes of 1972 and 1974 stood out as a true show of labor unity, bringing about industrial victory and political weakening of government (Richards 1997). Unions' growth included previously unorganized groups of service-sector employees. In the end, state efforts to impose a restrictive framework amounted to an overall defeat: the government decided to reinstate its interventionist approach, relying on nationalizations and incomes policy to face the decline of the economy.

However, the return of the Labour Party to power between 1974 and 1979 came along with an increasing polarization of the party system at a time when economic recession and increasing unemployment rates gave further boost to unions and unemployed mobilization (Aldcroft and Oliver 2001, 88). Within the Conservative Party, the New Right faction of Thatcher voiced a strong opposition against protection of jobs, nationalization of failing industries, and central control of wages and prices. When Labour voluntary policy collapsed under the pressure of public-sector strikes of 1978–1979, Thatcher won full power to deliver its antilabor project. She announced the restructuring of nationalized industries and restrictive stances against their shop floor, showing that the New Right government was prepared to face closures, redundancies, and confrontations. The solidarity within the labor movement, just recovered on occasion of the mobilizations of a few years earlier, was put under unprecedented strains. Protests took place especially throughout the northern regions owing to extensive job losses in labor-intensive industries such as steel, coal, railways, and energy. The miners' mobilization of 1984–1985 stood out probably as the strongest response to the New Right. And yet, it ended up in complete defeat under extreme state repression and divisions within the labor movement (Bagguley 1992; Richards 1997).

Relationships between workers and the unemployed proved to be extremely complex. Local activism of the unemployed was channeled through the creation of a national network of locally run unemployed centers. On the one hand, unions encouraged the unemployed to join these centers in an effort to channel their mobilization and gain full legitimacy in the eyes of workers who were victims of industrial restructuring. Unions also wanted to control this grassroots potential so as to avoid the risk that it could fall under communist influence, just as it had happened between the two world wars (Forrester and Ward 1986 and 1990). On the other hand, the unemployed could gain organizational capacities that they had lost within the general context of political consensus and the post–World War II drastic fall of unemployment rates. The TUC provided the necessary financial resources for the constitution and working of centers. The number of these centers grew to over 200 in a few years, and widespread "People's Marches for Jobs" were organized in 1981 and 1983. Nevertheless, exchanges between the two sides of the labor movement stood out for their exclusively instrumental nature, fostering no genuine overarching unity between unions and the unemployed (Lewis 1989 and 1990). While marching in continuity with their 1920s "hunger marches," the unemployed failed to acquire a substantial influence within the unemployed centers. At the same time, unions reinforced these structures as service providers and advice centers about social security. The economic dependence of the unemployed also meant that unions had more force to impose their leadership on centers and shape rules for representation in their management committees.

Hence, the unemployed centers developed mostly as groups mobilizing on behalf of the unemployed, or at times simply concerned with the issue of unemployment. They were part of the broad political coalition against the conservatives' decisions over unemployment, but certainly not the expression of the collective will of the unemployed themselves (Kingsford 1982). Yet, the unemployed made some important attempts to gain control of "their own" organizations. In some case they did stand against increasing co-optation by the unions, preventing TUC leaders from gaining full control of the unemployment centers (Bagguley 1991). What is more, the National Unemployed Centres Combine (NUCC) was set up on the occasion of the first large marches for jobs at the beginning of the 1980s. NUCC worked as a national point of reference for many unemployed centers with the aim of translating their local activism into a powerful and independent force of the unemployed themselves.

Mass work dismissals following throughout the 1980s enabled the New Right to target more easily the different components of the labor movement so as to bend it to obedience and detonate the dangerous mix of rising unemployment and protests (Gamble 1994). Unemployment rates went over 10 percent between

1981 and 1987, with the number of unemployed people peaking between 1983 and 1986 at over three million (Pissarides 2006). A series of policies thus aimed to constrain potential mobilization. Decision-making over unemployment was strengthened at the national level. The Manpower Services Commission (MSC) was provided with a stronger role to develop, under government guide, programs for the unemployed. In addition, many unemployed centers were built and maintained through the funding of MSC and local authorities so as to decrease their disruptive role in case of industrial disputes. The necessity to attract MSC funding also implied that centers had to be managed by a joint committee of local trade unionists, representatives of local authorities, and even local voluntary organizations, rendering it difficult for the unemployed to sit on management committees. That is, centers often became dependent on both the central state, in the form of MSC funding, and at the local level, in the form of local institutions' support. Orientation toward the local state increased over time, but this did not imply decreasing dependence. It is sufficient to say that many centers of unemployed workers disappeared virtually overnight with the reorganization of the local government in the mid-1980s. The abolition of the Greater London council alone was enough to bring down numerous unemployed centers that were concentrated in the capital.

The New Right finally won the acquiescence of the unemployed. Restrictive interventions lasted well into the 1990s. Entitlements to, and provisions of, unemployment benefits were increasingly reduced, culminating in 1996 with the abolition of the national unemployment insurance scheme and its replacement with the more restrictive jobseeker's allowance. Since the early 1990s, unemployed groups became too weak to place their claims within the public space. For example, three marches were organized in the mid-1990s throughout the Midlands, Yorkshire, and the northeast to protest against the introduction of the jobseeker's allowance[3]; yet, these marches were overall unreported in the national press. Many unemployed centers gradually withdrew from political engagement, often bringing to end their whole organizational experience.[4] The legacies of the New Right victory could also be assessed at the individual level, for example, considering the higher rates of unemployment, as well as the higher numbers of disabled, long-term sick, and early retired people, in regions where it had won the bitter industrial disputes (Beatty, Fothergill, and Herrington 1997).[5]

Final Phase: Pro-unemployed and New Labour Long-lasting Pacification

The New Labour, still in government at the time of writing, has stood out for its ambiguous relationship of continuity and breaking with the New Right. On the one hand, New Labour has further developed the effort of Thatcherism, aimed at tackling needs of global economic competition and efficiency (Pierson 1994). For instance, New Labour has shared the New Right belief in a flexible labor market, asserting Britain as one of the least-regulated among the OECD members, with different measures to promote part-time work, fixed-term, freelance, and temporary contracts. It has further undermined unions' power, increased work incentives for claimants of unemployed benefits, and contracted out public services. Following the fundamental tenet of "no rights without responsibilities" (Giddens 1998), the New Labour "third way" has put emphasis on self-initiative, duties, and personal commitment, thus bridging much of the gulf with the New Right. Some scholars have thus argued that under New Labour the idea of welfare contractualism has systematically undermined that of welfare rights (Dwyer 2004). On the other hand, the British state under New Labour has invested extensively in the development of measures to tackle social exclusion. The introduction of a "working families tax credit" and a new "child care tax allowance," alongside with increases in "income support" for families and "child benefit" for the first child, have aimed to redress effectively the dramatic rising of people living on incomes of less than half the average, which had reached the highest peak with the New Right in power. In addition, reforms of the labor market and new mechanisms to tackle unemployment have gained top priority in the government agenda so as to move more people from welfare to work. The wide number of reforms have included programs for the provision of a higher level of training and education, changes to the system of national contribution, a national minimum wage, and, in particular, the New Deal.

The New Deal was launched so as to help people find work, providing them with the possibility of undertaking training in the prospect of a stable employment. Although it was soon extended to older people, to single parents, and to the disabled, the New Deal started as a specific policy directed at young unemployed people through the implementation of a set of actions. These actions refer to advice and guidance to improve job searching, training and education to improve participants' skills, as well as provision of work experiences in environmental task forces, in voluntary service, or in subsidized private employment. The success of the program has thus depended on its achievement in enhancing participants' skills, increasing the chance of continuing work when out of subsidies. New Labour has thus reversed some fundamental tenets of the New Right project, such as the very low priority accorded to full employment, the aversion for redistribution, and in particular, rejection of partnership between different interests. Yet, it has operated within a political space that continues to be shaped according to the legacies of the New Right, for example, with very few access points for the labor movement, its communities, organizations, institutions, and in particular, for the unemployed themselves. The New Deal program, however, has relied not only on governmental bodies and local authorities, but also on the direct involvement of a large volume of voluntary groups, private corporations, charities, and independent organizations. Crucial exchanges have been fostered between the state and a wide range of groups from civil society, while institutional intervention and financial help have been channeled toward a wide range of nongovernmental organizations. In sum, in a situation of full demobilization of the unemployed and increasing levels of economic and social exclusion, the state has opened space for the intervention of a wide range of probeneficiary organizations, which act in the name of the unemployed but do not necessarily include or have strong connections with the unemployed themselves.

Accordingly, there has been an impressive development of interactions between actors from the policy domain and civil society organizations. On the one hand, the state and its policy elites have been interested in the support that pro-unemployed organizations can provide in terms of welfare services, production of knowledge, sharing of expertise, and public legitimization. On the other hand, pro-unemployed organizations have obtained in exchange a privileged access to higher political positions and financial resources, thus reinforcing their organizational strength and public acknowledgment. Indeed, a crucial point is that independent organizations working on behalf of the unemployed have been unwilling to forge fully consensual relations, but rather, have worked in an overall context of competitive cooperation (Cinalli 2007b). The pro-unemployment voluntary sector has engaged directly with government provisions and policies such as the New Deal and various schemes aiming to increase the employability of the unemployed. That is, the difference between the New Right and the New Labour could hardly be any clearer. Whereas the long years of Thatcherism signed a long cycle of contentious protest with widespread recourse to strikes, marches, pickets, and occupations before the final demobilization of the unemployed could be achieved, New Labour has fostered the pacification of unemployment politics through the involvement of a large sector of civil society. Co-optation through public funds for stakeholders and direct state intervention have enabled the replacement of ideological and class conflicts with more manageable interactions among organized groups, leaving no space for direct mass participation and protest of the unemployed themselves, and more broadly of the labor movement.

Hence, the unemployed have lost further capacity for mobilization, offering no more than some negligible contribution to the public debate (Cinalli and Statham 2005). The voluntary pro-unemployed sector has shown no interest in mobilizing the unemployed in mass protest action: it has worked especially to develop more extensive exchanges with policymakers. Due to the weakening of the whole labor movement, the unemployed have attempted to shape new patterns in terms of their alliances. For example, on the occasion of the most contentious mobilization under New Labour, dismissed dockers in Liverpool did not enjoy the support of their own union, but rather that of women's groups, environmentalists, human rights groups, and other independent organizations mobilizing on issues of housing, disability, peace, and social justice.[6] Indeed, the unemployed may have lost their interest in a unified and powerful labor movement, compensating this loss with extensive interactions, and gradual integration, with other social movements (Touraine, Wieviorka, and Dubet 1987).

As regards top-down opportunities, New Labour has aimed to recompose work conflicts and pacify the labor market policy field. It has thus opened an important space for the concrete intervention of a wide range of probeneficiary organizations, while constraining direct mobilization of the unemployed. Once again the impact of the state has had a key role: during the last decade,

188 • Manlio Cinalli

some unemployment centers that had survived the process of demobilization decided to engage in government projects. For example, the old unemployment center in Sheffield has changed its name to "centre for full employment" (CFU), accepting to cooperate fully with government in supporting programs that reinsert unemployed people back into the labor market.[7] Put simply, the opening up of institutional channels of access has led pro-unemployed organizations to strengthen their direct forms of institutional involvement in the political process; it has attracted a wider range of pressure groups and specialist organizations willing to seize the new opportunities; and it has even encouraged a probeneficiary transformation of the few unemployed organizations that were still active in the field.

Conclusion

This chapter has focused on main aspects of unemployment politics in Britain between its early appearances in the nineteenth century and current New Labour approach. In particular, an important part of the argument has been dedicated to the discussion of three main phases of unemployment politics. The first phase runs from the second half of the nineteenth century until World War II. The definite irruption of unemployment politics in the late nineteenth century was matched by the emergence of a unified labor movement with no clear distinction between workers and the unemployed. Yet, following a long wave of unsuccessful protests, this period ended with a crucial deepening of the distinction between workers and the unemployed. The second phase started with the isolation of the unemployed. Their split with workers could hardly be counterbalanced through alternative alliances with the radical left at a time of escalating Cold War. In addition, they had to face a government that by then knew well how to constraint their mobilization. This phase ended with a missed occasion to reconstruct full solidarity within the labor movement. The miners' mobilization of 1984–19-85 marked the final defeat of the unemployed under New Right repression and labor movement divisions. Finally, the third phase refers to the New Labour years between the late 1990s and the present. This phase has stood out for the new impetus that successive governments have provided for pro-unemployed organizations, bringing about a long-lasting pacification in the overall field.

This chapter has focused on "opportunities" and "networks" so as to discuss the role of state policies and interorganizational alliances within the field of contention. The interplay between these two factors is noticeable across the three phases, and in particular, when comparing unemployment politics under the New Right and the New Labour. Under the New Right, Britain as the cradle of welfare was utterly transformed through monetarism, anti-union provisions, economic restructuring in large work-based industries, and the imposition of a strong belief in laissez-faire. In particular, the willingness of the New Right to sacrifice the wealth of some sections of the population for restoring a healthy British economy brought about mass work dismissals, public expenditure restraints, and finally, the eventual acquiescence of workers and the unemployed to the new rules of the global market. At the same time, the restrictive stance of political context was followed by a large volume of difficulties in terms of labor movement relationships. Exchanges between unions and the unemployed were instrumental. The unemployed had little control of their own organizational structures, since unions could impose their own leadership and prevent them from gaining substantial influence.

By contrast, the New Labour has elaborated crucial reforms to deal with social exclusion, provide better opportunities of education, and revive mechanisms for tackling unemployment. Not only has this opening up of institutional channels led probeneficiary organizations to strengthen their direct forms of involvement on behalf of the unemployed, but it has attracted a wider range of pressure groups and specialist organizations willing to seize the new opportunities. The voluntary pro-unemployed sector has reinforced political strength and public acknowledgment through a privileged access to decision-making and institutions. Consequently, pro-unemployed organizations have shown no interest to mobilize the unemployed in mass protest action, but have worked especially to develop more extensive exchanges with policy elites. As regards the unemployed themselves, they have concentrated their direct intervention at the local level, usually as a mere outcome of specific industrial disputes. Overall, state responsiveness, the overall centralization of the policy process, as well as the new impetus of pro-unemployed organizations to target relevant policymakers have weakened the participation of the unemployed, discouraging them from using direct political action.

Ultimately, this chapter has argued that the British unemployed have become politically unable to place their claims into the public space. They are today the "objects," rather than the "protagonists," of discussions and decisions over unemployment. The study of networks and opportunities can account for the final transformation of a crucial field for competition between capital and labor into a consensual space that is immune to mobilization and disruptive protest. The politics of unemployment in Britain is no longer contentious but fully pacified, and the unemployed themselves have not a key role to play. In spite of drastic increases in the unemployment rates in the latter half of the decade starting in 2000, it should take an unlikely transformation of networks and opportunities to see them again as protagonists within "their own" field.

Notes

1. A large team of researchers engaged in the UNEMPOL project has focused on the relative mismatch between unemployment rates and mobilization of the unemployed across different European countries, focusing on the relation between political institutional approaches to employment policy and political conflicts mobilized by collective actors over unemployment in the public domain. Research reports and selected publications are available online at http://ics.leeds.ac.uk/eurpolcom/unempol (last accessed October 15, 2009).
2. The UAB was to be appointed by the minister of labor with the aim of determining new nationalized benefit scales, which were thus removed from local democratic control.

3. Interview with NUCC leader Derby, February 2004.
4. Only about fifty unemployed centers were operative by the mid-2000s, with very loose connections with the NUCC, which was politically marginalized, owing to increasing funding constraints and political conditions that forced centers to demobilize and to adapt to government strategies. Interview with NUCC leader Derby, February 2004.
5. For example, in 2002 the unemployed rate in the southeast was only half of same rate in the region of Yorkshire, irrespective of whether the computation was appraised through "claimant count" (1.8 percent vs. 4.0 percent) or using estimates also accounting for "hidden unemployment." For more details, see Fothergill (2002).
6. Interview with leader of the Women of the Waterfront (WOW), Liverpool, March 2006.
7. Interview with CFU leader Sheffield, February 2004.

References

Aldcroft, Derek H., and Michael J. Oliver. 2001. *Trade Unions and the Economy: 1870–2000*. Aldershot: Ashgate.
Atkinson, Anthony B. 1975. *The Economics of Inequality*. Oxford: Oxford University Press.
Bagguley, Paul. 1991. *From Protest to Acquiescence? Political Movements of the Unemployed*. London: Macmillan.
———. 1992. Protest, Acquiescence and the Unemployed: A Comparative Analysis of the 1930s and 1980s. *British Journal of Sociology* 43(3): 443–61.
Baxandall, Phineas. 2001. When is Unemployment Politically Important? Explaining Differences in Political Salience Across European Countries. *West European Politics* 24: 75–98.
Beatty, Christina, Steve Fothergill, and Alison Herrington. 1997. *The Real Level of Unemployment*. Centre for Regional Economic and Social Research. Sheffield: Sheffield Hallam University.
Berclaz, Julie, and Marco Giugni. 2005. Specifying the Concept of Political Opportunity Structures. In *Economic and Political Contention in Comparative Perspective*, ed. Maria Kousis and Charles Tilly, 15–32. Boulder: Paradigm Publishers.
Brown, Kenneth D. 1971. *Labour and Unemployment: 1900–1914*. Newton Abbot: David and Charles.
Cinalli, Manlio. 2007a. Between Horizontal Bridging and Vertical Governance: Pro-Beneficiary Movements in New Labour Britain. In *Civil Societies and Social Movements: Potentials and Problems*, ed. Derrick Purdue, 88–108. London: Routledge.
———. 2007b. The Impact of "Relational structures" upon Collective Action: A Comparison of Unemployment and Asylum in New Labour Britain. *Sciences Po Working Papers* 23. http://www.cevipof.msh-paris.fr/publications/notes_etudes.html (last accessed October 15, 2009).
Cinalli, Manlio, and Paul Statham. 2005. Final Report for the United Kingdom. *Final Report for the 5th Framework Programme of the European Commission*. UNEMPOL. http://www.eurpolcom.eu/exhibits/ch3-UK.pdf (last accessed October 15, 2009).
Cole, George D. H., and Margaret I. Cole. 1937. *The Condition of Britain*. London: V. Gollancz.
Cronin, James E. 1979. *Industrial Conflict in Modern Britain*. Totowa: Rowman and Littlefield.

Croucher, Richard. 1987. *We Refuse to Starve in Silence: A History of the National Unemployed Workers' Movement, 1920–46*. London: Lawrence & Wishart.

Deacon, Alan. 1977. Concession and Coercion: The Politics of Unemployment Insurance in the Twenties. In *Essays in Labour History, 1918–1939*, Vol. 3, ed. Asa Briggs and John Saville, 9–35. London: Croom Helm.

Demazière, Didier, and Maria-Teresa Pignoni. 1998. *Chômeurs : du silence à la révolte*. Paris: Hachette.

Diani, Mario. 1992. Analysing Social Movement Networks. In *Studying Collective Action*, ed. Mario Diani and Ron Eyerman, 107–35. London: Sage.

Diani, Mario, and Doug McAdam. 2003. *Social Movements and Networks. Relational Approaches to Collective Action*. Oxford: Oxford University Press.

Dwyer, Peter. 2004. Creeping Conditionality in the UK: From Welfare Rights to Conditional Entitlements. *Canadian Journal of Sociology* 29(2): 265–87.

Eisinger, Peter K. 1973. The Conditions of Protest Behavior in American Cities. *American Political Science Review* 67(1): 11–28.

Evans, Neil. 1999. "South Wales has been Roused as Never Before": Marching against the Means Test, 1934–1936. In *Crime, Protest and Police in Modern British Society: Essays in Memory of David J.V. Jones*, ed. David W. Howell and Kenneth O. Morgan, 176–206. Cardiff: University of Wales Press.

Flanagan, Richard. 1991. *"Parish-Fed Bastards": A History of the Politics of the Unemployed in Britain, 1884–1939*. New York: Greenwood.

Forrester, Keith, and Kevin Ward. 1986. Organising the Unemployed? The TUC and the Unemployed Workers' Centres. *Industrial Relations Journal* 17(1): 46–56.

———. 1990. Trade Union Services for the Unemployed: The Unemployed Workers' Centres. *British Journal of Industrial Relations* 28(3): 387–95.

Fothergill, Steve. 2002. *Hidden Unemployment*. Centre for Regional Economic and Social Research: Sheffield Hallam University.

Fulcher, James. 1991. *Labour Movements, Employers and the State*. Oxford: Clarendon Press.

Gamble, Andrew. 1994. *The Free Economy and the Strong State*. London: MacMillan.

Giddens, Anthony. 1998. *The Third Way: The Renewal of Social Democracy*. Cambridge: Polity Press.

Giugni, Marco. 2008. Welfare States, Political Opportunities, and the Mobilization of the Unemployed: A Cross-National Analysis. *Mobilization* 13(3): 297–310.

Giugni, Marco, and Michel Berclaz. 2003. Political Opportunities for the Mobilization of the Unemployed: Insights from Switzerland. Second ECPR Conference. *Section on social movements, contentious politics, and social exclusion*. September 18–21, Marburg, Germany. http://www.eurpolcom.eu/exhibits/marburg-2003.pdf (last accessed October 15, 2009).

Harris, José. 1984. *Unemployment and Politics: A Study in English Social Policy, 1886–1914*. Oxford: Clarendon Press.

Harrison, Royden. 1965. *Before the Socialists: Studies in Labour and Politics, 1861–1881*. London: Routledge & K.Paul.

Hinton, James, and Richard Hyman. 1975. *Trade Union and Revolution: The Industrial Politics of the Early British Communist Party*. London: Pluto Press.

Hobsbawm, Eric J. 1969. *Industry and Empire: From 1750 to the Present Day*. Harmondsworth: Penguin.

Howell, Chris. 2005. *Trade Unions and the State: The Construction of Industrial Relations Institutions in Britain, 1890–2000*. Princeton: Princeton University Press.

Kelly, John. 1998. *Rethinking Industrial Relations*. London: Routledge.

Kidd, Alan J. 1984. The Social Democratic Federation and Popular Agitation amongst the Unemployed in Edwardian Manchester. *International Review of Social History* 29(3): 336–58.

Kingsford, Peter. 1982. *The Hunger Marches*. London: Lawrence & Wishart.

Jahoda, Marie, Paul F. Lazarsfeld, and Hans Zeisel. 1971. *Marienthal: The Sociography of an Unemployed Community*. London: Tavistock.

Kriesi, Hanspeter, Ruud Koopmans, Jan Willem Duyvendak, and Marco Giugni. 1995. *New Social Movements in Western Europe. A Comparative Analysis*. Minneapolis: University of Minnesota Press.

Levy, Jack. 1989. The Diversionary Theory of War: A Critique. In *Handbook of War Studies*, ed. Manus I. Midlarsky, 258–88. London: Allen and Unwin.

———. 1998. The Causes of War and the Conditions of Peace. *Annual Review of Political Science* 1: 139–65.

Lewis, Paul. 1989. The Unemployed and Trade Union membership. *Industrial Relations Journal* 20(4): 271–9.

———. 1990. *Trade Union Policy and the Unemployed*. Aldershot: Avebury.

Macmillan, Harold. 1971. *Riding the Storm, 1956–1959*. London: Macmillan.

McNeill, William. 1982. *The Pursuit of Power: Technology, Armed Force and Society since A.D. 1000*. Chicago: Chicago University Press.

Meacham, Standish. 1977. *A Life Apart. The English Working Class, 1890–1914*. London: Thames & Hudson.

Melucci, Alberto. 1984. Movimenti in un mondo di segni. In *Altri codici*, ed. Alberto Melucci, 417–48. Bologna: Il Mulino.

———. 1989. *Nomads of the Present*. London: Hutchinson Radius.

Phelps Brown, Henry. 1975. A Non-Monetarist View of the Pay Explosion. *The Three Bank Review* 105: 6–7.

Pierson, Paul. 1994. *Dismantling the Welfare State? Reagan, Thatcher, and the Politics of Retrenchment*. Cambridge: Cambridge University Press.

Pissarides, Christopher A. 2006. Unemployment in Britain: A European Success Story. In *Structural Unemployment in Western Europe: Reasons and Remedies*, ed. Martin Werding, 209–36. Cambridge: MIT Press.

Piven, Frances F., and Richard A. Cloward. 1977. *Poor People's Movements: Why They Succeed, How They Fail*. New York: Pantheon Books.

Reiss, Matthias. 2011. From Poor Relief to Politics: The Protest of the British Unemployed in the 1870s and 1880s. In *Unemployment and Protest: New Perspectives on Two Centuries of Contention*, ed. Matthias Reiss and Matt Perry, 75–107. Oxford: Oxford University Press.

Richards, Andrew. 1997. *Miners on Strike: Class Solidarity and Division in Britain*. Oxford: Berg.

Ross, Arthur M., and Paul T. Hartman. 1960. *Changing Patterns of Industrial Conflict*. New York: Wiley.

Scally, Robert J. 1975. *The Origins of the Lloyd George Coalition: The Politics of Social Imperialism, 1900–1918*. Princeton: Princeton University Press.

Schulte Beerbühl, Margrit. 2011. The March of the Blanketeers: Tragic Failure or Pioneer of Unemployed Protest? In *Unemployment and Protest: New Perspectives on Two Centuries of Contention*, ed. Matthias Reiss and Matt Perry, 59–74. Oxford: Oxford University Press.

Silver, Beverly J. 2003. *Forces of Labor: Workers' Movements and Globalization since 1870*. Cambridge: Cambridge University Press.

Stearns, Peter N. 1975. *Lives of Labour*. London: Croom Helm.

Stedman-Jones, Gareth. 1984. *Outcast London: A Study in the Relationship between Classes in Victorian Society*. London: Penguin.

Tarrow, Sidney. 1994. *Power in Movement. Social Movements, Collective Action and Politics*. Cambridge: Cambridge University Press.

Taylor, Alan J.P. 1954. *The Struggle for Mastery in Europe, 1848–1918*. Oxford: Clarendon Press.

Thompson, Paul. 1967. *Socialists, Liberals and Labour: The Struggle for London, 1885–1914*. London: Routledge & K.Paul.

Tilly, Charles. 1978. *From Mobilization to Revolution*. Reading: Addison-Wesley.

Touraine, Alain, Michel Wieviorka, and François Dubet. 1987. *The Workers' Movement*. Cambridge: Cambridge University Press.

Ward, Stephanie. 2011. "The Workers Are in the Mood to Fight the Act": Protest against the Means Test, 1931–5. In *Unemployment and Protest: New Perspectives on Two Centuries of Contention*, ed. Matthias Reiss and Matt Perry, 245–64. Oxford: Oxford University Press.

Webb, Sidney, and Beatrice P. Webb. 1920. *The History of Trade Unionism*. New York: Longmans.

Whiteley, Paul F., and Stephen J. Winyard. 1987. *Pressure for the Poor: The Poverty Lobby and Policy Making*. London: Methuen.

Whiting, Richard. 2007. The reform of working life in Britain, 1963–1971. *The Historical Journal* 50: 423–48.

CHAPTER 8

Organizing the Unemployed in Ireland

Frédéric Royall

The object of this chapter is to assess issues concerning—and examples of—the mobilization of unemployed people in the Republic of Ireland from the mid-1980s to the mid-2000s.[1] In fulfillment of this aim, the first part gives an overview of labor market developments and discusses briefly the particular social and political contexts in which Irish employment and unemployment policies were formulated during that period. Next, the mobilization of unemployed people is assessed via their main organizational forum, the Irish National Organization of the Unemployed (INOU). This section focuses on two areas: mobilizing factors and forms of action. The final part of the chapter discusses some issues and challenges with respect to the mobilization of the unemployed in the prevailing very difficult economic climate.

Economic and Labor Market Policy Developments

From the 1930s, Irish society was weighed downed by a "republican dogma" that contributed to a sustained period of economic sluggishness: industrial and agricultural underperformance, mass emigration, and chronic unemployment (Lee 1989; Barry 1999).[2] By the late-1980s, however, the country's fortunes were beginning to improve. The economic guidance of the European Economic Community (EEC) helped the country's political elite to forge a domestic social and political consensus on the best ways to pull the economy from despondency and to reenergize it. These guidelines gave Irish public authorities limited political options but whose choices were fixed within specific European policy objectives that fostered economic growth (Laffan 1989; Fitzgerald 2000) and led to the "Celtic Tiger" miracle (Valarasan-Toomey 1998; Sweeney 1999). As of the mid-1990s, the economy grew at a steadily increasing rate, inflation stabilized,

Table 8.1 Unemployment in Ireland (1980–2008) (annual averages)

1980	1982	1987	1990	1993	1998	2000	2003	2006	2008
90,000	115,000	226,000	172,000	220,000	127,000	75,500	82,100	85,600	115,500
6.0%	10.7%	16.9%	12.9%	15.7%	7.8%	4.2%	4.6%	4.4%	6.7%

Sources: Central Statistics Office, various years, Labour Force Surveys; Breen et al. (1990), Table 7.1.

public debt was reigned in, net outward migration rates were reversed, and, in some cases, social security benefits improved markedly.

With respect to the labor market, public authorities of the 1980s were spurred into action by the severity of the economic crisis that pushed unemployment to a peak rate of 16.9 percent in 1987 (OECD 1989; Johns 1993). Table 8.1 summarizes the unemployment rates between 1980 and 2008. Bolstered by improved international economic conditions and various EEC economic guidelines, public authorities carried out a series of labor market and economic reforms (OECD 1991, 1995, and 1999): wage restrictions, income tax decreases, limits on and reviews of access to unemployment benefits and allowances, and promotion of "active" labor market measures (O'Connell and McGinnity 1997; Tille and Yi 2001; Glyn 2002). From 1989 to 1993 the labor market stabilized and the unemployment rate started to fall moderately at first, then more dramatically. For instance, the rate of unemployment fell from 14.7 percent in 1994, to 7.8 in 1998, and then to 3.7 by 2001.[3] Employment prospects also improved markedly. For example, the employment rate increased from 45.4 percent in 1994, to 59.7 in 1998, and to 66.3 in 2005.[4] This compares to a drop of an average of 0.5 percent per year during the 1980s. In addition, the mean growth rate of the economy was 9 percent for the period 1994–2002. Gross national product averaged 5.8 percent from 1997 to 2003 and the gross domestic product 7.6 percent (Department of Finance 2004).

Some economists consider that the phenomenal economic change of fortunes may be explained by the coming together of a number of factors external in origin: improvements in the international economic climate; a strengthening of the common European market and, consequently, the influx to Ireland of (especially American) capital investment; favorable demographic shifts; long-term benefits of fiscal stabilization of the late 1980s; better educational levels, which improved the skills of the workforce; and a massive transfer of European Structural Funds from Brussels (Barry 1999; Nolan, O'Connell, and Whelan 2000; Hamilton 2005). But it is also important to underline the key role played by two major domestic developments: first, the establishment of "social partnership" and, second, domestic implementation of European labor market guidelines. It is to these points that I now turn.

Social Partnership

In the first case, social partnership refers to multiannual wage, industrial relations, and labor market agreements drawn up between the main social and economic actors (originally employers and trade unions) and central public authorities. These types of collective agreements are not novel in Ireland. Collective agreements evolved from a series of weak and ineffective centralized agreements in the 1970s to decentralized negotiations in the 1980s (Wallace, Gunnigle, and McMahon 2004, 377–410). Then from 1987 onward, a new model emerged—through state guidance—based on reenergized, coordinated pay policy and national-level bargaining (Roche 1989). In a sense, the partnership process was an end product of the severe financial and economic travails of the 1980s and it had two major implications. First, social partnership helped reduce industrial conflict, ensure moderate wage increases, improve economic growth rates, reduce inflation, stabilize the conditions for foreign direct investment, and decrease the rate of unemployment. Second, social partnership also had a considerable influence on the extent and the forms of the collective action of the unemployed.

If differences arose between the political parties at the beginning on the rationale of—and need for—social partnership, all were in agreement nonetheless that radical measures needed to be put in place to drag the country out of its economic despondency. Undoubtedly, employers and the trade unions shared a sense of patriotic duty and were cognizant of the fact that the country's future depended on their reaching a consensus on economic issues. But even if employers and trade unions understood the importance of coming to agreement in the short-to-medium term, one should not underestimate the fact that a firm political hand was required to translate this token desire into a coherent economic strategy. It must be borne in mind that since 1987 all the main political parties participated in an official capacity in drawing up and in putting in place at least one of the multiannual social partnership agreements.[5] So, political elites played a key role in the social partnership process not only by establishing its institutional bases but also by ensuring the stability and longevity of this tripartite institution.

Trade unions, though aware of and preoccupied with increases in the rates of unemployment and the attendant negative social consequences, had become to a large extent social and economic interest groups similar to many others by the early 1980s, catering primarily to the interests of their membership and adopting appropriate defensive strategies.[6] This is particularly true on the issue of unemployment. For example, Tony Monks (1994), general secretary of the INOU from May 2000 to December 2001, argues that when involved in discussions or negotiations with other social and economic interests or when initiating strike actions, self-interest and the defense of its membership often caused the trade union movement to overlook the needs of disadvantaged groups—such as the unemployed—in pursuit of the best available conditions for its membership. Brian Kenny (1990), a poverty activist, generally supports this viewpoint.[7] As a result, unemployed people often looked with trepidation at the timid commitment of the trade union movement to the issue of the interests of the unemployed—before and even in the immediate aftermath of its inclusion in the social partnership process (Bond 1990). Some unemployment activists even perceived the trade union movement's role in social partnership as an example of state-led strengthening of trade union corporatism and detrimental to the cause of the unemployed.[8] Unemployed people's wariness of the trade union movement's role in labor market affairs was mirrored by sentiments expressed by the public at large. For example, in an opinion poll in early 1993, only 11 percent of respondents strongly agreed with the view that trade union demands on behalf of people at work added to the difficulties in tackling unemployment—39 percent agreed, 30 percent disagreed, and 8 percent strongly disagreed.[9]

The trade union movement's stance on unemployment issues may be understood because of the context in which it was embedded. By the 1980s, the Irish trade union movement was at an important juncture. In a period characterized by decentralized wage agreements, sustained decline in membership, increasing rates of unemployment, and the failure of many domestic, unionized companies, most trade unions faced a bleak future. In addition, some newly established domestic and international companies insisted upon nonunionism or on single-union recognition agreements, particularly in the electronic and aeronautical sectors (e.g., Ryanair).[10] As a response to international competitive pressures, management/union relations were typified by "a new emphasis on industrial relations restructuring" (Roche and Gunnigle 1995, 14).[11] In this context, the inclusion of some of the major trade unions in the social partnership process gave them the opportunity to recover some lost ground and to attempt to exert an influence on public policy issues that were of paramount importance to them—unemployment, education, wage policy, and so on—and to put forward their preferred social and political demands: income tax reform, increases in social security benefits, job creation, and so on. Moreover, the political elites were cognizant of the fact that the participation of the main trade unions in the social partnership process was essential since it was felt that these unions could play a key role in supporting the policy measures needed to reenergize the economy through wage restrictions, industrial relations stability, social consensus, and so on. For this reason, public authorities increased the political might of the services and industrial trade unions to the detriment of agricultural unions and landowners—the social groups that had been up to then two of the main economic and political actors.[12] In general, however, the Irish trade union movement has not emerged unscathed from the major social and economic changes that have taken place especially since the mid-1980s. It is not entirely surprising in such circumstances that its capacity to play a key role in protest events has waned.

Labor Market Guidelines

With respect to the second case—implementation of European Union labor-market guidelines—the fact that the country adhered to the Maastricht convergence criteria contributed to the success of centralized agreements from the beginning of the 1990s. The political elites recognized that the country's economic viability depended on its integration with the rest of Europe and that the European context played a key role in ensuring the success of social partnership. Later, when Ireland joined the Economic and Monetary Union in 1999 and it no longer had direct control over its monetary and exchange policies, adjustments to external events could only be carried out through fiscal policy measures or wage adjustments. This gave even more importance to the success of the social partnership agreements as a means by which to promote sound economic management. In short, from 1987 a consensus emerged on the need to fight against inflation (especially in 1987 and in 1988) then on the need to implement "active" labor market measures (from the end of the 1980s) via corporatist arrangements between the state and the main social partners—in the beginning chiefly the employers' federation and the main industrial, service-sector, and agricultural trade unions and, much later, community and voluntary organizations.

These social partnership agreements gave public authorities the political scope to implement a number of European Commission-led labor market initiatives. For example, as unemployment levels became a common concern across the European Union by the mid-1990s, the Irish government welcomed the 1997 European Council Luxembourg Summit, which established guidelines to coordinate member states' employment strategies. In the Irish case, the European Employment Strategy—generally known as the Luxembourg Process—allowed governments' labor market policy to move toward a specific European path and to focus on state-led activation strategies. Following these guidelines, Irish public authorities sought to pursue a number of policy objectives: active labor market programs, preventative measures to reduce the number of people becoming long-term unemployed, job creation, better labor supply through increasing adaptability and mobility, and "making work pay" among other priorities (Department of Enterprise, Trade and Employment 2003). One key Irish government commitment was to "eliminate long-term unemployment as soon as circumstances permit but, in any event, not later than 2007"[13] and the 2004 Irish national employment action plan outlined progress made under the ten guidelines specifically in conjunction with the "Sustaining Progress" social partnership agreement (Department of Enterprise, Trade and Employment 2004).

The social partnership corporatist arrangements and the implementation of European Union-led labor market guidelines had a profound effect on the mobilization of the unemployed especially in consideration of the fact that in 1997 some community and voluntary sector organizations—as well as the INOU—were included in the social partnership process. This inclusion process was construed in some quarters as a means by which the government sought to "ensure the fairness necessary for social cohesion, an essential underpinning to successful policy implementation" (McCarthy 1999, 9). In essence, the main political parties in government—the various coalition or minority governments from 1987—wanted above all to avoid conflict with the main social actors and sought to remain true to the "republican dogma" of social cohesion and consensus. Fianna Fáil especially—the principle coalition partner in various governments since the 1980s and the most nationalist party with the exception of today's Sinn Féin—had recourse to such a mechanism as a means by which to remain loyal to its historical political mission as the party of social integration. Thus, Fianna Fáil helped the economic recovery by promoting and supporting the social and political consensus that accompanied economic success—through the institutionalization of social partnership.

In this way, the social and economic measures that were introduced from the end of the 1980s were institutionalized and deepened during the 1990s and industrial and social peace was ensured. In short, what emerged from the end of the 1980s was a consensus on the main economic issues of the day—or at least on the short-term political priorities to be put in place (Lutz 2003)—and the Irish discarded the profound pessimism that loomed over them during the 1980s. By the year 2000, economic prosperity was confirmed and optimism well established, and the Irish largely supported the social partnership arrangements and the European Union-led labor market initiatives that they felt ensured economic prosperity (Hardiman 2002).[14]

Conditions for the Mobilization of the Unemployed

The argument thus far is that the Irish social and political contexts—themselves strongly influenced by the European integration process—provide a framework in which the unemployed may mobilize and, where necessary, help shape the collective action repertoires that are used.

Constraints

In Ireland, as elsewhere in Western Europe, mobilization by unemployed people has often been considered to be improbable. The psychological and cognitive obstacles unemployed people encounter, the prevalence of social isolation, their attitudes of resignation, fatalism, or culpability, and the absence of collective identity are some of the reasons that contribute to their political apathy thus militating against spontaneous collective action (Whelan 1991). But in light of recent European examples of the collective action of the unemployed as described in this volume, such a view would need to be revised. A number of theoretical approaches have attempted to analyze the conditions that are conducive to the collective actions of the unemployed (Baglioni et al. 2008; Giugni, Berclaz, and Füglister 2009). One pioneering approach was that of Bagguley (1991) who argues that unemployed people's passive or militant behavior depends on the way they are organized, on the one hand, and on the nature of their relations with the state, on the other. Other authors make the case that unemployed people's passivity may be better explained by reference to the role of the trade union movement in unemployment affairs. For instance, Rafferty (1990) points out that the Irish trade union movement tended to act on behalf of workers and of the unemployed on the "mistaken" belief that both groups shared the same interests and objectives. He suggests, therefore, that the trade union movement acted against the establishment of an independent unemployment movement. Bagguley's and Rafferty's analyses underline the fact that the mobilization of the unemployed depends very much on favorable political opportunities but also, more specifically, on the ways the state and social actors—and above all the trade unions—address unemployment. I will only look briefly at these points as they refer to the Irish case.

The Irish system is noted for being phenomenally centralized with little or no discretion or power accorded to local public authorities (Barrington 1980, 30–56; Coombes, Rees, and Stapleton 1991). In addition, the nature of Irish party politics militates against radical and long-term departures from prevailing economic and social policy guidelines. For example, Hardiman (1987) argues that "the structure of party competition made it difficult for governments to develop an appropriate strategy of response to distributional conflict" (169). In this context, challenges to economic or social orthodoxy—by low-resourced groups, for example—were, more often than not, condemned to failure. These political and administrative constraints complicated matters for the mobilization of the unemployed. Specifically with regard to labor market affairs, since the 1960s the Irish state has progressively taken responsibility for unemployment through a network of highly structured locally based agencies. These agencies have traditionally been the first point of call for unemployed people seeking benefits, jobs, training courses, and so on. Organizations of the unemployed have never been able to offer services of a comparable extent and quality. Consequently, the state's local welfare, benefits, and labor market offices impacted positively on the daily lives of the unemployed, but it can be argued that they had a negative effect on the capability and willingness of the unemployed to mobilize against prevailing policy decisions. This is because local agencies only delivered services. They had no power. Protest actions against toothless local agencies were generally seen as pointless exercises and the unemployed were not willing or able to mobilize against the central decision-making levels (Allen 1998, 131–42).

Moreover, it was difficult for mobilization to emerge in a politically constrained setting. Irish central public authorities are also noted for the expedient ways by which they deal with challengers to authority (Breen et al. 1990, 20–52).[15] This accounts for the suspicion many marginalized and disadvantaged people harbored toward the state and for the belief of many unemployed people that collective action was ineffective because it would more than likely lead to state repression not compromise.[16] In such circumstances it is entirely understandable that only several hundred people at most participated in the few unemployment demonstrations that took place at the end of the 1980s—at a time of record levels of unemployment.

In addition, many unemployment activists were deeply wary of being too closely associated with the state to avoid compromising their position and independence.[17] Economic recession and the spectacular rise in mass unemployment in the 1980s brought about a reevaluation of the perception and of the place and role of the state in the management of social and economic affairs and, thereby, of unemployed people's links with state agencies. Public authorities progressively devolved responsibility for the implementation of many policy measures—such as training, placement, and the provision of information—to decentralized nongovernmental organizations (NGOs) (Duggan and

Roynane 1992; Commins 1993). However, when the issue arose of allowing NGOs to participate in labor market affairs, public authorities ensured that key decision-making mechanisms and financial and administrative control remained securely in their preserve: NGOs delivered services; the state kept ultimate control (Royall 2005, 73–90). This devolution process occurred because the participation of NGOs in the management of economic affairs was invariably sought as a means by which to manage a turbulent environment for which other, more conventional, instruments of public intervention were excluded as undesirable or inefficient (Kooiman 1993). Along with the new climate of economic management procedures, pressures came to bear on the trade union movement and on the community and voluntary sector to reassess their roles in social and economic affairs. For trade unions this involved changes in the fulfillment of their roles and functions as major social and economic actors. For community and voluntary interests this involved, at times, increased participation in the provision and management of key services to and facilities for unemployed people.

This transfer of responsibility from the state to the trade union movement for a role in economic management and for the provision of social and economic services had major repercussions on the unemployed. As the community and voluntary sector came to play a greater role in economic and social affairs from the late 1970s, the "historical role" of the trade union movement as defenders and representatives of workers and of the unemployed was increasingly put into question. Challenges to the trade union movement led it to reaffirm its position and, thereby, to undermine nontrade union-led initiatives in support of the unemployed (Rafferty 1990). One of the ways the trade union movement did this was by creating a network of relatively well-resourced centers for the unemployed where unemployed people could have access to a number of services—personal development courses, welfare information sessions, and so on.[18] These ICTU Centers offered many services complementary to those offered by state agencies, but they were also "competing" with the services on offer in some emerging locally based organizations of the unemployed. For this reason, some unemployment activists saw the trade union movement as a rival to be treated with caution (ibid.).

As for the community and voluntary sector, the transfer of responsibility for the provision of social and economic services gave it the opportunity to mark its presence by offering a wide range of services to disadvantaged people—including the unemployed—through participation in many Irish state and European-financed projects (Ó Cinnéide 1985; Curtin and Varley 1995). Indeed, as dissatisfaction rose with the trade union movement's role and stance on unemployment during the 1980s, many unemployed people felt that community and voluntary organizations were more successful in addressing a number of issues of particular importance to them such as housing, social welfare, health care, or education. For some activists, the participation of the community and voluntary sector in the management of economic affairs gave them the opportunity to distance themselves from the omnipresence and the dominance of the trade union movement.[19]

INOU's Role

It is in this context, characterized by the dominance of the state and of its agencies on society, but also by a sharp rise in the rate of unemployment and of poverty, that an organization of the unemployed was established largely independent of the trade union movement—the INOU. Prior to the INOU's foundation in February 1987 by a number of mainly Dublin-based community and voluntary activists, no national organization existed to represent the unemployed or to speak on their behalf on national labor market issues. When issues of unemployment arose, the trade union movement was considered by some to be representative of the unemployed and saw its role very much in that light (Royall 2005, 116–18). Of the many small community and voluntary groups that existed prior to the INOU, most of them focused on local issues, had limited financial and human resources, and dealt with unemployment as only one of a number of social issues affecting their communities such as urban decay, crime, illiteracy, or drug use. Though composed of a few locally based groups in 1987, the INOU steadily increased membership over the years. By 1995, the INOU had over 200 affiliates. Ten years later, a number of groups had left the INOU whereas others had joined, and the number of affiliates was now approximately 170, ranging from community and voluntary organizations, local unemployment organizations, to ICTU-affiliated centers for the unemployed.

The INOU profited from the participation of the community and voluntary sector in the fight against unemployment for two reasons. First, as an integral part of the community and voluntary sector, it was able to gain from the experience and expertise of activists from already established organizations. Second, this sharing of experience allowed the INOU to be organized in a more professional manner so as to overcome various obstacles—personal, psychological, financial, organizational, institutional, and so on. However, the INOU was never in a position to become a major and lasting force for protest. In spite of several attempts the organization was incapable of mobilizing people on a wide scale. In this regard, Mike Allen (1998, 299–320), general secretary of the INOU from 1987 to May 2000, refers to the disappointment he felt time and again in the 1990s when calls for mobilization were frustrated by the reluctance of INOU members or sympathizers to participate in such initiatives. Few protest events took place from the mid-1980s to the late 1990s. For example, the INOU did periodically organize some collective-action events such as protest events in 1998 against the Employment Action Plan and on the theme of "Share the Wealth," rallies in 1999 against job cuts, or demonstrations in 2002 against cuts in the Community Employment Scheme.[20] But protest activities were not the INOU's mainstay and its leadership preferred to focus on what it considered to be constructive forms of dialogue with social partners. According to Eric Conroy—INOU general secretary from 2002 to 2007—protest events did not generate a critical mass of protesters and the views of the INOU leadership were more effectively presented through dialogue with relevant public authorities.[21] This change in focus led to wide-ranging debate and took a long time to establish itself. In addition, Allen (1998) states that "undoubtedly some [community and trade union] officials tried to undermine the [INOU], but equally there were other officials and unions without whom the INOU would not have survived" (135). Implicit in this statement is the conclusion that the INOU enjoyed a long-standing bittersweet romance with the trade union movement. The interests of the trade union movement and those of the INOU were often intertwined and cooperation thrived despite the wariness of some activists (Kenny 1990, 34–5).

On its establishment it was expected that the INOU would become a national organization regrouping the campaigning activities of local affiliates and organizing pressure group activities at central level. In other words, the INOU would campaign on unemployment issues at a national level while local affiliates would provide services and therefore build up local expertise and contacts. But the INOU soon moved away from the confines of the public relations exercises, which the founding planning group had intended it to pursue. Tensions ensued with some community-based affiliates and, at times, with ICTU-affiliated centers for the unemployed as it was felt that the INOU was tackling issues for which it had no brief and which were the traditional preserve of the trade union movement and best handled by it. By the mid-1990s, the INOU became the main pro-unemployed national organization and its aims were threefold: to represent the interests and views of unemployed people and their dependants at the national level; to improve the standard of living for those without work and for their dependants; and to build on the common interests between the unemployed and workers in the trade union movement. In short, it sought to promote constructive collaboration with rival organizations and to establish formal, democratic structures in which various views could be aired, debated, and addressed.

INOU's Strategy

The INOU encouraged the unemployed to overcome their reluctance to engage through initiatives undertaken in two areas—campaigning and service provision. Allied to this was the desire to stir the unemployed to act collectively and for the organization to receive maximum public exposure so as to enhance its status as a defender of the unemployed and to establish itself as an authoritative figure on issues of concern to unemployed people. For strategic reasons, the INOU shied away from direct action and sought to discourage it (Allen 1998, 278–88). It preferred skilful public relations work, formal and informal contacts with civil servants and elected representatives, and publicity measures such as organizing colloquiums, publishing newsletters, distributing pamphlets, engaging in public debates, or issuing press releases of annual pre-budget submissions or statements to the media in response to government initiatives such as the Special Task Force on Jobs, the Industrial Policy Review, the annual national employment action plans, the national antipoverty strategy, or the Employment Equality Act.[22] The INOU also published a number of economic reports and information booklets that reviewed Irish or

European Union policies and outlined the INOU's position in respect to them. Moreover, a number of high-visibility campaigns were initiated against the inadequacies of some active labor market programs (1998–2004),[23] outdated social welfare legislation (1999),[24] negative effects of the Treaties of Maastricht and of Amsterdam (in 1992, 1995 and 1998),[25] or cuts in various labor market schemes such as the Community Employment and Jobs Initiative Schemes (2003 and 2004).[26] In this respect, the INOU often issued statements of rhetoric highlighting the successes of its actions. Examples include the claims that it was instrumental in the government's decision in 1995 to allocate ten million pounds to the community employment programs,[27] that it played a vital part in the review of national agreements on unemployment-related issues in 1996,[28] that it had secured important changes for community employment workers,[29] that it played a key role in "Partnership 2000,"[30] or in highlighting its role in the "Sustaining Progress" agreement.[31] Former INOU general secretary Conroy describes these various campaigning activities as of paramount importance to the INOU and to the unemployed.[32]

Moreover, Allen (1998) highlights the importance of acquiring expert knowledge and shows how the INOU suffered in its early years through insufficient research and analysis:

> This was a crucial lesson for the organization... By meeting the protesters and showing that we couldn't prove some of our arguments, they [Department of Social Welfare officials] undermined our position... We needed more than just a list of grievances; we needed an analysis and we needed answers. (138)

The use of persuasive discourse focusing on the unemployed and on society at large was instrumental in this respect. As Fillieule (1993) observes, persuasion is an important element in a mobilization campaign and its effectiveness from the point of view of mobilizing individuals is a key element because "low-resourced groups... usually can't have recourse to coercive strategies (such as strike action)" (134).

To this end, many INOU campaigns were initiated primarily to highlight the deep-set nature of the social and economic problems the unemployed faced and to focus attention on the various public and semi-state agencies allegedly responsible for them. Several campaigns pointed to the responsibility of the agencies of the state (e.g., Foras Áiseanna Saothair, Forfás, or the Department of Social Welfare) for high levels of unemployment or for the inadequate services or benefits provided to the unemployed such as job creation, information for job seekers, social welfare allowances, or training programs. Many other INOU campaigns focused on state agencies because public authorities had taken responsibility not only for direct labor market intervention but also for maintaining financial and administrative control. The unemployed were, thereby, particularly dependent on agencies of central public authorities for information on employment and unemployment-related affairs, for the provision of many vital services, and for financial assistance programs and measures.

Also used were symbolic representations of unity. The INOU often ran campaigns of unity such as "Share the Wealth" in 1998 or "Applications Welcome" in 1999. Another important strategy for symbolic effect was the use of the moral leverage of well-known personalities. The support by high-profile public figures was crucial in helping INOU leaders gain public sympathy, in highlighting the role of social and economic factors with respect to unemployment, in stressing the responsibility of social and economic interests to resolve the problems, and instrumental in convincing unemployed people that it was successful in defending their interests. For example, the moral support of religious personalities such as Sister Stanislas Kennedy, Father Seán Healy, or that of celebrities such as television presenter Gay Byrne, singer Christy Moore, or Nobel laureate Séamus Heaney were instrumental in changing what Allen (1998) assesses as the public's negative views of the unemployed (274–98). Indeed, INOU actions endeavored to influence the public's perception of the issue and to highlight the issues facing unemployed people.[33] Equally important was the ongoing support of the Conference of Religious in Ireland to the work of the INOU. As a result of these campaigning initiatives and the public support they generated, by the late 1990s INOU officials were often solicited to air their views on various labor market issues and invited to participate in state-constituted committees, forums, and boards including social partnership (Allen 1998, 292–6).

Important as they may have been, the INOU-led initiatives that sought to improve the role and status of the unemployed in Ireland were only one type of the required measures to help to create the group's cohesion with a view to initiating collective action. The INOU and its affiliates also sought to provide a number of services. Examples include the establishment of playschool facilities, training courses, literacy courses, canteen services, counseling services, telephone "welfare to work" advice services, production and dissemination of practical information about social welfare and other entitlements, and so on (INOU 2006). In the short term, these various service-orientated initiatives were of considerable importance not least because they introduced the unemployed to the means that the INOU and its affiliates had at their disposal and which they were prepared to use to help unemployed people in difficulty. Equally important is the fact that the initiatives created a process legitimizing the role of the INOU, thereby helping it to survive as an organization by receiving financial support for its various initiatives or by recruiting new members. By promoting service-orientated activities, the INOU also became an active participant in the unemployment policy sector often securing key administrative functions in the provision of services to the unemployed. As McGinn and Allen (1991) point out:

> Associations of the unemployed constitute an important sector of voluntary activity. They are engaged in work that is essential to large numbers of Irish people...Welfare rights advice and educational courses are the most commonly provided services...At least half the associations have a drop-in facility, help with the preparation of curriculum vitaes and job applications and support for community enterprises...Associations also engage in public education and campaigning on issues affecting unemployed people. (4)

In short, the INOU focused many service-orientated activities on simplified, locally based objectives and on the immediately perceptible problems unemployed people encountered, on the one hand, and directed many of its campaigning activities at national level, on the other. In doing so, it underlined the difficulties many unemployed people faced and the urgency of finding collective solutions to the problems. It focused on relatively small targets, but required that public authorities present immediate responses such as the provision of affordable housing, increases in social welfare payments, improved training or retraining facilities, provision of inexpensive electricity or gas supplies, or reductions in the cost of public transportation. It is revealing in this respect that Allen (1998, 297) considers that the INOU was successful in one of its main objective—legitimacy—in that it was invited to participate in the social partnership process in 1997.[34]

Key Issues and Challenges in a Rapidly Changing Context

We now turn to a discussion of various issues and challenges that are likely to have a bearing on the mobilization of the unemployed. So far we have seen that the unemployed pursued objectives of better living conditions and of higher status for a number of important reasons. Of historical significance was the fact that various INOU actions were organized beyond the direction of the trade union movement and carried out within a politically difficult setting. Equally crucial is the fact that aside from overcoming many unemployed people's individual acts of fatalism, the INOU also had to prevail over a number of basic organizational problems. There was a constant shortage of well-qualified administrative personnel, ongoing financial difficulties, inadequate premises, a dearth of office supplies, as well as a lack of coherent structures. Local corporatist tendencies and deep-set rivalries shot through with personal, religious, and political divisions also made the INOU's task eminently arduous in the early years (Monks 1994; O'Neill 1994).

Lack of Critical Mass for Political Activism

As a result of this situation, the INOU had to address the major issue of the lack of a critical mass of active members. It is particularly tricky in Ireland to obtain official membership figures of Irish unemployment organizations since these organizations are extremely reluctant to publicize them. For example, INOU members can be either organizations or individuals and the organization's website identified 107 such affiliates in June 2006 rising to 172 by November 2008.[35] But there are data—in the public domain at least—that show how these two categories are broken down and it is impossible to know the number of individual members or how many of these members are unemployed. Obtaining an "official" number of the unemployed people involved in protest (or other collective) actions is also a tricky exercise. One reason for this difficulty is that given the fickle nature of the unemployed, INOU leaders and other unemployment activists were generally reluctant to organize protest events—or to give numbers in attendance when they did so—in case poor attendance would hinder rather than promote their cause. In addition, government records are not in the public domain as there is a thirty-year embargo on all such documents including police records. No empirical study has ever been carried out in Ireland on protest events and media reports of the number of unemployed participants in any type of collective action has always been, at best, anecdotal and purely speculative. The most recently reliable indication of the number of participants in unemployment protest events dates from the 1950s (Kilmurray 1988). At that time, several thousand unemployed people participated in a number of such events.[36] Since then, records of the numbers in attendance at protest events have been poor, incomplete, or unreliable.

So despite these various types of difficulties and obstacles, it is laudable that by the early 1990s especially, the unemployed in Ireland were able to address the serious issues of weak structures, disparate objectives, and negative collective identities and to organize. But could this situation have been possible without the key resources that the INOU provided? It is probably unlikely. The INOU brought something special to the cause of the unemployed as Allen (1998) shows when referring to the enormity of the tasks INOU officers and activists faced (131–42). Indeed, Allen writes movingly of the personal and organizational difficulties he experienced in attempting to initiate collective action.

Instrumental in respect of the role of the INOU is that throughout the 1980s and 1990s opinion polls showed that there was considerable public goodwill toward the organization. By the early 2000s, however, the INOU seemed to need to work much harder to make itself relevant and, despite the very constructive work of current and past INOU officers, ongoing issues of concern abound. One such issue is whether access to the social partnership process—or even the INOU's close links with civil servants and elected officials—did not put a check on the organization's demands and therefore indirectly stunted mobilization. This issue was hotly debated in some quarters. Moreover, as the INOU became increasingly reliant on state subsidies—particularly from the Department of Social and Family Affairs—the question arises as to whether the INOU dampened some of its demands in order to continue to receive such funding or even to keep participating in various state-funded or state-managed programs. Another area of concern refers to resource issues. Here, resources do not only refer to material goods—essentially money—but also to "the knowledge of organizing and mobilizing people politically" such as leadership qualities, legitimacy, and social relations (Bagguley 1992, 448). As a rule, the INOU provided an important and ongoing organizational resource to the cause of the unemployed—knowledge on how to organize and to mobilize politically. But in 1999 and early 2000, many long-serving INOU officers/activists left the organizations to move on to other pursuits thereby depriving the INOU of key leadership qualities and know-how. This matter of staff turnover was hugely important in terms of the vitality and the effectiveness of the organization and it became an issue of ongoing concern even if a certain level of staff stability was subsequently reestablished.

All these concerns point to the fact that when Ireland entered a period of sustained economic growth in the mid-1990s, the INOU also entered a period of major challenges. As public authorities willingly acceded to some of the INOU's demands—job creation, increased social welfare benefits, decreased levels of unemployment, and so on—some of the organization's original aims and objectives needed to be reviewed and redirected as indeed happened in the early 2000s.[37] But as it became commonly acknowledged that the INOU was well established and that—via the INOU—the unemployed had attained a forceful voice in their defense, the mobilization of the unemployed still faced key challenges in other areas.

Long-term Viability of the INOU

As Tilly (1986) has shown, the forms and repertoires of collective action are molded by the political and institutional structures in which they are embedded. This is clearly the case in an Irish context given that social and political centralization had a major impact on the way public affairs and "protest" activities—including those of the INOU—were carried out. Let us consider these points briefly while also taking note of Bagguley's (1991) main thesis that unemployed people's political quiescence or militancy are determined by changes in their relationship with the state and by changes in the ways people and organizations try to mobilize them.

It must be conceded that the INOU is not a decentralized organization run and controlled by the unemployed and so, Bagguley's (1991) comment seems apt: "Only in those places and at those times where the political organizations of the working classes have stressed decentralized collective action, as opposed to centralized and technocratic forms of action, have political movements of the unemployed been able to develop" (3). Contrary to this view, the INOU tried neither to transform the social and political order nor to influence local state agencies (Bagguley 1992, 449). Rather, it was always a centralist, technocratic organization run for the unemployed where the emphasis was on rights campaigning, on providing services, and on influencing the national institutions of the state. It could well be that by following such objectives, the INOU indirectly distanced itself from the immediate concerns of—locally based—unemployed people and that these very people felt physically and even philosophically detached from some of the organization's centrally focused aims or initiatives.

Equally important is the fact that the Irish state's main form of control in the social welfare system is through income maintenance schemes and that local authorities have no role to play in such affairs since all decisions and responsibilities are taken and are assured at the central level (Peillon 2001b, 16–18). Although local welfare assistance and benefits offices impact positively on the daily lives of the unemployed, they generally have had a negative effect on the capability and willingness of the unemployed to mobilize in spite of the INOU's best efforts. Protest actions were seen as ineffective and the unemployed were either not willing or not able to mobilize in significant numbers against central decision-making levels (Allen 1998, 274–9). Moreover, as the INOU focused its campaigning activities above all on the central decision-making authorities, it contributed in no small way to the lack of mobilization at the local level. This trend is acknowledged by former general secretaries of the INOU. Thus Allen suggests that "current political structures allow other forms of access to decision-making which can produce better results for unemployed people than marching down the street in ever smaller numbers" (280) and Conroy states that the INOU works "efficiently in the corridors of power."[38] In such circumstances, it is increasingly difficult to describe the INOU as a "political movement." As a consequence, one major challenge is to consider how the organization may continue to make itself relevant to its target—essentially locally based—public.

This point is all the more important given that major social and economic changes have taken place in Ireland since the mid-2000s. The Irish political system remained largely stable and highly centralized in the 1980s and 1990s, but full employment, sustained economic growth, as well as certain cultural changes all had a bearing on the conditions in which the collective action of the unemployed was initiated. For example, Bagguley (1991) considers that certain cultural resources promote or inhibit the development of political protest by the unemployed: "high levels of class solidarity and belief in the efficacy of participation in collective action, for example, are positive elements…Ideological beliefs that obscure relations of domination will tend to retard the development of protest" (37). In the Irish case, there is little historical evidence of widespread feelings of class solidarity. On the contrary, it is commonly acknowledged that other dominant traits of Irish political culture—paternalism, religion, authoritarianism, and so on—had an overbearing influence on economic development (Lee 1989; Coakley 1992) and on the mobilization of the unemployed (Royall 2005, 19–20). But recent research suggests that some of these influential cultural traits are weakening (Nic Ghiolla Phádraig 1995) and so questions must be raised as to the extent to which Irish "republican" ideological beliefs are still fully relevant and carry on obscuring relations of domination in society.[39]

Equally important is the extent to which these traits continue to impact negatively on the development of protest, in general, and on that of the unemployed, in particular. For example, in his research on societal conflict, Gurr (1970) has highlighted the role of subjective dynamics in the case of minority groups—and especially feelings of relative deprivation—to account for collective action. So, it may be argued that despite a very long period of economic difficulties (1920s–1980s), the Irish were never as frustrated by their relatively deprived economic status as that which occurred in other richer countries—such as France—where rates of unemployment were historically far lower but where changes in people's economic conditions were felt strongly at a political level at least. This may be because despite the prevalence of poverty in Ireland, the country was generally considered to be an example of a highly integrated and socially cohesive society (Peillon 1982; Durkheim 2004). But in the 1990s, the country experienced an economic boom and a late, but intense, entry into modern life. Both factors shook the country's traditional value system and codes and unraveled its frameworks of social cohesion. At the same time, various traditional "safety valves"—the role of the state, the prevalence of community and family support structures, the role and place of the Catholic Church and of its moral teachings and codes, the culture of acceptance/deference, and so on (Royall 2005, 35–59)—no longer cushioned, at least to the same degree, the effects of social and economic deprivation.

So, following the economic boom and consequent social change of the 1990s, will the major economic difficulties of the late 2000s give rise to increasing levels of frustration?[40] During the 1990s and early 2000s the possibility of a drop in social standing through job loss was not a source of major worry for the great majority of the population following a significant upswing in job creation and a sharp drop in the rate of unemployment. However, social problems did not disappear as if by magic and research shows that these problems worsened at an alarming rate for many socially and economically marginalized people. Indeed, studies that show the marked improvement in the economic status of most people in Ireland since the early 1990s are counterbalanced by other studies that indicate an equally significant rise in social and economic polarization and inequality during the same period (Allen 2000; Nolan, O'Connell, and Whelan 2000; Kirby 2002; Hillyard, Rolston, and Tomlinson 2005). In other words, Ireland went from being a society characterized by relatively widespread poverty but with a strong degree of social cohesion to one that was far more affluent but also more socially and economically polarized. In the current climate of economic recession and rapidly rising rates of unemployment, will levels of frustration and demand increase, especially for the most economically deprived, and will social and economic change impact on the way the marginalized act collectively?[41]

Allied to these issues is the fact that Ireland saw a spectacular rise in inward population flows from the mid-1990s to the mid-2000s: asylum seekers, returning emigrants, and between 2004 and 2007 a major influx of immigrants from the twelve new European Union member states.[42] Despite a severe economic downturn since early 2008, it is not clear at this point the extent to which immigration can or will have a significant impact on the mobilization of the unemployed. One reason for this is that as of the third quarter of 2008 new immigrants were only slightly swelling the ranks of the unemployed.[43] Equally important is the fact that recent non-Irish immigrants are arguably not yet fully integrated into Irish society and therefore do not have access or recourse to the same social and political networks.[44] Profound social change is in train and new immigrants will undoubtedly contribute to deepen the transformation of the Irish value systems—the role of work, the status and influence of religion, divisions across social classes, and so on.

Seen in this light, the Irish situation has evolved very much since the early 1990s.[45] Although national political opportunities do not really seem to favor the mobilization of the unemployed, the income maintenance system has greatly improved the lot of many marginalized people even if it has not altogether decreased the incidence of inequality. As the economy grew, rates of unemployment fell, standards of living rose, and new demands and new expectations arose. Pro-unemployed organizations also entered a new era.[46] In the current context of economic difficulties, rising levels of expectation may help explain the phenomenal success of the INOU-organized demonstration in June 2002 along with other antipoverty and equality bodies against government-proposed changes to the Community Employment Scheme. This protest event brought together several hundred people—employed and unemployed alike. A key challenge, therefore, is for the INOU to consider the role that it may play to ensure that a rise in disadvantaged/marginalized Irish people's levels of subjective frustration can be channeled into contentious action.

Conclusion

This chapter has investigated issues concerning—and examples of—the mobilization of unemployed people in the Republic of Ireland since the mid-1980s. The argument is that despite the lack of political opportunities for successful mobilization, the INOU was instrumental in improving the role and status of the unemployed so as to help facilitate the group's cohesion. The final part of the chapter explored a number of key issues and challenges that may have a bearing on the role and status of the unemployed and on the initiation of collective action. The section explored in particular whether economic recession, a rise in levels of unemployment, along with an increase of demands placed on public authorities could lead to an upsurge in the incidence of social conflict and, thereby, to the mobilization of the unemployed. This issue is of course conditional upon the ways that deprivation and opportunities are successfully transformed into collective action.

Notes

1. This chapter is based on qualitative empirical research: opinion polls, interviews, and the Irish National Organization of the Unemployed (INOU) archival documents.
2. For a discussion of this "republican dogma," see Whyte (1974) and Coakley (1992).
3. See the Central Statistics Office's seasonally adjusted standardized unemployment rates as presented in the *Quarterly National Household Surveys*: http://www.cso.ie/statistics/LabourForce.htm (last accessed November 4, 2008).
4. See also http://epp.eurostat.cec.eu.int/portal/page?_pageid=1090,30070682,1090_33076576&_dad=portal&_schema=PORTAL (last accessed August 16, 2008).
5. Even the Labour Party, which initially opposed the principle of social partnership, changed its position from 1993 onward. The various agreements were negotiated with different combinations of parties in office. The first (Programme for National Recovery, 1987–1990) was negotiated by the minority Fianna Fáil government; the second (Programme for Economic and Social Progress, 1990–1993) by a Fianna

Fáil–Progressive Democrats coalition; the third (Programme for Competitiveness and Work, 1994–1997) by a Fianna Fáil–Labour Party coalition; the fourth (Partnership 2000, 1997–2000) by a Fine Gael, Labour Party, and Democratic Left coalition; the fifth, sixth, and the most recent (Programme for Prosperity and Fairness, 2001–2003, Sustaining Progress, 2004–2007, and Towards 2016) by minority coalitions.
6. For a review of the historical development of the Irish trade union movement, see McCarthy (1980).
7. To compare the Irish situation with that of England, see Lewis (1990, 24–37).
8. Interview with Mick Rafferty, Dublin, February 11, 1993. See also Monks (1994).
9. Survey carried out on January 3, 1993, for the *Irish Times* by the opinion poll agency MRBI (Code MRBI 4099/93).
10. This general tendency was pursued up to and beyond the 1990s. For example, at a time of sustained economic growth, a tendency arose to increase the difficulty in ensuring unionization in newly created jobs. From 1995 to 2005, "unions have found it extremely difficult to secure members in sectors largely dominated by USA-based investors, particularly in computers and electronics, call centers and financial services." http://www.eiro.eurofound.ie/2005/10/feature/ie0510201f.html (last accessed November 4, 2008).
11. In addition, Roche and Gunnigle (1995) argue that: "For the foreseeable future unions will continue to play a pivotal role in Irish industrial relations and will have a major impact on the outcome of new industrial relations and human resources strategies. But intensified competitive pressures, new managerial strategies for marginalized unions or adopting the nonunion option pose for Irish unions arguably their most serious strategic challenge since they became pillars of Irish industrial relations in the first three decades after Independence" (31). For another assessment of the Irish trade union movement, see Wallace (2003).
12. Despite positive moves in terms of social partnership, the position of the Irish trade union movement in society at large has declined since the mid-1990s. For example, Central Statistics Office analyses show that although total trade union membership increased by 20 percent from 1994 to 2004, by the second quarter of 2007, 31.5 percent of all employees in Ireland were unionized compared to 37.4 percent in 2003 and 46 percent in 1995. In terms of union density (i.e., membership as a proportion of the labor force), private sector union density was approximately 22 percent at the end of 2005 compared to public sector union density in the region of 80 percent. This imbalance is accounted for by the fact that unions have been gaining members in the public sector but losing members in the private sector. One development of serious concern to the trade union movement is the decrease in the level of unionization among young people: in the twenty–twenty-four age group it was 15.4 percent in 2007 compared to 19.2 percent in 2005 and 38.8 percent in 1994; and in the twenty-five–thirty-four age group it was 25.8 percent in 2007 compared to 29.7 percent in 2005 and 46.8 percent in 1994. See http://www.cso.ie/releasespublications/documents/labour_market/current/qnhsunionmembership.pdf (last accessed November 4, 2008).
13. http://europa.eu.int/comm/employment_social/missoc/2003/022003/irl_en.pdf (last accessed November 5, 2008).
14. See also the results of major European opinion polls: Eurobarometer, 2003/4. *Eurobarometer: Public Opinion in the European Union*. Brussels, European Commission (nos. 59–61), http://europa.eu.int/comm/public_opinion/standard_fr.htm (last accessed October 25, 2008).

15. On the issue of state/society interactions, see Kriesi et al. (1992).
16. Interview with Seán Lambe, unemployment activist, Dublin, March 4, 1993.
17. Interview with John Ryan, head of the Limerick Centre for the Unemployed, Limerick, October 21, 1992.
18. These Centers for the Unemployed were established by the Irish Congress of Trade Unions (ICTU).
19. For a discussion of the strengths and weaknesses of the community and voluntary sector in Ireland, see O'Sullivan (1999).
20. Interview with Eric Conroy, Dublin, April 15, 2005. See the following issues of the *INOU Bulletin* 8(8), October 1998; 8(9), November 1998; and 12(2), May/June 2002. See also the *Irish Times*, August 7, 1999.
21. Interview with Eric Conroy, Dublin, April 15, 2005.
22. *INOU Bulletin*, 10(7), September 1999; *INOU Bulletin*, 8(7), September 1998.
23. *INOU Bulletin*, 14(2), March/April 2004.
24. *INOU Bulletin*, 10(7), September 1999.
25. *INOU Bulletin*, 8(3), May 1998.
26. *INOU Bulletin*, 15(2), February/March 2005.
27. *INOU Bulletin*, 7(4), May 1995.
28. *INOU Bulletin*, 7(15), May 1996.
29. *INOU Bulletin*, 11(7), March 2000.
30. *INOU Bulletin*, 9(1), January 1997.
31. *INOU Bulletin*, 13(2), February/March 2003.
32. Interview with Eric Conroy, Dublin, April 15, 2005.
33. Contrary to the situation in France and Germany in recent years, no survey has ever been carried out in Ireland as to the public's perception of the collective action of unemployed people. Studies in Ireland addressed the issue of unemployment from a mainly party political perspective, i.e., on the public's assessment of the Irish government's or the European Union's policies on issues such as unemployment, poverty, crime, and so on. Such studies have shown that public opinion in Ireland has historically supported governmental policy measures to fight unemployment and on job creation. For example, in a cross-national study of public opinion and welfare state regimes from 1976 to 1996, John Lapinski et al. (1998) found that Ireland ranked high in support for governmental intervention to mitigate against the effects of unemployment or of governmental support of the unemployed. Evidence from the 1990s suggests that active labor market governmental policies have gained public approval while support for the marginalized social actors waned. For an overview of Irish public opinion on unemployment matters, see http://www.tcd.ie/Political_Science/IOPA/ (last accessed November 8, 2008). See also the various studies commissioned by the Combat Poverty Agency.
34. On the various types of impact or outcomes of collective action and on the notion of "procedural gains," see Gamson (1975).
35. See http://www.inou.ie (last accessed November 5, 2008).
36. The protest rallies were organized following layoffs in the Dublin-based building industry by a number of—unionized—unemployed workers with links to the Communist Party of Ireland. See also the *Irish Press*, August 1–13, 1953, and the *Sunday Independent*, March 10, 1957.
37. For example, the organization's initial objectives to address mass and structural unemployment slowly became less relevant. These objectives were soon to be replaced by a preoccupation with youth unemployment including long-term unemployment and with European social policy.

38. Interview with Eric Conroy, September 9, 2005.
39. For a discussion of the impact of political and institutional factors on civil society in various European countries, see chapter 2 of Balme and Chabanet (2008).
40. For a discussion of objective deprivation and the unemployed, see Baglioni et al. (2008).
41. On these points, see Chabanet and Royall (2009).
42. Figures compiled by the Department of Social and Family Affairs show that 251,032 people from the ten EU accession states were issued with personal public service (PPS) numbers from May 1, 2004, to July 31, 2006. A PPS number is required for a person to take up a job. See the *Irish Times*, August 10, 2006.
43. Asylum seekers are not entitled to work in Ireland. Immigrants from EU accession countries are predominantly employed in nonunionized sectors. The government introduced a number of restrictions on entitlements to welfare benefits in May 2004. Migrant workers from EU accession states must prove that they have "resided habitually" in Ireland as a qualifying requirement for all social assistance benefits. The restrictions assume that a person is not habitually resident if he/she has been living in Ireland for less than two years. Some reports indicate a significant rise in the incidence of poverty, homelessness, and social exclusion among many recently arrived east European immigrants. See the *Irish Times*, August 7, 2006. Irish Central Statistics Office data show that the economic slump is leading many EU immigrants to return to their country of origin. See the *Irish Times*, September 26, 2008.
44. Recent research suggests that new immigrants to Ireland avail to a very little extent the services of unemployment centers and when they do it is invariably for purposes of gathering information on welfare or employment entitlements (see Royall 2009). This may well be because as of the third quarter of 2008 new immigrants from the twelve new EU accession countries were primarily in employment. A February 2006 report by the Allied Irish Bank showed that there was no evidence of job displacement from Irish workers in favor of immigrant workers from new EU accession countries.
45. It is interesting to note that the level of protest events has increased significantly since the mid-1990s. See Peillon (2001a).
46. Berclaz, Füglister, and Giugni (2004) suggest that the most generous welfare states seem to provide more favorable conditions for the mobilization of the unemployed than liberal or restrictive states. In the former types of countries, people who experience economic difficulty are more inclined to be very demanding of public authorities; the opposite seems to be the case in countries with a residual welfare system. For a typology of various welfare state regimes, see Esping-Andersen (1990). For a discussion of the Irish case, see Peillon (2001b). In this sense, improvements in the rights of the minority/disadvantaged groups in Ireland open up an interesting avenue of research and suggest that, in time, a higher level of social conflict is likely to arise.

References

Allen, Kieran. 2000. *The Celtic Tiger: The Myth of Social Partnership*. Manchester: Manchester University Press.
Allen, Mike. 1998. *The Bitter Word*. Dublin: Poolbeg.
Bagguley, Paul. 1991. *From Protest to Acquiescence? Political Movements of the Unemployed*. London: Macmillan.

Bagguley, Paul. 1992. Protest, Acquiescence and the Unemployed: A Comparative Analysis of the 1930s and 1980s. *British Journal of Sociology* 43(3): 443–61.

Baglioni, Simone, Britta Baumgarten, Didier Chabanet, and Christian Lahusen. 2008. Transcending Marginalization: The Mobilization of the Unemployed in France, Germany, and Italy in a Comparative Perspective. *Mobilization* 13(3): 323–35.

Balme, Richard, and Didier Chabanet. 2008. *Collective Action and European Democracy*. New York: Rowman and Littlefield.

Barrington, Tom. 1980. *The Irish Administrative System*. Dublin: Institute of Public Administration.

Barry, Frank, ed. 1999. *Understanding Ireland's Economic Growth*. Basingstoke: Macmillan.

Berclaz, Michel, Katharina Füglister, and Marco Giugni. 2004. États-providence, opportunités politiques et mobilisation des chômeurs: Une approche néo-institutionnaliste. *Swiss Journal of Sociology* 30: 421–40.

Bond, Larry. 1990. National Agreements and Social Reform. INOU conference, October 20, Dublin, Ireland.

Breen, Richard, Damian Hannan, David Rottman, and Christopher Whelan. 1990. *Understanding Contemporary Ireland: State, Class and Development in the Republic of Ireland*. London: Macmillan.

Chabanet, Didier, and Frédéric Royall. 2009. Economic recession and the Mobilization of the Unemployed: France and Ireland Compared. *French Politics* 7(4): 268–93.

Coakley, John. 1992. Society and Political Culture. In *Politics in the Republic of Ireland*, ed. John Coakley and Michael Gallagher, 23–39. Galway: PSAI Press.

Commins, Patrick. 1993. *Combating Exclusion in Ireland: A Mid-way Report 1990–1994*. Dublin: The European Community Programme to Foster the Social and Economic Integration of the Least Privileged Groups.

Coombes, David, Nicholas Rees, and John Stapleton. 1991. *Economic Development Networks: Consultation of Economic and Social Interests for Purposes of Local Economic Strategy*. London: LRDP.

Curtin, Chris, and Tony Varley. 1995. Community Action and the State. In *Irish Society: Sociological Perspectives*, ed. Patrick Clancy, Sheelagh Drudy, Kathleen Lynch, and Liam O'Dowd, 379–409. Dublin: Institute of Public Administration.

Department of Enterprise, Trade and Employment. 2003. *National Employment Action Plan, Ireland 2003–2005*. Dublin: Stationery Office.

Department of Enterprise, Trade and Employment. 2004. *National Employment Action plan, Ireland 2004*. Dublin: Stationery Office.

Department of Finance, 2004. *Economic Review*. Dublin: Stationery Office. August.

Duggan, Carmel, and Tom Roynane. 1992. *Services for the unemployed in the Areas of Information, Advice, Guidance and Counseling in Ireland: National Systems, Local Case Studies and the Issues Arising*. Dublin: Work Research Centre.

Durkheim, Émile. 2004 [1893]. *De la division du travail social: Étude sur l'organisation des sociétés supérieures*. Paris : Presses universitaires de France.

Esping-Andersen, Gøsta. 1990. *The Three Worlds of Welfare Capitalism*. Princeton: Princeton University Press.

Fillieule, Olivier. 1993. Conscience politique, persuasion et mobilisation des engagements, L'exemple du syndicat des chômeurs, 1983–89. In *Sociologie de la protestation: Les formes de l'action collective dans la France contemporaine*, ed. Olivier Fillieule, 123–55. Paris: L'Harmattan.

Fitzgerald, Rona. 2000. Ireland and Economic Integration, 1985–95. In *The Neutrals and the European Integration 1945–95*, ed. Rolf Steininger and Michael Gehler, 173–91. Vienna: Böhlau.

Gamson, William. 1975. *The Strategy of Social Protest*. Homewood: Dorsey Press.

Giugni Marco, Michel Berclaz, and Katharina Füglister. 2009. Welfare States, Labour Markets and Political Opportunities for Collective Action in the Field of Unemployment. In *The Politics of Unemployment in Europe: Policy Responses and Collective Action*, ed. Marco Giugni, 133–50. Farnham: Ashgate.

Glyn, Andrew. 2002. *Labour Market Success and Labour market Reform: Lessons from Ireland and New Zealand*. Center for Economic Policy Analysis, New School University (New York), Working Paper 2002–03.

Gurr, Ted Robert. 1970. *Why Men Rebel*. Princeton: Princeton University Press.

Hamilton, Rob. 2005. Education, Demographics and the Irish Economic Miracle. *Central Bank of Ireland Quarterly Bulletin* 2: 103–29.

Hardiman, Niamh. 1987. "Consensual Politics": Public Goods and Collective Action in Ireland. In *Political Stability and Neo-Corporatism*, ed. Ilja Scholten, 153–76. London: Sage.

———. 2002. From Conflict to Co-ordination: Economic Governance and Political Innovation in Ireland. *West European Politics* 25(4): 1–24.

Hillyard, Paddy, Bill Rolston, and Mike Tomlinson. 2005. *Poverty and Conflict in Ireland: An International Perspective*. Dublin: Combat Poverty Agency.

INOU. 2006. *Working for Work: Exploring Welfare, Work, Education and Training Options for Unemployed People*. 13th edition. Dublin: INOU.

Johns, Christopher. 1993. Ireland's Record—Last in the Class? *Studies* 80(32): 9–23.

Kenny, Brian. 1990. Representing the poor. INOU conference, October 20, Dublin, Ireland.

Kilmurray, Evanne. 1988. *Fight, Starve or Emigrate: A History of the Unemployed Associations in the 1950s*. Dublin: Larkin Unemployed Centre.

Kirby, Peadar. 2002. *The Celtic Tiger in Distress: Growth with Inequality in Ireland*. Basingstoke: Palgrave.

Kooiman, Jan, ed. 1993. *Modern Governance: New Government—Society Interactions*. London: Sage.

Kriesi, Hanspeter, Ruud Koopmans, Jan Duyvendak, and Marco Giugni. 1992. New Social Movements and Political opportunities in Western Europe. *European Journal of Political Research* 22: 219–44.

Laffan, Brigid. 1989. While You're Over There Get Us a Grant: The Management of the Structural Funds in Ireland. *Irish Political Studies* 4: 43–57.

Lapinski, John, Charles Riemann, Robert Shapiro, Matthew Stevens, and Lawrence Jacobs. 1998. Welfare State Regimes and Subjective Well-Being: A Cross-National Study. *International Journal of Public Opinion Research* 10(1): 2–24.

Lee, Joe. 1989. *Ireland 1912–85: Politics and Society*. Cambridge: Cambridge University Press.

Lewis, Paul. 1990. *Trade Union Policy and the Unemployed*. Aldershot: Avebury.

Lutz, Karin. 2003. Irish Party Competition in the New Millennium: Change or Plus ça Change? *Irish Political Studies* 18(2): 40–59.

McCarthy, Charles. 1980. The Development of Irish Trade Unions. In *Trade Unions and Change in Irish Society*, ed. David Nevin, 26–38. Dublin: Mercier Press.

McCarthy, Dermot. 1999. *Building Partnership*. Dublin: Department of the Taoiseach.

McGinn, Pat, and Mike Allen. 1991. *Organizing against Unemployment: The Strength and Weaknesses of Organizations of the Unemployed in Ireland.* Dublin: INOU.

Monks, Tony. 1994. Representing the Long-term Unemployed: The Role of the Unemployed People's Organizations. *LEDA Circuit on Local Responses to Long-term Unemployment*, June 23–25, Dundee, Scotland.

Nic Ghiolla Phádraig, Máire. 1995. The Power of the Catholic Church in Ireland. In *Irish Society: Sociological Perspectives*, ed. Patrick Clancy, Sheelagh Drudy, Kathleen Lynch, and Liam O'Dowd, 137–54. Dublin: Institute of Public Administration.

Nolan, Brian, Philip O'Connell, and Christopher Whelan. 2000. *Boom to Bust: The Irish Experience of Growth and Inequality.* Dublin: Institute of Public Administration.

Ó Cinnéide, Séamus. 1985. Community Responses to Unemployment. *Administration* 33(2): 231–57.

O'Connell, Philip, and Frances McGinnity. 1997. *Active Labour Market Policy in Ireland.* London: Ashgate.

O'Neill, Jim. 1994. *Five Years of INOU Development: An Evaluation of the Irish National Organisation of the Unemployed.* Dublin: INOU, Unpublished Report.

O'Sullivan, Eoin. 1999. Voluntary Agencies in Ireland—What Future Role? *Administration* 45(4): 54–69.

OECD. 1989. *Economic Survey: Ireland.* Paris: OECD.

———. 1991. *Economic Survey: Ireland.* Paris: OECD.

———. 1995. *Economic Survey: Ireland.* Paris: OECD.

———. 1999. *Economic Survey: Ireland.* Paris: OECD.

Peillon, Michel. 1982. *Contemporary Irish Society: An introduction.* Dublin: Gill and Macmillan.

———. 2001a. The Constitution of Protest as Sign in Contemporary Ireland. *Irish Political Studies* 16: 95–110.

———. 2001b. *Welfare in Ireland: Actors, Resources and Strategies.* Westport: Praeger.

Rafferty, Mick. 1990. Community Responses to Unemployment. In *Community Work in Ireland: Trends in the 80's, Options for the 90's*, ed. Combat Poverty Agency, 216–34. Dublin: Combat Poverty Agency.

Roche, William. 1989 [2nd ed.]. State Strategies and the Politics of Industrial Relations in Ireland since 1945. In *Industrial Relations in Ireland: Contemporary Issues and Developments*, 115–31. Dublin: Department of Industrial Relations.

Roche, William, and Patrick Gunnigle. 1995. Competition and the New Industrial Relations Agenda. In *New Challenges to Irish Industrial Relations*, ed. Gunnigle Patrick and William Roche, 1–34. Dublin: Oak Tree Press.

Royall, Frédéric. 2005. *Mobilisations de chômeurs en Irlande (1985–1995).* Paris : L'Harmattan.

Royall, Frédéric. 2009. Political Challengers, Service Providers or Service Recipients? Participants in Irish Pro-unemployed Organizations. In *The Politics of Unemployment in Europe: Policy Responses and Collective Action*, ed. Marco Giugni, 117–32. Farnham: Ashgate.

Sweeney, Paul. 1999 [2nd ed.]. *The Celtic Tiger: Ireland's Continuing Economic Miracle.* Dublin: Oak Tree Press.

Tille, Cédric, and Kei-Mu Yi. 2001. Curbing Unemployment in Europe: Are There Lessons from Ireland and the Netherlands? *Current Issues in Economics and Finance* 7(5): 1–6.

Tilly, Charles. 1986. *La France conteste de 1600 à nos jours.* Paris: Fayard.

Valarasan-Toomey, Mary. 1998. *The Celtic Tiger: From the Outside Looking In.* Dublin: Blackhall.

Wallace, Joseph. 2003. Unions in 21st Century Ireland—Entering the Ice Age? Industrial News Conference, *No Vision no Future?*, February 27, Dublin, Ireland.

Wallace, Joseph, Patrick Gunnigle, and Gerard McMahon. 2004 [3rd ed.]. *Industrial Relations in Ireland*. Dublin: Gill & Macmillan.

Whelan, Christopher. 1991. *Social Class, Unemployment and Psychological Stress*. Dublin: The Economic and Social Research Institute.

Whyte, John. 1974. Ireland: Politics without Social Bases. In *Electoral Behavior: A Comparative Handbook*, ed. Richard Rose, 619–51. New York: The Free Press.

CHAPTER 9

Political Opportunities and the Mobilization of the Unemployed in Switzerland

Michel Berclaz, Katharina Füglister, and Marco Giugni

Switzerland has long avoided the problem of unemployment, being characterized by a situation of virtual full employment. Even in the period of the economic crisis of the mid-1970s, unemployment never went above a "physiological" level. This was made possible, among other things, by the strategy of using women and the foreign labor force as a "buffer" in order to reduce unemployment in bad economic times (Bonoli and Mach 2001). Given this situation, it is legitimate to wonder if it is worth at all to discuss about the political mobilization of the unemployed. After all, why bother to examine the behavior of the unemployed in a country in which the situation of the labor market is fine and the unemployed form a small group, a country in which in other words the "problem" is not there?

Yet there are reasons to address this issue. First of all, the situation in Switzerland has changed quite dramatically in the early 1990s, when unemployment rates increased to reach levels that, to be sure, remain lower than most other European countries, but that can no longer be ignored by political authorities and public opinion alike. This new situation has led to a number of changes in the existing legislation on the unemployment insurance (most notably, through the revisions of the law in 1990, 1995, and 2002). Most importantly, the new situation has created a potential for mobilization not only of the people most directly concerned by unemployment—that is, the unemployed themselves—but also for other collective actors such as parties, unions, and other interest groups, which is worth analyzing in depth. This mobilization potential, however, has largely remained latent. To be sure, the political mobilization of the unemployed is a relatively rare phenomenon everywhere in Europe. Yet, in cross-national perspective, the Swiss unemployed emerge as quite an inactive social group (Giugni 2008).

Why are the unemployed in Switzerland politically so inactive? Drawing in particular from the social movement literature, several explanatory factors may be mentioned. First, the unemployed might simply not be interested in political mobilization. These are people who, quite understandably, are more worried about their economic situation and who struggle to get a job rather than becoming involved in some kind of political activity. Second, the low level of mobilization may be due to the lack of an "objective" condition that gives rise to grievances about the situation of the labor market. The political mobilization of the unemployed in Switzerland may be lagging behind that observed in other countries because unemployment is lower and therefore the number of jobless people does not create a "critical mass" large enough for a social movement to form.[1] Third, the low level of mobilization of the unemployed would stem from the (missing) social construction of the "problem" of unemployment as well as the discursive practices relating to collective action itself and to its relation to societal issues. In other words, the unemployed may have difficulties in motivating people for action, identifying causes and consequences (prognostic frames) of a given problem, defining unemployment as an unjust condition, blaming the political authorities or someone else for this condition, and so forth.[2] Fourth, a strong collective identity to be engaged in the struggle for better conditions might be lacking.[3] Fifth, there might be a lack of internal resources.[4] As compared to other social groups and movements, the unemployed are certainly very badly equipped in terms of resources and organizational structures, which resource mobilization theory has shown as being a necessary condition for protest to occur. Finally, the structure of political opportunities may not be favorable to the emergence of a movement of the unemployed.[5]

These explanatory factors are likely to be interrelated and to have a cumulative impact on the political mobilization of the unemployed. We argue in particular that, in Switzerland, all these aspects—the low level of interest in politics by unemployed, their low level of resources, the lack of a collective identity, and the framing of the unemployment issue in the public domain, which tend to discourage the unemployed to mobilize—stem from a specific political opportunity structure relating to certain characteristics of the Swiss welfare state. Indeed, the low level of mobilization of the unemployed in Switzerland represents a puzzle in light of the characterization of the generally open political opportunity structure for the mobilization of social movements in this country, which should and indeed does lead to much protest, although a moderate one (Kriesi et al. 1995). We argue that the unemployed face a specific political opportunity structure, stemming from the dominant conception of the welfare and the way in which the unemployment issue is framed in the public domain, which goes in the opposite direction, that is, in the direction of limiting the space for their mobilization. Before we elaborate this argument further, a brief overview of the situation with respect to unemployment and the policy responses to it is in order.

The Emergence of the "Problem" of Unemployment and Policy Responses

In Switzerland, unemployment became a relevant political issue during the 1990s. This country has, compared to other European countries, a very short history of unemployment. Until the 1990s the Swiss labor market was in a situation of nearly full employment, with a number of registered unemployed below 1 percent of the active population. The low unemployment rate of Switzerland was until the 1970s partly due to anticyclical policies that were based on foreigners and women, two categories that were pushed out of the labor market when the economic situation worsened (Bonoli and Mach 2001). This solution was no longer applicable after changes in the immigration practice and the better integration of women in the labor market. More generally, labor market regulations in Switzerland are traditionally characterized by the combination of a liberal type of regulation and relatively generous unemployment social benefits as well as by the combination of a comparatively lower trade union power due to a low unionization rate and a tradition of negotiation among social partners. These features have allowed Switzerland to keep a low rate of unemployment, even with a very weak growth as it has been the case in recent years.

However, the situation of unemployment changed quite dramatically in the early 1990s, when a deteriorating economic situation had also an impact on the Swiss labor market. In 1991, 68,000 persons were unemployed, which corresponds to 1.8 percent of the active population.[6] A first peak of unemployed was reached in 1997, when 162,000 persons were without a job (4.1 percent). After a short period of economic recovery, the number of unemployed rose again and reached in 2003 the highest level ever with 186,000 people without job, which corresponds to an unemployment rate of 4.1 percent. In addition, parallel to the rate of unemployment, the number of underemployed people (i.e., people who have a part-time job) is also increasing. At the same time, the public opinion has become to view unemployment as a relevant political issue in the 1990s. While for decades unemployment was not among the main worries of the Swiss population, starting from 1990 it has become a priority issue. For example, unemployment was considered the most important problem by Swiss citizens in 2003.[7]

The development of welfare policies took place later in Switzerland than in other European countries.[8] In general, the Swiss social policy is very static as reforms take a long time to find a way through the federal structure and the procedures of direct democracy. Unemployment policies are an example of the late development of welfare policies: a basis for a mandatory unemployment insurance was included in the Constitution in 1975 and the related legislation was implemented in 1982. However, important changes in legislation and practice occurred in the 1990s, when the unemployment rate rose significantly and the social security system was subject to economic pressure. Responding to increasing unemployment rates and to the emerging public debate, unemployment-insurance legislation was revised a first time in 1990 and then again in 1995, and 2002. Urgent measures and changes were also introduced in 1993, 1999, and 2000. Pointing to the reactive nature of the state response to the new situation, sociologist Duvanel (2002) has stressed the fact that, as unemployment started to grow, the law has been in a situation of constant revision and adaptation. This is also a consequence of the Swiss welfare state, which is not built on a model or societal project, but rather emerged in a pragmatic way as a response to conjunctural evolutions (Fragnière and Christen 1988).

The main changes implied by all these revisions concern the amount and duration of social benefits, the conditions for eligibility, and, in the 1995 revision, a shift toward active measures. The latter are meant to help the reinsertion of jobless people in the labor market through formation and training as well as other forms of individual aid. They also aim to put an end to the passive perception of unemployment allowances. The open question is whether these measures are interpreted as help to insertion into the labor market or rather as a punishment for being "inactive." Since the Swiss unemployment social benefits system is insurance-based, these moves toward an obligation to furnish a counterpart to social benefits can be interpreted as a tightening of the management of unemployment and control of the unemployed. This might mark the beginning of a fundamental shift from welfare to workfare (Cattacin et al. 2002).

The 1995 revision introduced a related important change with the creation of a new placement system: the Regional Placement Bureau, a special office devoted to the reinsertion of the unemployed. This office personifies the ambiguity of activation measures (Duvanel 2002; Valli, Martin, and Hertz 2002).[9] They are conceived as help to the unemployed in their quest for a job, but at the same time they can force them to take a job or a course and have the power to sanction the unemployed by suspending their right to allowances in case of misbehavior. Similarly, the most recent changes have followed a trend toward the tightening of the conditions of the unemployed. For example, the definition of the jobs the unemployed are supposed to accept has been broadened, the level of social benefits compared to the salary one had when employed has been brought down from 80 to 70 percent, the duration of social benefits has been shortened from 520 to 400 opening days, the necessary contribution period required to be eligible for social benefits has been increased from six to twelve months.

As compared to other European countries, the level of social benefits for a lack of job is relatively high in Switzerland. However, one major criticism can be held against the legislation on unemployment. According to Cattacin et al. (1999), it does not take into consideration long-term unemployed that no longer fulfill the requirements of unemployment insurance. More generally, the Swiss situation with respect to the institutional approaches to unemployment is kind of paradoxical: comparatively, unemployment social benefits are high, and the objective conditions of unemployed are better that in most other European countries, but at the same time strong stigmata are associated with the condition of being unemployed.[10] The unemployed are easily suspected of being responsible for their situation. Thus, since 1992, the law was clearly oriented toward the fight against abuses (Duvanel 2002).[11] Furthermore, workfare conditions are progressively being installed and the unemployed have to face an institutional mistrust concerning the reasons for their condition, putting them in a situation in which they have to constantly prove that they are not responsible for it and that they are doing everything in order to get out of it. In other words, the problem of unemployment is becoming the problem of the unemployed (Valli, Martin, and Hertz 2002).

To summarize, at least concerning unemployment, the Swiss welfare state can be characterized as having rather restrictive policies both in terms of the formal criteria of eligibility to social rights and provisions and the obligations relating to eligibility (Berclaz, Füglister, and Giugni 2004). We argue that these characteristics lead to an unfavorable opportunity structure for the political mobilization of the unemployed.

The Specific Opportunity Structure in the Unemployment Political Field

The idea that contentious politics is channeled in important ways by existing political opportunity structures is one of the most consistent findings of social movement theory today. State-related aspects such as the degree of openness of the institutionalized political system, the prevailing strategies of the authorities toward protest, and the configuration of power within the institutional arenas are most often used to explain the emergence of social movements as well as cross-national variations in the extent and forms of protest (Kitschelt 1986; Kriesi et al. 1995; McAdam 1996; Tarrow 1998; McAdam, Tarrow, and Tilly 2001). In this perspective, Switzerland offers social movements many opportunities, both formal and informal, to mobilize, which lead to high levels of mobilization and moderate action repertoires (Kriesi et al. 1995). As a result, the mobilization of the unemployed should be more important and moderate than in countries in which opportunities are less favorable, such as, for example, France.

However, recent work on immigration and ethnic relations politics has stressed the role of what we may call specific (or perhaps better, sectoral) political opportunity structures (Berclaz and Giugni 2005), which impinge upon the claim-making of actors who intervene in this political field (Koopmans et al. 2005). In addition, this work points to the need to distinguish between the institutional and discursive side of such specific opportunities. Institutional opportunities can be defined as options for collective action that provide actors with different chances and pose different risks from one context to the other (Koopmans 2004). They determine the access provided by the political system to challengers for their mobilization. Discursive opportunities can be defined as the chances that movement identities and claims have to gain visibility in the mass media, to resonate with other actors' claims, and to gain legitimacy in public discourses (Koopmans et al. 2005). In other words, they define which political positions are more likely to become visible in the public domain, which identities and claims are more likely to find an echo with respect to other claims, and which identities and claims are more likely to be considered as legitimate in public discourses.

Following this perspective, we explore the role of specific opportunities for claim-making in the field of unemployment in order to examine to what extent the actors, interests, and collective identities involved in the employment political field are influenced by certain aspects of their institutional and discursive context. To do so, we focus on the characteristics of the welfare state as a specific political opportunity structure shaping the claim-making and structuring the public discourse on unemployment (Giugni, Berclaz, and Füglister 2009; Giugni 2010). We argue that the prevailing view of the welfare state in a given country impinges in significant ways upon the "contentious politics of unemployment"—that is, the public debates and collective mobilizations pertaining to unemployment—in that country. Dominant conceptions of the welfare state define a political opportunity structure that enlarges or constrains the options for action by collective actors that intervene in this field.

Although the specific opportunity structure in the field of unemployment politics has both an institutional and a discursive side, here we focus on the discursive context and the framing of the issue of unemployment. We argue that the specific ways in which the issue of unemployment is framed in the (dominant) public discourse provide discursive opportunities that channel the claim-making by the unemployed. We further suggest that these ways of framing the issue of unemployment, in turn, stem from the prevailing conception of the welfare state and, more specifically, from the prevailing view concerning the rights and duties of the unemployed in Switzerland.

Discursive opportunities point to the fact that the mobilization of collective actors in a given political field does not depend solely on a more-or-less favorable institutional context. It stems also from certain cultural and discursive conditions. In the social movement literature, it is the so-called framing approach that has most thoroughly dealt with these aspects (Gamson, Fireman, and Rytina 1982; Snow et al. 1986; Snow and Benford 1992; Gamson 1992 and 1995; see Benford and Snow 2000 and Snow 2004 for reviews). This approach stresses the linkages between existing interpretations of objective facts and events, on the one hand, and participation into social movements, on the other; between the movements' interpretive and discursive frames and mobilization. However, the focus in this theoretical tradition is put on how political mobilization depends on the cognitive processes that underlie the evaluation of a given situation, of possible solutions, and motivations for action (Snow et al. 1986), as well as the creation of feelings of identity, injustice, and agency (Gamson 1995). In other words, at least in its original formulation (Snow et al. 1986), this approach looks at the ways in which collective action frames emerging from within social movements can help their efforts at mobilization. The concept of discursive opportunities can be seen as an attempt to bridge this literature with the political opportunity approach by looking at how framing processes occurring outside the movements and stemming from institutional settings and arrangements channel the movements' mobilization.

Public Discourse on Unemployment

The main goal of our analysis is to explore some of the possible linkages between the Swiss approach to unemployment, on the one hand, and the opportunities for mobilization provided by the structure of public discourse on unemployment issues, on the other. One potential linkage lies perhaps in the stronger presence of employer's organizations and groups in claim-making in the field (table 9.1).[12] These organizations are among the most important actors overall, and definitively the most important among civil society actors (20.7 percent of all claims). Labor organizations and groups, in contrast, are much less present (8.7 percent of all claims). Furthermore, employers' organizations and groups are not only the most active type of actors among civil society actors, they are also those whose claims are most detrimental to the rights and position of the group of the unemployed. This can be seen in the right-hand column of the table, which shows the average discursive positions of the categories of actors considered. The average position of the employers (-.31) stands in strong opposition to those, for example, of the labor sector (.80) and nonstate welfare actors (.91), which are most in favor of an improvement in the rights and position of the unemployed. In such a situation, organized unemployed not only finds little support by political allies within the institutional areas (institutional opportunities), but also encounter an unfavorable discursive context to the extent that their collective identity and claims receive little visibility in the mass media, they do not resonate with the claims of other collective actors, and they have little chances to achieve legitimacy in a public discourse dominated by actors who frame the issue of unemployment mainly in economic rather than in social terms and who tend to make claims that are detrimental to the rights and position of the unemployed (discursive opportunities).

Table 9.1 Actors involved in claim-making in unemployment politics in Switzerland (1995–2002)

	Percentages	*Average discursive position*
State and party actors	54.1	.45
Governments	13.7	.55
Legislative and political parties	26.4	.47
Judiciary	1.7	.32
State agencies	9.6	.35
Other state actors	2.84	.16
Civil society actors	44.2	.21
Labor organizations and groups	8.7	.80
Employers' organizations and groups	20.7	−.31
Unemployed organizations and groups	0.3	(1.00)
Nonstate welfare organizations and groups	2.2	.91
Other civil society actors and groups	12.3	.52
Other and unknown actors	1.7	.69
Total	100%	.35
N	2019	2019

Note: Figures in brackets have less than ten cases.

The average discursive positions suggest a further hypothesis concerning the absence of the unemployed, one that takes into account the behavior of other actors, this time not acting "against" the unemployed, but on behalf of them. If we look at the table, we can see that, in addition to labor organizations and groups as well as nonstate welfare organizations and groups, there is an important share of claims made by other civil society actors and groups, which have a relatively high average discursive position. In other words, a rather important sector of the civil society participates in the public debates on unemployment (12.3 percent of all claims) with the aim of improving the rights and position of the unemployed (average discursive position of .52). Thus, other collective actors might act on behalf of the unemployed, who remain absent from the public domain in part due to the unfavorable discursive context stemming from the central place of employers' organizations and groups in the public debates. However, the actors that generally take a position that aims at an improvement of the conditions of the unemployed, such as, for example, the trade unions, speak first for the workers and only then make claims aiming the unemployed. In order to be heard, the unemployed have to share an alliance with actors that only defend their interests in the second place. Furthermore, nonstate welfare organizations and groups focus their involvement on the integration of the unemployed into the labor market, whereas their political commitment stays quite weak. Therefore, even if these organizations can be seen as potential allies for the unemployed, such an alliance does not give much visibility to the claims of the unemployed in the public sphere.

The important role played by the economic milieus and the political organizations that defend their interests can also be seen by having a closer look at the claim-making by political parties (table 9.2). Right and center-right parties dominate the scene (58.9 percent against 39.2 percent for left parties), although the socialists are the most active single party, followed by the Free-democratic party. Extreme-right parties are much less active, indeed nearly absent from the public debates on unemployment. The crucial issues for these parties lie

Table 9.2 Distribution of claims in unemployment politics by party in Switzerland (1995–2002)

	Percentages	Average discursive position
Left parties	*39.2*	*.68*
Socialist party	32.5	.67
Greens	5.4	.73
Other leftist parties	1.2	(.60)
Right and center-right parties	*58.9*	*.28*
Christian-democratic party	11.3	.46
Free-democratic party	33.0	.24
Swiss people's party	11.3	.13
Other right and center-right parties	3.2	.54
Extreme right parties	*2.0*	*(.25)*
Total	100%	.43
N	406	406

Note: Figures in brackets have less than ten cases.

elsewhere, most notably in immigration politics and in the safeguarding of national sovereignty and identity.

Discursive positions can also be used to have a sense of the policy positions of actors with respect unemployment and the constituency of the unemployed. They provide a picture of the alliance and opposition systems as they express themselves through the claim-making in unemployment politics. In other words, they allow us to observe the multiorganizational field of unemployment in the public domain. If we look at the average discursive position of actors (tables 9.1 and 9.2), we observe the presence of a polarized situation with two quite distinct camps: a "pro-unemployed" camp who is clearly in favor of measures that improve the rights and position of the unemployed (made above all by labor as well as nonstate welfare organizations and groups, state agencies, and other sectors of the civil society) and a camp who is more conservative in this respect (made above all by employers' organizations and groups), with the state (except for state agencies) somewhere in between. These two camps are reflected in the traditional left-right opposition in the party system, with the extreme right that is in a way out of play, as we said. The organized unemployed must deal with this situation in their claim-making and their mobilization is channeled by this pattern of positioning by other collective actors, for example, by leaving little room for claims that are made by other actors on their behalf. Clearly, the specific opportunity structure in the field of unemployment politics is an unfavorable one in this respect.

We expect the thematic focus of claims to be the aspect most directly linked to institutional approaches to unemployment and the related structure of discursive opportunities (table 9.3). If we look at the general categories, the main pattern seems at the same time quite clear and reflecting the principal features seen thus far: socioeconomic issues regarding the labor market are by and large the most important thematic focus of claims in unemployment politics in Switzerland (71 percent of all claims). Actors who intervene in this field tend to locate the problem of unemployment and its solution in the market and the economy, as can be seen in the high proportion of claims concerning macr-economic issues (32.5 percent). This does not mean that the state plays a marginal role, but its role is largely seen as consisting in regulating the labor market, as the share of claims focusing on state policy regarding the labor market attests. Claims focusing on welfare systems and social benefits (14.9 percent), just as those concerning individual insertion in the labor market (11.9 percent), are much less important. Among the former, the largest share deals with unemployment insurance, which is little surprising for a country that has a strongly Bismarckian welfare model based on the insurance system of social benefits. Furthermore, during the 1990s there have been a number of revisions of the law on unemployment insurance, each time creating a public debate.

The framing of the problem of unemployment mainly in socioeconomic terms, of course, reflects in part the crucial role played by the economic milieus and the organizations defending their interests in the public debates on unemployment. However, the main point for our present purpose is that this provides

Table 9.3 Thematic focus of claims in unemployment politics in Switzerland (1995–2002)

	Percentages
Socioeconomic issues regarding the labor market	71.0
Macroeconomic issues	32.5
Economic development policy	12.0
State policy regarding the labor market	17.0
State policy regarding the labor forces	3.5
Work conditions	5.8
Targeted employment measures	0.1
Welfare systems and social benefits	14.9
Unemployment insurance	13.2
Social aid	1.3
Nonstate welfare systems	0.1
Targeted reactive measures	0.2
Individual insertion in the labor market	11.9
Active/insertion measures	7.4
Training/formation	0.6
Educational issues	3.9
Issues regarding the constituency of unemployed	1.8
Associational life	0.4
Individual/psychological attitudes/dispositions	0.2
Other issues regarding the unemployed	1.1
Other issues	0.3
Total	100%
N	2019

the unemployed with a discursive opportunity structure that gives more visibility, resonance, and legitimacy to claims that focus on the (labor) market rather than the group of the unemployed. This can also be seen in the low share of claims focusing on issues regarding the constituency of the unemployed, which by definition placed the group at center stage (1.8 percent). Furthermore, within the general category of socioeconomic issues concerning the labor market, claims on state policy regarding the labor market (i.e., the phenomenon of unemployment) are much more frequent than claims on state policy regarding the labor forces (i.e., the group of unemployed). This indicates a framing of the problem of unemployment that is more economic than social, a framing that puts forward economic regulation rather than social citizenship.

Finally, we can look at the object actors of claims in unemployment politics (table 9.4). Object actors are those actors whose interests are affected by the (realization of the) claims. In other words, this is the constituency that is at the center of the contentious politics of unemployment. An interesting feature of the Swiss situation in this respect is the important place taken by workers and employees as objects of claims (54.8 percent of all claims). This can once again be interpreted as reflecting an institutional approach to unemployment, which focuses on the economy rather than on the social groups of excluded, an approach that stems in part from the historically low levels of unemployment

Table 9.4 Object actors of claims in unemployment politics in Switzerland (1995–2002)

	Percentages
Workers/employees	*54.8*
Precarious workers/employees	4.1
Workers/employees of same company	31.0
Illegal workers	0.2
Other and unspecified workers/employees	18.6
Unions	0.3
Unemployed	*45.2*
Young unemployed	6.2
Old-age unemployed	0.9
Women unemployed	0.5
Migrant unemployed	1.2
Disabled unemployed	0.6
Long-term unemployed	3.6
Unemployed recently made redundant	5.3
Social welfare recipients	2.6
Other and unspecified unemployed	24.3
Total	100%
N	2019

in this country, but which we may also interpret as a result of the specific opportunity structure in this field. In particular, workers and employees of a company represent nearly one-third of all objects, suggesting an approach that aims not only to find the solutions to unemployment in the functioning of the economy, but also at the local level. This may be seen as reflecting a reactive rather than a proactive approach to the problem of unemployment and a search for short-term rather than long-term solutions. Furthermore, when the group of unemployed is the object of claims, this occurs above all in general terms (24.3 percent of claims referring to other and unspecified unemployed).

To summarize, in Switzerland the unemployed do not find much support from state actors and political parties. The discourse is dominated by the economic aspects of unemployment and largely eschews its social aspects. The public discourse on the contentious politics of unemployment in Switzerland is expressed in a discussion around the conditions of the workers and focuses on the economic dimension. The unemployed themselves constitute, in this perception, individuals that have temporarily lost their job. This kind of framing gives little visibility, resonance, and legitimacy to collective identities and claims that focus on the social and structural aspects of unemployment. In such a framing scheme, the solution to the problem is seen in a good functioning of the labor market, and leaves little space for policy solutions focusing on the individuals already excluded from the labor market. Most importantly, such an institutional and discursive context constrains the formation of organizations and networks of unemployed, their activities and forms of action, and their policy impact.

Organizations and Networks

To examine the organizational structures of the unemployed in Switzerland we can again use information gathered in the UNEMPOL project. The networks of voluntary associations play a crucial role in the civil society's development since they create channels of communication and of exchange between individuals and organizations. In addition, a dense social network can constitute a resource for a minority group in terms of social capital, a resource that may help establish a basis for trust and action (Putnam 1993, 2000). The number and type of unemployed organizations is particularly important because they provide the infrastructure upon which a collective identity can rest. This is especially true for groups that are structurally fragmented like the unemployed, which face difficulties creating a collective identity (Fillieule 1993).

Generally speaking, the organizational structures of the unemployed are quite fragile. The unemployed constitute a deprived population affected by three types of deprivation: economic, social, and political. Economic deprivation stems from the diminished economic resources following the loss of a regular income. Social deprivation comes from the lack of remunerated work, which in contemporary society has a central position as a social integrator and a marker of social position. Political deprivation can be seen in the lower degree of confidence in democratic institutions and the lower degree of political participation. To these three aspects, we may add a fourth one—psychological deprivation (see Jahoda, Lazarsfeld, and Zeisel 1933; Schnapper 1981)—seen, for example, in the feelings of uselessness and isolation. Taken together, these four types of deprivation make the unemployed, like other "poor people's movements," less likely to produce structures and organizations that favors their political mobilization. As a result, the organizational structures of the "movements of unemployed" tend to be weaker and more short-lived than that of other movements.

To be sure, unemployed associations have indeed been created, but they are not very structured, have poor resources, and lack visibility in the public sphere. The level of organization and mobilization is dependent on the most active members, and the strong turnover among members and especially in the leadership weakens these organizations considerably. Furthermore, it is difficult for potential partners to work with them, as the contact persons and the political orientation of the organizations change quite often. The interviews we have conducted with unemployed organizations and with other actors involved in the field show that the most active unemployed organizations are those that are not run by the unemployed themselves.[13] This underscores the crucial role of leadership and political entrepreneurs for a social movement (Oberschall 1973), especially so if other resources are scarce or even lacking completely. The analysis of Duvanel (2002), who has spent two years of participant observation in an unemployed organization, confirms this point as well as the difficulties faced by unemployed in collective action.

Most unemployed organizations are local. National structures that have sometimes been created are very weak, dependent on the involvement of local members, and are often short-lived. In addition, often unemployed and pro-unemployed organizations do not engage in political activities, but restrain themselves to help jobless people, avoiding the use of their scarce resources in political-oriented action. Thus, neither unemployed nor pro-unemployed organizations have the sufficient means, willingness, and visibility to mobilize in an effective way the unemployed or on behalf of the unemployed. As a result, the unemployed must rely on existing actors that are not "specialized" in supporting the unemployed (unions and leftist parties). In fact, for this type of actors, unemployed are not a priority. This does not mean that unemployment is not an important issue, but that the unemployed as a constituency group are not central in their political agenda. The way the debate is framed puts the unemployed at the margin of public discourse on unemployment.

In addition to single organizations, the network structure is also an important aspect of the organizational structures of the unemployed that deserves to be analyzed. Using our interview data, we can see the position of unemployed organizations in the network of relationships among actors in the field of unemployment. When we asked the selected organizations to mention the most important actors in the field, unemployed organizations were seldom mentioned, if at all, except for one notable exception: the ADC Chaux-de-Fonds (ADC NE), the organization that launched a successful referendum against the decision of the federal government to reduce the level of unemployment social benefits in 1996. This organization ranks thirteenth among a list of forty-two actors. However, this respectable ranking seems to be more an homage for that action than a recognition of the actual importance of the organization.

We also asked actors to mention those they try to influence, collaborate and disagree with. Focusing on collaborations, we can see that unemployed organizations (ADC BS, ADC GE, ADC NE, ADC VD, *Surprise*) are peripheral actors in the network structure in the field. They collaborate to a certain degree among each other as well as with leftist parties (mostly at the local level) and unions (figure 9.1). The most interesting aspect in this respect is perhaps that unions represent an important bridge between unemployed organizations and other actors. In other words, they play the role of brokers in the network structure. Yet these potential allies do not consider the unemployed as a crucial issue, although they are indeed interested in the issue of unemployment. Finally, we should note the very weak degree of collaboration among unemployed organizations and welfare organizations that are fully or partly devoted to giving direct aid to the unemployed.

Concerning influence and especially disagreements, unemployed organizations are even more isolated, as other actors tend to ignore them. The relationship is asymmetrical, as unemployed organizations mention actors they have tried to influence or disagreed with, but the reverse is not true, that is, they are not mentioned back by those actors. Thus, organizations of the unemployed are not only weak and loosely structured, but also peripheral in the unemployment political field. Given these organizational structures, in what kind of activities has the unemployed engaged in?

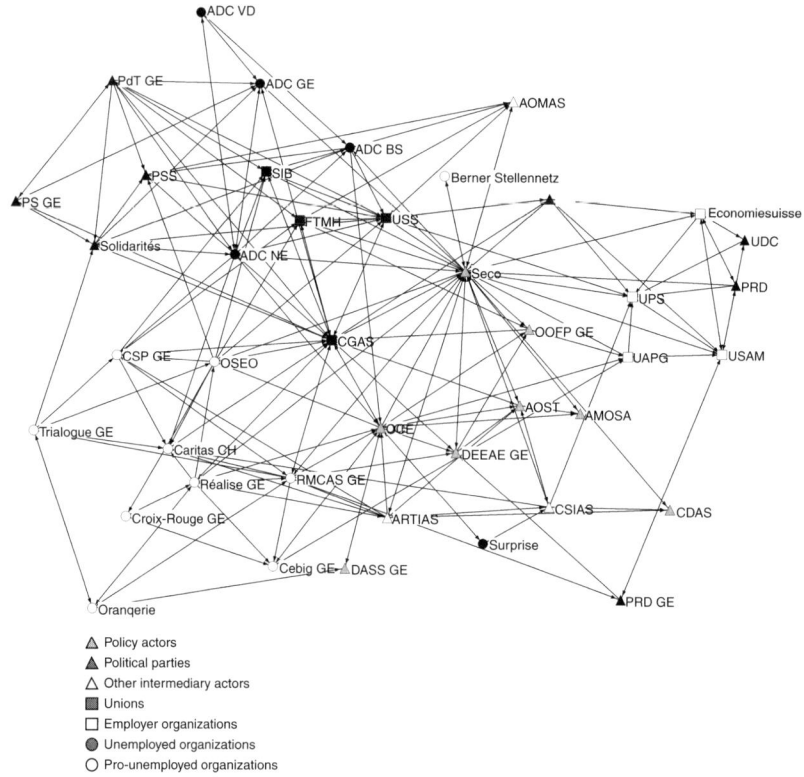

Figure 9.1 Network of collaborations in the unemployment political field in Switzerland.

Activities and Forms of Action

The unemployed in Switzerland display a very low level of mobilization. If we look at the claim-making data, unemployed organizations and groups account for far less than 1 percent of all claims. Thus, unemployed are virtually absent from the public domain as claim-makers and their actions are rarely reported in the media. One would be tempted to say that the low level of mobilization of the unemployed is obvious in a country that has one of the lowest unemployment rates in Europe. However, this explanation seems not very convincing in light of the developments that occurred since the early 1990s, both in the unemployment rate and in the public perception of this issue. Others would explain such a low level of mobilization with the very characteristics of the groups of the unemployed. For example, as Rosanvallon (1995) writes, "The difficulty to mobilize and to represent the excluded is explained by the fact that they first define themselves through the failures of their existence, through a negativity therefore" (203; our translation). According to this view, the unemployed do not form a social group with common interests. Similarly, other authors have pointed to the lack of a collective identity among the unemployed, or at least to the difficulty to build one, which would make their political mobilization very unlikely (e.g., Faniel 2003).

While we agree that a low level of common interest and a weak collective identity make the mobilization of the unemployed particularly difficult, we think that the extremely low level of mobilization of the unemployed in Switzerland is due to other reasons as well. In particular, it depends on the weakness of preexisting networks and organizations, which are crucial factors in shaping collective interests and identities. Preexisting networks and organizations as well as collective interests and identities, in turn, are influenced by the institutional approaches to unemployment, which characterize a given polity and which provide a set of institutional and discursive opportunities channeling the extent and forms of the claim-making of the unemployed. As we try to show, in Switzerland such a specific political opportunity structure is particularly unfavorable to the mobilization of the unemployed.

However, the political activities of an organization are not limited to overt protest or other forms of mobilization in the public domain, such as those usually reported in the media. Other channels of influence and mobilization exist. To deal with these other channels and how the unemployed use them in Switzerland, we can look at the information that we can draw from the interviews with unemployed organizations. In the interviews, unemployed organizations were asked to tell whether they use different forms of action in political activities aimed to defend their rights and interests, either on a regular or on an occasional basis (table 9.5).[14] Unemployed organizations are forced to limit the range of their actions due to their poor resources. For example, they use media-related strategies, some on a regular basis. Informing the public does not occur on a regular basis (only one organization, among those we interviewed, said it uses this form of action regularly). Lobbying and consultations are more frequent, but not used on a regular basis. Unemployed organizations usually try to influence the policymakers by informing them about the situation faced by the unemployed, and the government asks about the position of unemployed organizations. Policy and intermediary actors have made it quite clear that the surprising success of an unemployed organization in launching a referendum against a change in the unemployment law has strengthened the position of unemployed

Table 9.5 Form of actions used by different types of actors in Switzerland

	Policy actor		Intermediary		NGOs		Unemployed	
	National	Local	National	Local	National	Local	National	Local
Media related	1.00	0.95	0.97	0.97	1.00	0.55	1.00	0.85
Informing the public	0.25	0.37	0.57	0.73	0.40	0.10	0.60	0.25
Negotiating/lobbying	0.92	0.92	1.00	0.94	1.00	0.94	1.00	0.83
Consultation	0.67	0.92	0.96	0.79	0.75	0.40	0.00	0.69
Court-action	0.25	0.75	0.30	0.67	0.00	0.38	1.00	0.75
Political campaigns	n/a	n/a	0.56	0.72	0.50	0.04	0.33	0.33
Mobilizing the public	n/a	n/a	0.44	0.79	0.44	0.17	0.13	0.69

organizations, as it made their views more important in light of the political authorities and favored the establishment of consultation procedures, pointing to what Kitschelt (1986) has called a procedural impact. These organizations also make frequent use of court action on behalf of the unemployed whose social benefits have been reduced or suspended. Campaign contributions are quite low and mainly restricted to nonfinancial forms of contributions, again due to their limited resources. Concerning the mobilization of the public, unemployed organizations are quite active, although not on a regular basis. They are especially active in direct fund-raising and are dependent on this source of money to survive and carry on their activities in favor of the unemployed. They also use protest activities, but not very often, as can also be inferred from the low level of mobilization observed in the claim-making data.

These figures show that the organizations of the unemployed do engage in various types of activities, although this is based on a self-evaluative criterion, which tells us nothing about the actual frequency of use of the various forms of action. We probably are on the safe side if we say that unemployed organizations are less active than, for example, intermediary organizations, even with regard to these less publicly visible activities. In any event, the comparatively lower level of mobilization of the unemployed in Switzerland seems to confirm that their political activities have much difficulty to gain visibility in the public domain and that the unemployed have little legitimacy to enter the public discourse. This may have two main reasons. First, the unemployed have trouble developing collective identities and organizational structures that may help them to engage in political mobilization. Second, the discourse and actions of the unemployed are not always listened to and considered legitimate by other actors as well as by the media, at least mainstream media. Can they have an impact on such an unfavorable question?

Policy Impact

According to the description made so far, the political mobilization of the unemployed in Switzerland is unlikely and remains very weak. We described a group that is more a social category than a social group, lacks a collective identity, has weak organizational structures, whose resources are scarce at the political, social, and economic levels, and faces a hostile institutional and discursive context. Concerning the final aspect, we maintain in particular that the way the debate is framed, mainly in economic terms and focusing on workers threatened by unemployment, has made the unemployed a marginal object in public discourse in the unemployment political field. In such a context, the unemployed face difficulties in mobilizing, and even when they do mobilize they have trouble entering the public domain through media coverage. Furthermore, they have a peripheral position within the network structure in the field.

However, sometimes unemployed mobilization does occur and can even be successful. For example, in the early 1990s, when unemployment started to rise, there were some instances of mobilization by the national federation of unemployed organizations (FEDAC), which was able to set up a protest march attended by more than 10,000 people in February 1993, during a parliamentary session dealing with issues relating to unemployment. To do so, however, they took advantage of the support of trade unions. As a result, the FEDAC felt it had been instrumentalized by the unions, which took a central stage position during the protest (Duvanel 2002). Other smaller activities took place, but on the whole the protest was quite limited and short-lived (ibid.).

Perhaps the most interesting instance of successful mobilization by organized unemployed in Switzerland, however, took place in 1996. In that year, all the conditions for mobilization were present and organized unemployed took advantage of a window of opportunity. That year the parliament passed a change of the unemployment law that was quite detrimental for the rights of unemployed. Their potential allies did not believe in any chance of success and refused to launch a referendum, which, together with the popular initiative is one of the main instruments in the hands of actors from the civil society to challenge policy proposals. An unemployed organization (the ADC NE) then decided to launch a referendum single-handedly. Using its own structures and networks, which in fact were not very strong, it managed to contact other local unemployed organizations, far-leftist parties, and small unions. Quite surprisingly for most observers, the unemployed were able to collect more than the 50,000 signatures required to bring the referendum to the popular vote. This represents a first major success of this campaign. In the following stages of the process, unions and the socialist party took the responsibility for leading the campaign. Again quite surprisingly, the referendum was accepted by voters in 1997, although with a narrow margin.[15]

This example suggests that often the unemployed must rely on their own structures and resources, and sometimes are indeed able to do so, but it also shows the relative weakness of such structures and resources, as well as the relative disinterest or lack of confidence of the potential allies that are leftist parties and unions. Yet this successful mobilization would not have been possible without the instruments provided by direct democracy, which is an important aspect of the general political opportunity structure in Switzerland (Kriesi et al. 1995). At the same time, this example shows the weakness of the alliance structures of the unemployed. The fact that the major successful mobilization by the unemployed occurred without the initial support by political allies suggests that institutional actors do not have a specific interest in establishing alliances with unemployed organizations.

Thus, this mobilization is in a way paradoxical; it represents the peak of the mobilization of the unemployed in Switzerland, but it also shows their weakness. The windows of opportunity were characterized by a rare mix of contingent situations: a change in the unemployment law, growing unemployment, higher levels of public awareness, and the absence of political allies. The unemployed do not have a tradition of mobilization in Switzerland, but they can occasionally achieve mobilization in very rare and particular conditions. In this case, the weapons offered by the political system were crucial, both for the mobilization and for its success. The unemployed remained inside the institutional rules of the game. The mobilization of the unemployed in Switzerland seems to be a contingent reaction to a contingent situation.

This successful mobilization did not only have a substantial impact on legislation, but it also had what Gamson (1990) has called "acceptance" and Kitschelt (1986) "procedural impact." Some of the actors we interviewed in out study pointed to the fact that, after that day, unemployed organizations are more often consulted during the legislative process. However, we should not overestimate the actual power of the ADC NE as well as that of the other ADCs, as the collective interests represented by unions and especially by employer's associations are obviously the dominant ones.

We should also note that a referendum launched by leftist parties and unions aimed to fight another change of the unemployment law threatening to deteriorate the rights of unemployed was defeated by popular vote in 2003. However, at that time the situation of the labor market was better than in 1996, although it was worsening again. Furthermore, the parliament used the weapon of policy instruments, in the form of a number of proposed legislative changes aimed at improving the situation of the unemployed. This suggests that the possibilities for successful mobilization by the unemployed vary in time and that certain conditions in the economic, social, and political environment can facilitate their task. Here we have focused on political conditions.

Conclusion

The most striking characteristic of the political mobilization of the unemployed in Switzerland is their virtual absence from the public domain as collective actors. To be sure, the level of mobilization of jobless people is quite low everywhere. Yet the Swiss unemployed seem to be particularly inactive, both with regard to their claim-making in the public domain and the less visible forms of actions that are carried by organizations. We have suggested that the weak mobilization by the unemployed is the result of a cumulative effect of a number of factors, going from the lack of interest that unemployed have in political participation, to the difficulty of creating a collective identity, to the scarce resources they have at their disposal to mobilize, to the specific way the issue of unemployment is framed in the public domain. However, here we have focused on the role of specific (institutional and especially discursive) opportunities deriving from the prevailing conception of the welfare state.

Another characteristic of the unemployed in Switzerland, partly resulting from the unfavorable political context, is their disorganization and lack of internal resources. There are few unemployed organizations, and the existing ones dispose of very limited material resources. This also depends on the fact that it is difficult to ensure a sustained flow of resources and to find a permanent leadership, given the conjunctural nature of unemployment. It is difficult, in such a situation, to create organizations that go beyond episodic collective action and allow the interests of the unemployed to be represented in the long run. As a result, what is needed in order to warrant more stable organizational structures is external resources and leadership. This organizational weakness, in turn, further contributes to the low level of mobilization.

The lack of organization probably goes hand in hand with the difficulty of building a strong collective identity. Again, this may result in part from the specific way in which the issue of unemployment is framed in the public domain. The analysis of the claims made in the field of unemployment politics suggests that the unemployed are seen mostly as people having lost their job temporarily. In the prevailing view, unemployment is not a social problem in itself. This kind of framing leaves little room for the creation of a collective identity of unemployed and also little legitimacy to the organizations and groups defending the interests and rights of the unemployed. In brief, unemployment, rather than the unemployed as a social category whose interests and rights are threatened, is at the center of public discourse. This provides more opportunities for the mobilization of actors who stress the (economic) solution of the problem of unemployment than those who focus on the social condition of the constituency group.

In light of these characteristics, it is at best imprudent to speak of a social movement of the unemployed in Switzerland. At the same time, however, some instances of mobilization have indeed taken place, although they have remained sporadic and quite limited in numbers. Furthermore, the rare episodes of contention made use of the institutional channels provided by the Swiss political system, such as direct democracy, like in the example just evoked. Most importantly, the lack of internal organization and coordination, as well as the weak collective identity, prevents us from saying that there has been a movement of the unemployed in Switzerland. The most important of such episodes of contention is perhaps the launching of the referendum against the decision of the Federal government to reduce the level of unemployment social benefits in 1996, an effort that, moreover, was successful. This suggests that, in spite of an unfavorable institutional and discursive environment stemming from the dominant conception of the welfare state and the way in which the issue of unemployment is framed in Switzerland, in spite of weak organizational structures, and in spite of a weak collective identity, protest activities of a marginal social group can nevertheless emerge, although not in a consistent fashion.

Appendix: List of Interviewed Actors

Acronym	Name	English translation
Policy actors		
SECO	Secrétariat d'État à l'Economie	State Secretariat for Economic Affairs
AOST	Association des offices suisses du Travail	Association of the work offices in Switzerland
CDAS	Conférence des directrices et directeurs cantonaux des affaires sociales	Conference of the directors of social affairs
DEEAE	Département de l'Economie, de l'Emploi et des Affaires extérieures GE	Department for economic, work, and foreign affairs of Geneva

Continued

Appendix Continued

Acronym	Name	English translation
DASS	Département de l'Action sociale et de la Santé du canton de Genève	Department for social affairs and health of Geneva
OCE	Office cantonal de l'Emploi GE	Regional Labor Office, Geneva
OOFP	Office de l'Orientation et de la Formation professionnelle	Office for professional training, Geneva
AMOSA	Observatoire du marché de travail de la Suisse orientale, Argovie et Zoug	Observatory of the labor market, German part of Switzerland
Intermediary actors		
PSS	Parti socialiste suisse	Swiss social-democrat Party
PRD	Parti radical-démocratique suisse	Liberal democratic party of Switzerland
PDC	Parti démocrate-chrétien suisse	Christian democratic party of Switzerland
UDC	Union démocratique du centre	Switzerland's people's party
PRD GE	Parti radical-démocratique Genève	Liberal democratic party of Geneva
PS GE	Parti socialiste Genève	Social-democrat party of Geneva
	Solidarités Genève	Solidarity party of Geneva
PdT	Parti du travail Genève	Labor party of Geneva
Employers' organizations		
USAM	Union suisse des arts et métiers	Swiss industry union
	Economiesuisse	Economiesuisse
UPS	Union patronale suisse	Swiss employers' association
UAPG	Union des associations patronales genevoises	Union of employers' association of Geneva
Trade unions		
USS	Union syndicale suisse	Swiss Labor Union
FTMH	Fédération des travailleurs de la métallurgie et de l'horlogerie	Federation of metal and clock-making workers
SIB	Syndicat de l'industrie et du bâtiment	Trade Union for Industries and Construction
CGAS	Communauté genevoise d'action syndicale	Community of Genevan trade unions
Interregional policy counselors		
CISAS	Conférence suisse des institutions d'action sociale	Swiss conference of social aid institutions
AOMAS	Association des organisateurs de mesures du marché du travail en Suisse	Association of providers of active labor market measures
ARTIAS	Association romande et tessinoise des institutions d'action sociale	Association of social aid institutions, French and Italian parts of Switzerland.
Pro-unemployed NGOs		
	Caritas	Caritas
OSEO	Œuvre suisse d'entraide ouvrière	Swiss workers relief organization
	Hospice général RMCAS	Social aid and minimal income services

Continued

Appendix Continued

Acronym	Name	English translation
CSP	Centre social protestant	Protestant social centre
	Croix-Rouge genevoise	Red Cross Geneva
	Cebig	Professional competences assessment centre
	L'Orangerie	*L'Orangerie*
	Association réalise	Assocation Realize
	Maison du Trialogue	House of the Trialogue
	Berner Stellennetz	Jobnetwork Bern
Unemployed organizations		
ADC GE	ADC (Association de défense des chômeurs Genève)	Unemployed association Geneva
ADC NE	ADC Chaux-de-Fonds	Unemployed association La Chaux-de-Fonds
ADC BA	ADC Bâle	Unemployed association Basel
ADE VD	ADE (Association des demandeurs d'emploi Lausanne)	Unemployed association Lausanne
	Surprise Strassenmagazin	Street magazine Surprise

Notes

We thank Didier Chabanet and Jean Faniel for their detailed comments on a previous draft. The Swiss Federal Office for Education and Science is gratefully acknowledged for its financial support of the Swiss part of the UNEMPOL project, on which the data presented in this essay are based.

1. This kind of explanation reflects what are often been called grievance theories, which stress the impact of discontent as a source of collective action (e.g., Turner and Killian 1957; Kornhauser 1959; Smelser 1962; Gurr 1970). These theories have lost much of their popularity among students of social movements and have largely been discarded in favor of resource mobilization or opportunity theories. However, given the strong and direct link between the economic situation and unemployment, it is worth asking whether, in this field, the objective condition does not play a role. In fact, a simple correlation between the unemployment rate (the most straightforward indicator of objective condition in this field) and the level of mobilization of the unemployed in the six countries of the UNEMPOL project suggests that such a role is at best very limited (Giugni 2008).
2. In the social movement literature, this kind of explanatory factors has been stressed by the framing perspective (e.g., Gamson, Fireman, and Rytina 1982; Snow et al. 1986; Snow and Benford 1992; Gamson 1992, 1995; see Benford and Snow 2000 and Snow 2004 for reviews).
3. Various authors, especially among proponents of the new social movements approach, have pointed to the role of identity for social movement mobilizations (e.g., Melucci 1996; Polletta 1997; see Polletta and Jaspers 2001 for a review).
4. This is an aspect that has been stressed forcefully by resource mobilization theory since the 1970s (e.g., Oberschall 1973; McCarthy and Zald 1977; Tilly 1978; see Edwards and McCarthy 2004 for a review).
5. This perspective has been stressed by political process theorist, in particular by focusing on such aspects of the political institutional context as the openness of the

state, the prevailing strategy of the authorities to deals with challengers, and the structure of political alignments and the presence of allies within the institutional arenas (Kitschelt 1986; Kriesi et al. 1995; McAdam 1996; Tarrow 1998; McAdam, Tarrow, and Tilly 2001; see McAdam 1996 and Kriesi 2004 for reviews).

6. This figure comes from the Swiss Labor Force Survey (SLFS). In Switzerland two indicators are commonly used to analyze the situations of unemployed: The statistics of the unemployed registered at the regional job placement offices drawn up by the State Secretariat for Economic Affairs (SECO) and the statistics of the unemployed recorded by the Swiss Federal Statistical Office (SFSO). The data of the latter are collected by means of the SLFS, an interview based on a household sampling, which is conducted annually since 1991 in order to obtain data about working environment and professional life in general. To ensure the international comparability of the so collected labor market indicators, the SLFS organizes its interviews according to the recommendations of the ILO and the norms of the OECD.

7. This information is based on a survey carried out by the GfS research institute (Arbeitslosigkeit macht zunehmend Kummer. *NZZ* 292, December 16, 2003).

8. For an explanation of the delay in the development of the Swiss welfare state, see Armingeon (2001, 152–5).

9. These authors also noticed that these measures might point out a difference between "good unemployed," who show good behavior and goodwill, and "bad unemployed," who do not comply with the new rules and demands.

10. Such a situation of mistrust toward the unemployed, but at the same time a relatively generous level of compensation may be explained in political economic terms. Switzerland has both a flexible labor market and an open economy. Small countries with open economies must develop trade-off policies for their population to accept the risks and side effects of such openness (Katzenstein 1984, 1985). The relative generosity of the unemployment scheme may be in part a result of this trade-off policy. In addition, the flexibility of the labor market is very valuable for employers. As a result, they might be willing to accept a generous unemployment law as long as it does not interfere with labor market regulations. More generally speaking, labor market regulations are an important explanatory factor of the situation of unemployment in a given country.

11. Duvanel (2002) quotes an important political personality who told him that Switzerland has chosen the repressive way concerning unemployment (18).

12. The data shown in table 9.1 and in the other tables that follow were gathered in an international research project financed by the European commission and the Swiss Federal Office for Education and Science through the 5th Framework program of research of the European Union. This is the UNEMPOL project (*The Contentious Politics of Unemployment in Europe Project: Political Claim-making, Policy Deliberation and Exclusion from the Labor Market*), which includes six countries: Britain (study supervised by Paul Statham, University of Leeds), Switzerland (Marco Giugni, University of Geneva), France (Didier Chabanet, University of Lyon), Italy (Donatella della Porta, European University Institute, Florence), Germany (Christian Lahusen, University of Bamberg), and Sweden (Anna Linders, University of Cincinnati and University of Karlstad). See the project's website (http://www.eurpolcom.eu/unempol/) for further information. The data on claim-making in the field of unemployment politics were retrieved by content analyzing the major national quality newspaper (*Neue Zürcher Zeitung*) for the 1990–2002 period (only data pertaining to the 1995–2002 period are used here).

The coding was done following a sampling procedure. Specifically, we coded all claims reported in the Monday, Wednesday, and Friday issues and found in international, national, and economic sections of the newspaper (in addition to the front page). In addition, in order to improve coverage, claims reported in the issue consulted and which took place up to two week before or which will take place up to two weeks after the date of appearance of that issue were also coded. The unit of analysis is the single political claim, broadly defined as a strategic intervention, either verbal or nonverbal, in the public space made by a given actor on behalf of a group or collectivity and which bears on the interests or rights of other groups or collectivities. In other words, a claim is the expression of a political opinion by verbal or physical action in the public domain. If it is verbal, a claim usually consists of a statement, an opinion, a demand, a criticism, a policy suggestion, and so on addressed to the public in general or to a specific actor. A political claim can take three main forms: (1) political decision (law, governmental guideline, implementation measure, etc.), (2) verbal statement (public speech, press conference, parliamentary intervention, etc.); and (3) protest action (demonstration, occupation, violent action, etc.). All claims taking one of these forms have been coded, provided that they fell in the unemployment issue field. For each claim retrieved we coded a number of relevant variables. The most important are: the location in time and place of the claim, the actor who makes the claim and its policy position relating to the issue at stake, the form of the claim, the thematic focus of the claim, the target of the claim, and the object of the claim (i.e., the constituency group).

13. We have carried out forty-two semi-structured interviews with main national and local actors within the contentious field of unemployment in Switzerland, focusing on direct action and involvement of the actors in the public and policy domains. Interviews have been conducted with: (1) policy actors and state institutions; (2) intermediary actors such as political parties, unions, and employers' organizations; (3) nongovernmental organizations, welfare organizations, and probeneficiary charities; and (4) groups promoting direct mobilization/participation of the unemployed themselves. The interview schedule for each category of actors has been specifically designed to analyze where these actors locate themselves in relation to other actors within the same field. They include not only qualitative in-depth questions (examining, e.g., the framing of the issues and the "perceived" role of legislative provisions and policies for structuring actors' demands) but also sets of standardized questions that aim to investigate action repertoires, mobilization and communication strategies, institutions on which demands are made, as well as relationships of influence, cooperation, and disagreement among different types of organizations in the field. It should be emphasized that the questionnaire has also gathered information on how actors from the public and policy domains see the potential influence of increasing European integration in the unemployment field. Interviewees have thus been asked to give more open-ended prognostic statements, thus allowing for comparison of the opinions expressed by actors of different types. See the appendix for the full list of organizations interviewed.

14. Table 9.5 shows the distribution of standardized categories of forms of action across different types of actors. It aims to capture the relative importance of the different forms of action in relation to each other in a comparable way. Since the categories of forms of action are comprised of different numbers of forms of action and since there are different numbers of actors in each type of actor, the values in the table

were standardized using the following steps: (1) add up all mentions (regular and occasional combined) of forms of action within a given category by type of actor; (2) divide by the number of forms of action in the category; and (3) divide by the number of actors in each type of actor.

15. See Duvanel (2002) for a detailed account of the mobilization process. This author stresses in particular the difficulty, apart from a few exceptions, in contacting other unemployed organizations, as there was not many of them, especially in the German part of Switzerland, and that it was difficult to get in touch and work with them, as they were often no longer active or very small both in terms of members and resources. For example, the FEDAC became an empty shell in 1996, no longer having an active role and being largely dependent of the participation of local members that were mostly inactive. The signature campaign was an example of a mixture of amateurism and efficiency, use of scarce resources, and overwhelming in its success. Furthermore, both the gathering of the signatures and the vote displayed significant difference between the French-speaking and the German-speaking parts of the country. It was easier to gather the signatures in the French-speaking part.

References

Armingeon, Klaus. 2001. Institutionalizing the Swiss Welfare State. *West European Politics* 24: 145–68.

Benford, Robert D., and David A. Snow. 2000. Framing Processes and Social Movements: An Overview and Assessment. *Annual Review of Sociology* 26: 611–39

Berclaz, Julie, and Marco Giugni. 2005. Specifying the Concept of Political Opportunity Structures. In *Economic and Political Contention in Comparative Perspective*, ed. Maria Kousis and Charles Tilly, 15–32. Boulder: Paradigm Publishers.

Berclaz, Michel, Katharina Füglister, and Marco Giugni. 2004. États-providence, opportunités politiques et mobilisation des chômeurs: Une approche néo-institutionnaliste. *Swiss Journal of Sociology* 30: 421–40.

Bonoli, Giuliano, and André Mach. 2001. The New Swiss Employment Puzzle. *Swiss Political Science Review* 7: 81–94.

Cattacin, Sandro, Matteo Gianni, Marcus Mänz, and Véronique Tattini. 1999. Workfare, Citizenship and Social Exclusion. In *Citizenship and Welfare State Reform in Europe*, ed. Jet Bussemaker, 58–69. London: Routledge.

———. 2002. *Retour au travail*. Fribourg: Editions Universitaires.

Duvanel, Blaise. 2002. *La Suisse et ses chômeurs*. Genève: IES Editions.

Edwards, Bob, and John D. McCarthy. 2004. Resources and Social Movement Mobilization. In *The Blackwell Companion to Social Movements*, ed. David A. Snow, Sarah A. Soule, and Hanspeter Kriesi, 116–52. Oxford: Blackwell.

Faniel, Jean. 2003. Belgian Unemployed and the Obstacles to Collective Action. Second ECPR Conference, *Section on Social Movements, Contentious Politics, and Social Exclusion*, September 18–21, Marburg, Germany.

Fillieule, Olivier. 1993. Conscience politique, persuasion et mobilisation des engagements: L'exemple du syndicat des chômeurs, 1983–1989. In *Sociologie de la protestation*, ed. Olivier Fillieule, 123–57. Paris: L'Harmattan.

Fragnière, Jean-Pierre, and Gioia Christen. 1988. *La sécurité sociale en Suisse*. Lausanne: Réalités sociales.

Gamson, William A. 1990. *The Strategy of Social Protest*. 2nd ed. Belmont: Wadsworth Publishing.

———. 1992. The Social Psychology of Collective Action. In *Frontiers of Social Movement Theory*, ed. Aldon D. Morris and Carol McClurg Mueller, 53–76. New Haven: Yale University Press.
———. 1995. Constructing Social Protest. In *Social Movements and Culture*, ed. Hank Johnston and Bert Klandermans, 85–106. Minneapolis: University of Minnesota Press.
Gamson, William A., Bruce Fireman, and Steven Rytina. 1982. *Encounters with Unjust Authority*. Homewood: Dorsey Press.
Giugni, Marco. 2008. Welfare States, Political Opportunities, and the Mobilization of the Unemployed: A Cross-national Analysis. *Mobilization* 13: 297–310.
Giugni, Marco, ed. 2010. *The Contentious Politics of Unemployment in Europe*. Houndmills: Palgrave.
Giugni, Marco, Michel Berclaz, and Katharina Füglister. 2009. Welfare States, Labour Markets, and the Political Opportunities for Collective Action in the Field of Unemployment: A Theoretical Framework. In *The Politics of Unemployment in Europe: Policy Responses and Collective Action*, ed. Marco Giugni, 133–49. Farnham: Ashgate.
Gurr, Ted Robert. 1970. *Why Men Rebel*. Princeton: Princeton University Press.
Jahoda, Marie, Paul F. Lazarsfeld, and Hans Zeisel. 1933. *The Arbeitslosen von Marienthal*. Leipzig: Hirzel.
Katzenstein, Peter. 1984. *Corporatism and Change*. Ithaca: Cornell University Press.
———. 1985. *Small States in World Markets*. Ithaca: Cornell University Press.
Kitschelt, Herbert. 1986. Political Opportunity Structures and Political Protest: Antinuclear Movements in Four Democracies. *British Journal of Political Science* 16: 57–85.
Koopmans, Ruud. 2004. Political. Opportunity. Structure. SomeSsplitting to Balance the Lumping. In *Rethinking Social Movements*, ed. Jeff Goodwin and James M. Jasper, 61–73. Lanham: Rowman and Littlefield.
Koopmans, Ruud, Paul Statham, Marco Giugni, and Florence Passy. 2005. *Contested Citizenship*. Minneapolis: University of Minnesota Press.
Kornhauser, William. 1959. *The Politics of Mass Society*. NewYork: Free Press.
Kriesi, Hanspeter. 2004. Political Context and Opportunity. In *The Blackwell Companion to Social Movements*, ed. David A. Snow, Sarah A. Soule, and Hanspeter Kriesi, 67–90. Oxford: Blackwell.
Kriesi, Hanspeter, Ruud Koopmans, Jan Willem Duyvendak, and Marco Giugni. 1995. *New Social Movements in Western Europe*. Minneapolis: University of Minnesota Press.
McAdam, Doug. 1996. Conceptual Origins, Current Problems, Future Directions. In *Comparative Perspectives on Social Movements*, ed. Doug McAdam, John D. McCarthy, and Mayer N. Zald, 23–40. Cambridge: Cambridge University Press.
McAdam, Doug, Sidney Tarrow, and Charles Tilly. 2001. *Dynamics of Contention*. Cambridge: Cambridge University Press.
McCarthy, John D., and Mayer N. Zald. 1977. Resource Mobilization and Social Movements: A Partial Theory. *American Journal of Sociology* 82: 1212–41.
Melucci, Alberto. 1996. *Challenging Codes*. Cambridge: Cambridge University Press.
Oberschall, Anthony. 1973. *Social Conflict and Social Movements*. Englewood-Cliffs: Prentice-Hall.
Polletta, Francesca. 1997. Culture and its Discontents: Recent Theorizing on Culture and Protest. *Sociological Inquiry* 67: 431–50.
Polletta, Francesca, and James M. Jasper. 2001. Collective Identity and Social Movements. *Annual Review of Sociology* 27: 283–305.

Putnam, Robert D. 1993. *Making Democracy Work*. Princeton: Princeton University Press.
———. 2000. *Bowling Alone*. New York: Simon and Schuster.
Rosanvallon, Pierre. 1995. *La nouvelle question sociale*. Paris: Seuil.
Schnapper, Dominique. 1981. *L'épreuve du chômage*. Paris: Gallimard.
Smelser, Neil J. 1962. *Theory of Collective Behavior*. New York: Free Press.
Snow, David A. 2004. Framing Processes, Ideology, and Discursive Fields. In *The Blackwell Companion to Social Movements*, ed. David A. Snow, Sarah A. Soule, and Hanspeter Kriesi, 380–412. Oxford: Blackwell.
Snow, David A., and Robert D. Benford. 1992. Master Frames and Cycles of Protest. In *Frontiers in Social Movement Theory*, ed. Aldon D. Morris and Carol McClurg Mueller, 133–55. New Haven: Yale University Press.
Snow, David A., E. Burke Rochford, Jr., Steven K. Worden, and Robert D. Benford. 1986. Frame Alignment Processes, Micromobilization, and Movement Participation. *American Sociological Review* 51: 464–81.
Tarrow, Sidney. 1998. *Power in Movement*. 2nd ed. Cambridge: Cambridge University Press.
Tilly, Charles. 1978. *From Mobilization to Revolution*. Reading: Addison-Wesley.
Turner, Ralph H., and Lewis M. Killian. 1957. *Collective Behavior*. Englewood Cliffs: Prentice-Hall.
Valli, Marcello, Hélène Martin, and Ellen Hertz. 2002. Le "feeling" des agents de l'État providence: analyse des logiques sous-jacentes aux régimes de l'assurance chômage et de l'aide sociale. *Ethnologie Française* 33: 221–31.

CHAPTER 10

The Mobilization That was Not: Explaining the Weak Politicization of the Issue of Unemployment in Poland

*Catherine Spieser and
Karolina Sztandar-Sztanderska*

By combining mass unemployment, a high level of restrictive changes in policies addressing the unemployed, and a low level of political and social conflict connected to these issues, Poland appears as a puzzling case in the European landscape. During 1989–1990, the revolutions that brought to an end decades of communist rule in Central and Eastern Europe were accompanied by a wave of hope for rapid material gains from economic restructuring. Similar expectations for an improvement in well-being accompanied European Union (EU) accession fifteen years later. In this context, the rise of unemployment, which is often associated with a failure of government policies, could be interpreted as a nonachievement of the new political regime.

There were several reasons to believe that this would prove a particularly salient issue likely to trigger political and social mobilization. First, unemployment appeared as both a new and a massive phenomenon. While it had been officially inexistent for half a century of communist rule,[1] Poland has faced a peak of mass unemployment from the end of the 1990s, in a context of increasing social differentiation and inequality. One decade after the fall of communism, the level of unemployment approached 20 percent and Poland had the lowest rate of employment in the EU when it joined in 2004. While an improvement at the aggregate level has been observed since, which may in part be attributed to growing migration outflows, unemployment remains a strikingly common experience since half of the Polish households have been confronted with it in the past five years, according to survey data (CBOS 2007). Second, Poland has a tradition of labor militancy. Trade unions, chiefly *Solidarność*, born as an independent workers' movement in 1980, have long been active players in Polish society and politics, from the early days of anticommunist protest and democratization, to the definition of public policies later on. They have at times managed to make strong claims in the political arena and less frequently mobilized around them in the streets. Some conditions for social mobilization were thus seemingly met in Poland, where the political salience of unemployment could be expected to be particularly high, especially given its sudden rise, the legacy of labor militancy, and the existence of potentially powerful unions who retained symbolic power even as membership eroded.[2]

However, the relatively dramatic situation in Poland was neither conducive to intense political conflict regarding the policies pursued, nor did it give rise to social mobilization in the name of a specific social group, the unemployed who are the obvious losers of postcommunist transformations. In other words, it was exceptionally *not contentious* by comparison with other European countries. Social and economic transformations in the postcommunist period, dominated by the rebirth of capitalism and the institutionalization of market economy and society, have proved an overall peaceful rather than conflictual process. In Central and Eastern Europe at large, political contention as well as social protest was more limited than expected in light of what had been observed in Latin American countries in the face of transformations similar in scope (Greskovits 1998). In Poland itself, social protest has remained low and no social movement concerning the unemployed in particular has emerged; the few occurrences of strikes and street mobilization that could be observed concerned primarily the defense of rights and status of pensioners or workers in specific sectors. While there is statistical evidence of an intense objective grievance in the form of double-digit unemployment rate, the prevailing discourses on unemployment did not allow this to become a sufficient condition for collective mobilization.

This chapter attempts to explain this relative quiescence.[3] We propose three complementary explanations for the low visibility and absence of mobilization of the unemployed themselves, the weak mobilization of existing sociopolitical collective actors on the issue of unemployment, and the generally low level of conflict in relation to policies concerning unemployment observed in Poland. First, the representations that the unemployed have of themselves, and the way they are described in the public discourse make it difficult for them to be perceived as a legitimate social group, let alone to mobilize collectively to defend their rights. Second, social policies may, or may not, provide incentives for collective action. In Poland, in the 1990s, new socioeconomic policies brought about a peaceful institutionalization of unemployment (Spieser 2007). The study of the policy response to labor market adjustment shows that policies managed to circumscribe conflicts by providing specific compensation benefits to the groups that were prone to mobilization, at the expense of more universal measures such as the unemployment benefit, which became characteristic of a minimalist welfare state. Finally, the political momentum is unfavorable: the priorities at stake, the inherited and emerging configuration of actors, and the exceptional times of postcommunist transformations constituted an overall adverse context for mobilization over the issue of unemployment.

Social Representations of Unemployment and the Unemployed

Social representations play a significant role in explaining the presence or absence of collective mobilization, first and foremost by framing the issue of unemployment in a certain way. The nature of the public debate may create unfavorable conditions by delegitimizing the rights and actions of several groups. More importantly, the terms used in the debate can shape the ways in which people think about a social reality and how they act in relation to it (Bourdieu 1993 and 1996). Some actions might simply become unthinkable. The public discourse on unemployment significantly contributes to orienting attitudes, although this should not be overestimated by relying on an assumption that people unquestioningly believe in what they are told and that they appropriate mechanically the vision of the reality provided by medias (Thompson 1995; Lemieux 2001; Wolton 2002). This point is supported by the analysis of two types of empirical material: on the one hand, the public and media discourse on the issue of unemployment in Poland (Portet 2006; Sztandar-Sztanderska and Zieleńska 2008) and on the other, the diaries written by the unemployed (Zawadzka 2005).[4] We investigate whether the public discourse and the ways in which the unemployed tell their stories leaves any space for them to think in terms of group interest, which is a necessary—though not sufficient—condition to undertake any collective action.

The Terms of the Debate on the Scope of Unemployment

Two recurrent issues are especially important from the point of view of collective mobilization: whether and how unemployment is questioned as a social problem and how the unemployed are portrayed as a group. Particular attention should be paid to the opinion and discourses of experts and academics since they have a large echo in the media and contributed to shaping this debate.

The central theme is whether unemployment is or is not a problem at all, or in a more nuanced version, whether its importance is not simply exaggerated by different factors, for instance, fallacious data. In this discussion, the voice of experts and academics is crucial, but surprisingly, their far-reaching statements are rarely backed by serious empirical or theoretical evidence. Despite this fact, they were not actually questioned due to an omnipresence of neoliberal arguments and the good reputation of the authors. The following fragments were written by Marek Góra, an economics professor at the Warsaw School of Economics and one of the architects of the Polish pension system, who has regularly worked as an expert for Polish authorities, foreign governments, or the OECD in the area of pension or labor market reform:

> The unemployment of 19–20 percent supposes the interference of extraordinary factors, which have been for some reasons activated in Poland, but have not been

activated in the same way in any other country, including countries with comparable characteristics. It seems however impossible to grasp such factors and there is no other option than to...think that there is something wrong at the level of data. (Góra 2004, 124; quoted by Portet 2006)[5]

Personally, I use a simplified formula providing an actual level of unemployment in Poland. I call it the 3/4 principle. It means, without entering into details, that I consider that the unemployment rate is similar to values of this indicator in other countries and it is at the level of 3/4 of what results from official statistics. (Góra 2004, 126–7; quoted by Portet 2006)

Opinions of the nonreliability of labor market statistics have been widely quoted or reformulated by journalists in even more radical terms by giving them a whiff of conspiracy theory as, for instance, in the following article published in the daily newspaper *Dziennik*:

The Central Statistical Office has announced false data on the unemployment. A problem with the unemployment rate is the same as with a public transport. It is not so disastrous—as it is said to be—but too many people free ride. The Central Statistical Office has published information that the unemployment was still over a level of 15 percent, but it has once again forgotten to take into account free riders. (Pietrzak 2006)

At first glance, this argument is supported by the importance of the informal economy in Poland and common knowledge that a part of registered unemployed work illegally in order to earn their living. According to the Labor Force Survey, 10 percent of the registered unemployed actually worked in 2005, and 11.6 percent in 2007.[6] More significant, though less pronounced in media reports: a share of those registered as unemployed is not able to take up a job or not willing to do so (20 percent in the second quarter of 2005, up to 37.8 percent in 2007). Pietrzak (2006) unfairly disregards the fact that the same Central Statistical Office he accuses of falsifying data on registered unemployment regularly publishes data on a so-called economic unemployment, which includes people who are not necessarily registered as unemployed, but who do not work more than one hour a week, look for a job, and are capable of taking it up within two weeks. According to this data, the number of registered unemployed remains higher than the total number of unemployed in the economic sense. However, 30.7 percent of the latter group decide not to register at all at the public employment office (second quarter of 2007), probably as a result of social stigma and a disbelief in the efficiency of public labor administration. This phenomenon of non-take-up of social rights is entirely ignored by the media, even though it has a massive character.

Generally speaking, the public debate on unemployment is characterized by two features. First of all, it is often organized over a symbolic division between so-called real and false unemployed (Portet 2006). Second, as the previous example reveals, different definitions of unemployment are implicitly referred to and frequently confused. They are rarely compared to conventionally accepted definitions of economic and registered unemployment or mixed with each other, which makes it difficult to understand where the differences in terms of numbers come from. The media follow logic of scoop rather than providing tools for an analysis of complex social and economic mechanisms (Bourdieu 1996). As a consequence, the reflection on unemployment focuses on the question of guilt and responsibility for the situation. The media offer several explanations: it is the fault of the people who present themselves as unemployed, although some researches show that this is not the case (see, e.g., Czapiński and Panek 2005 and 2007); it is also a fault of the workers of public employment offices, who—according to this interpretation—refrain from using legal sanctions against these "false unemployed" (Czapiński and Skrzydłowska-Kalukin 2007); and finally, it is a fault of the Central Statistical Office, which misinforms the public instead of providing them with reliable data.

In this atmosphere of mutual accusations, the politics of the definition of unemployment pass unnoticed. One of the most prominent examples of this strategy can be found in the report entitled *Social Diagnosis* (*Diagnoza Społeczna*) (Czapiński and Panek 2003, 2005, and 2007), frequently quoted by the media.[7] Every publication is accompanied by a scandal about the level of unemployment, since the researchers establish it at a much lower rate than the registered unemployment rate:

> We can divide all registered unemployed into two groups: true and false unemployed. Then we can split the group of false unemployed into people who are not interested in work (not searching for one and/or not able to take it up), people who are working illegally or who have an income higher than 900 PLN [~250 euros in the end of 2007] from any other sources. Similarly to previous series of our research, false unemployed constitute a significant part of unemployed (1/3 in 2003 and 2005, more than a half in 2007). (Czapiński and Panek 2007, 309)

Surprisingly, the new results are never seen as the consequence of redefining the criteria of unemployment. The authors adopt a definition that is, in fact, a strange mix of the usual definitions of economic and registered unemployed (people have to fulfill the criteria included in the administrative definition and be registered as unemployed in a local employment office) with another, not justified in their text, the criteria of income.

Individual Responsibility and the Negative Self-assessment of the Unemployed

This discussion pays little attention to structural factors that can explain the various, often complex, strategies pursued by jobless people. This applies with respect to unemployment and social deprivation more generally. A recent interview with Marta Danecka—a lecturer in the Institute of Political Studies in the Polish Academy of Sciences—published in one of the most prominent daily newspapers, *Gazeta Wyborcza,* under the title "My poverty, my fault" (Danecka and Leszczyński 2008) perfectly illustrates this tendency. Generally, few authors focus on systemic barriers such as the absence of transport infrastructure and care institutions, the mismatch between the education system and labor market demand, and the importance of the situation on the local labor market (Sztandar-Sztanderska and Zieleńska 2008), or analyze the pitfalls of the design and implementation of social and labor market policies. Commentators find more explicative the fact that people are passive or active, unwilling or willing, lazy or hard working (Czapiński and Skrzydłowska-Kalukin 2007; Danecka and Leszczyński 2008). The individualistic and often psychological language of the debate makes it also difficult to define the problem in political terms and to speak of the scope of responsibility of the actors involved in the making of employment policies and the definition of the duties and rights of citizens.

The nature of the public debate on unemployment in Poland is therefore one factor making the rise of a specific mobilization over this issue unlikely. Even though it is not a sufficient condition to prevent collective action, it gains explicative value when combined with the factors enlisted in the subsequent parts of this chapter. Normative assumptions underlying this discourse, such as a belief in the superiority of every remunerated activity over unemployment or full responsibility of individuals for their status in the labor market, also influenced reforms in social and labor market policy. However, it is still to be investigated whether the unemployed in their private life adopt the categories and normative presuppositions that are being imposed upon them by the public discourse and whether the analysis of their life stories gives us any more hints about potential collective action.

The analysis of the way in which the unemployed see their lives reveals that they have an extremely pessimistic vision of their situation, as shown by the results of a comparative study of diaries from the 1990s and 1930s conducted by Zawadzka (2005).[8] First of all, individualistic terms so frequently used in the public debate are also present in unemployed diaries and the strategy of blaming the victim seems to have resonance in the way they interpret their situation. The individualization of blame is a new tendency in the 1990s: "While people in the 1930s sought the causes of their miserable condition in social, market and political mechanisms, today they rather seek for internal causes and take all the blame for their present situation upon themselves" (ibid., 45). Second, the social stigma attached to being unemployed makes collective action unthinkable. In order to act collectively, they should be ready to define themselves publicly as unemployed, whereas in their everyday life they feel so humiliated that they sometimes choose to sever social relations rather than confessing their difficult situation and asking for support. According to their confessions, being unemployed is nothing to be proud of, but is rather a proof of personal failure, so there is no basis for positive identification with a group. Instead of showing any sense of community, unemployed are very careful to distinguish themselves from other subcategories—they often call dregs of society. Finally, the way they see their future and the way they depict the political sphere and political action are other discouraging factors. The comparison between the diaries of unemployed written in the 1930s and the late 1990s shows that while the first group believed in possibilities of the improvement of their situation arising from the action of public institutions or the adoption of new political solutions, the present unemployed are extremely skeptical about promises given by politicians, who are believed to be dishonest, cynical, and beyond people's reach (ibid., 33). Generally speaking, this empirical evidence confirms previous findings that the unemployed are not eager to fight for their rights and there should be other stimulus than joblessness for such a mobilization to take place.

However, public opinion polls suggest that Polish citizens in general have a more nuanced vision of unemployment (CBOS 1998 and 2006). Responses on the main causes of the unemployment indicated, in the first place, a generally bad labor market situation. In 1998, the most frequent answer to the open-ended question "What makes people unemployed?" was "liquidation of workplaces/enterprises" (33 percent) and "a lack of job offers" (29 percent). In 2006, 90 percent of respondents chose "a lack of workplaces" among the proposed answers (closed question). In 1998, only a minority considered unemployment a consequence of laziness or a lack of willingness to work (18 percent) or different preferences—living on benefits, working illegally, and generally of having too high expectations toward work (6 percent). Other stated reasons include a mismatch of qualifications and education with the labor market (10 percent) and a lack of qualifications or profession at all (8 percent). In this respect, the results from 2006 differ considerably, but they cannot be easily compared.[9] In 2006 respondents mentioned as causes of unemployment: a mismatch between educational system and demand for labor ("graduating from schools after which there are no work proposals," 67 percent), a lack of qualifications that are needed in the market (51 percent), but also profitability of working illegally (56 percent) and family assistance (52 percent). It is significant that despite the frequent accusations of improper unemployment registration in the public discourse, the majority of respondents did not agree with statements seeing unemployment as the effect of benefits and social aid or the absence of motivation to find a job. Neither did they believe that the unemployed can make a good living without regular employment. However, this does not necessarily translate into support for policies seeking to alleviate the effects of joblessness: according to another survey, only half of the Poles agree that the government "should spend money on unemployment benefits" (45 percent in 1997 and 52 percent in 2006) (ISSP 1997 and 2006).

The psychologization and individualization of both public and personal discourses on unemployment have several origins. On the one hand, it is embedded in a wider social process of individualization (Jacyno 2007). In this view, these discourses are simply manifestations of a larger trend of perceiving one's life situation and the broader social reality as the effect of individual actions and consequently to consider unemployment or poverty as a personal defeat. On the other hand, a detailed historically oriented explanation taking into account institutions, which analyzes how employment and joblessness were interpreted during and after communism, allows to show whether, when, and how the understanding of these phenomena changed. In the following sections we provide some elements of this context-oriented explanation with respect to the absence of mobilization in the name of the unemployed.

Labor Market Policies Designed to Avoid Social and Political Mobilization

The representations of unemployment prevailing in today's Poland are embedded in a specific historical, political, and institutional context. After the communist regime had guaranteed a universal right to work, unemployment was an unprecedented phenomenon to be addressed, especially when it appeared on a mass scale at the end of the 1990s. Since 1989, policies have above all sought to ease labor market adjustment to facilitate the rise and prosperity of a capitalist market economy.

Welfare legislation, the rights and benefits derived from the social security system, and political conflicts on its reform constitute a specific opportunity structure, so that "the mobilization of the unemployed is constrained by the way in which the welfare state is historically and collectively defined" (Giugni 2008, 301). First, unemployment is an institutional construction. The unemployed are identified as a group primarily by legal and statistical definitions related to labor market policies, which single them out as a category of beneficiaries (Salais, Baverez, and Reynaud 1986; Zimmermann 2001; Baxandall 2002). When no unemployment status or support system exists, the unemployed have no existence as a category of public intervention, which undermines their capacity to appear as a social group, especially in a political, ideological, or cultural context, which is unfavorable to them. Since unemployment was unknown in communist Poland, the way in which it was institutionalized after 1989 is crucial. Second, social policies serve to pacify conflicts. The welfare state pools and redistributes social risks arising in the labor market (Esping-Andersen 1990). In European postwar history, the most generous welfare systems resulted from the mobilization of class-based trade unions and political parties. Institutions such as social insurance were set up in response to demands for social protection under a threat of class conflict. More generally, governments seek to reach an equilibrium in which unemployment becomes socially and politically acceptable while policies remain economically viable, thereby defining a country-specific trajectory of adjustment.

Yet the relation between policies and mobilization is a complex and two-way one. On one hand, group mobilization may express demands for protection from the turmoil of market adjustment, a call for policy intervention when current income, rights, or benefits are deemed insufficient, which may contribute to shaping policies. On the other hand, existing welfare policies, with the set of rights, benefits, and obligations that they institutionalize, generate expectations over gains or losses that influence the collective mobilization of the groups concerned, especially in the face of an agenda of reform. Mobilization can be expected to be highest when benefits are generously granted and assorted with few obligations (Berclaz, Füglister, and Giugni 2004).

This section reviews the role of policies in the institutionalization of unemployment, the management of mass dismissals through exit to inactivity, and the slow emergence of a broader government program of action against unemployment, including active labor market policies eventually seeking to add obligations to social rights.

The Recent Institutionalization of Unemployment

Unemployment became a "new" problem to be addressed by policymakers and an issue on the political agenda only in 1989, with little experience to build upon.[10] Thus, unemployment compensation and labor market policies do not have a long history in Poland. In the first decade, they essentially contributed to a peaceful institutionalization of unemployment: the people most exposed in emerging capitalism,[11] and therefore most likely to oppose socioeconomic reforms, were compensated by adequate measures in a way that satisfied them at least temporarily.

From the recommodification of labor to the rise of unemployment

A quick look back at the origin of the unemployment category is enlightening. Prior to 1989 everybody had a constitutional right to work and unemployment had been made illegal (Mlonek 1999). As a result, the concept of unemployment was rarely used as an analytical category and inexistent as a category of public intervention. While at a marginal level a form of frictional unemployment (the gap between one's job and the successive one, when one changes jobs) could be found, the stock of explicit unemployment was never significant as few people remained without a job for a long time.[12] In that context, the definition of unemployment was written in the law only in 1989. The fact that such a conception of unemployment was the only existing one in the analyzes of labor allocation carried out before 1989 probably explains the somewhat prolonged belief of many Polish analysts and policymakers that unemployment was a natural side effect of transition that would resolve itself through market mechanisms.

Aiming to dismantle the "command economy," the first democratically elected government undertook to restore market mechanisms in the allocation of jobs and workforce. Unemployment grew as a result of the combination of uncertain economic conditions, wide-scale economic restructuring, adjustment to changing market environment, hardening budget constraints on large state-owned enterprises, and dismissals becoming an option with the changing governance of work. The Employment Act of 1989, revised in 1991, set the basis for new labor market governance and institutions compatible with a capitalist market economy: a network of public employment offices; an unemployment compensation scheme; and a dedicated Labor Fund to finance labor market programs. When setting the conditions of eligibility for unemployment compensation, the laws of 1989 introduced an initially broad definition of unemployment, which was subsequently restricted on several occasions in later years. By 2004, the legal definition of unemployment had become much more precise; the eligibility was restricted to Polish or EU citizens aged between eighteen and sixty (women) or sixty-five (men) years of age, not employed, not involved in training or in any kind of paid work, not entitled to an old-age or

Table 10.1 Employment and unemployment in Poland (1990–2008, percent of active population)

	1990	1991	1992	1993	1994	1995	1996	1997	1998	1999	2000	2001	2002	2003	2004	2005	2006	2007	2008
Registered unemployment rate	6.1	11.4	14.3	16.4	16.0	14.9	13.2	10.3	10.4	13.1	15.1	17.5	20.0	20.0	19.0	17.6	14.8	11.2	9.5
Employment rate (LFS)	n/a	n/a	53.3	52.1	51.0	50.7	51.2	51.5	51.0	48.0	47.4	45.5	44.1	44.0	45.1	45.9	47.5	49.5	51.0

Source: Employment services (data end of year) and labor force survey (Q4).

invalidity pension, not owing more than two hectares of land, but willing and available to start full-time work immediately, and registered with the local employment office.[13]

In 1989, the initial government proposal for an unemployment benefit scheme assumed a moderate increase in the number of unemployed (300,000), a forecast that it was advised to increase considerably by international advisors. In reality, registered unemployment jumped from 55,000 people (0.2 percent) to 1,125,000 (6.1 percent) within twelve months: more than one million people became unemployed in 1990 alone. The registered unemployment rate increased steadily along the 1990s to peak at a level of 20 percent in 2002–2003 (see table 10.1). A trend of unemployment accumulation is clearly identifiable as by 2003 more than one in two registered job seekers had been without a paid job for more than a year. The trend reversed with EU accession: the decrease of unemployment from 2005 corresponds both to the large numbers of Poles who emigrated to the United Kingdom, Ireland, and Sweden, which had opened their labor markets from 2004, and to an increase of job creation in Poland itself.

The introduction and gradual restriction of the unemployment benefit

In the early 1990s, policymakers were concerned that the surge of unemployment and a temporary deterioration of economic conditions could put regime change at risk. An unemployment benefit was swiftly introduced as the major instrument of the initial policy response, in view of alleviating the consequence of losing one's job. While from the outset, the government response included both passive and active labor market policies, the first largely prevailed. However the unemployment benefit proved a short-lived solution. The Law on Employment, subsequently revised as Law on Employment and Unemployment in 1991, established policies for unemployment benefits, employment services, and limited active labor programs.[14] They were financed by the Labor Fund, with a budget relying primarily on state subsidies (up to three-quarters of the total), and to a lesser extent on social contributions.

The first measures were generous. The level of benefit was calculated on the basis of the last remuneration and length of unemployment with a starting level of 70 percent (within the limit of the average wage) during the first three months, subsequently falling but with no limit in time. In practice, the benefit could not be lower than the minimum wage nor higher than the average wage. In the context of the time, when a significant rise of unemployment was expected, this was a generous and costly scheme, which would quickly become unsustainable. It is highly likely that the initial generosity of the scheme aimed to achieve a peaceful institutionalization of unemployment in Poland: "The government, seeking to gain social acceptance for its far-reaching reforms, was more interested in a temporary solution" (Gardawski 2002, 2). This law did not contain any eligibility condition related to previous employment and young graduates entering the labor market were entitled to a special benefit even in the absence of employment history (MPiPS 1995, 9; Gardawski 2002).

From 1991 onward, various measures aimed at introducing stricter eligibility conditions and reduce the length of the unemployment benefit. First, a twelve-month limit was introduced, with the possibility of extending the benefit to eighteen months in total for people with a long employment history. The level of the benefit was linked to the local unemployment situation. Both the lower and upper limit of the benefit amount was lowered drastically: it could be as low as 33 percent of the average wage. Restrictions on the benefit for unemployed graduates were also introduced in parallel. The relation between the level of the benefit and one's wage in the last job was completely eliminated in 1992: the unemployment benefit became a flat 36 percent of the average wage in the national economy. As a result, it was perceived as a measure of social assistance, rather than an entitlement deriving from one's contributions paid to a social insurance fund. In 1996, the mode of calculation of the benefit level was reformed so that it would allow for adjustment independently of a set level of the average wage, which made it possible for further lowering of the benefit to wage ratio (Gardawski 2002). In 2004, the rules were amended again. Although the Polish system is formally an unemployment insurance with obligatory contributions calculated as a percentage of salary, the benefit has now become a flat amount, which varies only slightly according to work experience.[15] Generally speaking, the unemployment benefit is granted for six months, but this can be extended in districts (*poviats*) marked by a level of unemployment higher for people who have a long working career behind them.

While 79 percent of the unemployed received income support from the unemployment insurance in 1990–1991, the proportion of the unemployed covered by the benefit has significantly decreased since 1992 (table 10.2). In 1999, there were 2.3 millions unemployed, out of which only one in four (554,000) received an unemployment benefit, against 3.2 millions unemployed (almost one million more) and only 539,000 beneficiaries in 2002 (one in six). The proportion of unemployed people entitled to the benefit fell down to, and stabilized at 14 percent in 2004. Such a drastic reduction of the eligibility for the unemployment benefit was triggered by the combination of the limited duration of the benefit and an increasing unemployment duration. With many unemployed remaining jobless for a long time (more than half for longer than a year from 2002), the number of beneficiaries declined mechanically over the years to become a marginal proportion of the unemployed. Those who stopped being eligible for benefits over time are unlikely to receive any other form of income replacement and may only qualify for basic social assistance such as food aid. As Gardawski (2002) noted, in 2000, the average *annual* subsistence allowance paid by the social services barely amounted to *one month* of the average wage. Survey data on the economic means of the unemployed confirms that social assistance is not a valid alternative source of income (ISSP 1997).

Meanwhile, the level of the unemployment benefit, which is determined by the Ministry of Labor and Social Policy, decreased in a severe manner (table 10.2). The replacement rate, an indicator showing the level of the benefit in relation to wages,[16] stood at 76 percent of the minimum wage and

Table 10.2 Unemployment benefit coverage and replacement rate in Poland (1990–2007)

	1990	1991	1992	1993	1994	1995	1996	1997	1998	1999	2000	2001	2002	2003	2004	2005	2006	2007
Entitled to benefit (% of the unemployed registered)	79	79	52	48	50	59	52	30	23	24	20	20	17	15	14	14	14	14
Unemployment benefit (% of Polish average wage)	19.6	34.2	37.9	36.0	37.0	36.7	33.4	32.0	30.5	23.8	23.3	23.1	23.4	22.9	22.0	21.9	21.5	20.0

Source: Ministry of Economy and Labor (data end of year).

30.5 percent of the average wage in 1998, whereas one decade later it accounted for only 49 percent of the minimum wage (2008) and 20 percent of the average wage (2007). Both developments had an important social impact: further impoverishment of those who remained in unemployment for a long time. In 1997, according to survey data, only 22 percent of the unemployed mentioned the unemployment benefit as their main source of economic support; 50 percent relied primarily on partner or family support; and only 5 percent on social assistance (ISSP 1997).

Policies Facilitating Labor Market Exit while Bypassing the Unemployment Status

Generally speaking, in Poland, neither the worsening economic situation of the unemployed nor the reforms restricting the unemployment benefit triggered specific collective mobilization. However, social protest appeared as a real threat to the process of marketization when a large number of workers with a strong tradition of mobilization were facing a deterioration of their work situation. In effect, "the political threat posed by unemployment" above all lies in the discontent of politically influential workers in employment who risk losing their jobs (Baxandall 2003, 253). This was mostly the case in two instances: in the process of restructuring of strategic sectors in which workers had enjoyed a privileged status and as far as workers with a long career behind them and no future in the new market society were concerned. In view of avoiding social conflict, these categories of people were often granted special compensation that bypassed the standard unemployment benefit.

This resulted in a segmentation of policies addressing unemployment: the jobless were not covered by one universal scheme, but split among a variety of compensation or social security mechanisms, which some saw as a deliberate government strategy to "divide and pacify" (Vanhuysse 2006) groups opposing market reforms. Without going that far, these policy choices clearly gave more favorable conditions to the groups that had the biggest capacity to mobilize against economic transformations, workers with a long career under the previous regime who had no future in the capitalist economy, and workers in strongly unionized sectors such as heavy industry and mining. Aside these particularistic schemes, the universal unemployment benefit set up as early as in 1990 quickly became marginal as a result of successive reforms. The unemployed, hardly identifiable as a social group, neither developed a collective consciousness nor uniform interests in the face of welfare reforms; the few protest actions that could be observed were embedded in the opportunity structure of specific industrial sectors and concerned primarily the conditions of collective dismissals and early retirement for these workers.

Collective dismissals and severance payments
Trade unions, which gathered the workers facing the threat of becoming unemployed, were potentially the strongest organized opposition group since and retained a significant mobilization capacity in sectors such as steel or mining.

Particularly visible because of their mass scale and the protests they occasionally triggered, collective dismissals were perhaps considered more illegitimate and a more immediate grievance than the remote existence of unemployment, often associated with individual failure.[17] In some cases of large company or sector restructuring, the conditions of unemployment, or more precisely, the conditions of dismissal led to intense negotiations. The *Act on Dismissals* of 1989 setting the rules of large workforce reductions and measures to protect affected employees imposed some obligations on the employer (notification of the trade unions in advance, stating the reasons for redundancies and the number of people concerned; informing the local employment office and developing a program for retraining and reemployment). Dismissed employees would receive redundancy payments of up to three months of wages. Under the influence of powerful unions, restructuring plans involved intense negotiations and complex agreements.

As an example, in the years 1994–1997, under the threat that the miners' unions would block the restructuring of the whole sector, particularly generous social packages were granted to them in the form of a significant one-off severance payment.[18] The mining sector provides an interesting illustration of negotiated compensation. Concentrated in Upper Silesia,[19] the mines and steelworks had a tradition of strong local trade unions and better than average welfare entitlements; they enjoyed more state support than elsewhere. Restructuring was contentious, for employees were strongly attached to the mines, which gave access to various benefits and social institutions. As a result, dialogue and coordination among the unions and employers came high on the agenda. In spring 1995, representatives of sociopolitical, professional, local government, and economic circles agreed to cooperate in a program for restructuring and development in Upper Silesia. A four-year reform plan prepared by the Ministry of Industry in 1996 granted special social transfers and other subsidies. The regional leader of *Solidarność* presented an alternative scenario calling for more involvement of the national government and a wider consultation of regional and local actors. The outcome reflected the traditional power structure of actors in the region, that is, the prominence of industrial actors linked to the biggest plants, which made it difficult to envisage innovative solutions. Half a dozen successive restructuring plans were drawn up but most of them were never fully implemented due to industrial conflict. Nevertheless, the workforce was reduced from a million people in the 1980s to a quarter of this by 2003. Conflicts over collective dismissals were eventually avoided by granting generous packages reflecting the bargaining power of the miners unions: there are reports of sums exceeding 10,000 euros to secure a definitive exit of mining employment (Gardawski 2003).

This contrasts with the steel industry, where employment was reduced in the same proportion, but under very different conditions. Until 1998, jobs were lost principally to retirement or disability benefits, or transferred to other entities and in 1999 a social package led to further jobs reductions, among which slightly less than half were transferred to other companies and the rest made redundant (Towalski 2003). In 2003, a second social package for steelworks, focusing on activation, was adopted by the government and endorsed by the sectoral tripartite team. Its major innovation was to facilitate reemployment in other industries, by linking severance payments to enrolment in training contracts. By Polish standards, restructuring in the steel sector is an unusually positive example of working social dialogue in a developmental perspective; in comparison with the mining sector, this process was also remarkably peaceful and conflicts were scarce,[20] a contrast that can be traced back both to the different role played by the unions (opposing, or even obstructing restructuring of the mines while cooperating in the steel sector), and to the ultimate objective (closing down the mines as opposed to reducing workforce to build smaller, competitive steel-melting plants).

Organizing exit from employment and the labor market at once: early retirement
As in Western Europe in the past (Kohli et al. 1991; Ebbinghaus 2006), early retirement provided a widely used alternative to manage mass dismissals, reducing their visibility by the same token. While it existed as a privilege before 1989, its function changed as it became a mechanism for employment adjustment. In addition, after 1990, the pension system continued to allow a long list of professions to retire earlier with full pension rights (Czepulis-Rutkowska 1999, 152). Social plans accompanying firm restructuring made extensive use of measures allowing to peacefully get rid of redundant workers and put them on the two kinds of inactivity pensions available: old-age retirement and disability. In 1991, a regulation targeting people who would be unable to find new employment allowed those who had been working for thirty-five (women) or forty years (men) to retire with full rights regardless of age if they had been made redundant (ibid.). An additional, preretirement benefit, financed on the labor fund, was later created to bridge the period between becoming unemployed and the legal retirement age, targeting especially the long-term unemployed (Czepulis-Rutkowska 1998, 196).

Evidence of the scope of early retirement in practice is provided by several indicators that capture the people moving from work or unemployment to retirement before the legal retirement age. The number of people retiring significantly exceeded those reaching retirement age in several given years. In 1991 and 1992, around 40 percent of all pensioners had not yet reached the legal retirement age (Golinowska 1994, 33-35; Orenstein 1995, 191). In 1996 again, 39.5 percent of all men and 28 percent of women who retired had not yet reached retirement age.[21] In 1999, one-third of the male workers who retired were below sixty, the percentage decreasing to one-fourth in 2001.[22] In 1999, still, more than 10 percent of men who were receiving an old-age pension were below sixty. While the number of employed people fell by 14 percent between 1989 and 1996, the number of pensioners of all kinds[23] rose simultaneously by 34 percent. Pensions clearly played the role of an additional unemployment benefit scheme. In 2003, out of around one million of unemployed who were receiving some kind of benefit (less than 30 percent), slightly more than half received a preretirement benefit, while only the remaining part received a proper unemployment benefit.[24] Over half a million people were receiving a preretirement benefit or allowance in 2003. A similar story can be told concerning disability benefits. In 2002, these were distributed to 13 percent of the working-age population (twenty–sixty-four), and up to 18 percent of those aged between forty and fifty-five (Burns and Kowalski 2004, 6–7). This suggests that invalidity, even though it required a medical examination certifying unfitness to work, was also used for preretirement. The government attempt to reform the scheme and strengthen controls in 2003 met with little success.

Therefore, the standard unemployment benefit was only one among several policy instruments used to address rising unemployment, and not necessarily the prevailing one. With the heavy reliance on severance payment to ease dismissals in strategic sectors on one hand, and on inactivity pensions (early retirement and disability) to ease the exit of the labor market of a generation of workers with outdated skills on the other one, governments privileged selective schemes at the expense of universal ones. This contributed to the lack of visibility of the unemployed.

One difficulty in characterizing the emerging Polish welfare state is that policies have been in flux for the past twenty years: labor market policies were being shaped, reformed, and fine-tuned. In the early 1990s, a mix of universal and corporatist features could be identified: an insurance-based income replacement scheme with universal eligibility, but decreasing levels of benefits. In later years, policies concerning unemployment resemble those in a minimalist welfare state: the eligibility criteria have become more restrictive and the duration of compensation was shortened, the coverage rate of the unemployment benefit and activation measures is low, the social insurance logic is fading, and support to the unemployed is not always perceived as fully legitimate. Unemployment was institutionalized as a social status giving limited rights to those without a job in Poland in the early 1990s while policies heavily relied on inactivity benefits to ease exits of the labor market. It appears that policies dealt with the potential political threat posed by unemployment more efficiently than they dealt with the social deprivation associated with joblessness. The unemployed remained extremely vulnerable given that they tended to stay in unemployment or inactivity with limited chances to move back to employment and hardly any possibility of obtaining income replacement support. From 2002 to 2004, the European guidelines and instruments allowed to reestablish labor market policies as a central area of public policy and triggered a re-orientation in favor of activation. However, the obligations actually imposed on the unemployed like the opportunities to benefit from activation measures remain scarce overall. Poland tends toward a minimalist or residual welfare state (Esping-Andersen 1990), which is possibly the least favorable context for mobilization on unemployment (Berclaz, Füglister, and Giugni 2004).

The Politics of Institutionalizing Market Economy and Society

Both policy changes and political mobilization are embedded in a specific political system. Factors such as "the degree of openness of the institutionalized political system" or "the configuration of power within institutional arenas" can encourage or impede the mobilization of social movements (Kriesi 2004). The low level of conflict over the issue of unemployment in Poland is also rooted in the politics of postcommunist transformations since 1989. In comparison with West European countries, Poland has gone through a period of extraordinary politics from the fall of communism till EU accession in 2004. The early years of that period were marked by democratic consolidation and the construction of a market economy, and the later ones by the preparation for EU membership. Both processes have provided a major policy direction that reduced the margin of maneuver of many actors, and left little space for the emergence of new collective actors seeking to influence policymaking aside partisan organizations. First, a sense of extraordinary politics has long dominated a relatively linear policy trajectory aiming to build not only a well-functioning market economy but also a "market society" based on economic individualism (Spieser 2009). Second, the configuration of actors was favorable neither to the promotion of the interests of the unemployed nor to their mobilization. This is illustrated by the example of the trade unions, which were potentially the closest to the concerns of the unemployed yet also pivotal actors in the transformations processes.

Extraordinary Politics and the Compromise on Prioritizing Macroeconomic Policies

The profound changes that affected Poland since 1989 have a systemic nature and a revolutionary magnitude. They constitute "*a complete* transformation, *parallel in all spheres*: in the economy, in the political structure, in the world of political ideology, in the legal system and in the stratification of society" (Kornai 2006, 217; emphasis in the original). The shift to a capitalist economy and a democratic political system in a nonviolent, peaceful, and yet tremendously accelerated process (ibid., 217–18) involved a shift of policy paradigm much more radical than the neoliberal turn observed in parts of Western European since the 1980s. Democratic Poland embarked on a path in which governments and society were "negotiating neo-liberalism" (Bandelj 2008, 47), seeking an arrangement to balance economic and social change under significant constraints. This particular historical path has far-reaching consequences that should not be underestimated in comparative studies.

At the end of 1989, Polish policymakers decided to embark on a macroeconomic stabilization plan and a rapid liberalization inspired by neoliberal orthodoxy. The "shock therapy" line of reform was presented as the only possible one (Balcerowicz 1995) and focused on quickly resolving the stabilization of public finance and bringing inflation down, which was a precondition for significant changes in any other policy area. During the first decade, the priority was largely understood as "liberating markets from the state" (Bruszt 2001) and withdrawing the state from the sphere of economic activity (Balcerowicz 1995). This included eliminating the guarantees of communism without making any serious attempt to propose an acceptable alternative system of needs satisfaction (Ksiezopolski 1993, 180). The need for a major social policy reform was clearly underestimated and a widespread belief was that market mechanisms alone would be sufficient to trigger the inevitable adjustments as long as the bases for economic recovery were guaranteed. A series of compensation measures for those who lost jobs and income were adopted in the early years. The introduction of an initially generous unemployment benefit unsustainable for the government budget, significant severance payments, and the use of pensions to absorb labor market adjustments follow this rationale of conflict avoidance. However, these were merely ad-hoc measures with a one-off effect. The strategy of the first postcommunist governments was to build a pluralist democracy and set down the lines for a market economy, all the more as there was a clear and broad consensus in this direction. Social policy was primarily seen as a burden on the reform process; its ultimate goal remained controversial and confusion reigned over its definition (ibid.).

Social policies were brought back onto the agenda by an increasingly adverse public opinion, the resurgence of industrial conflict in 1992–1993, the electoral reversal of 1995, when the former communist party came back to power, and the severe deterioration of labor market conditions. However, the cost-cutting agenda and the orientation toward a liberal welfare system prevailed even when the postcommunist left was in office. In 1997–1998, a major social reform operating a shift to an actuarial pension system relying heavily on pension funds was passed thanks to a large consensus among usually opposed partisan organizations.[25] The cost-cutting agenda was further pursued by a social democratic alliance who returned to power in 2001. Therefore, the general direction of economic policy, just like major welfare reforms relied on a broad interparty consensus. The orientation of labor market policies was little politicized. Unemployment became an increasingly salient issue from the mid-1990s as the figures rose. Yet on this too, government elites from both the social-democratic side and the liberal side agreed that the priority was to bring it down and that the best strategy to achieve this was twofold: increasing labor law flexibility and lowering the cost of labor. While much effort was put in these reforms, support to the unemployed—which presented the disadvantage of being costly for the state budget already in bad shape—was clearly a lesser priority. The unions themselves focused on retaining long-existing entitlements, rights, and benefits, for instance, early retirement pensions, at the expense of the new branch of unemployment insurance. Besides, in the face of high unemployment they found it difficult to formulate credible claims. The fight against unemployment was high on the political agenda from the end of the 1990s, but the struggle for the unemployed was not.[26] The policy debate tended to focus on the argument of an excessive rigidity of the Labor Code and labor costs, the reform of which was presented as a way to foster job creation by various governments including social democratic ones (Spieser 2009).

The Place of the Trade Unions within the Configuration of Actors

Mobilization on the issue of unemployment is influenced by the existing configuration of actors intervening in the field of socioeconomic policies. The set of allies, adversaries, and attentive observers, their capabilities, perceptions, and positions constitute a context of interaction in which new social movements may develop—or not (Kriesi 2004, 74). This also determines which issues are raised and how they may be addressed. In Poland, a Polish communist regime, which guaranteed some entitlements in the name of class struggle, was brought to an end by an independent workers movement—*Solidarność*—calling for better living standards and more freedom. In that context, state social spending is inevitably associated with the social order of the past. The trade unions are the organizations that most actively sought to incorporate and represent transition losers and provided them with a way to channel discontent "into a formal grievance capable of being redressed" (Ost and Crowley 2001, 4). However, they never managed to achieve a common stance in favor of measures aiming to alleviate the effect of unemployment.

This is first explained by the special role, unusual ideational stance, and strategy of the independent union. *Solidarność* gave its leading figures to the first democratic government, which undertook to design and implement neoliberal reforms. A question worth looking into is why it embraced so quickly and so firmly a neoliberal approach to economic reform. In a climate of dramatic economic crisis, it came to power very suddenly, and to some extent, unexpectedly (Orenstein 2001). Due to the underground character of its activities during most of the 1980s, it had neither trained political elites nor a comprehensive economic program; it was generally unprepared to govern. Leszek Balcerowicz was appointed because he appeared as a technician with firm ideas on the necessary reforms, a man with an economic program. He became deputy prime minister for economic affairs with free hands to implement his ideas.

Meanwhile, union leaders at the national level undertook the task of calming down and reassuring the members of their organizations. Lech Wałęsa, then president of the national *Solidarność* union, said that shock therapy would cause a downturn for three months and then things would get better, and called for strikes to be suspended despite the rapid erosion of real wages (Rainnie and Hardy 1995, 273; Ost 2001, 85). For the national leadership of *Solidarność*, the primary role of the union was to act as a protective umbrella for economic reforms over other functions and objectives. By 1992, the priority was still to avoid political backlash, but the government started to realize that this would only be possible by catering to the increasing number of people exposed to job and income security, hence the extension of emergency compensation measures (Orenstein 1995).

More generally, throughout the 1990s, the trade unions were weakened by their ideological fragmentation. On the one hand, *Solidarność* is the continuation of an anticommunist social movement of the 1980s. Although this was a matter of debate in the early 1980s, the 1987 program was officially based on the creation of a market economy and it emphasized property rights (Weinstein 1996 and 2000). Before the economic reforms had even started, "instead of building a strong union, *Solidarność* set out to build a weak one... that would follow the government as it pursued a painful economic reform" (Ost 2001, 82). The union has remained a deeply anticommunist Christian one to date, broadly adhering to, rather than challenging the features of a liberal market economy. On the other hand, OPZZ,[27] the other large union federation, is the successor of the former official communist union, and has remained much more closely linked to egalitarian and solidaristic values. OPZZ activists tend to have a more left-wing radical discourse. Its natural political ally is the social-democratic (and former communist) party. Compared to *Solidarność*, OPZZ has always been more dependent on its allied party and lacked "a program it could call its own" (Gardawski 1996, 101) with respect to the direction of reforms. The history of opposition prior to 1989, when some were jailed and others rewarded for their loyalty noticeably undermined cooperation between OPZZ and *Solidarność* for a long time.

Trade unions also face organizational problems and declining membership and they lack expertise. Although social policy is certainly the area to which they devote most attention, they have a limited capacity to react to government proposals in this area. In 2005, OPZZ had no more than five experts competent on these issues in its national office, while *Solidarność* counted less than ten in its own national office, most of them based in Gdańsk. It lost most of its experts to the corresponding ministries from 1990 to 1992, and then again to a lesser extent when its political group returned to power in 1997 (Ost 2001, 91). The involvement of trade unions in national politics and consultative institutions contributed to building a commitment to change but brought few direct policy gains as they were either restrained by their reduced bargaining capacity or self-restraining in their claims.

In the run up to the parliamentary election of 1996, following the return of the former communist in office under a social-democratic banner, *Solidarność* opted for a strategy of direct involvement in politics. An electoral alliance named *Akcja Wyborcza Solidarność* (AWS—Electoral Action Solidarity) was created in June 1996 at a meeting gathering trade union representatives and leaders of right-wing parties. The declared main goal of the party was "creating a broad electoral bloc, capable of winning the next parliamentary election" and its political program was to be based on the goals of the trade union (Wenzel 1998, 144). In reality, however, the program of AWS turned out to be a composite assembly of the platforms of various parties plus that of the trade union. Although the alliance was dominated by *Solidarność*, some demands of the trade union significantly departed from the claims of a few constituent parties, in particular with respect to pursuing neoliberal economic policies (ibid., 145–6). Overall, however, this political strategy had a rather negative impact on representing labor interests in the policymaking process, as *Solidarność* could only be an ally of liberal and conservative parties. It also came at the price of a divorce from grassroots organizations: the union became a vertically fragmented federation, with a widening divide between the center and the regional and sectoral branches. It was abandoned after 2001. The relatively passive stance of Polish trade unions on issues related to unemployment and the unemployed is thus not only the outcome of structural difficulties; it also reflects their deliberate ideological choices and political strategies.

Finally, formal corporatist institutions played a minor, unexpected role. Mimicking the arrangements found in Germany, Austria, or Nordic Europe, Poland developed its own tripartite body for social dialogue, which aimed to give the trade unions a forum but also an incentive to be reasonable in their claims and privilege dialogue over conflict. However, this was a state initiative rather than one of the unions and employers' organizations. The expectation was that it would allow overcoming the legacy of branch corporatism inherited from the communist regime (Hausner 1994, 138) and foster consensus on socioeconomic reforms. In response to the industrial conflicts of 1992–1993, the minister of labor and social policy Jacek Kuroń attempted to establish a social pact to deal with the privatization and restructuring of state enterprises (Hausner 1996, 112),[28] which later became a Tripartite Commission with a broader scope. However, it was only consultative and failed to play a major role in formulating principles of socioeconomic policy or labor relations (ibid.). The relations of the trade unions with government were determined by their party alliances: they tended to side with the government and accept government proposals when their allied parties were in office, or, on the contrary, systematically oppose when they were not. For many years OPZZ and *Solidarność* rarely cooperated in the national Tripartite Commission. In 2002–2003, an attempt to establish a broad social pact failed. The major outcome of Polish state-led neocorporatism was to legitimize the reforms carried out by the government, rather than influence them (Avdagic and Crouch 2006). Nevertheless, it did monopolize the resources of the trade unions available for policy-related work. Paradoxically, this malfunctioning labor inclusion through institutionalized social dialogue also contributed to closing the political arena to new or alternative organizations that were not officially recognized as representative; a context that makes it difficult for any other actor—for instance, an organization representing the unemployed—to make itself heard.

Conclusion

In our search for explanations for the low level of mobilization of the unemployed in Poland, we have identified a variety of factors that, combined, produce a climate in which not only the mobilization of the unemployed themselves is unlikely, but also mobilization on their behalf is discouraged. First, social representations are not favorable to the emergence of a group consciousness among the unemployed and undermine their willingness to engage in collective action. The dominant discourse is rejecting the idea of unemployment as a pressing social problem, diminishing its importance and putting forward arguments emphasizing individual strategies and responsibilities. The unemployed appear to integrate some of these arguments and blame themselves rather than referring to the status of a victim, although public opinion polls reveal a more compassionate picture.

Second, the welfare system that has been gradually taking shape in Poland has provided an unfavorable terrain for mobilization. On one hand, it has given the unemployed no real group existence, since it relied heavily on inactivity benefits (early retirement, disability, and severance payments) to facilitate exit from the labor market. On the other, after early ad-hoc measures serving to accommodate the interests of the most exposed or most militant workers to buy social peace, policies toward the unemployed have become minimalist in terms of benefits and eligibility, a context in which mobilization of the unemployed is unlikely (Berclaz, Füglister, and Giugni 2004, 436). Even in those years when unemployment appeared as a salient social and economic problem, unemployment insurance has not really managed to become a fully legitimate branch of the welfare state. Rather, it has become marginalized in the welfare system. According to survey data, only half of the Poles agree that the government "should spend money on unemployment benefits" while more than 80 percent think that government should provide a job for everyone and "spend money on retirement" (ISSP 1997 and 2006). Instead of triggering reactions emphasizing mutual rights and duties among state, society, and jobless people, the institutionalization of a residual welfare state reinforces the idea that support should be restricted to a very limited number of people. As a consequence, it focuses on people who will easily find employment, a further stigmatization of the unemployed, in particular beneficiaries with multiple problems and a culture of self-blame that decreases their chances for job insertion (Dean 2003; Dean et al. 2005; Bonvin and Farvaque 2007; Sztandar-Sztanderska, 2009).

Finally, at a more general level, both the broad political agenda and the configuration of actors constituted an adverse context for collective mobilization on behalf of the unemployed. The trade unions were either not willing or unable to do so for ideological reasons, because they pursued other goals, or simply because they lacked the capacity to do so. The extraordinary politics of postcommunist transformations resulted in a relative consensus, partly implicit and ambiguous, on the orientation of policies that legitimized the construction of a "market society" based on individualism and emphasizing one's responsibility for one's fate (Spieser 2009).

These factors, we have argued, contribute to the absence of mobilization in relation to unemployment. Yet this does not mean that unemployment was never considered a government failure and a motive for some kind of protest action. The way in which individuals and groups in society react to deteriorating socioeconomic conditions can be mapped using Tilly's repertoire of contention and Hirschman's voice and exit categories. Building on these, Greskovits (1998) distinguishes five types of social responses to economic stress under transformations: (i) riots and violent demonstrations; (ii) strikes; (iii) resisting market mechanisms and seeking rents; (iv) "going informal" (tax evasion, illegal employment, and criminality); (v) protest voting (voting against government for extremist or populist parties, and abstention) (75–6). The first three options rely on collective action and presuppose a group interest, while the two last constitute essentially individual strategies. In Poland, there were overall very few observations of demonstrations and strikes in connection to high unemployment or the situation of the unemployed. The search for rents and protection (as mentioned earlier), in the form of a specific arrangement and selective benefits, was the strategy privileged by unions in sectors where they were especially strong. However, the main response to changing conditions in Poland seems to have been an individual, rather than a collective, one, taking two possible forms: exit through immigration, which became easier and more significant from 2004 onward, or protest voting, identifiable in the sudden rise of populist parties in 2005. Incidentally, the Kaczyński brothers who came to power in 2005 promoted a very statist policy agenda and a return to traditional and solidarity values ("solidaristic Poland" as opposed to "liberal Poland").[29] This suggests that protest against government policies was directed above all via the electoral channel, rather than collective action, an argument also supported by the lower support for candidates advocating free market reforms in regions with higher unemployment (Bell 1997) and the fact that no government majority had ever been reconducted in office by the ballot at the time of writing.

Notes

1. There was only one dramatic, faraway historical precedent: the deep economic crisis in the 1930s, which led the unemployment rate to exceed 30 percent among industrial workers in certain Polish territories.
2. The unionization rate barely reached 17 percent in 2004 according to the most optimistic figures (European Commission 2004).
3. This approach arguably entails a few obstacles: it is impossible to describe an inexistent phenomenon and to rigorously establish what causes its nonoccurrence. Therefore, this chapter primarily aims to propose a set of possibly country-specific explanations for the distinctiveness of the Polish case. This study of developments in Poland gains explicative value when read in contrast of the case studies of unemployed movements in other countries. Its major input is to shed light on the role of the discursive context, general political dynamics, and specific welfare policies in facilitating or hindering social mobilization.
4. These diaries were written by the unemployed in response to two competitions organized by a research center, the Institute for Social Economy (Warsaw School of Economics), which aimed to collect and publicize qualitative data on this group of people. They constitute an invaluable source of information on individual life paths and perceptions. The diaries written for the first edition of the competition in the 1930s, published in the form of a book, attracted the attention of a wide public, were commented upon in the press, and analyzed by social scientists, whereas the diaries collected during the second competition in the late 1990s and published in 2005 passed rather unnoticed.
5. All quotations in this chapter not originally in English are the authors' translations from the original language.
6. The data used in this paragraph refers to the second quarter of 2005 and 2007 and is cited by Grotkowska (2008).
7. Social Diagnosis is the first well-known social science research project cofinanced to an important extent by the private sector in Poland (except its first edition, which was mainly funded by the government). It is published every two years since 2003 and each new release is a media event. All results and databases are available on the website: http://www.diagnoza.com/ (last accessed September 1, 2009).
8. For more information on this material, see note 4.

9. In the 1998 survey, the question was formulated as an open-ended one, against a closed question with a list of proposed answers, among which the respondent could choose several ones in 2006. This difference between the two surveys concerns several items.
10. The experience of unemployment in Polish history in the 1930s is only referred to by academic observers, it is not part of the cognitive frame in which policymakers and other actors reason two or more generations later.
11. Or, as we show later, most prone to mobilization.
12. Frictional unemployment was estimated as not exceeding half a percentage point in the People's Republic of Poland (Mlonek 1999). However, universal employment was achieved at the price of a higher number of workers than needed in many productive units, which is sometimes interpreted as hidden unemployment.
13. Law on employment promotion and labor market institutions of 2004.
14. Small business loans, loans to employers for creating jobs, training, public service employment, and wage subsidy programs.
15. In practice, the Ministry fixes the amount of the standard unemployment benefit for people who have worked between five and twenty years; those who have worked less than five years receive 80 percent of the standard benefit and those with more than twenty years work experience are entitled to 120 percent.
16. Because the unemployment benefit is calculated as a flat amount unrelated to one's previous wage, the reference indicators are the minimum wage and the average wage in the Polish economy. This should not be confused with the replacement rate used in contexts where the benefit is calculated on the basis of one's previous individual wage, which takes into account individual wages.
17. This is reflected in public opinion surveys highlighting a broad consensus on the idea that "the government should provide jobs for everyone," but an important divide on the provision of an unemployment benefit, which is supported by only half of the respondents (ISSP 1997 and 2006).
18. In counterpart, they lost the right to the unemployment benefit (Gardawski 2002).
19. At the outset of transition, sixty-four out of Poland's sixty-six deep coalmines and one of the two major steelworks were located in Upper Silesia (Blazyca 2002, 26).
20. Most strikes in this sector date back to the first half of the 1990s.
21. ZUS, quoted by Müller (1999, 101).
22. ZUS figures.
23. Including those receiving a disability benefit.
24. Ministry of Economy and Labor data, August 2004.
25. A part of the legislation package was passed by a social-democratic alliance and the rest by a coalition of the Solidarność alliance with centre right parties in the following legislature.
26. Policies aiming to fight unemployment and policies targeting the unemployed reflect two different visions of the problem. A good account of this in the French context is found in Pierru (2005).
27. The acronym stands for "All-Poland Trade Union Federation."
28. "Pact for State Enterprise Transformation," also named "Kuroń pact" after its initiator. This is the only working example of a relatively comprehensive social pact in Poland.
29. Declaration of the coalition on a common program under the leadership of Law and Justice and Self Defense parties, "Solidarne Państwo", Warsaw, April 27, 2006.

References

Avdagic, Sabina, and Colin Crouch. 2006. Organized Economic Interests: Diversity and Change in an Enlarged Europe. In *Developments in European Politics*, ed. Paul M. Heywood, Erik Jones, Martin Rhodes, and Ulrich Sedelmeir, 196–215. London: Palgrave.

Balcerowicz, Leszek. 1995. *Socialism, Capitalism, Transformation*. Budapest: Central European University Press.

Bandelj, Nina. 2008. Negotiating Neo-Liberalism. Free-Market Reform in Central and Eastern Europe. In *Globalization and Transformations of Local Socioeconomic Practices*, ed. Ulrike Schuerkens, 46–74. New York and London: Routledge.

Baxandall, Phineas. 2002. Explaining Differences in the Political Meaning of Unemployment across Time and Space. *Journal of Socio-Economics* 31(5): 469–502.

———. 2003. Postcommunist Unemployment Politics. Historical Legacies and the Curious Acceptance of Job Loss. In *Capitalism and Democracy in Central and Eastern Europe. Assessing the Legacy of the Communist Rule*, ed. Grzegorz Ekiert and Stephen E. Hanson, 248–88. Cambridge: Cambridge University Press.

Bell, Janice. 1997. Unemployment Matters: Voting Patterns during the Economic Transition in Poland, 1990–1995. *Europe-Asia Studies* 49(7): 1263–91.

Berclaz, Michel, Katharina Füglister, and Marco Giugni. 2004. États-providence, opportunités politiques et mobilisation des chômeurs: Une approche néo-institutionnaliste. *Swiss Journal of Sociology* 30: 421–40.

Blazyca, George, ed. 2002. *Restructuring Regional and Local Economies: Towards a Comparative Study of Scotland and Upper Silesia*. Aldershot: Ashgate.

Bonvin, Jean-Michel, and Nicolas Farvaque. 2007. A Capability Approach to Individualised and Tailor-Made Activation. In *Making it Personal. Individualising Activation Services in the EU*, ed. Ben Valkenburg and Rik van Berkel, 45–66. Bristol: Policy Press.

Bourdieu, Pierre, ed. 1993. *La misère du monde*. Paris: Seuil.

Bourdieu, Pierre. 1996. *Sur la television*. Paris: Liber.

Bruszt, László. 2001. Market Making as State Making: Constitutions and Economic Development in Post-communist Eastern Europe. *Constitutional Political Economy* 13: 53–72.

Burns, Andrew, and Przemyslaw Kowalski. 2004. *The Jobs Challenge in Poland: Policies to raise Employment*. OECD Economics Department Working Papers. Paris: OECD.

CBOS. 1998. *Opinie o przyczynach bezrobocia i bezrobotnych. Komunikat z badań*. Warsaw: CBOS.

———. 2006. *Stosunek do bezrobocia i bezrobotnych. Komunikat z badań*. Warsaw: CBOS.

———. 2007. *Społeczny zakres bezrobocia w Polsce. Komunikat z badań*. Warsaw: CBOS.

Czapiński, Janusz, and Tomasz Panek, ed. 2003. *Diagnoza społeczna 2003. Warunki i jakość życia Polaków*. Warsaw: Wyższa Szkoła Finansów i Zarządzania.

———. 2005. *Diagnoza społeczna 2005. Warunki i jakość życia Polaków*. Warsaw: Wyższa Szkoła Finansów i Zarządzania.

———. 2007. *Diagnoza społeczna 2007. Warunki i jakość życia Polaków*. Warsaw: Rada Monitoringu Społecznego.

Czapiński, Janusz, and Katarzyna Skrzydłowska-Kalukin. 2007. Nie ma kto pracować w Polsce. *Dziennik*, September 19.

Czepulis-Rutkowska, Zofia. 1998. Changes in Pension System. In *Social Policy in the 1990s. Legal Regulations and Their Prospected Results*, ed. Golinowska Stanisława, 194–209. Warsaw: IPiSS.

———. 1999. The Polish Pension System and its Problems. In *Transformation of Social Security: Pensions in Central-Eastern Europe*, ed. Katharina Müller, Andreas Ryll, and Hans-Jürgen Wagener, 143–58. Heidelberg and New York: Physica.

Danecka, Marta, and Adam Leszczyński. 2008. Moja bieda, moja wina. *Gazeta Wyborcza*, May 31, http://wyborcza.pl/1,76842,5263676,Moja_bieda__moja_wina.html (last accessed September 1, 2009).

Dean, Hartley. 2003. Re-conceptualising Welfare-To-Work for People with Multiple Problems and Needs. *Journal of Social Policy* 32(3): 441–59.

Dean, Hartley, Jean-Michel Bonvin, Pascale Vielle, and Nicolas Farvaque. 2005. Developing Capabilities and Rights in Welfare-to-Work Policies. *European Societies* 7(1): 3–26.

Ebbinghaus, Bernhard. 2006. *Reforming Early Retirement in Europe, Japan and the USA*. Oxford: Oxford University Press.

Esping-Andersen, Gøsta. 1990. *The Three Worlds of Welfare Capitalism*. Cambridge: Polity Press.

European Commission. 2004. *Industrial Relations in Europe 2004*. Luxembourg: Office for Official Publications of the European Communities.

Gardawski, Juliusz. 1996. *Poland's Industrial Workers on the Return to Democracy and Market Economy*. Warsaw: Friedrich Ebert Stiftung.

———. 2002. Unemployment Benefits Examined. *EIROnline*, October 29.

———. 2003. Difficult Restructuring of Coal Mining Continues. *EIROnline*, October 1.

Giugni, Marco. 2008. Welfare States, Political Opportunities, and the Mobilization of the Unemployed: A Cross-National Analysis. *Mobilization* 13(3): 297–310.

Golinowska, Stanisława.1994. *Social Policy and Social Conditions in Poland: 1989–1993*. Warsaw: IPiSS.

Góra, Marek. 2004. Trwale wysokie bezrobocie w Polsce. Refleksje, próba częściowego wyjaśnienia i kilka propozycji. In *Elastyczny rynek pracy w Polsce : jak sprostać temu wyzwaniu?*, ed. Michał Boni, 123–44. Zeszyty BRE Bank-CASE, 73. Warsaw: CASE.

Greskovits, Bela. 1998. *The Political Economy of Protest and Patience. East European and Latin American Transformations Compared*. Budapest: Central European University Press.

Grotkowska, Gabriela. 2008. Polityka w obszarze rynku pracy w działaniu: ciągłość i zmiana—komentarz. Conference *Prezentacja projektu badawczego CAPRIGHT: Resources, Rights and Capabilities: In Search of Social Foundations for Europe*, May 5, Warsaw, Poland.

Hausner, Jerzy. 1994. Interest Organization and Industrial Relations in Central and East European Countries. *Yearbook of Polish Labour Law and Social Policy*, 135–46. Krakow: Jagellonian University Press.

———. 1996. Models of the System of Interest Representation in Post-socialist Societies: The Case of Poland. In *Parliaments and Organized Interests: The Second Steps*, ed. Attila Agh and Gabriella Ilonszki, 102–20. Budapest: Hungarian Centre for Democracy Studies.

International Social Survey Programme (ISSP). 1997. Role of Government III. Extracted via the ZACAT portal: http://zacat.gesis.org/webview/index.jsp (last accessed September 1, 2009).

International Social Survey Programme (ISSP). 2006. Role of Government IV. Extracted via the ZACAT portal: http://zacat.gesis.org/webview/index.jsp (last accessed September 1, 2009).

Jacyno, Małgorzata. 2007. *Kultura indywidualizmu*. Warsaw: PWN.

Kohli, Martin, Martin Rein, Anne-Marie Guillemard, and Herman Van Gunsteren. 1991. *Time for Retirement. Comparative Studies of Early Exit from the Labor Force*. Cambridge: Cambridge University Press.

Kornai, Janos. 2006. The Great Transformation of Central Eastern Europe. *Economics of Transition* 14: 207–44.

Kriesi, Hanspeter. 2004. Political Context and Opportunity. In *The Blackwell companion to social movements*, ed. David A. Snow, Sarah A. Soule, and Hanspeter Kriesi, 67–90. Oxford: Blackwell.

Ksiezopolski, Miroslaw. 1993. Social Policy in Poland in the Period of Political and Economic Transition: Challenges and Dilemmas. *Journal of European Social Policy* 3(3): 177–94.

Lemieux, Cyril. 2001. Une critique sans raison ? L'approche bourdieusienne des médias et ses limites. In *Le travail sociologique de Pierre Bourdieu. Dettes et critiques*, ed. Bernard Lahire, 205–29. Paris: La Découverte.

Mlonek, Krystyna. 1999. *Bezrobocie w Polsce w XX wieku w świetle badań*. Warsaw: Krajowy Urzad Pracy.

Müller, Katharina. 1999. *The Political Economy of Pension Reform in Central-Eastern Europe*. Cheltenham and Northampton: Edward Elgar.

Ministry of Labour and Social Policy (MPiPS). 1995. *Promocja aktywności zawodowej młodzieży. Program przeciwdziałania bezrobociu wśród młodzieży*. Warsaw: Ministerstwo Pracy i Polityki Socjalnej, Krajowy Urzad Pracy.

Orenstein, Mitchell A. 1995. Transitional Social Policy in the Czech Republic and Poland. *Czech Sociological Review* 3(2): 179–96.

———. 2001. *Out of the Red: Building Capitalism and Democracy in Postcommunist Europe*. Ann Arbor: University of Michigan Press.

Ost, David. 2001. The Weakness of Symbolic Strength: Labour and Union Identity in Poland. In *Workers after Workers' States. Labor Politics in Postcommunist Europe*, ed. Stephen Crowley and David Ost, 79–96. Boston and Oxford: Rowman & Littlefield.

Ost, David, and Stephen Crowley, ed. 2001. *Workers after Workers' States. Labor Politics in Postcommunist Europe*. Boston and Oxford: Rowman & Littlefield.

Pietrzak, Michał. 2006. GUS podał nieprawdziwe dane o bezrobociu. *Dziennik*. Warsaw : Axel Springer, 25.09.2006, http://www.dziennik.pl/gospodarka/article7649.ece?service=print (last accessed September 1, 2009).

Pierru, Emmanuel. 2005. *Guerre aux chômeurs ou guerre au chômage*. Bellecombe-en-Bauges: Editions du Croquant.

Portet, Stéphane. 2006. Les paradoxes de la flexibilité du temps de travail en Pologne. PhD thesis, Institut des sciences sociales, Université de Toulouse-Le Mirail.

Rainnie, Al, and Jane Hardy. 1995. Desperately Seeking Capitalism: Solidarity and Polish Industrial Relations in the 1990s. *Industrial Relations Journal* 26(4): 267–79.

Salais, Robert, Nicolas Baverez, and Bénédicte Reynaud 1986. *L'invention du chômage*. Paris: Presses universitaires de France.

Spieser, Catherine. 2007. Labour Market Policies in Post-Communist Poland: Explaining the Peaceful Institutionalisation of Unemployment. *Politique Européenne* (21): 97–132.

———. 2009. Institutionalising Market Society in Times of Systemic Change. The Construction and Reform of Social and Labour Market Policies in Poland in a Comparative Perspective. PhD thesis, Department of Political and Social Sciences, European University Institute, Florence.

Sztandar-Sztanderska, Karolina. 2009. Activation of Unemployed in Poland. From Policy Design to Policy Implementation. *International Journal of Sociology and Social Policy* 29 (11/12): 624–36.

Sztandar-Sztanderska, Karolina, and Marianna Zieleńska. 2008. Twoja bieda, państwa wina. *Gazeta Wyborcza*, July 20, http://wyborcza.pl/1,76842,5426343,Twoja_bieda __panstwa_wina.html (last accessed September 1, 2009).

Thompson, John B. 1995. *The Media and Modernity: A Social Theory of the Media*. Stanford: Stanford University Press.

Towalski, Rafał. 2003. "Activation Package" Agreed to Accompany Iron and Steel Restructuring, *EIROnline*, October 30.

Vanhuysse, Pieter. 2006. *Divide and Pacify. Strategic Social Policies and Political Protests in Post-Communist Democracies*. Budapest: Central European University Press.

Weinstein, Marc. 1996. The Remaking of the Polish Industrial Relations System: The Institutional and Ideational Antecedents of Firm-level Employment Practices. PhD Thesis, Sloan School of Management, Massachussets Institute of Technology.

———. 2000. Solidarity's Abandonment of Worker Councils: Redefining Employee Stakeholder Rights in Post Socialist Poland. *British Journal of Industrial Relations* 38(1): 49–73.

Wenzel, Michał. 1998. Solidarity and Akcja Wyborcza "Solidarnosc." An Attempt at Reviving the Legend. *Communist and Post-Communist Studies* 31(2): 139–56.

Wolton, Dominique. 2002. Une critique de la critique: Bourdieu et les médias. *Sciences Humaines*. Numéro spécial Pierre Bourdieu.

Zawadzka, Anna. 2005. Bezrobotni z dwudziestolecia międzywojennego i z końca wieku: problemy, postawy, narracje. Analiza pamiętników bezrobotnych. *Kultura i społeczeństwo* 2: 29–50.

Zimmermann, Bénédicte. 2001. *La constitution du chômage en Allemagne*. Paris: Maison des Sciences de l'Homme.

Index

Accornero, Aris, 133, 152
Aganzo, Andrés, 156, 162, 163, 165, 171, 173
Agh, Attila, 273
Agrikoliansky, Eric, 164, 173
Ahmad, Akhlaq, 113, 119, 128
Ahtisaari, Martti, 109
Alapuro, Risto, 127, 128
Albrechtsen, Helge, 91, 105
Aldcroft, Derek H., 179, 183, 190
Allen, Kieran, 211, 215
Allen, Mike, 201, 203, 204, 205, 206, 207, 208, 210, 215, 218
Alliances, 3, 9, 16–19, 22, 29–30, 33, 43–46, 69–79, 81, 83, 91, 101–104, 111–118, 126, 156, 168–170, 176, 177, 187–188, 227–228, 233, 237, 244, 265–268
Alterglobalization, 7, 8, 15, 50, 99–100
  See also Antiglobalization; Countersummit
Anarchist movements, 16, 19, 98–100, 103, 156, 164
  See also Far left
Andreasson, Kristiina, 128
Andreosso-O'Callaghan, Bernadette, 26
Antentas Collderram, Josep Maria, 159, 173
Antiglobalization, 76, 135, 144–150, 156, 164–170
  See also Alterglobalization
Arcq, Étienne, 106
Armingeon, Klaus, 242, 244
Atkinson, Anthony B., 182, 190
Aubry, Martine, 53
Avdagic, Sabina, 268, 272
Aznar, José María, 7, 156, 163, 166, 167, 168

Bagguley, Paul, 2, 13, 15, 18, 20, 24, 30, 41, 53, 67, 84, 103, 106, 155, 160, 173, 176, 177, 178, 180, 181, 184, 190, 200, 208, 209, 210, 215, 216
Baglioni, Simone, 2, 6, 14, 24, 131, 150, 152, 200, 215, 216
Balcerowicz, Leszek, 264, 266, 272
Balme, Richard, 24, 215, 216
Bandelj, Nina, 264, 272
Bar-On, Shani, 2, 24
Barrington, Tom, 201, 216
Barry, Frank, 195, 196, 216
Bassolino, Antonio, 141
Bauer, Heinz, 66, 72, 88
Baumgarten, Britta, 4, 24, 57, 58, 62, 73, 75, 82, 84, 85, 86, 152, 216
Baverez, Nicolas, 254, 274
Baxandall, Phineas, 175, 190, 254, 260, 272
Beatty, Christina, 185, 190
Bell, Janice, 270, 272
Benford, Robert D., 19, 27, 42, 56, 226, 241, 244, 246
Berclaz, Julie, 190, 225, 244
Berclaz, Michel, 10, 16, 21, 24, 175, 176, 191, 200, 215, 216, 217, 221, 225, 226, 244, 245, 254, 263, 269, 272
Bergman, Solveig, 113, 128
Bermeo, Nancy, 24, 26, 174
Béroud, Sophie, 7, 45, 46, 51, 52, 53, 54, 55, 155, 168, 173
Berta, Giuseppe, 132, 152
Bieber, Anne, 82, 84
Blair, Tony, 9, 64, 74
Blazyca, George, 271, 272
Böhnisch, Tomke, 79, 84

Bond, Larry, 197, 216
Bonoli, Giuliano, 221, 223, 244
Bonvin, Jean-Michel, 269, 272, 273
Boumaza, Magali, 43, 53
Bourdieu, Pierre, 1, 24, 29, 53, 249, 251, 272, 274, 275
Bourneau, François, 37, 53
Brand, Karl-Werner, 87
Braun, Dietmar, 51, 54
Breen, Richard, 196, 201, 216
Brenke, Karl, 73, 84
Briggs, Asa, 191
Bruszt, László, 264, 272
Burgess, Katrina, 158, 173
Burns, Andrew, 263, 272
Byrne, Gay, 206

Cadiou, Stéphane, 43, 53
Calle, Angel, 162, 164, 173
Cameron, David, 2, 24
Capdevielle, Jacques, 45, 54
Capron, Michel, 106
Caroyez, Philippe, 94, 106
Carrieri, Mimmo, 133, 152
Castel, Robert, 42, 54
Cattacin, Sandro, 224, 244
Chabanet, Didier, 1, 2, 3, 21, 24, 29, 54, 56, 99, 104, 106, 147, 151, 152, 163, 173, 215, 216, 241, 242
Charles, Nickie, 119, 128
Chevènement, Jean-Pierre, 51
Christen, Gioia, 224, 244
Christmas bonus, 4, 15, 29, 40–41, 45, 99
Church(es), 16, 68, 69, 70, 72, 76, 77, 83, 116, 118, 123, 127, 165, 211, 218
    See also Religious actors
Cinalli, Manlio, 8, 175, 176, 187, 190
Civil society, 9, 100, 114–118, 122, 125, 127, 175–176, 186–187, 215, 227–229, 232, 237
Clancy, Patrick, 216, 218
Cloward, Richard A., 2, 15, 26, 41, 48, 56, 135, 136, 142, 153, 176, 178, 192
Coakley, John, 210, 212, 216
Coenen, Harry, 27, 58, 87
Cognitive Frame/framing, 11–13, 19–22, 226
    Resources, 42, 160, 200
Cohen, Valérie, 50, 54
Cole, George D.H., 181, 190
Cole, Margaret I., 181, 190

Colicchio, Pasquale, 95, 96, 106
Collderram, Antentas, 173
Collovald, Annie, 52, 54
Commins, Patrick, 202, 216
Communist
    Organisations, 3, 4, 7, 9, 18–20, 26, 30–34, 37, 39–40, 51–52, 56, 95, 99, 102–103, 111–112, 133, 141–142, 146, 162–163, 171, 181–184, 214, 247–249, 265
    See also PCF
    Regime, 254, 264–269
Constancias, Hubert, 48
Coombes, David, 201, 216
Corporatism/t
    See (Neo)corporatism/t
Correia, Fatima, 97, 106
Counterstigmatization, 131, 138
Countersummit, 15, 164, 167
    See also European Marches against unemployment, job insecurity, and social exclusions; European Summit; G8 Summit
Court-action, 4, 23, 50, 125, 236
Cremer-Schäfer, Helga, 79, 83
Cress, Daniel M., 131, 152
Crettiez, Xavier, 51, 54, 173
Cronin, James E., 179, 180, 182, 190
Crouch, Colin, 268, 272
Croucher, Richard, 2, 18, 20, 24, 30, 54, 103, 106, 180, 181
Crowley, Stephen, 266, 274
Curtin, Chris, 202, 216
Czapiński, Janusz, 251, 252, 272
Czepulis-Rutkowska, Zofia, 262, 273

Danecka, Marta, 251, 252, 273
Daniel, Christine, 51, 54
Deacon, Alan, 180, 191
Dean, Hartley, 269, 273
De Barros, Françoise, 33, 54
Dechezelles, Stéphanie, 43, 53
Demazière, Didier, 1, 3, 24, 39, 51, 52, 54, 138–139, 142, 152, 159, 173, 177, 191
Denis, Jean-Michel, 55
Deprivation
    Political, 232
    Relative, 79, 104, 210
    Social, 2, 9, 39, 79, 161, 211–213, 232, 251, 263

Derichs-Kunstmann, Karin, 82, 84
Desanti, François, 49
Dethyre, Richard, 47, 52
De Vries, David, 2, 24
De Waele, Jean-Michel, 106
Diani, Mario, 176, 177, 191
Díaz-Salazar, Rafael, 173
Disruptive protest(s), 48, 176, 178–179, 185, 189
Dohet, Julien, 103, 106
Drudy, Sheelagh, 216, 218
Dryon, Philippe, 98, 106
Dubet, François, 187, 193
Dubois, Vincent, 36, 42, 54
Duchesne, Sophie, 23
Dufour, Christian, 18, 24
Dufour, Pascale, 54
Duggan, Carmel, 201, 216
Dunezat, Xavier, 120, 128
Durkheim, Émile, 210, 216
Duvanel, Blaise, 224, 232, 237, 242, 244
Duyvendak, Jan Willem, 192, 217, 245
Dwyer, Peter, 186, 191

Ebbinghaus, Bernhard, 77, 84, 91, 106, 262, 273
Ebersold, Serge, 36, 54
Edwards, Bob, 241, 244
Ehrholdt, Andreas, 57, 62, 79
Eick, Volker, 70, 84
Eisinger, Peter K., 177, 191
Ekiert, Grzegorz, 272
Elena y Peña, Joaquin, 174
Elias, Norbert, 131, 138, 152
Emirbayer, Mustafa, 19, 25
Entrepreneur(ship), 71–79, 80, 81, 232
Esping-Andersen, Gøsta, 20, 25, 112, 128, 215, 216, 254, 263, 273
European
　Commission, 167, 199
　Economic Community, 195, 196
　Employment Strategy, 22, 100, 199
　Marches against unemployment, job insecurity, and social exclusions, 2, 99, 100, 103–104, 147, 163–164
　Social funds, 122, 159
　Social policy, 214
　Summit, 166, 199
　See also Countersummit
　Treaty(ies), 3, 36, 205
　Union integration process, 3, 11, 12, 36, 114, 148, 198, 200, 205, 215, 243, 247, 257, 264
Evans, Neil, 181, 191
Evans, Richard J., 30, 54
Eyerman, Ron, 191

Faniel, Jean, 1, 2, 5, 6, 16, 24, 25, 47, 51, 92, 93, 94, 95, 96, 97, 98, 99, 100, 101, 102, 103, 104, 106, 151, 234, 241, 244
Far left, 3, 7, 16, 40, 95, 98–104, 162–166, 188, 237
　See also Communist; Maoists; Trotskyist/m
Farvaque, Nicolas, 269, 272, 273
Fernández, Álvarez, 2, 25
Ferrara, Luciano, 139, 142, 152, 153
Ferrera, Maurizio, 132, 152
Fillieule, Olivier, 40, 51, 53, 54, 150, 152, 164, 173, 205, 216, 232, 244
Fireman, Bruce, 226, 241, 245
Fitzgerald, Rona, 195, 217
Flanagan, Richard, 2, 25, 179, 181, 191
Folsom, Franklin, 2, 25
Form(s) of action, 5, 10, 23, 35, 50, 103, 142, 155, 195, 209, 231, 234–236, 238, 243–244
　See also Court-action; Disruptive protest(s); Repertoire of action
Forrester, Keith, 184, 191
Fothergill, Steve, 185, 190, 191
Fragnière, Jean-Pierre, 224, 244
Franck, Cécile, 165, 173
Franco (General), 7, 156, 157, 162
Freeman, Jo, 85
Fritzell, Johan, 128
Füglister, Katharina, 10, 16, 21, 24, 200, 215, 216, 217, 221, 225, 226, 244, 245, 254, 263, 269, 272
Fulcher, James, 177, 180, 191

G8 Summit, 8, 149, 169
Gallagher, Michael, 216
Galland, Olivier, 1, 25
Gallas, Andreas, 60, 66, 67, 69, 70, 71, 73, 78, 83, 84
Gallie, Duncan, 21, 25
Gallino, Luciano, 132, 152
Gamble, Andrew, 184, 191

Gamson, William, 53, 54, 79, 85, 131, 139, 141, 152, 214, 217, 226, 238, 241, 244, 245
Gardawski, Juliusz, 257, 258, 261, 267, 271, 273
Garraud, Philippe, 35, 54
Geary, Dick, 30, 54
Gehler, Michael, 217
Gerlach, Luther P., 80, 85
Gerstlé, Jacques, 55
Gianni, Matteo, 244
Giddens, Anthony, 186, 191
Ginsborg, Paul, 135, 139, 142, 149, 152
Giraud, Olivier, 51, 54
Giugni, Marco, 2, 10, 16, 21, 23, 24, 25, 72, 85, 106, 175, 176, 190, 191, 192, 200, 215, 216, 217, 218, 221, 222, 225, 226, 241, 242, 244, 245, 254, 263, 272, 273
Globalization, 7, 13–15, 165–166
Glyn, Andrew, 196, 217
Gobin, Corinne, 46, 53
Golinowska, Stanisława, 262, 273
González, Felipe, 163
Goodwin, Jeff, 19, 25, 245
Góra, Marek, 249, 250, 273
Gotovitch, José, 106
Grehn, Klaus, 69, 70, 85
Grell, Britta, 70, 84
Greskovits, Bela, 248, 269, 273
Grievances, 31, 44, 58, 59, 63–65, 79, 92, 177, 205, 222
Grote, Jürgen R., 77, 87
Grotkowska, Gabriela, 270, 273
Gualmini, Elisabetta, 133, 152
Guillemard, Anne-Marie, 274
Gunnigle, Patrick, 197, 198, 213, 218, 219
Gurr, Ted Robert, 13, 25, 104, 106, 210, 217, 241, 245

Hamel, Pierre, 87
Hamilton, Rob, 196, 217
Hamman, Philippe, 43, 53
Hanagan, Michael, 85
Hannan, Damian, 216
Hanson, Stephen E., 272
Hardiman, Niamh, 200, 201, 217
Hardy, Jane, 266, 274
Harris, José, 179, 191
Harrison, Royden, 178, 191
Hartman, Paul T., 183, 192
Hassel, Anke, 77, 85, 87
Hausner, Jerzy, 268, 273
Healy, Seán, 206
Heaney, Séamus, 206
Hege, Adelheid, 18, 24
Heiskala, Risto, 109, 125, 128, 129
Helin, Vesa, 113, 128
Herrington, Alison, 185, 190
Hertz, Ellen, 224, 225, 246
Heywood, Paul M., 272
Hietanen, Elina, 128
Hillyard, Paddy, 211, 217
Hinton, James, 181, 191
Hoareau, Charles, 39, 54
Hobsbawm, Eric J., 14, 15, 25, 134, 135, 136, 137, 152, 179, 191
Höhfeld, Jörg, 82, 84
Hokkanen, Liisa, 113, 128
Holli, Anne Maria, 120, 128, 129
Howell, Chris, 177
Howell, David W., 191
Huovinen, Pasi, 114, 128
Hvinden, Bjørn, 128
Hyman, Richard, 181, 191

Identity, 1, 31, 58, 131, 147, 150, 176, 178, 200, 222, 226–227, 229, 232, 234–236, 238, 239, 241
Ilonszki, Gabriella, 273
(Im)migrant(s), 43, 113, 119, 124, 137, 143, 149, 165, 166, 170, 211, 215, 231
Inés, María, 25
Interwar Mobilizations, 8, 18, 20, 29–35, 175, 179–182

Jacobs, Lawrence, 217
Jacyno, Małgorzata, 253, 274
Jahoda, Marie, 1, 25, 65, 85, 177, 192, 232, 245
Januarius, Joeri, 91, 107
Jasper, James M., 245
Jenkins, J. Craig, 65, 71, 85, 152
Jenkins-Smith, Hank, 135, 153
Jobert, Bruno, 36, 54
Johns, Christopher, 196, 217
Johnson, Victoria, 85
Johnston, Hank, 85, 245
Join-Lambert, Marie-Thérèse, 47, 55
Jones, Erik, 272

Jospin, Lionel, 44, 48
Julkunen, Raija, 113, 114, 125, 126, 128
Juppé, Alain, 48
Juppi, Pirita, 129

Kaczyński (brothers), 270
Kalander, Marina, 16, 25
Kalela, Jorma, 128
Kantelhardt, Uwe, 60, 67, 70, 73, 75, 83, 85
Kathleen, Lynch, 216, 218
Katzenstein, Peter, 242, 245
Keinänen, Päivi, 111, 112, 113, 128
Kelly, John, 177, 191
Kennedy, Stanislas, 206
Kenny, Brian, 197, 204, 217
Kerbo, Harold R., 2, 25
Keßler, Martin, 27, 79, 85
Kiander, Jaakko, 128
Kidd, Alan J., 178, 192
Kieser, Albrecht, 73, 85
Killian, Lewis M., 241, 246
Kilmurray, Evanne, 208, 217
Kingsford, Peter, 184, 192
Kinnunen, Petri, 128
Kirby, Peadar, 211, 217
Kitschelt, Herbert, 16, 25, 72, 85, 87, 139, 152, 225, 236, 238, 242, 245
Kittler, Klaus, 84, 85
Kivikuru, Ullamaija, 128
Klandermans, Bert, 41, 55, 85, 152, 245
Klippstein, Norbert, 83, 84, 85, 86
Kohl, Helmut, 61, 64, 74
Köhler, Holm-Detlev, 172, 173
Kohli, Martin, 262, 274
Konttinen, Annamari, 129
Kooiman, Jan, 202, 217
Koopmans, Ruud, 166, 173, 192, 217, 225, 245
Kornai, Janos, 264, 274
Kornhauser, William, 241, 245
Kotakari, Ulla, 110, 129
Kourchid, Olivier, 2, 18, 25, 31, 32, 51, 55
Kousis, Maria, 190, 244
Kowalski, Przemyslaw, 263, 272
Kriesi, Hanspeter, 55, 72, 85, 139, 153, 173, 177, 192, 214, 217, 222, 225, 237, 242, 244, 245, 246, 264, 266, 274
Krzeslo, Estelle, 98, 106

Ksiezopolski, Miroslaw, 264, 274
Kull, Silke, 73, 86
Kvist, Jon, 128

Laffan, Brigid, 195, 217
Lagneau, Éric, 48, 55
Lahire, Bernard, 274
Lahusen, Christian, 4, 24, 57, 58, 75, 82, 85, 86, 152, 216, 242
Lapinski, John, 214, 217
Lazarsfeld, Paul F., 1, 25, 65, 85, 177, 192, 232, 245
Le Grignou, Brigitte, 49, 55
Lee, Joe, 195, 210, 217
Lefèvre, Josette, 46, 51, 53
Lefresne, Florence, 22, 25, 106
Leisering, Lutz, 83, 86
Lemieux, Cyril, 249, 274
Léonard, Évelyne, 106
Leszczyński, Adam, 251, 252, 273
Lévy, Catherine, 22, 25, 51, 55
Levy, Jack, 179, 192
Lewis, Paul, 184, 192, 213, 217, 246
Linders, Annulla, 16, 25, 242
Lipponen, Paavo, 109
Lipsky, Michael, 16, 25, 43, 55, 86
Locke, Cybèle, 2, 26, 105, 107
Loikkanen, Heikki A., 128
Lorence, James J., 2, 26
Louis, Marie-Victoire, 1, 25
Luhtakallio, Eeva, 6, 109, 119, 120, 125, 128, 129
Lustiger-Thaler, Henri, 87
Lutz, Karin, 200, 217

Määttänen, Sanna, 126
Mach, André, 221, 223, 244
Macmillan, Harold, 183, 192
Maloney, William, 24
Mänz, Marcus, 244
Manzano, Virginia, 2, 25
Maoists, 95, 102
March(es) of the Unemployed, 9, 23, 32–33, 35, 51, 97, 99, 136, 139, 142, 164, 180, 184, 185, 187
 See also European Marches against unemployment, job insecurity, and social exclusions
Martin, Hélène, 224, 225, 246
Martin, Jean-Philippe, 45, 55

Martin, Virginie, 35, 53
Marwell, Gerald, 65, 67, 86
Massow, Martin, 68, 86
Mathers, Andy, 2, 26, 99, 107
Mathieu, Lilian, 36, 52, 55
Matonti, Frédérique, 56
Matthies, Aila-Leena, 110, 129
Maurer, Sophie, 13, 26, 29, 40, 42, 50, 52, 55, 96, 107, 131, 137, 138, 151, 153
Mayer, Margit, 70, 84
Mayer, Nonna, 164, 173
McAdam, Doug, 16, 26, 27, 67, 72, 86, 87, 139, 153, 176, 177, 191, 225, 242, 245
McCarthy, Charles, 213, 217
McCarthy, Dermot, 199, 217
McCarthy, John D., 26, 27, 65, 86, 87, 88, 241, 244, 245
McClurg Mueller, Carol, 245, 246
McElligott, Anthony, 18, 26
McGinn, Pat, 206, 218
McGinnity, Frances, 196, 218
McMahon, Gerard, 197, 219
McNeill, William, 178, 192
Meacham, Standish, 179, 192
Media coverage, 3, 20, 37, 47–50, 53, 60, 63, 67, 73, 75, 76, 78, 99, 100, 110, 116, 123–126, 127, 142, 161, 204, 208, 225, 227, 234–236, 249–251, 270
Melucci, Alberto, 175, 192, 241, 245
Mercier, Nicole, 172, 174, 217
Meyer, David S., 72, 86, 131, 139, 141, 152
Meynaud, Hélène, 45, 54
Michel, Louise, 50
Midlarsky, Manus I., 192
Mikko, Kautto, 128
Minkoff, Debra C., 72, 86
Mitterrand, François, 36
Mlonek, Krystyna, 255, 271, 274
Monks, Tony, 197, 207, 213, 218
Moore, Christy, 206
Morales, Rafael, 169, 174
Morelli, Anne, 106
Moreno, Luis, 160, 174
Morgan, Kenneth O., 191
Morris, Aldon D., 245, 246
Mouchard, Daniel, 39, 42, 55, 165, 174
Mouriaux, René, 45, 52, 53, 54, 55
Müller, Katharina, 271, 273, 274
Mundo, Yang, 87

Neidhardt, Friedhelm, 66, 86
(Neo)corporatism/t, 5, 44, 59, 74, 77–78, 80, 112, 117, 118, 148–149, 198–199, 207, 263, 268
Ness, Immanuel, 16, 26, 93, 107
Networks, 1, 3, 9, 14–15, 22, 35–43, 58–62, 66–71, 76, 80, 81, 103, 115–117, 126–127, 131, 142–148, 156, 161–166, 170, 171, 176–178, 184, 188, 189, 201, 202, 211, 232–237, 241, 255
Nevin, David, 217
Nic Ghiolla Phádraig, Máire, 210, 218
Nikolaus, Kurt, 75, 85, 86
Nolan, Brian, 196, 211, 218
Nylund, Marianne, 110, 120, 129

Oberschall, Anthony, 232, 241, 245
Ó Cinnéide, Séamus, 202, 218
O'Connell, Philip, 196
O'Dowd, Liam, 216, 218
Oliver, Michael J., 179, 183, 190
Oliver, Pamela, 65, 67, 86
Olson, Mancur, 65, 86
O'Neill, Jim, 207, 218
Opp, Karl-Dieter, 65, 86
Opportunity structure(s)
  Discursive(s), 19, 61, 126, 222, 225–231, 235, 236, 238, 239, 270
  Political, 12, 16, 25, 58–59, 71–79, 80–81, 112, 139–142, 225–226
  Specific, 16, 225–231, 254
  Window(s) of, 10, 59, 77, 81, 237
Orenstein, Mitchell A., 262, 266, 274
Oschmiansky, Frank, 73, 86
Ost, David, 266, 267, 274
O'Sullivan, Eoin, 214, 218
Ourabah, Fodil, 52

Pagat, Maurice, 36, 37, 52
Panek, Tomasz, 251, 272
Pape, Klaus, 84, 85
Passy, Florence, 245
Patou, Charles, 49, 55
Paugam, Serge, 1, 21, 25, 26, 29, 55
Paulus, Wolfgang, 66, 68, 86
PCF, 4, 18, 30–34, 36, 39, 40, 46
Peillon, Michel, 209, 210, 215, 218
Peltokoski, Jukka, 129
Pereyra, Sebastian, 2, 27
Pérez Quintana, Vicente, 162, 174

Index • 283

Pérez Torres, Francisco Miguel, 161, 174
Pernot, Jean-Marie, 51, 55
Perrineau, Pascal, 43, 55
Perrot, Michelle, 51, 55
Perry, Matt, 2, 18, 23, 24, 26, 27, 31, 32, 33, 51, 55, 58, 86, 106, 107, 192, 193
Peter, Michael, 73, 84
Phelps Brown, Henry, 179, 192
Piekkola, Hannu, 114, 128
Pierru, Emmanuel, 2, 18, 26, 29, 30, 31, 43, 52, 55, 56, 271, 274
Pierson, Paul, 185, 192
Pietrzak, Michał, 250, 274
Pigenet, Michel, 23, 26, 32, 51, 56, 105, 107
Pignoni, Maria-Teresa, 3, 24, 39, 51, 52, 54, 56, 138–139, 142, 152, 159, 173, 177, 191
Pilgram, Arno, 58, 65, 84, 87
Pissarides, Christopher A., 185, 192
Piven, Frances Fox, 2, 15, 26, 41, 48, 56, 135, 136, 142, 153, 176, 178, 192
Pleyers, Geoffrey, 15, 26
Polavieja, Javier G., 18, 26, 158, 174
Police repression, 30, 32, 33, 48, 147
Political impact, 6, 21, 35, 48, 50, 79, 214–215, 231, 236–238
Political socialization, 13, 30, 39–40, 182
Polletta, Francesca, 241, 245
Pont Vidal, Josep, 167, 174
Portes, Alejandro, 135, 138, 153
Portet, Stéphane, 249, 250, 274
Pouchadon, Marie-Laure, 50, 56
Pouget, Émile, 50–51
Public
  Arena/sphere, 40, 50, 59, 72, 149, 228, 232
  Debates, 47, 72, 79, 109, 124, 155, 182, 187, 204, 223, 226, 228–229, 249, 250, 252
  Discourses, 225–231, 236, 239, 248, 249, 252, 253
  Opinion, 4, 5, 19, 20, 23, 30, 43, 47–48, 63, 73, 99, 109, 144, 214, 221, 223, 253, 265, 268, 271
  Perception(s)/representation(s), 110, 124, 234, 249–253
Purdue, Derrick, 190
Putnam, Robert D., 232, 246
Pyykkönen, Miikka, 129

Radical left
  See Far left
Raevaara, Eeva, 120, 128, 129
Rafferty, Mick, 200, 202, 213, 218
Rainnie, Al, 266, 274
Rees, Nicholas, 201, 216
Rein, Harald, 59, 61, 64, 66, 67, 68, 69, 75, 86
Rein, Martin, 274
Reiss, Matthias, 2, 24, 26, 27, 58, 86, 106, 107, 178, 192, 193
Reister, Hugo, 59, 62, 68, 71, 83, 85, 86
Religious actors, 206–207
Reman, Pierre, 106
Remondino, Fabrizia, 142, 153
Repertoire of action, 23, 35, 104, 142, 164, 200, 209, 225, 243, 269
Revolution-Thursday, 6, 114, 124
Reynaud, Bénédicte, 254, 274
Reyneri, Emilio, 132, 153
Rhodes, Martin, 272
Richards, Andrew, 2, 16, 18, 26, 27, 30, 56, 93, 107, 157, 158, 172, 174, 183, 184, 192
Riemann, Charles, 217
Rink, Dieter, 87, 96
Riots, 23, 124, 179, 269
Roche, William, 197, 198, 213, 218
Rochford, E. Burke, Jr, 56, 246
Rodríguez Cabrero, Gregorio, 156, 160, 174
Roger, Antoine, 43, 93
Rolke, Lothar, 1, 27, 66, 87
Roller, Edeltraut, 71, 87
Rolston, Bill, 211, 217
Rosanvallon, Pierre, 234, 246
Rose, Richard, 219
Rosenzweig, Roy, 2, 27
Ross, Arthur M., 183, 192
Rossmann, Ulrike, 88
Roth, Roland, 58, 62, 71, 76, 82, 87
Rothardt, Dieter, 68, 83, 87
Rottman, David, 216
Royall, Frédéric, 2, 10, 13, 24, 26, 27, 52, 56, 127, 129, 195, 202, 203, 211, 215, 216, 218
Roynane, Tom, 202, 216
Rucht, Dieter, 82, 87
Ryll, Andreas, 273
Rytina, Steven, 226, 241, 245

Sabatier, Paul A., 135, 153
Salais, Robert, 254, 274
Salmon, Jean-Marc, 40, 56
Sánchez León, Pablo, 156, 162, 174
Santoro, Serena, 139, 142, 153
Saville, John, 191
Scally, Robert J., 179, 192
Scherer, Wolfgang, 59, 61, 64, 66, 67, 68, 69, 75, 86
Schmid, Günther, 73, 86
Schmid, Manfred G., 64, 87
Schmitter, Philippe C., 77, 87
Schnapper, Dominique, 1, 27, 232, 246
Scholten, Ilja, 217
Schröder, Gerhard, 22, 57, 58, 62, 64, 73, 76, 77, 79, 80
Schuerkens, Ulrike, 272
Schulte Beerbühl, Margrit, 178, 192
Scotson, John L., 152
Scruggs, Lyle, 91, 107
Sedelmeir, Ulrich, 272
Segrestin, Denis, 172, 174
Seiler, Daniel-Louis, 106
Sensenbrenner, Julia, 135, 138, 153
Serrano del Rosal, Javier G., 158, 174
Shaffer, Richard A., 2, 25
Shapiro, Robert, 217
Siisiäinen, Martti, 6, 109, 112, 114, 116, 128, 129
Silver, Beverly J., 178, 192
Simpura, Jussi, 128
Skrzydłowska-Kalukin, Katarzyna, 251, 252, 272
Smelser, Neil J., 241, 246
Snow, David A., 19, 27, 42, 56, 85, 131, 138, 152, 153, 173, 226, 241, 244, 245, 246, 274
Social acceptance, 47–49, 257
    See also Media coverage; Public discourses/opinion(s)
Social capital, 37, 65, 67, 232
Social partner(ship), 7, 12, 17, 44, 50, 64, 77–81, 167, 196–200, 203, 206–208, 212, 213, 223
Sommier, Isabelle, 51, 54, 173
Soule, Sarah A., 85, 153, 173, 244, 245, 246, 274
Spieser, Catherine, 11, 247, 248, 264, 265, 269, 275, 276
Springhorn-Schmidt, Margrit, 66, 72, 88

Staggenborg, Suzanne, 170, 174
Stapleton, John, 201, 211
Statham, Paul, 175, 187, 190, 242, 245
Stearns, Peter N., 178, 192
Stedman-Jones, Gareth, 178, 193
Steinert, Heinz, 58, 65, 84, 87
Steininger, Rolf, 217
Stevens, Matthew, 217
Stigmatization, 1, 5, 10–11, 19–20, 37, 42, 52, 54, 55, 64, 72, 79, 125, 131, 163, 224, 250–253, 269
    See also Counterstigmatization
Streeck, Wolfgang, 77, 87
Strümpel, Burkhard, 84
Svampa, Maristella, 2, 27
Sweeney, Paul, 195, 218
Sztandar-Sztanderska, Karolina, 11, 247, 249, 252, 269, 275

Tainio, Risto, 113, 129
Talejo Vázquez, Felix, 170, 174
Tarrow, Sidney, 16, 27, 55, 72, 80, 87, 92, 100, 107, 111, 129, 177, 193, 225, 242, 245, 246
Tartakowsky, Danielle, 23, 26, 31, 32, 51, 56, 105, 107
Tattini, Véronique, 244
Taylor, Alan J.P., 179, 193
Taylor, Gary, 128
Taylor, Verta, 52, 56, 101, 107
Teixeira, Ruy, 65, 67, 86
Thatcher, Margaret, 9, 183, 185, 187
Thompson, John B., 249, 275
Thompson, Paul, 178, 193
Thorez, Maurice, 31
Tille, Cédric, 194, 218
Tillon, Charles, 32
Tilly, Charles, 80, 85, 87, 177, 190, 193, 209, 218, 225, 241, 242, 244, 245, 246, 269
Tilly, Chris, 85
Tocqueville, Alexis de, 13
Todd, Malcolm, 128
Tomlinson, Mike, 211, 217
Touraine, Alain, 187, 193
Towalski, Rafał, 261, 275
Traxler, Franz, 77, 87
Trotskyist/m, 4, 19, 40, 95, 99, 102–103
Tuchszirer, Carole, 51, 54, 160, 167, 172, 174
Turner, Ralph H., 241, 246

Uljas, Päivi, 111, 112, 129
Unemployed
  Long-term, 57, 62, 65, 67, 97, 118, 126, 139, 199, 218, 224, 231, 262
  Young, 39, 94, 95, 96–97, 104, 114, 119, 186, 231
Unemployment benefit system, 9, 11, 12, 17, 23, 35, 44, 51, 82, 83, 89–95, 105, 111–112, 132, 185, 221, 223–224, 229–230, 258, 265, 269
UNEMPOL, 81, 151, 189, 232, 241, 242
Uske, Hans, 73, 75, 87
Uusitalo, Hannu, 128

Valarasan-Toomey, Mary, 195, 218
Valli, Marcello, 224, 229, 246
van Berkel, Rik, 16, 27, 58, 87, 272
Vandaele, Kurt, 91, 107
van den Oord, Ad, 2, 27, 30, 56
van Deth, Jan, 24
Van Gunsteren, Herman, 274
Vanhuysse, Pieter, 260, 275
Vanthemsche, Guy, 91, 107
Varley, Tony, 202, 216
Vauhkonen, Ilse, 127, 129
Vergely, Michel, 37
Vielle, Pascale, 273
Villanen, Sampo, 127, 129
Vincent, Catherine, 157, 174
Visser, Jelle, 18, 27, 91, 106
Vlek, Ruud, 16, 27, 58, 87
von Klippstein, Michael, 83, 84, 85, 86
von Winter, Thomas, 65, 88

Wacker, Ali, 66, 67, 88
Wagener, Hans-Jürgen, 273
Wałęsa, Lech, 266
Wallace, Joseph, 197, 213, 219
Walsh, Edward J., 79, 88
Ward, Kevin, 184, 191
Ward, Stephanie, 181, 193

Webb, Beatrice P., 179, 193
Webb, Sidney, 179, 193
Weber, Max, 114, 126, 129
Weinstein, Marc, 266, 275
Welfare state, 5–7, 17, 20–21, 61–64, 73, 111–114, 133, 156, 159–160, 214–215, 222–226, 238–239, 242, 248, 254, 263, 269
Wenzel, Michał, 267, 275
Werding, Martin, 192
Western, Bruce, 91, 107
Whelan, Christopher, 196, 200, 211, 216, 218, 219
Whiteley, Paul F., 181, 193
Whiting, Richard, 183, 193
Whyte, John, 212, 219
Wieviorka, Michel, 187, 193
Willemez, Laurent, 50, 56
Willems, Ulrich, 88
Willmann, Christophe, 31, 56
Winyard, Stephen J., 181, 193
Wöhrmann, Eduard, 68, 83, 87
Wolski-Prenger, Friedhelm, 27, 60, 66, 67, 68, 69, 70, 71, 72, 73, 75, 81, 83, 85, 87, 88
Wolton, Dominique, 249, 275
Worden, Steven K., 56, 246
Workfare, 9, 224
Wright, Vincent, 24, 89

Yi, Kei-Mu, 196, 218

Zald, Mayer N., 26, 27, 52, 65, 86, 87, 88, 152, 241, 245
Zawadzka, Anna, 249, 252, 275
Zediri-Corniou, Malika, 52
Zeisel, Hans, 25, 65, 85, 177, 192, 232, 245
Zieleńska, Marianna, 249, 252, 275
Zimmermann, Bénédicte, 254, 275
Zoll, Rainer, 66, 72, 88
Zorn, Annika, 67, 88